The Political Roots of Racial Tracking in American Criminal Justice

The race problem in our criminal justice system persists because we enable it. The tendency of liberals to point a finger at law enforcement, racial conservatives, the War on Drugs, is misguided. Black as well as white voters, Democrat as much as Republican lawmakers, President Obama as much as Reagan, both Congress and the Supreme Court alike...all are implicated. We all are "The Man."

Whether the problem is defined in terms of blacks' overrepresentation in prisons or in terms of the disproportional use of deadly police force against blacks, not enough of us demand that something be done. The absence of public outrage stems from the belief that blacks are prone to violence, that there is a serious violent crime problem in the country and that, as a result, racial unevenness in criminal law enforcement is understandable, even if regrettable.

Mass media plays a key role in this fictional narrative, despite mountains of social science research to the contrary. Ultimately, however, politicians continually leverage it for electoral gain through anti-crime policies and strategies that scarcely promote public safety, yet virtually debilitate large portions of black America. The *Political Roots of Racial Tracking in American Criminal Justice* is the story of how the race problem in criminal justice is continually enabled in the national crime policy process, and why.

Nina M. Moore is a political science professor at Colgate University. She was recently named in The Princeton Review's *The Best 300 Professors* in the United States. Her research, teaching, and writing focus on racial inequality, public policy, and governance processes. Moore was appointed by Governor David Patterson to a four-year term on the New York State Commission on Judicial Conduct (2009–2013) and by the New York State Senate to the Advisory Council on Underage Alcohol Consumption and Youth Substance Abuse (2010–present). She is the author of *Governing Race: Policy, Process, and the Politics of Race.*

The Political Roots of Racial Tracking in American Criminal Justice

NINA M. MOORE

Colgate University

CAMBRIDGE
UNIVERSITY PRESS

CAMBRIDGE
UNIVERSITY PRESS

32 Avenue of the Americas, New York, NY 10013-2473, USA

Cambridge University Press is part of the University of Cambridge.

It furthers the University's mission by disseminating knowledge in the pursuit of education, learning, and research at the highest international levels of excellence.

www.cambridge.org
Information on this title: www.cambridge.org/9781107654884

First published 2015

Printed in the United States of America

A catalog record for this publication is available from the British Library.

Library of Congress Cataloging in Publication data
Moore, Nina M., 1966–
The political roots of racial tracking in American criminal justice / Nina Moore.
pages cm
Includes bibliographical references and index.
ISBN 978-1-107-02297-3 (hardback) – ISBN 978-1-107-65488-4 (pbk.)
1. Discrimination in criminal justice administration – United States. 2. Racial profiling in law enforcement – United States. 3. Crime and race – United States. 4. Criminal justice, Administration of – United States. 5. United States – Race relations. I. Title.
HV9950.M64 2015
363.2'308900973–dc23 2014043071

ISBN 978-1-107-02297-3 Hardback
ISBN 978-1-107-65488-4 Paperback

For my parents,
Charles L. and Nora L. Moore

Contents

Figures

Tables

Preface

In a society under the forms of which the stronger faction can readily unite and oppress the weaker, anarchy may as truly be said to reign as in a state of nature, where the weaker individual is not secured against the violence of the stronger; and as, in the latter state, even the individuals are prompted, by the uncertainty of their condition, to submit to a government which may protect the weak as well as themselves; so, in the former state, will the more powerful factions or parties be gradually induced, by a like motive to wish for a government which will protect all parties, the weaker as well as the more powerful.

James Madison
Federalist No. 51

The race problem in the American criminal justice system endures because the public and policymakers enable it. Racial justice advocates' tendency to point the finger of blame chiefly at police officers, prosecutors, and criminal court judges is, therefore, misguided. The same can be said of the conventional wisdom that traces the root of the problem to racist politicians, racial conservatives, Republicans, Presidents Reagan and Bush, and the like. Regardless of whether we define the problem as having to do with unequal treatment in the process or with the gross overrepresentation of minorities in the process, the bottom line is that very few American citizens and policymakers care enough to mobilize around it. It can be argued that the disinterest is not entirely unfounded, even if its foundation is faulty. Considering the steady flow of informational cues in the public arena about blacks and crime, there is little wonder why most voters and lawmakers are convinced the current state of affairs is reasonable, even if regrettable. The story told in this book is the story of how racial concerns are consistently ignored in the national crime policy process, and why.

Seldom do we consider at length the part played by the body politic as a whole – that is, the combined influence of average citizens, courts, lawmakers, lobbyists, academics, and mass media. Instead, the black law enforcement experience is typically examined by way of a legal, socio-logical, or criminological lens. The usual take-away from these angles is that discriminatory law enforcement is to blame, or that criminal law is structured in ways that disproportionately ensnare minorities, or that blacks commit more crime due to structural and cultural causes. This book endeavors to extend the scope of the study of race and criminal jus-tice to include a systematic probe of the national political context within which the intersection of race, crime, and criminal justice is negotiated. From a political science perspective, the necessity of probing the political context of a public policy problem is a virtual given. That is where we usually find the primary reason some policy problems are allowed to per-sist while others are redressed. Logically, then, that is where we should also expect to learn of the national political forces that help sustain the racial status quo in American criminal justice. Thankfully, the public pol-icy process literature provides extremely helpful insights.

It is important that we come to grips with the full range of forces that enable racial tracking in criminal justice, given that the problem has broader implications not only for the black community but for the coun-try as a whole. The costs to blacks are incalculable in economic, social, political, psychological, and emotional terms. How does one even con-cretize, let alone tally, the entire range of losses that stem from the fact that criminal law is disproportionally enforced against blacks and that the treatment that blacks receive in the criminal process is devoid of the leniency and consideration accorded their white counterparts? Add to this the many decades the problem has persisted, the many ways in which it has manifested itself, and the many lives affected directly and indirectly, and it becomes apparent that the issue figures rather largely in the fabric of black life in the United States.

Racially uneven enforcement of criminal law is important also because it gives rise to fundamental questions about democratic process and minor-ity interests. What are the conditions under which minority concerns will be advanced or protected in a political system based on majority rule? What are the most effective political strategies for securing policy change that improves the lot of disadvantaged racial minorities in a democratic setting? What can be expected when minority policy interests are, or at least are perceived to be, in conflict with those of the majority? It is questionable whether a democratic society founded on principles of liberty and equality can legitimately claim to be so when its greatest power – the power to punish, imprison, and exterminate – is used in ways that chiefly debilitate already marginalized minority communities on a continual and widespread basis. This is precisely why striking a balance between minority interests and majority interests lay at the heart of the Founders' plan for a limited constitutional democracy. This balancing of interests was of utmost concern to the father of the U.S. Constitution, James Madison, in his classic statements on American democratic governance in *Federalist Nos. 10* and *51*.

Our collective responsibility to discover how best to achieve such balance – in this case, how to maintain "law and order" without crippling the black community in the process – inheres regardless of the proximal cause(s) of racially disparate outcomes. If the problem stems partly from excessive black criminality brought on by socioeconomic disadvantage, it is no less of a problem in that millions of young lives are destroyed before they begin. If racially discriminatory enforcement plays but a minuscule role, its relevance to any degree means the life course of potentially thousands of citizens is negatively impacted due, at least partly, to the color of their skin. The mere fact that minority groups are disproportionally the aggrieved in police brutality complaints, yet jails and prisons are mostly filled with these same groups, speaks volumes about both the perception and the reality of "liberty and justice for all" in the United States. For these reasons and more, discovering the political pathway to a more evenhanded approach to criminal law enforcement is as much a matter of protecting treasured Americans ideals as it is one of improving the plight of blacks in the criminal justice system.

This book contends that a critical first step toward fully understanding racial tracking is to grasp its political roots. It presents a two-part research analysis that carefully highlights, first, the extent and nature of racial differences in American criminal justice and, second, the national political undercurrents that help sustain it. This book undertakes a systematic examination of a wide range of mostly primary quantitative and qualitative data stretching across several decades. The analysis advances two basic conclusions. The first is that there are two racially distinct modes of criminal law enforcement in the United States: one white, one black. Meaning, the manner in which law enforcement officials interface with black citizens differs in striking ways from that with similarly situated whites. The distinctive nature of the black law enforcement experience consists of much more than the numerical imbalance in traffic stops, arrests, sentencing, and imprisonment that often dominates scholarly and popular discussions of race and policing. On average, when black citizens (including those never arrested) encounter law enforcement, they can expect to receive more intrusive, physically harmful, and unsympathetic treatment than would white citizens. A key point of this book, then, pertains to the many ways in which the *nature* of the black law enforcement experience departs from that of whites with respect to everything from initial contact with police officers, to plea negotiations with prosecutors, to pretrial criminal court decisions, to the behind bars prison experience, and more. It documents a form of racial tracking within the American criminal justice system whereby one track is reserved mostly for whites and a separate track for blacks.

The second, more central, argument of the book is that the American public and policymakers play a pivotal role in fueling this dualism in law enforcement. Without their tacit consent, its proximate structural causes would have been dismantled or at least seriously tackled long ago. The handful of lawmakers who champion the cause of criminal justice reform along racial lines have yet to muster the political support and resources needed to score a transformative legislative victory. They have not done so because Americans – black and white alike – are unconvinced racial tracking should be a top criminal justice policy priority. Their stance is not entirely attributable to a lack of clarity as to what the underlying causes are or whether the problem is amenable to public policy reform. Scholars have supplied massive empirical insight into the problem and ample reason for the public to believe it is fixable. The public and policymakers' relative indifference is partly fostered, instead, by a scripted message transmitted by mass media about black criminality. The message supplies compelling reasons for the public and policymakers to conclude that racially uneven criminal justice outcomes are not a fundamental public policy concern, and most certainly not as concerning as the need to fight crime. Helping make the message that much more palatable is the public's already ingrained predisposition toward individualist explanations over and above structural determinism.

It is my sincere hope that this book, together with existing works, helps generate and sustain a serious public dialogue about the considerable role mainstay national politics play in continually enabling racial tracking in American criminal justice. Unfortunately, space and time limitations make it impossible to address every important question on the subject; so, necessarily, more than a few go unanswered. Not taken up here is the law enforcement experience of other marginalized groups in the United States besides blacks, particularly those that other studies have shown also to diverge substantially from whites'. Differences along the lines of ethnicity, immigration status, religion, and sexual orientation also exist; sometimes one form of group disadvantage is compounded by another. The fact that Latinos constitute the largest ethnic minority in the United States as of the 2000 census makes a comprehensive analysis of the national political backdrop of their law enforcement experience indispensable to a full understanding of race-ethnicity, criminal justice, and politics in the United States. Remarkably few policing incidents in recent years involving individual Latino suspects and arrestees have dominated national headlines, let alone spurred federal legislative action or wide-scale public reaction. And, when there is a rash of controversy surrounding treatment of Latinos by law enforcement officials, the issue is often conflated with immigration politics and only loosely connected to the embedded tension between minority status and criminal law enforcement. Hopefully, this book will contribute in some way to the vibrant current of literature on the Latino law enforcement experience. It uses the black law enforcement experience as a basis for developing an integrative theoretical framework, which helps explain the dynamic interplay between identity and national trends in judicial, legislative, partisan, interest group, and voters' crime policy positioning.

Given that the chief aim of this book is to explore at length the political factors that sustain racial tracking in criminal justice, it does not join the longtime debate about the proximate causes that generate racial disproportionalness in criminal justice. A fairly exhaustive review of the mainstream theories of racial disparity in criminal justice that have been put forth over the years is presented in Chapter 8, but this discussion is offered solely for the purpose of grounding the book's claims about the wealth of expert knowledge available on the subject and, more importantly, the intellectual wherewithal for the public and policymakers to act. No attempt is made here to settle the decades-old dispute as to whether police officers and other law enforcement agents engage in deliberate discrimination, whether the system is designed to entrap the poor and minorities, whether blacks commit more crime, whether structural or cultural factors are determinative, and so on. The sheer complexity of the causation question precludes its resolution in the space of a single work, and it is complicated further by the fact that existing studies are not mutually exclusive of one another. What the review in Chapter 8 does assert, nonetheless, is that within and across the vast literature on immediate causes, there is substantial evidence that validates macro-context theories of racial differences in criminal justice. Notwithstanding particularized scholarly disagreements over which societal factors matter most, there is a meeting of minds around the basic idea that they matter.

Rather than choose from among the many well-grounded macro-level theories of racial unevenness in criminal justice or endeavor to disprove any one of them, this study proceeds with the understanding they all have some credence. The underlying premise of this study is this: whatever the immediate institutional and structural factors that account for blacks' overrepresentation and differential treatment within the criminal justice process, all such factors are amenable to policy reform. Some more readily than others. Accordingly, this book takes up the next logical line of inquiry, which to date remains largely unchartered territory. It asks: Why the lack of policy reform in this area? Why so little political attention to the societal forces that enable racial unevenness in law enforcement? More precisely, what part do voters, lawmakers, and interest groups play in aiding and abetting racial tracking and its underlying drivers? To sum up, chiefly at issue in the pages to follow is the extent to which national politics are as much a piece of the puzzlement of race and criminal justice as are the remaining forces ably identified by scholars across the disciplines.

The book is divided into three parts, comprising eight chapters. The first part is composed of two chapters. The opening chapter presents a systematic descriptive analysis of what I term "racial tracking" in the criminal justice system. The term is intended to convey the fact that blacks are not only disproportionally entangled in the criminal process but are also subject to a less lenient form of criminal processing. Chapter 1 argues that in order to adequately comprehend the role of race in American criminal justice, we have to gauge both aspects of this duality. Blacks are more likely to be arrested, convicted, and sentenced to prison, *and* blacks are more likely to be on the receiving end of harsh, heavy-handed, and disadvantageous treatment during their encounters with law enforcement, compared to whites. In short, the average black citizen more often experiences the worst criminal law enforcement has to offer, including a sizable number who are never arrested, let alone found guilty of a criminal act. Thus, Chapter 1 establishes the fact that there are two racially distinct modes of law enforcement – one black, one white.

Qualitative and quantitative distinctions in the black law enforcement experience are evident at each of the major stages of the process, namely the police and investigation stage, the prosecution stage, the court stage, and the prison stage. (The broader societal impacts of these distinctions are taken up later in the book.) A range of nationally representative statistical data are used in Chapter 1 to construct a concise yet comprehensive profile of racial tracking. Much of the data are primary and drawn from several national databases. They permit a probe of more than 100 indicators of black and white interface with criminal justice, from the initial point of contact up to and including the behind-bars experience. Among the data sources chiefly relied on are Bureau of Justice Statistics databases and reports, the *Uniform Crime Reports*, the National Crime Victimization Survey, *Sourcebook of Criminal Justice Statistics*, National Association for the Advancement of Colored People (NAACP) reports, U.S. Civil Rights Commission reports, and several other government and non-government sources.

A layout of the policy process theory offered in this book to help explain racial tracking is in Chapter 2, where a delineation of its broader public policy impact is also found. Chapter 2 also contains an introductory overview of how the theory is applied in the remaining chapters, along with details on the analytic focus, data, and methodology of the analyses in Chapters 3 through 8. The second part of the book focuses on the institutional behaviors and policies that help sustain racial tracking. Chapter 3 considers the role of U.S. Supreme Court rulings on race and law enforcement from 1932 to 2005. Chapters 4 and 5 take us inside Congress. A detailed look at the substance and fate of the racial justice policy agenda from 1988 to 2012 is provided in Chapter 4. Chapter 5 examines modern crime laws enacted between 1968 and 1994, the demise of racial justice in the context of those proceedings, the impact of these policies on the racial divide in criminal justice, and the political motives driving Congressional adoption of these mainstay laws.

With special attention to the role of political parties, public opinion, scholarly research, mass media, and ideological traditions, the third part probes the political roots of the institutional responses examined in the second part. Chapter 6 highlights the partisan politics of race, crime, and criminal justice from 1968 to 2012. National public opinion and the degree to which it is conducive to racialized criminal justice are analyzed in Chapter 7. The discussion in Chapter 8 presents a relatively comprehensive cross-disciplinary review of scholarly studies put forth to explain racial disparities in criminal justice, media treatment of this expert knowledge, and how the American public's conception of individualism effectively mediates (and trumps) both.

This book has been several years in the making and could not have reached the finish line without the help of many, more than I can list by name here. Any mistakes, misfires, or shortcomings in its pages are entirely my own. Funding from an institutional grant of the Mellon Foundation supported the fieldwork portion of the study. The Colgate University Faculty Research Council supplied monies for development and administration of the original national surveys used in this study. I am indebted to the legislative staff, attorneys, civilian review board members, and law enforcement officials who took time out of their busy schedules to meet with me, exchange e-mails, or send materials. Christine Demetros and Lydia Turnipseed of Syracuse University Law School were a great help during my search for hard-to-find court documents. Paige Harrison of the Bureau of Justice Statistics pointed me in the right direction for locating various prison data sources. I am enormously grateful also for the indispensable help of several student research assistants. Elise Aronson assisted with several parts of the project. At various junctures, the project benefited also from the excellent efforts of Li Zhou, Calla Yee, Carly Ackerman, Steffy Parver, Kathleen Shaughnessy, Michelle Cohen, and Samuel Flood.

During the early stages of the work, my thinking was sharpened enormously by the critical feedback of fellow panelists at the Midwest Political Science Association 2010 Annual Meeting and also Lani Guinier on the courts chapter. Michael Tonry and my ever-supportive colleague in the Political Science Department at Colgate University, Michael Johnston, were kind enough to chime in on the overarching message of the book. Their seasoned advice helped me develop a clearer framework and pitch for the book proposal. Michael Hayes took the time to provide an excellent preliminary lay of the land of the policy process literature. Also appreciated are the feedback comments of anonymous readers for sample chapters. My participation for a number of years in the hearings and deliberations of the New York State Judicial Conduct Commission afforded me a perspective on the inner workings of state courts and on judicial decision making that I could never have gained through reliance on academic research methods alone. To the following I am indebted for their critical feedback on select chapters: Tawanna Brown, Agber Dimah, Debra Earl, and Linda Upshaw.

A very special thank you is owed to my editor at Cambridge University Press, Robert Dreesen, who encouraged me to focus on producing my best. His supportive words eased my anxiety during the final phase of the writing process. For me, they were also a license to say what needed to be said in the book, and how it needed to be said. I sincerely hope he does not regret reassuring me that how long or how lengthy the project proved to be was not all that mattered. On the personal front, I have been blessed with parents, sisters, and brothers who supply a steady flow of good old-fashioned common sense. Sometimes without knowing it, they reminded me of the wholesomeness of family and good people at precisely those times when the research and writing for this book shined an almost blinding spotlight on all that remains undone in this policy sphere. I dedicate this work to my parents, Charles and Nora Moore, the two most conscientious people I will ever know. Finally, Dennis was always at-the-ready with a healthy dose of laughter, provocative questions, and philosophical musings. He is the best son in the universe.

The audience will, hopefully, find the discussion and analysis in this book are grounded in a firm empirical foundation, but I concede it is not a purely academic exercise for me. My having lived in the largest housing project in the United States during my teenage years undoubtedly influenced my thinking about race, crime, and justice. After spending one night in one of the twenty-eight sixteen-story concrete buildings that composed the Robert Taylor Homes, then–U.S. Housing and Urban Development Secretary Henry Cisneros declared Chicago public housing likely the most violent in the country.[1] William Julius Wilson used the Robert Taylor Homes in his groundbreaking study of the urban underclass to illustrate the growing problems of social dislocation in the inner city. In *The Truly Disadvantaged*, Wilson observed that in 1983, "only a little more than 0.5% of Chicago's more than 3 million people lived in the Robert Taylor Homes"; however, "11 percent of the city's murders, 9 percent of its rapes, and 10 percent of its aggravated assaults were committed in the project."[2]

One cannot come of age under such severe circumstances and settle on a reductionist perspective on race and criminal justice. A black-versus-white paradigm will not do, and neither will an us–versus–"the man" perspective or any other version of us-versus-them. "Project kids," as we were called, grow up as part of a multi-tiered minority. We were a minority (black), within a minority (segregated by race: 99.99 percent black), within a minority (poor), within a minority (mired in concentrated poverty). There was still yet another layer of minority identity for me beyond these, as my family was a two-parent, devoutly religious household in a sea of so-called broken homes, my father gainfully employed, and our tenancy shorter than most. As to the overall Robert Taylor community, we lived quite literally at the intersection of race, crime, and the American version of justice during the 1980s. The greater visibility of drug use and trafficking, the rapid emergence of violent splinter gangs, and the launch of the national War on Drugs all converged on our small section of the city like a perfect storm during the 1980s. And as with any perfect storm, those at the center were subject to multiple cross-pressures.

On the one hand, I experienced up close and personal my friends being forced to submit to random police pat-downs and searches and – in full view of the public – pull down their pants or spread-eagle on the concrete ground. Several years after my family's exodus came the police sweeps proposed by a Democratic president and coordinated by Chicago Housing Authority police; Chicago city police; Illinois state police; the Federal Bureau of Investigation; the Drug Enforcement Administration; the Bureau of Alcohol, Tobacco, and Firearms; and the U.S. Marshals. The sweeps subjected entire households to unannounced, warrantless police searches, during which residents were forced to remain seated and still in their living rooms while the police rifled through their bedrooms and personal belongings in hopes of finding criminal evidence. Widespread arrests for petty offenses were typically all that resulted. None of the humiliating dragnets made so much as a dent in the infamously high violent crime rate in the area. They did, however, manage to fortify the wedge between residents and law enforcement officials – black and white officials alike.

Just as impactful as my firsthand observations of police excess and ineffectiveness was having experienced the devastating loss of a childhood friend to violent crime. Viewed from a strictly personal vantage point, it is the kind of experience from which one never fully recovers. From an analytical perspective, the murder of my friend Alfreda Creekmore symbolized many of the recurring themes that preoccupy studies of race, crime, and justice. She was brutally raped and beaten to death with a steel pipe, virtually beyond recognition. Freda, the victim, was young, gifted, and black. Her assailant, Michael Madden, was also black and was deemed a serial offender, according to court papers.[3] His pattern of criminal activity was known beforehand to local police and to his victims but not published to the community at large until after the fact. News of Freda's brutal murder occupied all of a few sentences in local newspapers. There were no marches, demonstrations, or name-brand civil rights leaders demanding anything, neither in regard to the perpetrator nor the police. Following seventeen hours of interrogation and forced injection of a tranquilizer used to treat psychosis, police obtained a confession from Madden, a conviction, and a forty-five-year sentence. Madden's appeal alleging Fifth and Sixth Amendment violations was eventually rejected.

In the wake of my friend Freda's murder and Madden's conviction, things returned to abnormal. Violent crime in the area continued on course. So did the intensity of intrusive but scarcely effective policing. And so did the widespread arrests and, eventually, mass prison commitments. In time, this vicious cycle reached the point where the only viable solution local, state, and federal policymakers could fathom was to completely demolish the Robert Taylor Homes projects and, in the process, dismantle what community had managed to survive more than thirty years in the midst of it all. Looking back, there is no question in my mind that we were all complicit. We all played a role in perpetuating the vicious cycle, if only by virtue of our failure to mobilize and actively demand meaningful change. It is my belief that, as a country, we all continue to play much the same role, with much the same dire consequences, but on a much wider scale. My personal and professional goal in writing this book is to help shed light on what we all bring to the table, to expose our collective obligation to do more, and to bring into sharper focus why we have not.

I

Racial Tracking

Two Law Enforcement Modes

Scholarly assessments of the black experience in American criminal justice tend to center on numerical disparities in arrests, sentencing, and incarceration. With few exceptions, little to no attention is devoted to the many ways in which the substantive elements of the average black law enforcement experience systematically diverge from that of whites.[1] The fact that blacks encounter the very worst treatment the system has to offer is most often the stuff of newspaper headlines. High-profile incidents such as those involving Rodney King, Amadou Diallo, the Scott sisters, Professor Henry Louis Gates, and Oscar Grant are occasions on which civil rights leaders, organizations, and demonstrators sound the alarm to expose what they see as a system rife with callousness and low regard for blacks and their civil liberties.[2] The infamous ordeals of the Rodney Kings and Oscar Grants of the world, in their view, are symptomatic of a much deeper and more widespread pathology – one that lurks behind the much talked about statistical overrepresentation. The rare emergence of such high-profile incidents, however, makes it difficult to assail the notion they are nothing more than isolated incidents or, at best, the kind that occur only in places like Los Angeles, Chicago, New York, and other hotbeds of policing controversy. The preoccupation with racial disparities thus continues to dominate the already limited discourse on experiential differences in the criminal process.[3]

National data help prove it is actually the "processing" differential that is the most persistent and pervasive feature of the black–white divide in criminal justice. These data show that for the average black citizen, arrestee, and convict, their modes of interface with criminal justice actors diverges in notable ways from their white counterparts'. Blacks can reasonably expect a markedly different brand of justice. More precisely, the chances they will receive harsher, more intrusive, more injurious, more demeaning, and generally disadvantageous treatment *during* their encounters with officials within the system far outweigh the chances they will receive leniency or special consideration. Virtually the opposite is true for whites. The version of justice they encounter is more consonant with law enforcement's "serve and protect" pledge. What scarce compassion the system parcels out is allocated in large measure to whites, not blacks. More so than differences in degree, then, it is differences in kind that chiefly distinguish the average black law experience from the white law experience. In fact, national data actually do not bear out certain of the more common accusations lodged against law enforcement, such as racial profiling, overzealous prosecution, starkly different sentencing, and the like, though such allegations have been proven in various cities and other localities. At the same time, there is much systematic evidence to corroborate the more egregious treatment-related allegations often made by or on behalf of blacks and thus ample reason to look beyond the problem of overrepresentation when weighing the significance of race in American criminal justice.

Whether concretized in terms of numerical imbalances or processing differences, racially disparate outcomes exist at every stage of the criminal process, including the arrest and investigation, prosecution, adjudication, and imprisonment stages. Inasmuch as racial differentiation is pervasive throughout the system, it is arguable there are two racially distinctive law enforcement modes – one that operates among blacks and another for whites. In this study, I refer to this phenomenon of dual processing and unevenness as "racial tracking."

In what follows, we examine a wide range of nationally representative data to demonstrate the existence of racial tracking in the American criminal justice system. Taken together, the selected indicators establish the system is fundamentally structured along racial lines. Much of the data are primary, quantitative, drawn from several national databases, and representative of state (not federal) criminal justice systems.[4] They permit a concise yet uniquely in-depth and comprehensive perspective on the extent of divergence between the average law enforcement experience of black and white Americans on a national scale, to complement existing analyses of local and state law enforcement trends.[5] We also learn from the data in this chapter that the pervasive racial dualism in law enforcement is not new but has existed for decades. A look at the broader social and economic impact of racial tracking is reserved for Chapter 2.

The discussion here begins with a look at the arrest and investigation stage, where the actions and decisions of police officers are front and center. Next examined is the prosecution stage. Following this is a probe of the decisions rendered by state criminal courts, from pretrial through final disposition. Then, a look at the prison experience of black and white convicts. Last, we probe the long-standing history of racial tracking.

Officer Un-Friendly to Blacks: Race at the Arrest and Investigation Stage

The version of policing that the average black citizen encounters is one that, to an unusual degree, involves him being suspected of criminal activity, stopped for unarticulated reasons, subject to intrusive investigatory tactics, subject to excessive physical force, and at greater risk of being killed by a police officer. There is also the well-studied surer prospect of being arrested. Police officers' decisions have a ripple effect throughout the formal criminal process as well, insofar as they launch the official process of assigning criminal culpability by way of an arrest. However, their impact extends well beyond this. Because police officers' contact with citizens in general is more frequent than that of other actors in the criminal justice system, what officers do and how they behave also has wider and potentially deeper racial impacts than that of other law enforcement officials. In fact, the international human rights watch organization Amnesty International cited the United States in 1998 for human rights violations precisely because of repeated allegations of domestic police brutality, specifically police shootings, restraint techniques, and civil liberties abuses.[6] Thus, for citizens, scholars, and critics alike, the actions of police officers are a critical window into how the overall criminal justice experience of blacks and whites compare to one another. We turn now to an analysis of statistical data on public–police contacts, traffic stops, police use of force, arrests, and arrest-related deaths in order to establish the existence of racial tracking at the police and investigation stage.

For black citizens, there is a greater chance their interactions with police officers stem from being viewed as suspects by the officers. The data in Table 1.1,[7] from the Police–Public Contact Survey (PPCS) series administered by the U.S. Bureau of Justice Statistics, show that, compared to white citizens, the likelihood of face-to-face contact between a black citizen and an officer occurring because the officer suspects him of some kind of criminal activity is double that of whites'. Although being treated like a suspect right from the start is true of only 4.6 percent of

TABLE 1.1. *Citizens Who Had Face-to-Face Contact with Police, by Race, United States, 2005 (Percent within Race)*

Race of Citizen	Had Personal Contact (Number)	Reason for Contact					
		Police Initiated	Reported Crime	Police Assistance	Police Investigation	Suspected of Something	Traffic Stop (Driver)
Black	15.7 (4,377,317)	60.0	26.3	5.6	5.5	4.6	38.1
White	19.7 (31,664,301)	57.9	25.0	6.7	5.2	2.3	39.6
B-W Ratio	0.8	1.0	1.1	0.8	1.1	2.0	1.0
U.S.	18.5 (42,794,940)	58.8	25.1	6.4	5.4	2.6	40.1

blacks who reported at least one face-to-face contact, this percentage translates into more than 200,000 black citizens, hardly an insignificant number from a political and policy standpoint. In contrast, moreover, the chances of a black encounter with the police resulting from the officer providing help or assistance is slightly smaller than is the case for white encounters. Conversely, Table 1.1 also reveals blacks are as likely as whites to cooperate with police officers, either by way of reporting crime or taking part in a police investigation. This fact hints at a willingness on blacks' part to be partners in the fight against crime, which should not be surprising given the prevalence of criminal victimization in black communities (something detailed in Chapter 6). However, the potential for mutual partnership between black communities and police officers is arguably minimized by the fact that the latter disproportionally regards the former as criminal.

Those aspects of the black law enforcement experience that are comparable to whites' mostly pertain to the issue of frequency. According to the national data in Table 1.1, blacks' rate of contact with the police is not substantially different, something that runs counter to allegations of over-policing. As well, the police are just as likely to initiate contact with a black person as they are a white person, an important fact given police-initiated contacts dominate all citizen–police contacts. On the whole, then, what we can definitively say about the national portrait of the black law enforcement experience in the United States is that it does not necessarily entail over-policing, but rather a far less helpful version of policing.

TABLE 1.2. *Reason for Traffic Stop Contact, by Race, United States, 2005*
(Percent within Race)

Race of Citizen (Number)	No Reason Given	Speeding	Vehicle Defect	Record Check	Stop Sign/ Light Violation	Illegal Turn/ Lane Change	Roadside Check (Dui)	Seatbelt Violation
Black (1,667,758)	4.2	45.2	12.8	14.6	8.1	5.5	1.0	3.9
White (12,539,103)	1.5	55.7	8.7	10.2	6.7	5.6	2.4	4.8
B-W Ratio	2.8	0.8	1.5	1.4	1.2	1.0	0.4	0.8
U.S. (17,160,770)	1.8	53.7	9.4	10.5	7.3	5.8	2.2	4.7

Note: PPCS data pertain to stopped drivers only.

Further separating the black law enforcement experience from whites' is the unusual degree of seeming randomness in officers' decision whether to zero in on individual black citizens. The uncertainty and unpredictability we often hear voiced by blacks is partly borne out by data on what is the second most common catalyst for citizen–police encounters, namely traffic stops (which account for roughly 40 percent of all such encounters). Presented in Table 1.2,[8] traffic stop data unequivocally show that the likelihood of a black driver being stopped by a police officer for no reason at all is almost three times that of a white driver. Again here, the absolute percentage is small, only 4.2 percent. But, in real life this is the equivalent of more than 70,000 black drivers each year whose daily commute to work, home, or school is disrupted by a police officer for no apparent reason. This number takes on even greater significance when we consider what transpires during these stops.

The unsettling aspect of black drivers' experience with police is that of what more often happens to them during the traffic stops. As with all contacts, less concerning here as well is the frequency with which officers conduct traffic stops involving blacks, in that there is only a 1 point difference in the percentage of black and white police encounters tied to traffic, according to Table 1.1. According to Table 1.2, there is also minimal difference in the likelihood of each group of drivers being stopped as a result of citations that are somewhat easier to dispute in court, such as stop sign/light violations, illegal turn/lane change, and seat belt violations. Citations based on objective indicia[9] actually involve white drivers to a greater degree. At least according to national data, as far as traffic stops are concerned too, at the core of the "driving while black" phenomenon is not how often black drivers are stopped by the police. Rather, it is the officers' disproportional use of heavy-handed and intrusive tactics during stops involving black drivers and passengers.

For black drivers, being pulled over by the police entails risks and consequences that extend far beyond a traffic violation citation. Russell-Brown recounts the story of the first black female astronaut's encounter with police in her hometown, Nassau Bay, Texas. Mae Jemison was arrested, handcuffed, pushed face-down onto the pavement, and forced to remove her shoes and walk barefoot from the patrol car into the police station – all because of a traffic infraction.[10] Not only Mae Jemison, but all black drivers can reasonably worry that the worst that could happen to them will happen to them. For starters, black drivers are twice as likely to be handcuffed or arrested during the course of a traffic stop. They are anywhere from two to three times more likely to have either their vehicle or their person searched by a police officer. Fully 6 percent of traffic stops involving black drivers result in the vehicle being searched and better than 5 percent involve a physical search of the driver himself. This translates into more than 100,000 searched vehicles and more than 90,000 black drivers who are physically searched and/or patted down by police officers. One might be inclined to make much of the fact that Table 1.3 shows the rate of consent for black drivers is also greater. Except that "consent" under these circumstances may be more aptly presumed the making of fear, pressure, or a desire to expedite the stop and avoid being detained for a period of time.[11]

There is a measure of public humiliation that accompanies officers' greater use of intrusive tactics against blacks. Traffic stops usually take place in full public view where others can see, unlike most other kinds of police-initiated contacts. Any moderately observant adult living in the United States could scarcely escape witnessing at least once in their lifetime the spectacle of black drivers and/or passengers sitting on the curbside, squatting on the roadside, bent over the side or back of the car, or in handcuffs, while police officers search their personal belongings. For some black drivers, these searches also infringe on their civil liberties. As much is suggested by the data in Table 1.3,[12] which expose a gap between the number of black drivers who are subjected to a police search and the number that give their consent to such searches.

The harmful impact of the activities that occur during traffic stops involving black drivers are magnified still further by the fact that such

TABLE 1.3. *Police Actions During Traffic Stops, by Race, United States,*
2005 (Percent within Race)

Race of Citizen (Number)	No Action Taken	Verbal Warning	Written Warning	Traffic Ticket	Speeding Ticket	Arrested	Handcuffed
Black (1,667,758)	17.4	14.6	8.1	55.1	76.3	4.8	3.9
White (12,539,103)	13.4	19.1	9.3	56.1	69.8	2.2	1.9
B-W Ratio	1.3	0.8	0.9	1.0	1.1	2.2	2.1
U.S. (17,160,770)	13.3	18.1	8.7	57.3	43.1	2.5	2.2

Race of Citizen	Police Ask to Search Vehicle	Police Ask to Search Driver	Police Search Vehicle	Police Search Driver	Consent to Vehicle Search	Consent to Personal Search
Black (1,667,758)	4.6	3.6	6.1	5.4	4.8	3.8
White (12,539,103)	2.2	1.2	2.7	1.9	2.5	1.6
B-W Ratio	2.1	3.0	2.3	2.8	1.9	2.4
U.S. (17,160,770)	2.7	1.6	3.5	2.6	2.9	1.9

Note: PPCS data pertain to stopped drivers only.

stops occur under a cloud of uncertainty. A black person is not in a position to predict when or why a traffic stop will occur, at least not with the same degree of confidence as his white counterpart. The earlier discussion noted data in Table 1.2 that indicate blacks are three times more likely than whites to be stopped for no stated reason. Table 1.3 provides additional evidence on the random nature of black law enforcement encounters. It shows a noticeably higher percentage of traffic stops involving blacks result in no action at all being taken by police. Furthermore, although stopped black drivers (45.2 percent) are slightly less likely than whites (55.7 percent) to be stopped for speeding, they are slightly more likely (76.3 percent) to be ticketed for speeding as compared to whites (69.8 percent). Finally, the fact that government data show police officers are less likely to retrieve criminal evidence in searches of black drivers and passengers (3.3 percent), and substantially more likely to find incriminating evidence in searches of whites (14.5 percent),[13] underscores the

TABLE 1.4. *Police Use of Force in Traffic and Non-Traffic Contacts, by Race, United States, 2005*

Race of Citizen	In Traffic-Related Contacts		In Non-Traffic Contacts	
	% Within Race (Number)	% Within Contacts	% Within Race (Number)	% Within Contacts
Black	1.2 (25,295)	19	6.2 (138,222)	34
White	0.5 (83,911)	62	1.3 (193,469)	48
B-W Ratio	2.4		4.8	
U.S.	0.6 (135,318)		2.0 (404,840)	

Note: PPCS data pertain to police use of force during respondent's most recent contact.

conundrum blacks face in any effort to avoid such stops through law abidance alone.

Taken together, all of these findings related to traffic incidents – unexplained stops, no action taken, incongruent ticketing, and unfruitful searches – point to the conclusion the average black driver cannot exactly gauge whether, when, or why he or she will be added to the class of drivers stopped by the police, among other things.

To the higher level of uncertainty surrounding black citizens' interface with police we can add also greater physical harm, including a higher rate of fatalities. Irrespective of whether they encounter officers while driving, walking, or standing, the use of police force against blacks is markedly higher than it is for whites. This is depicted in Table 1.4.[14] In traffic-related contacts, the use of force against blacks is more than double that of whites. PPCS data also establish that, when adjudged against their share of the residential population in the United States, blacks are overrepresented among persons subject to police force. For non-traffic contacts, their share of police force is almost three times their share of the residential population. Finally, not shown in the table are PPCS force data that prove for the majority of respondents who reported the use of force in their most recent contact, actual physical force was used more often than other, verbal forms of force encompassed by the survey's definition of force, such as shouting, cursing, or threatening.

These percentages translate into more than 25,500 black drivers whose experience with law enforcement is relatable to that of the infamous Rodney King incident. More generally, though a majority of blacks

TABLE 1.5. *Arrest-Related Deaths, by Race, 2003–2005*

Race of Citizen	Number of Ards	% Share Ards	% Share U.S. Population	% Share Arrests
Black	639	31.9	12.1	27.8
White	879	43.9	69.5	69.8

are not physically beaten and kicked by four police officers, as in the case of Rodney King, or shot nineteen times, as in the case of Amadou Diallo, or shot in the back while face-down on the ground, as in the case of Oscar Grant, the fact that there is a very large number of such victims within the black community who are is crucial. There are thousands of Rodney Kings, Amadou Diallos, and Oscar Grants whose experiences are not memorialized on video footage or national news media.

The disproportionate use of deadly force against blacks is a game-changing feature of the black law enforcement experience. When a black person is killed by a police officer, the ripple effects in the black community are more jolting, wider, deeper, and longer-lasting. Police killings of blacks are such a penetrative phenomenon that they are the stuff of popular culture and folklore in the black community, starting with the 1960s chart-topping single "Inner City Blues" by late R&B singer Marvin Gaye. The song contains an infamous reference to "trigger-happy policing." It is a quip with a firm empirical foundation, in two ways. First, 93 percent of police homicides involve the use of a firearm. Second, blacks die while in the custody of law enforcement officials at a rate nearly double that of whites in custody.

We gain a firmer grasp of the relative odds of blacks versus whites dying while in the custody of law enforcement by examining data drawn from the most comprehensive of the three available databases on police homicides in the United States,[15] namely the Bureau of Justice Statistics' Deaths in Custody Reporting Program (DCRP). The DCRP maintains a record of all types of deaths that occur during the process of arrest. The data from these records, shown in Table 1.5,[16] reflect considerable racial unevenness in arrest-related deaths (ARDs). The context of the killing does not matter as much as one might think, at least not in terms of whether they are officially deemed a criminal suspect. Blacks' share of ARDs (32 percent) exceeds their share of persons arrested (27.8 percent). It exceeds even more so their share of the U.S. residential population (12 percent). Meanwhile, a very different story unfolds for whites, whose

TABLE 1.6. *Arrest-Related Death Rate, by Cause of Death, Race,*
2003–2005 (Per 100,000 Arrests)

Race of Citizen	Homicide	Intoxication	Suicide	Accident	Illness	Other
Black	11.7	3.6	1.2	2.1	1.5	2.5
White	7.0	1.2	1.9	0.7	0.7	0.9
B-W Ratio	1.7	3.0	0.6	3.0	2.1	2.8

share of ARDs (43.9 percent) is more than 25 percent lower than their share of persons arrested (69.8 percent). Finally, the ARD rate of roughly 22.6 for every 100,000 black U.S. residents is almost twice that (12.4 ARD) for whites.

The observed racial unevenness in arrest-related deaths maintains irrespective of the cause of death. No matter the method, blacks emerge as the most prone to die in law enforcement custody, according to Table 1.6.[17] They face an increased chance of dying due to intoxication, accident, illness, and even unspecified causes. Police homicide in particular is the cause of black ARDs at a rate nearly double that of whites. Viewed from a practical standpoint, the ARD data for the three-year 2003–2005 period showing 639 black deaths essentially mean that every other day, somewhere in America, a black person dies during an encounter with law enforcement. As we learned is true of traffic stops, there is a noteworthy "X" factor that figures into the picture of arrest-related deaths as well. Approximately one out of every ten black ARDs is classified under "other."

So, much like the data presented earlier, which indicate black drivers are more frequently stopped by law enforcement for no apparent reason, these data show they also die in the custody of law enforcement for no apparent reason as well.

Finally, the fact that black citizens are officially converted into criminal defendants by police officers at rates far greater than those of whites is so well known as to barely require elaboration. Even so, to lay out more fully here the racial divide in criminal justice and set the stage for the rest of the book, it is worth establishing the unevenness in arrest rates maintains no matter the angle from which it is viewed. Data from the Federal Bureau of Investigation's Uniform Crime Reporting Program (UCR), shown in Table 1.7,[18] reveal that no matter where they are – in the city or the suburbs, in metropolitan or non-metropolitan areas – the same story emerges. Whether young or old, being arrested by a police officer is

TABLE 1.7. *Arrest Rate, by Race, Age, Offense Category, and Geographic Area, 2009 (Per 100,000 Residents)*

	Black	White	B-W Ratio
Total	7,636	3,024	2.5
Over age 18	6,443	2,618	2.5
Under age 18	1,193	407	2.9
Violent crime	448	110	4.1
Property crime	1,025	378	2.7
Drug abuse violations	1,104	346	3.2
Cities	6,237	2,203	2.8
Suburban areas	2,512	1,280	2.0
Metropolitan counties	1,127	563	2.0
Non-metropolitan counties	272	259	1.1

a more likely event for blacks than for their white counterparts. Although the various dimensions of criminal process discussed so far are of great personal and practical consequence, an arrest is a police officer's single most important legal authority. It triggers the formal process of assigning criminal culpability. It entails, more specifically, a policeman's decision to affix blame for a crime to a particular individual. Therefore, because the authority to arrest is used more extensively against black individuals, it is the primary medium through which criminal law is enforced chiefly on black citizens.

What the foregoing analysis illustrates, in sum and substance, is the infamous "Officer Friendly" caricature traditionally used to symbolize police departments' pledge to "serve and protect" is a cultural icon that does not connote quite the same meaning for the black population in the United States as it does for whites. Officer Friendly has yet to develop the same rapport with blacks that he has cultivated over the years with whites.

The Color of Amnesty in American Criminal Justice

The racial dynamics of criminal process are more contained at the prosecution stage than they are at the police investigation stage; still, they are no less concerning. Despite the limited confines within which they appear, it is the departures from the norm in America at this stage that speak most forcefully to the relevance of racial influences here. The "norm" happens to be an incredibly beefed-up version of "law and order" justice. We live in an era in which being tough on crime is one of the most basic rules of politicking for politicians seeking to win public endorsement, and none more so than local and state prosecutors, almost all of whom are elected into office by voters. The political atmosphere demands they be tough, indeed relentless in their campaign against crime and criminals. This is exactly what the public gets, for the most part. The new normal in contemporary American justice revolves around imposition of the most exacting criminal punishments possible. One consequence of this is that the overwhelming majority of persons charged with a crime are eventually deemed guilty, either by way of a plea negotiation or a guilty verdict.

As well, today's prosecutors are armed with enormous independent power to fill jails and prisons, or not. This is an imbedded feature of the nature of prosecutorial power simply in the ordinary course of things. As Bynam perceptively observes, "The prosecutor controls the type of conviction sought. The prosecutor also controls the plea bargaining process and the dismissals of cases at the postindictment-preconviction stage. Most significantly, the prosecutor decides whether a trial proceeds to the penalty phase."[19] He further describes this control as a form of "unbridled discretion."[20] We can add to this observation that, thanks to the swell of mandatory sentencing laws[21] enacted over the past two decades in states across the country, the already "unbridled discretion" inherent in prosecutors' authority is magnified even more. Against this backdrop, therefore, the "norm" is best understood as prosecutors being tough and seeking tangible results through the exercise of their now considerably greater discretionary power.

Even after taking into account the nation's "tough on crime" norm, blacks' experience at the ever-more decisive prosecution stage is best understood as distinguishable. Here is what I mean. When downward departures from the "tough on crime" norm are made at the prosecution stage – that is to say, when there is a relaxation of the stringent "law and order" approach – it is whites who are the most frequent beneficiaries. Thus, even as prosecutors are expected to utilize their discretionary authority according to the rubric of a results-oriented legal and political framework, they do so in ways that serve to benefit whites more than blacks. There are options available to prosecutors that enable them to hold criminal defendants accountable for their alleged crimes but without simultaneously imposing the lifetime consequences ordinarily associated

TABLE 1.8. *Felony Prosecutions, by Offense Category, Race, United States, 1990–2004 (Percent within Race)*

Race of Defendant	Violent	Property	Drug	Public Order
Black	26.7	29.2	36.5	7.6
White	21.9	36.5	31.5	10.2
B-W Ratio	1.2	0.8	1.2	0.7
U.S.	25	30.9	35.4	8.8

Note: Most serious charge at initial appearance.

with a criminal conviction or lengthy imprisonment. Prosecutors can show mercy and leniency and, in doing so, mitigate the harsh, personalized ramifications of American criminal justice.

In what follows we examine national data on criminal prosecutions, in particular evidence of whether and how prosecutorial discretion is utilized in ways that vary along racial lines and in ways that are disproportionally advantageous for white defendants and convicts. The data are drawn from the most comprehensive national database on state prosecutions. The U.S. Department of Justice's *State Court Processing Statistics Series* (SCPS) tracks felony defendants' movement through criminal courts for the nation's seventy-five most populous counties.[22] Analysis of these data proves prosecutors are more likely to spare white defendants the full brunt of criminal justice than black defendants. That we observe this particular racial outcome in connection with what little amnesty exists at the prosecution stage serves to reinforce the chapter's argument regarding racial tracking in criminal justice.

The uneven distribution of sympathy means the system of justice encountered by black defendants and convicts is one that doles out fewer breaks at the prosecution stage than does the one encountered by white defendants and convicts.

Although these circumstances appear to validate the oft-heard complaint the system is "always trying to keep a brother down," in reality, it is more accurate to say the system does not operate so as to avoid or minimize "keeping a brother down." Indeed, it is the case that much of the evidence in Tables 1.8 through 1.11[23] suggests the system is no more inclined to "keep a brother down," than is true for non-black defendants and convicts. The main take-away from this group of tables is that racial disparities in the exercise of prosecutorial discretion are not manifest at every possible decision point, but are instead confined to certain types of decisions, namely those that grant mercy. There are

TABLE 1.9. *Felony Prosecutions, by Offense Type, Race, United States, 1990–2004 (Percent within Race)*

Race of Defendant	Murder	Rape	Robbery	Assault	Burglary	Larceny Theft	Motor Vehicle Theft
Black	1.0	1.5	8.6	12.7	7.7	9.3	2.6
White	0.6	1.6	3.5	11.4	9.7	10.7	3.3
B-W Ratio	1.7	0.9	2.5	1.1	0.8	0.9	0.8
U.S.	0.9	1.5	6.6	12.3	8.6	9.1	3.3

Race of Defendant	Forgery	Fraud	Drug Sales	Other Drug	Weapons	Driving-Related	Public Order
Black	2.7	2.4	19.1	17.4	3.5	1.5	2.7
White	3.7	3.5	11.5	20	1.9	4.4	3.9
B-W Ratio	0.7	0.7	1.7	0.9	1.8	0.3	0.7
U.S.	2.8	2.6	17.3	18.1	2.8	2.8	3.1

Note: Most serious charge at initial appearance.

minor racial differences tied to the decision whether to prosecute for violent, drug, property, and public order offenses, as shown in Table 1.8. Except in the case of robbery, murder, and drug sales, Table 1.9[24] shows unremarkable differences across the percentage of blacks and whites prosecuted for each of the individual offenses depicted. There are negligible racial differences in the likelihood of prosecutors reducing charges against black defendants from a felony to a misdemeanor or from an actual offense to an "attempt," according to Table 1.10.[25] According to Table 1.11,[26] there are small racial differences in prosecutors' tendency to "pile on charges" or not. Finally, from Table 1.16 we learn that prosecutors are almost as inclined to enter into plea agreements with black defendants (59.4 percent) as they are in cases involving white defendants (64.4 percent).

The gravamen of the case for racial tracking at the prosecution stages rests chiefly on the use of alternative methods of prosecution. It is here that the exceptions to the ordinarily stringent rule of criminal law are found. It is in these particular instances the point of departure between black and white defendants is especially poignant, such that prosecutors are more likely to "go easy" on white defendants. Listed in Table 1.12[27] are the alternative routes prosecutors have at their disposal to assign criminal responsibility to a criminal defendant and, in doing so, essentially give the defendant a "second chance." Known as "special assignments,"

TABLE 1.10. *Charge Reduction and Attempted Offense Felony Charge, by Race, United States, 1990–2004 (Percent within Race)*

Race of Defendant	Charge Reduction		Attempted Offense Felony Charge	
	Initial Charge Reduced to Misdemeanor	Initial Felony Charge Pursued (Not Reduced)	Attempted Offense	Complete Offense
Black	13.9	73.3	4.8	82.3
White	13.2	76.5	4.2	85.4
B-W Ratio	1.1	1.0	1.1	1.0
U.S.	13.4	75.1	4.9	83.6

Note: Adjudication charge.

TABLE 1.11. *Number of Felony and Misdemeanor Charges, by Race, United States, 1990–2004 (Percent within Race)*

Race of Defendant	One	Two	Four	Six	Eight or More
Black	43.8	27.1	7.2	1.9	2.6
White	43.6	26.4	6.9	1.9	2.9
B-W Ratio	1.0	1.0	1.0	1.0	0.9
U.S.	42.6	27.6	7.2	1.8	2.6

Note: At initial appearance.

these options are used when the prosecutor opts to either postpone or abandon altogether pursuit of charges and are enormously beneficial to the defendant.

One of the more common types of special assignments – diversion – entails the diversion or redirection of a defendant's adjudication to an alternative program. Such programs include drug treatment, psychiatric treatment, anger management, or other forms of counseling and preventative services. Crucially, a diversion often results in charges being dropped altogether, provided the defendant successfully completes the treatment program. "Deferred adjudication" is another type of special assignment, which carries even greater benefits than a diversion. With a deferment, charges are officially "deferred" for a period of time and, as long as the defendant stays out of trouble during that period, the charges are later dropped and the arrest record is usually expunged as well. Unlike a diversion, a deferment typically comes with only this stipulation, and no program requirements.

TABLE 1.12. *Alternative Prosecutions, by Special Assignment, Race, United States, 1990–2004 (Percent within Race)*

Race of Defendant	Special Assignment Made	Type of Special Assignment Made			
		Prosecutorial Diversion	Deferred Adjudication	Special Treatment Court Assignment	Other
Black	3.3	41.2	15.6	33.2	10.0
White	5.7	46.2	19.0	30.6	4.2
B-W Ratio	0.6	0.9	0.8	1.1	2.4
U.S.	4.4	46.6	18.3	29.1	6.0

According to Table 1.12, white defendants are about 40 percent more likely than blacks to have a special assignment made in their case. While the roughly 6 percent figure listed in the table seems small at first glance, based on the *State Court Processing Statistics* program data series, this translates into literally thousands more whites than blacks who can count on prosecutors handling their case with a measure of consideration and empathy.

Consenting to special assignments at the prosecution stage is not only a less frequent occurrence for black defendants, it also does not fit quite as neatly into the standard protocols of special assignments. For blacks, prosecutors tend to devise and consent to what are essentially "special" special assignments, according to Table 1.12. Whether for positive or negative purposes, we cannot tell from the data, but we know they are likely to come up with something different for blacks. Black defendants are almost two and a half times more likely to be granted assignments that vary from the most commonly used special assignments, such as diversion, deferments, and treatment courts. Furthermore, from Table 1.13[28] we get a glimpse of the kinds of treatment courts to which "special" defendants are redirected. What stands out in connection with this measure is the fact that blacks are three and a half times more likely than whites to be assigned to domestic violence court, a finding that does not necessarily jive with the fact that they are equally likely as whites to be prosecuted for assault. And, whereas Table 1.7 shows blacks are more than three times likelier to be arrested for drug abuse violations, Table 1.13 shows they are no more likely than whites to be redirected to drug court where, among other things, they would receive rehabilitative and preventative drug treatment and services.

TABLE 1.13. *Special Treatment Court Type, by Race, United States,*
1990–2004 (Percent within Race)

Race of Defendant	Domestic Violence Court	Drug Court	Other
Black	6.4	92.7	0.9
White	1.8	96.5	1.8
B-W Ratio	3.6	1.0	0.5
U.S.	3.6	95.1	1.3

In essence, there is something akin to a side door at the prosecution stage of the criminal process. Only a very small handful of criminal defendants are permitted to exit the criminal process out of this side door. Nationally representative data show unequivocally these lucky defendants are more likely white, by the thousands. Black defendants, by comparison, experience far less luck.

Judging Differences in Black and White

To fully appreciate whether, how, and at whose behest state criminal courts dispense justice along racial lines, we have to look at more than just the sentencing disparities that tend to define our perspective on this critical juncture in criminal process. The many rulings issued by judges throughout the trial court proceedings that precede imposition of punishment are as telling about racial inequality in adjudication as are the final judgment. Upon comparing the procedural decisions in cases involving black defendants to those involving whites, perhaps curiously, we learn that state criminal courts are not biased in favor of white defendants through and through, at least not according to national data. The category of court decisions for which we discern a marked racial divide happens to also be the one that interlocks with the politics of crime outside the court room. To the extent this is true, then, the court stage of the criminal process is arguably the least concerning within the process as far as racial progressivism is concerned, yet also the one that contains the clearest tell-tale signs of the criminal process' permeability to external political pressure. Tables 1.14 through 1.21 present nationally representative data from the SCPS data series. The data tell us a few things about race and state criminal court decision-making.

First, absent at the court stage are drastic racial differences in the way state criminal court judges dispose of the various motions and pleadings

TABLE 1.14. *Pretrial Release and Detention, by Race, United States,*
1990–2004 (Percent within Race)

Race of Defendant	Release vs. Detention		Reason for Detention		Release Supervision	
	Released	Detained	Denied Bail	Held on Bail	Supervised	Unsupervised
Black	60.4	37.6	7.5	31.4	14.4	85.6
White	67.1	31.5	5.9	25.5	15.8	84.2
B-W Ratio	0.9	1.2	1.3	1.2	0.9	1.0
U.S.	60.7	37.6	6.8	31.7	14.7	85.3

presented on behalf of black and white defendants. One way of getting at this is to examine judges' decisions regarding pretrial release and detention, using the data in Table 1.14.[29] Black defendants actually have a slight edge in connection with judges' ruling on whether to release a defendant pending trial. While they are minimally more likely than white defendants to be detained until their trial begins, the reasons for their detention is due as much to having been denied bail as to not having posted bail. In addition, when judges decide whether to require supervision for those defendants who are released pretrial, they do so in a racially balanced fashion. Black defendants who are released pretrial are no more or less likely to be subject to pretrial supervision than their white counterparts.

Second, the data supply a somewhat surprising answer to the question of whether there are marked differences in the type of pretrial release judges grant to black and white defendants. This is in many ways a question of whether the hurdles a black defendant must overcome to secure pretrial release are more imposing than those faced by a white defendant. The answer is "no," in light of the data in Table 1.15.[30] In fact, in one respect, black defendants appear to have somewhat of an advantage with respect to the types of non-financial releases granted by judges. They have a better chance of attaining an unsecured bond release and a significantly better chance of receiving an emergency release, which is normally granted as a result of overcrowded jails and prisons. Not only in connection with these two rarely used types of non-financial releases but also in connection with the two most commonly used types of non-financial releases we discern no remarkable bias against blacks. A black defendant faces an almost equal chance of being "ROR'd," that is to say released on his own recognizance or a verbal or written commitment to appear in court as required. A white defendant's prospects for attaining a conditional

TABLE 1.15. *Court Pretrial Financial and Non-Financial Release and Detention, by Race, United States, 1990–2004 (Percent within Race)*

Race of Defendant	Non-Financial Release			
	ROR	Conditional	Unsecured Bond	Emergency Release
Black	19	7.6	4.6	0.9
White	20.7	9.5	3.4	0.4
B-W Ratio	0.9	0.8	1.4	2.3
U.S.	20.1	8.0	3.4	0.5
Race of Defendant	Financial Release			
	Surety Bond	Full Cash Bond	Deposit Bail	Property Bond
Black	17.3	2.1	6.7	0.9
White	24.6	3.4	4.5	0.7
B-W Ratio	0.7	0.6	1.5	1.3
U.S.	19.4	2.6	4.8	0.7

release are slightly but not drastically better than a black defendant's, which means the former is slightly more likely to have to participate in a drug monitoring program or other types of pretrial services.

As to the two least desirable of the typical financial releases granted – surety bond and full cash bond – judges actually tend to require these financial releases primarily of white defendants, as shown in Table 1.15. This means judges more often impose on white defendants the requirement to post some form of collateral as a condition for their pretrial release. Conversely, deposit bonds and property bonds are used in ways that favor black defendants. Because a deposit bond is paid by the defendant directly to the court and eliminates the need for a bail bondsman, and a property bond permits a defendant to post property valued at the full bail amount, the financial and logistical challenges of black defendants' pretrial release are, by comparison, less burdensome.

The discretion exercised from the bench in the courtroom appears to be exercised in ways that minimally benefit black defendants. In most states, in disposing of pretrial motions and pleadings, judges are empowered to utilize their own judgment and to judiciously weigh the evidence and arguments presented by counsel. As an example, theirs is the decision whether to permit a defendant to post bail and not be confined prior to trial. Although many states require judges to offer defendants at least

TABLE 1.16. *Court Trial Outcomes, by Race, United States, 1990–2004*
(Percent within Race)

Race of Defendant	Dismissal	Acquittal	Guilty-Plea[a]	Guilty-Trial	Diverted-Deferral[a]
Black	29.3	1.3	59.4	5.2	4.7
White	23.2	0.7	64.4	3.5	8.2
B-W Ratio	1.3	1.9	0.9	1.5	0.6
U.S.	25.6	1.0	63.4	4.0	6.1

Note:

[a] This includes deferrals/diversions and plea arrangements reached after court trial proceedings commenced and also "No Contest" pleas. Data exclude "Other" and "Case pending."

two types of bail, it is judges who determine the amount of bail, based on their assessment of the public safety and flight risk posed by a defendant. In light of the preceding analysis, at a minimum, we can say judges' use of their discretion during pretrial lacks a clear and consistent racial imprint. Judges do not dispose of procedural matters in ways that increase the odds of a black conviction or prison sentence, according to the nationally representative data examined here.

The data in Table 1.16[31] lead to the same conclusion in regard to how judges eventually dispose of the criminal charges brought against defendants. The vast majority of those criminally charged reach a plea agreement with prosecutors, as shown in the table. For blacks, however, the SCPS data hint that they stand a better chance with judges. The chances of an acquittal for black defendants register at a rate twice that of whites (albeit an admittedly small percentage of blacks and whites are acquitted). The second most common trial outcome – dismissal – is also something experienced by blacks at a higher rate than whites. However, because many states require that judges consult with the prosecution in disposing of a case through dismissal, we have to look elsewhere to tease out judges' decisional tendencies in regard to final trial outcomes.

Table 1.17[32] allows us to do this by presenting comparative data on bench trials and jury trials. It reveals no major difference exists between judges' and juries' propensity to convict black and white defendants. However, a bench trial is much more likely to return a not guilty verdict for a black defendant than will a jury trial. Much more clearly in this instance, then, blacks are better off taking their changes with a judge as opposed to those deemed a jury of their peers.

TABLE 1.17. *Court Verdict, by Trial Type, Race, United States, 1990–2004 (Percent within Race)*

Race of Defendant	Convicted		Not Convicted	
	Bench	Jury	Bench	Jury
Black	80.5	76.2	19.5	23.8
White	87.1	79	13.0	21.0
B-W Ratio	0.9	1.0	1.5	1.1
U.S.	82.3	77.6	17.7	22.4

Note: Data exclude "Other" and "Case Pending."

TABLE 1.18. *Court Conviction, by Offense Category, Race, United States, 1990–2004 (Percent within Race)*

Race of Convict	Violent	Property	Drug	Public Order	Other Felony	Misdemeanor
Black	13.9	23.8	33.5	7.8	0.3	20.6
White	13.2	31.3	26.9	9.5	0.3	18.8
B-W Ratio	1.1	0.8	1.2	0.8	1.0	1.1
U.S.	14.5	26.1	31.4	8.6	0.3	19.0

For black defendants who are convicted, whether their conviction prospects hinge more or less on the type of offense they are charged with is captured by the data in Table 1.18.[33] There, we are able to ascertain whether black convictions exceed white convictions for certain types of crime. What we see, more precisely, are negligible to modest differences in the conviction rates of black and white defendants across the major offense categories. Violent crime and drug offenses are more likely to net convictions for blacks whereas convictions for property and public order offenses are more likely for white defendants. Inasmuch as these racial differences across crime types virtually mirror those observed earlier at the arrest and prosecution stages, they are not readily attributable to the court stage alone but rather are the direct byproduct of multiple decision points.

Right up until the point of sentencing, then, it seems black defendants receive mostly balanced treatment at the court stage or, more accurately, treatment that is not definitively more disadvantageous than that accorded to white defendants and convicts.

Sentencing is the point at which the racially balanced scales of court justice begin to tilt in favor of white defendants and against blacks. This observation is significant not only because it proves the existence of racial tracking also at the court stage; it is also noteworthy because it hints at external pressures that filter into the criminal process at this particular juncture more so than at the other junctures analyzed earlier. For sentencing decisions, judges must weigh defendants' character and potential for rehabilitation along with the nature of their crime. Judges must consider as well a mix of other things such as public safety, local community attitudes toward crime and punishment, and, alas and critically, mandatory sentencing laws. Such laws do more than just place parameters around judges' sentencing decisions. At times, they literally mandate that certain sentences be imposed in cases that fit the sentencing laws' predetermined criteria or formulas. The authority to decide whether to charge a defendant with a crime that is subject to determinate sentencing mandates is a decision that rests with prosecutors and grand juries, not judges. Thus the racial disproportionalness observed in connection with sentence types, sentence lengths, and death sentencing is fundamentally reflective, at least in part, of what is dictated beyond the courthouse. It is the most direct link in the criminal process to the politics of race and justice explored at length in the rest of the book.

Setting aside for now the political impetus behind the types of sentences imposed by judges, what we learn from the national data in Tables 1.19 through 1.21 is that a racial pattern is evident in sentencing outcomes. Blacks disproportionally experience the harshest forms of punishment doled out by the criminal justice system, a finding corroborated in other studies[34] as well. We observe from Table 1.19,[35] to start with, black convicts are 30 percent more likely to be sent to prison. The luckier convicts who receive the lighter forms of punishment, such as a fine or probation, tend to be white. Black convicts who are incarcerated for violent offenses will receive a prison sentence that is, on average, up to nine months longer than that of violent white convicts, according to Table 1.20.[36]

One of the main assertions of this chapter – that the criminal justice system reserves its harshest dispositions for blacks – could not be more evident than in the case of death sentencing. Much has been written about the causal dynamics of capital sentencing, a debate that hinges in large part on disagreement over the significance of other racial and nonracial factors, such as race-of-victim, defendant socioeconomic status, severity of crime, exacerbating or mitigating circumstances, and so on. We will examine some of the evidence parsed in this debate later in the book in Chapter 8. For now, we note only that, when viewed in terms

TABLE 1.19. *Court Sentence Type, by Race, United States,*
1990–2004 (Percent within Race)

Race of Convict	Prison	Jail	Probation	Fine	Other
Black	34.4	37	26.5	1.4	0.8
White	26.5	39.8	31.2	1.9	0.6
B-W Ratio	1.3	0.9	0.8	0.7	1.3
U.S.	31.3	40.9	25.5	1.6	0.8

TABLE 1.20. *Mean Sentence Length in Months, by Punishment Type,*
Offense Category, Race, United States, 2006

Race of Convict	Prison			Jail			Probation		
	Violent	Property	Drug	Violent	Property	Drug	Violent	Property	Drug
Black	108 mo.	49 mo.	51 mo.	7 mo.	6 mo.	5 mo.	44 mo.	36 mo.	38 mo.
White	99	46	50	7	6	5	44	37	34
B-W Ratio	1.1	1.1	1.0	1.0	1.0	1.0	1.0	1.0	1.1
U.S.	96	47	50	7	6	5	44	38	37

of proportionality to residential population makeup, there is little question that death sentencing in the United States is used excessively against black convicts. Whereas blacks make up roughly 13 percent of the U.S. population, black convicts claim an astounding 41 percent of the death row population.

The same imbalance is observed relative to executions. Black convicts are executed at a rate well more than triple blacks' share of the residential population. In contrast, white convicts' share of death row inmates and of executions is significantly lower than whites' share of the residential population. Now, just as in days of old, therefore, America's ultimate criminal punishment is borne disproportionally by those who have black skin. It is worth noting too Table 1.21[37] shows blacks claim a disproportionate share of those removed from death row each year, almost half. The removal figures shown do not include executions. They reflect successful death row appeals following a court finding of a flawed criminal trial, conviction, or death verdict. The higher rate of death row removals for blacks – when combined with the evidence showing higher rates of closed cases, dismissals, and acquittals for blacks – further reinforce the

TABLE 1.21. *Capital Punishment Sentencing, Execution, and Removal, by Race, 2009 (Number and Percent)*

Race of Convict	U.S. Residential Population (16+)	Total on Death Row as of 12/31/09	Executed	Removed from Death Row[a]
Black	13%	41%	40%	49%
White	80%	45%	46%	51%
Total number[b]	307 million	3,173	52	97

Notes:

[a] Excludes executions and includes persons of Hispanic/Latin origin.

[b] Includes American Indians, Alaska Natives, Asians, Native Hawaiians, and other Pacific Islanders.

idea that an unusual degree of seeming arbitrariness and unpredictability inheres in the criminal process experienced by blacks leading up to and including the court stage.

The Color Line Behind Bars

The disparity in incarceration rates is well known enough that the late black comedian Richard Pryor famously remarked in a joke about black men in prison "you go down there looking for justice; that's what you find: just us."[38] That Pryor was not too far off the mark is shown by the data in Table 1.22,[39] which reveal a black imprisonment rate six times that of whites and three times the national rate. The disparity is greatest for eighteen- and nineteen-year-olds, where blacks outnumber their counterparts more than ninefold. The prison system has custody of more than 100,000 black men in the prime of their life (i.e., thirty to thirty-four years old) but a significantly fewer number of white men in their prime. Even during their senior years, blacks far outnumber whites in the prison system. Drug-related offenses are a mainstay trap for blacks, as the rate at which they are sent to prison for drugs exceeds that of whites by eight to one.

Blacks now constitute a majority of the state and federal prison population, claiming fully 588,000 of the nation's 1,550,300 sentenced prisoners.

Besides a grossly disproportional black inmate population, what else do you find when you go to America's prisons? As against all of the attention devoted by critics to the racial disproportionalness in imprisonment

TABLE 1.22. *Sentenced Prisoners under State and Federal Jurisdiction, by Demographics, Offense Category, United States, 2010 (Rates Per 100,000 Residents)*

	Black		White		U.S.	
	Rate	Number	Rate	Number	Rate	Number
Total	1,551	588,000	253	499,600	502	1,550,257
Gender						
Male	3,107	561,400	465	451,600	953	1,446,000
Female	134	26,600	48	48,000	67	104,600
Age						
18–19	774	10,700	82	4,200	239	21,700
20–24	2,587	78,100	380	47,400	853	184,100
30–34	3,914	100,000	629	72,500	1,358	271,100
60–64	578	9,600	121	15,500	199	33,500
Offense						
Violent	767	290,900	120	236,000	239	736,800
Property	210	79,700	59	116,100	84	260,300
Drug	385	146,000	46	91,500	108	334,000

Note: These figures do not include persons in jail or persons in prison but not yet sentenced. The total number of persons incarcerated in public and private facilities as of 2010 was estimated at 2,266,800 as reported in: Glaze L. E. (December 2011). *Correctional Populations in the United States 2010* (NCJ 236319). http://www.bjs.gov

rates, what of the nature of blacks' experiences behind bars? Do the substantive differences evident throughout the initial stages of the criminal process appear behind bars? Do prison officials have a distinctive orientation toward the rehabilitation, health, safety, and parole-related concerns of black versus white prisoners? If indeed a black convict's prison experience compares unfavorably to a white convict's then we can say that from start to finish, the criminal justice process in the United States operates differently toward as well as *upon* black citizens, defendants, convicts, and prisoners.

Turns out, the racial markings of criminal justice are nowhere more apparent than in the lived experience within the nation's prisons. To compare the prison experience of black and white convicts, this discussion examines the rehabilitation training they receive, the medical screening and treatment they receive, the safety and discipline measures to which they are subject, and the amount of time they spend behind bars before being released by prison parole officials. The analysis draws

TABLE 1.23. *State Prison Experience: Discipline, Safety, and Mortality, by Race, United States, 2000–2009*

	Black	White	B-W Ratio	U.S.
Discipline (percent within race)				
Written up or found guilty of breaking rules	53.7	49.2	1.1	50.3
Subject to disciplinary action	92.3	90.8	1.0	91.5
Safety (percent within race)				
Injured in an accident	23.6	24.9	1.0	22.3%
Injured in an intentional assault	7.7	6.8	1.1	7.2
Sexually assaulted since admission	4.5	5.3	0.9	4.4
Mortality rate (per 100,000 inmates)				
Suicide	8.0	22	0.4	14
Homicide	2.0	5.0	0.4	4.0

on data from the only national prison survey series, the Bureau of Justice Statistics' *Survey of Inmates in State and Federal Correctional Facilities* (SISFCF), which is conducted by the U.S. Census Bureau and covers almost 3,000 variables on prisoners, prison activities, and prison services.

Analysis of these data indicates that serving time in prison is more of a waste of a black inmate's life than of a white inmate's. This does not apply to the circumstances of their imprisonment, at least not when measured in terms of safety, mortality, and disciplinary controls. In a place where cleavages are firmly entrenched along racial lines because of the prevalence of gangs and other identity groupings, blacks are actually safer than whites, according to the nationally representative SISFCF data in Table 1.23.[40] The life-threatening dangers of prison life are not shared equally by black and white prisoners, as whites are significantly more likely to die in prison, whether due to homicide or suicide. Neither is day-to-day physical safety a function of racial influences. Black and white prisoners are accidentally and intentionally injured and sexually victimized at comparable rates. Finally, prison officials are not significantly more prone to discipline black prisoners than white prisoners.

It is in connection with the rehabilitative capacity of the behind-bars experience that we observe the most vivid racial differences. Put simply,

TABLE 1.24. *State Prison Experience: Rehabilitation, by Race, United States, 2004 (Percent within Race)*

	Black	White	B-W Ratio	U.S.
Educational services				
Participated in vocational or job training program	29.2	25.8	1.1	27.2
Completed GED	37.2	51.3	0.7	38.1
Pre-release programs				
Employment counseling	15.0	12.4	1.2	12.8
Parenting classes	24.8	16.0	1.6	19.7
Life/skills community adjustment	34.1	29.4	1.2	28.6
Prison employment				
Work assignment inside prison	62.0	61.7	1.0	60.3
Monetary compensation for work	54.0	61.9	0.9	57.0
Time credits or privileges for work	30.1	27.9	1.1	28.7

for white convicts, prison programs yield the kind of long-term benefits that translate in the workplace so as to potentially make them better workers on release; for black convicts, they yield benefits that potentially make them better people. Of course, generally speaking, it can be argued that the goal of rehabilitating prisoners was abandoned by society long ago.[41] Even so, state governments continue to invest public monies into prison programing for at least the stated purpose of salvaging prisoners' human capital on release. This paradigm does not work the same way for black prisoners as it does for white prisoners. According to Table 1.24,[42] black prisoners are less likely to acquire traditional educational achievements (e.g., a General Education Diploma), while white prisoners complete standard educational programs at an appreciably higher rate, 30 percent higher. Thus, they benefit to a greater extent from their prison experience in the long run, because fewer than 5 percent of unskilled jobs in the central-city labor markets do not require a high school diploma, work experience, or other relevant skill.[43] Blacks participate to a nominally greater extent in pre-release programs, such as employment counseling, parenting classes, and life/skills community adjustment – helpful in the social world, but less so in the work world. Setting aside for now just who controls prisoner participation in rehabilitative programing, the main point of the discussion here is that, in the end, the prison experience is less productive for black convicts than for whites.

TABLE 1.25. *State Prison Experience: Medical Screening and Treatment, by Race, United States, 2004 and 2007 (Percent within Race)*

	Black	White	B-W Ratio	U.S.
Medical screening				
Medical screening at admission	73.9	71.9	1.0	72.9
Blood test since admission	86.2	87.4	1.0	86.6
Drug test since admission	66.8	66.4	1.0	64.3
AIDS test since admission	80.5	74.9	1.1	77.3
Medical treatment				
Medication for positive TB skin test	86.6	80.9	1.1	85.1
Seen by health professional for hepatitis	94.6	95.1	1.0	94.6
Counseling for mental or emotional problems	63.8	57.7	1.1	60.0
Required to participate in drug program	62.1	61	1.0	62.3
AIDS				
HIV positive	2.0	1.0	2.0	1.5
AIDS-related deaths (per 100,000 inmates)	14.0	5.0	2.8	9.0

Black convicts suffer from life-threatening illnesses at a rate nearly double that of whites. This observation does not coincide with a finding of differentiated health services. Medical screening, blood tests, and doctor's appointments are provided by prison officials at roughly the same rate for both groups, as shown in Table 1.25.[44] However, the data show the devastating effects of Acquired Immune Deficiency Syndrome (AIDS) are borne disproportionally by black inmates, something that further distinguishes prison's long-term impact on their lives. The rate of HIV infection for black prisoners is twice that of whites'. At first glance, the disproportionalness in HIV infection observed behind bars is similar to that outside of prison and, thus, suggestive of the possibility that more is at issue than the prison experience per se. However, the death rate for HIV-inflected black prisoners points to a more layered conclusion. National SISECF data show the rate of HIV-related deaths is considerably higher for all prisoners than it is for the general U.S. population. Crucially, for black prisoners, the already higher than usual death rate for prisoners is tripled. Table 1.25 shows the AIDS-related death rate for black inmates is nearly three times that of white inmates. Although

TABLE 1.26. *Percent of Maximum Sentence and Mean Months Served in State Prison, by Offense Category, Race, 2008*

Offense Category	% of Maximum Sentence Served			Mean Number of Months Served		
	Black	White	B-W Ratio	Black	White	Diff.
All	52.4	44.1	1.2	33 mos.	26 mos.	7 mos.
Violent	63.7	60.0	1.1	58	48	10
Property	46.0	38.5	1.2	23	20	3
Drug	42.1	31.6	1.3	24	18	6
Possession	40.0	31.1	1.3	18	14	4
Trafficking	42.4	28.2	1.5	28	20	8
Other Drug Offense	47.1	41.5	1.1	24	22	2
Public Order	54.5	42.2	1.3	24	19	5

white prisoners' suicide and homicide rates outpace that of blacks, black prisoner's increased vulnerability to life-threatening diseases carries with it considerable collateral effects that are eventually carried back to their families, homes, and communities.

The question of how much of their prison sentence black and white convicts end up serving before returning to their communities is ultimately a question of how extensively their human capital is depreciated and for how long. In regard to percentage of sentence served, moreover, there is a difference. Prison officials are more likely to deny parole to black prisoners. For cases in which the sentencing judge did not foreclose the possibility of early release, the decision whether to release a prisoner before the expiration of his sentence is typically made by parole boards, many of which are constituted in part by prison officials or which heavily weigh the input of prison officials regarding suitability for early release and parole. (Data from the National Corrections Reporting Program show it is rare for a state prisoner to serve out his entire sentence. Thus, the vast majority of prisoners are affected by release decisions.) Table 1.26,[45] which depicts the amount of time served in state prisons, makes clear blacks serve a larger proportion of their prison sentence. This is regardless of the type of offense for which they are imprisoned. For almost every type of crime, black prisoners must serve more time than their white counterparts. This is especially so with respect to drug trafficking, for which blacks serve 42 percent of their sentence and whites, 28 percent. This translates into a mean difference of eight months. For violent crimes, the 4 percent difference in time served translates into black prisoners spending an additional ten months behind bars for similar crimes and an additional six months for drug offenses.

Where the prison experience is concerned too, then, there are separate tracks for blacks and whites. The former leads to a longer stay in prison, less productive rehabilitation, and a greater chance of suffering lifelong repercussions.

Extended History of Racial Differences in Criminal Punishment

In closing, it is important to point out the racial divide in criminal justice is by no means a new phenomenon. The observed racial disproportional-ness extends virtually throughout American history. The racial disparity in arrests has existed for decades, as shown in Figure 1.1.[46] And, since national prison data first became available in the late 1920s, they have likewise manifest a persistent racial disparity, as shown in Table 1.27.[47] Although the black–white gap in imprisonment peaked to between 6:1 and 8:1 as of the 1990s and later, prior to this time, blacks were always at least three times to five times more likely than whites to be incarcerated. That the American criminal justice system is grounded in a long history

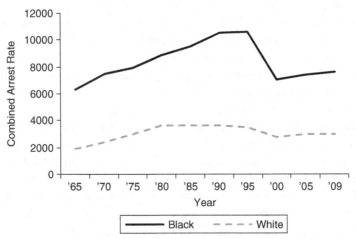

FIGURE 1.1. Combined Violent, Property, and Drug Arrest Rate, by Race, 1965–2009 (Per 100,000 Residents).

TABLE 1.27. *Rate of Imprisonment, by Race, United States,*
1930–2010 (Rates Per 100,000 Residents)

	1930	1940	1950	1960	1970	1980	1990	2000	2010
Black	124	137	114	143	85	199	1194	1729	1551
White	46	37	30	35	16	39	176	208	253
B-W Ratio	3	4	4	4	5	5	7	8	6
U.S.	54	48	38	47	24	59	297	480	502

Note: Data for 1930–1980 reflect prison admissions; data for 1990–2010 reflect sentenced prisoners. Not reflected in the table are persons in jail facilities or not yet sentenced.

of racial differentiation says something about the basic nature of the system itself. It is organized along racial lines and has been for some time.

Having observed the substantive components of racial tracking in the foregoing, we consider next its broader public policy impact and significance in Chapter 2.

2

Policy Process Theory of Racial Tracking

An Overview

Presently, the dominant theories put forth to explain the persistence of racial disproportionalness in American justice are offered in the fields of law, criminology, sociology, psychology, and economics. The available politics-centered accounts tend to emphasize racial bias or indifference – conscious and unconscious, institutional and noninstitutional. At the risk of oversimplifying, the politics-centered accounts may be summed up as attributing key racial justice outcomes mostly to actors within the criminal justice system, to racial conservatism, to rulings of the Burger-Rehnquist Courts, and/or to the Republican Party. In connection with the latter, Richard M. Nixon's "law and order" agenda and Ronald Reagan's War on Drugs each receive considerable attention.

Empirical analyses of systemic political forces and their role in enabling racial tracking are in short supply.[1] In fact, within the political science discipline generally, research studies explicitly purposed to provide an in-depth, systematic account of the perpetual interplay between race, crime, and criminal justice politics are rare. Yet, precisely because racial tracking is a major public policy concern, the policy process literature would seem an excellent starting place for any effort to explicate its causal roots more fully. In turn, racial tracking is an excellent case study for gauging the overall utility of existing theories of the public policy process and, particularly, their capacity to explain the lack of racial justice reform.

This study presents a public policy process-centered theory and analysis of racial tracking. The theoretical framework it advances constitutes an attempt to synthesize and expand upon what we know about how the policy process works. The analysis then applies the expectations derived from this framework to the intersection of race and criminal justice. Thus, the book endeavors to build upon as well as test the foundation laid by major models of policymaking. What it aims to contribute to the public policy literature is twofold. First is what I term here the "basic principles policy process framework." While this framework is anchored in the rich empirical insights as well as the disagreements within the study of policymaking, it also aims to amplify the commonalities across the varied perspectives. The benefit gained by identifying and articulating these commonalities is that the considerable breadth and depth of knowledge amassed in this subfield can be more readily fitted to other persistent societal problems. It can help to facilitate efforts to ascertain whether and how the policy process is implicated in regard to other ongoing macro-level problems.

Among the central questions of interest to this study, for which a policy process principles framework offers valuable guidance are: Why has the policy process failed to redress the longstanding racial divide in American criminal justice? Who or what entities within the policy process are chiefly responsible for the lack of attentiveness? How should we apportion political accountability in regard to the continued interaction between race and criminal law enforcement? The research presented in the remainder of this book illuminates how the answers to these questions are imbedded in a policy process lens. Meanwhile, the story of the political system's non-responsiveness to racial tracking contains some useful additives to the larger story of how public policy decisions are made in the United States. There are bits and pieces of the former that could be more fully and explicitly incorporated into the latter.

In short, racial tracking has a policy process tale of its own that is not only complementary but also supplementary to current understandings of policy process. Accordingly, the data and information examined in the chapters to follow expose also the public policy lessons imbedded in the intersection of race and criminal justice. In addition to the six principles extracted from past studies, I articulate also a seventh principle derived from the present work, one I term the "public origins principle." An integrative policy process theory of racial tracking is the final product of applying these seven principles to the book's research analysis. The twin theoretical aims of this book are to interject into the study of race and justice key insights gleaned from the public policy literature and to articulate one of the ways in which racial tracking adds to what we already know about how and why public policy problems are tackled in the United States (or not).

Of course, the foregoing discussion and what it promises is premised on the understanding that racial tracking is indeed a public policy matter. But, before proceeding as if it were, we begin by first establishing how it is so. Whereas Chapter 1 describes racial tracking, we review in this chapter its broader societal impact. Following this is a presentation of the basic principles process framework. Then, I present an overview of how the framework is applied in the remainder of the study to help explain racial tracking.

Racial Tracking as Public Policy

Based on the most rudimentary conception of what constitutes a public policy problem, racial tracking is appropriately classified as such. Affecting more than just the subset of blacks identified in Chapter 1's analysis, taken as a whole, racial tracking is a phenomenon that affects a sizeable portion of the American public in harmful ways that mark a meaningful divergence from societal norms, and on a continual basis. Further, to the extent that the short- and long-term consequences of racial tracking are socially and politically constructed, it is a phenomenon that is at least partly amenable to governmental policy intervention.[2]

Racial tracking is a public policy problem first in that it is operative on a massive scale. The criminal justice disparities laid out in the preceding chapter result in a fundamental alteration to the life course of millions of blacks. The probability of black citizens in the United States being imprisoned at least once in their lifetimes is remarkably higher than average. Nearly one in every five black citizens is projected to go to state or federal prison at least once, compared to only 3 percent of non-Hispanic whites.[3] For black males, there is a staggering one-out-of-three chance. Meanwhile, the already emergent net effect of racial tracking is similarly massive, as ex-prisoners now claim roughly 20 percent of the civilian noninstitutional black male population, compared to only 3 percent of the white male population. Ex-felons, defined as those who have been convicted of a felony, claim nearly 44 percent of the black male population, compared to about 9.5 percent of white males.[4] As of 2010, this translates into approximately 7,227,564 non-Hispanic black males and 9,216,674 white males. It should be noted this statistical portrait excludes the nearly 600,000 black males currently confined to jail and prison facilities, as well as those now en route to a felony conviction.[5]

To strengthen our grasp of the scale and policy significance of these numbers, consider the minimum numerical thresholds that trigger governmental action under the Voting Rights Act of 1965 (VRA), as amended. The VRA – designed to minimize racial-ethnic disparities and discrimination in elections – uses 5 percent as the base trigger for requiring states to provide voting materials in bilingual format. If more than 5 percent of the citizens of a state or political subdivision are of a single language minority or of limited English language proficiency, then the state is barred from providing voting materials in English only. The VRA also uses an absolute figure; it imposes the prohibition where more than 10,000 citizens are part of a language minority. In essence, with an eye toward racially and ethnically balanced participation in elections, the alarm set by Congress is triggered at 5 percent and 10,000 – a far cry from the 40 percent and 7 million now directly affected by racial tracking.

Concretizing the substantive elements of racial tracking's harmful impact and also its divergence from societal norms is a difficult task, partly because so much of its impact is of a psychological and emotional nature. What we can do, nonetheless, is weigh its tangible effects. Felony conviction and incarceration rates are the features of criminal justice known to carry the most serious consequences, but there are data that show *mere contact* with the criminal justice system can have significant repercussions as well. Records of "arrest," "conviction," and incarceration" convey a stigma differing in degree but not necessarily in kind.[6] The arrest rate of blacks is 250 percent greater than average; therefore, the personal, individualized repercussions of an arrest are felt disproportionally within black communities as well, and there are many negative consequences. Arrest records are part of one's "criminal record" or "rap sheet" and used by law enforcement to gauge propensity toward criminal behavior and, in some instances, help prove guilt. U.S. Equal Employment Opportunity Commission guidelines permit employers to decline to hire an applicant because of an arrest record, provided the employer asserts a business justification for doing so.[7] Because the Federal Fair Credit Reporting Act permits consumer credit reporting agencies to maintain and provide criminal record information, an arrest record functions as a handicap in a host of other ways. This is all separate from the more immediate fallout that results from sometimes lengthy pretrial detentions that can jeopardize employment, income, housing, and other critical aspects of one's life.

The direct and indirect costs of a conviction and of incarceration are jolting. Study after study has detailed the debilitating employment-related repercussions of a criminal record. A "felony conviction or time in prison makes individuals significantly less employable."[8] Schmitt and Warner clarify this effect is not simply that individuals who commit crimes are less likely to work in the first place; rather, felony convictions or time in prison has a net independent impact that lowers the employment prospects of ex-offenders below what they would otherwise be. In fact, the evidence indicates employers are more willing to hire almost any other marginalized group besides ex-offenders. While we know that minorities' overrepresentation in the criminal justice system means they suffer these employment effects or scars more frequently than whites do, Holzer and colleagues add that these scars are also more serious for minorities.[9] The economic consequences for minorities are different in degree and kind. Pager's work comparing the job prospects of nonviolent offenders with virtually identical educational and work experience credentials shows that black nonviolent offenders tend to receive fewer than half the job offers of their white counterparts.[10]

There are a number of existing policies and practices that directly facilitate the disadvantageous effects of incarceration on employment opportunities, those of black ex-felons more than white ex-felons. As to laws that bar employers from hiring ex-offenders in certain positions under the guise of protecting vulnerable populations, research studies show that some of these bans are chiefly punitive, more so than preventative.[11] For example, the theory of negligent hiring makes employers liable and subject to punitive damages for any risk created by their employees. Work by Holzer, Raphael, and Stoll further indicates employers are already far more wary of the liabilities induced by simply hiring black males, separate and apart from their fear of hiring black ex-convicts.[12] Moreover, parole restrictions often require ex-prisoners and parolees to live in the same communities from which they came, which are often predominantly minority communities with relatively few unskilled jobs. Some state laws go so far as to prohibit ex-offenders from obtaining driver's licenses, which are typically the most basic starting point for proving identity and residency in connection with submission of a job application or completion of new employee tax forms and other paperwork.

There are dozens of additional ways in which federal and state laws magnify the economic ramifications of racial tracking. Federal laws prohibit drug felons from living in federally funded public housing. Federal and state laws permit private agencies and landlords to deny housing under certain conditions, most notably in the case of a drug conviction. Ex-prisoners are expressly barred for a period of time from obtaining federally subsidized student loans and grants-in-aid to further their education. The income and salaries of the seven million black ex-offenders are likewise restricted by existing policies. The 1996 federal welfare law, Temporary Assistance to Needy Families (TANF), contains a specific provision that restricts access to public benefits for individuals with drug-related convictions.[13] Under the law, states must impose a lifetime ban on the receipt of TANF assistance and food stamps for drug felons, unless state legislation is enacted to opt out or modify the ban. Only a handful of states have opted out of the lifetime ban. This ban carries sizeable consequences for blacks, as nearly one out of every four sentenced black prisoners is incarcerated due to a drug conviction. Studies show that child support orders and the arrearages that accrue during a prison stay operate as a form of additional "taxes" on the earnings of many ex-offenders.

Although extraordinarily large numbers of black ex-offenders bear the most direct economic hardships, the black population and society as a whole also endure certain economic losses. Schmitt and Warner detail the extent to which the overall U.S. economy pays a price for the nation's incarceration policy in the form of reduced output of goods and services, which in their estimation equals as much as 0.4 to 0.5 percentage points of the GDP as of 2008, or roughly $57 to $65 billion.[14] If we apportion this amount according to blacks' 40 percent share of the existing sentenced prisoner population, we can say that the economic burden of racial tracking borne specifically by black America registers at up to $26 billion annually. Racial tracking drives up unemployment rates within black America, especially those of black males. The decline in employment rates facilitated specifically by incarceration rates is estimated at 4.7 to 5.3 percentage points for black males, compared to only 1.0 to 1.1 for white males.[15] It bears emphasizing this effect is on top of the normally higher unemployment rates of black males. As such, their plight within the criminal justice system diminishes their already lower socioeconomic prospects. In fact, about one-third of the employment gap between young white and young black men is attributable to racial differences in incarceration rates.[16] There is, then, a cyclical economic effect for black males that works as follows.

The racial disparities in criminal justice widen the racial disparities in socioeconomic viability, which in turn widen[17] the racial disparities in criminal justice, and so on.

The racial divide in criminal justice depletes what economists refer to as human capital, which is the agglomeration of work-related skills, education, and references from employment and acquaintances that enable one to maintain beneficial labor market participation. This outcome is observed at both the individual and aggregate levels. To the extent that racial tracking lowers the overall productivity of predominantly black neighborhoods, from the standpoint of potential job and business developers it thereby also diminishes the feasibility of business and job development projects within those communities. Finally, the black law enforcement experience has a "viral" effect that handicaps millions more who are not directly entangled within the criminal process. Those associated with ex-offenders suffer disadvantage too. Here, as well, federal and state policies are implicated. As an example, public housing rental leaseholders deemed to have associated with or hosted drug felons as guests are evicted and barred from public housing. Applicants to public-sector jobs and some private-sector jobs as well are typically required to disclose their familial or social relation to persons convicted of various crimes, and such disclosures can prove damaging.

Of special note is the deterioration of the black family structure brought on by the overrepresentation of blacks in prisons and jails. This particular aspect of its impact is a critical pathway through which its debilitating effects are diffused across the black population and perpetuated from one generation to the next.[18] To start with, the TANF ban on access to government assistance and food stamps is a ban that operates in practice on families and children, not simply the targeted ex-offender. A vast literature establishes the relation between income on the one hand, and educational, housing, and political outcomes on the other.[19] More poignantly, Wilson's work on the black urban underclass illustrates incarceration rates are a key factor lowering the black male marriageability index, which in turn increases the preponderance of single-parent households within black neighborhoods, a phenomenon that in turn helps engender the higher incidence of concentrated poverty and social dislocation there.[20]

Then there are the intergenerational dynamics. Not only does incarceration dismantle the relationship between parent and child, but also in many states parental rights during and after incarceration are terminated or severely curbed as a matter of practice. Especially important for our discussion is that this circumstance is most acute for blacks, given that approximately one in nine black children have a parent currently behind bars, compared to one in every twenty-eight of all minor children in the United States.[21] Researchers have documented extensively the still wider range of handicaps that compound loss of a parent to the system, including showing that the children of prisoners face a greater chance of academic failure, truancy, and eventually becoming prisoners themselves.[22] Given that the black residential population in the United States is, on average, younger than other racial subgroups, the collateral consequences of criminal justice bear disproportionately on black children.

In addition to the aforementioned psychological, economic, and collateral effects of racialized law enforcement are the political consequences that flow from it. Perhaps oddly, the black law enforcement experience renders the black electorate less able to mobilize within the electoral process on behalf of criminal justice reform, as Manza and Uggen carefully lay out in their study of felon disenfranchisement and American democracy.[23] Moreover, according to recent data compiled by the Brennan Center for Justice, all but fifteen states and the District of Columbia have enacted laws that prohibit persons convicted of a felony from participating in elections following their release from prison.[24] Among the states with felon disenfranchisement laws, four permanently disenfranchise all persons with felony convictions, unless and until government approves restoration on a per person basis. Seven permanently disenfranchise certain categories of ex-offenders, unless and until government restores the right on an individual basis. In the remaining twenty-four states, voting rights are restored only after completion of the sentence imposed, whether that entails completion of probation, parole, or a term in prison.

The Sentencing Project estimates that, as of 2013, such felon disenfranchisement laws result in the disenfranchisement of fully 2.2 million or 7.7 percent of the entire black adult population in the United States, compared to 1.8 percent of the nonblack population.[25] In three states – Florida (23 percent), Kentucky (22 percent), and Virginia (20 percent) – more than one in five black citizens are barred from participating in American elections. In essence, during a time when voter participation levels for the country as a whole hover near the 50 percent mark, erosion of the black electorate by way of criminal justice forces further mutes an already marginalized voice in national elections and politics.

The mass effects of racial tracking are observed not only in connection with the plight of the black population, black neighborhoods, and black families in the United States; the average nonblack citizen's interests are also intertwined with the problem. Recall, to start with, the annual loss in goods and services that ranges in cost up to $26 billion for black imprisonment annually. Alongside these economic losses, for taxpayers, blacks' overrepresentation in the criminal justice system also translates into hundreds of billions of dollars funneled out of public coffers to corrections. What is more, these dollars may be aptly described as poorly spent. The direct costs of maintaining the existing incarceration-centered crime policy to state taxpayers is, on average, up to $52 billion annually, according to data from both the Pew Center and the U.S. Bureau of Justice Statistics.[26] As much as 80 percent of these expenditures are allocated to institutional corrections (i.e., jails and prisons) and the remainder to community supervision (i.e., probation and parole). The per-prison-inmate cost reported by a sample of thirty-three states in 2009 was estimated at $29,000 annually.[27] This figure, multiplied by the nearly 600,000 sentenced black prisoners now behind bars, indicates some $17.4 billion is spent annually on black prisoners.

Ordinarily, one would expect greater public safety to be the return on an investment of this magnitude; however, both government and non-governmental data and analyses consistently show just the opposite. First of all, according to the Bureau of Justice Statistics, some 45 percent of black sentenced state prisoners were incarcerated in 2011 due to non-violent offenses.[28] Most had never been previously convicted. Thus, a sizeable portion of the black and white prison population never jeopardized public safety in the first place. Furthermore, up to 45 percent of those released from prison are re-incarcerated within three years, either for committing a new crime or for violating conditions governing their release. In terms of numbers, government data show that of the 668,800 new prison admissions in 2011, fully 205,787 were parole violators.[29] Because parole violations can stem from something as simple as failure to report to a parole officer in a timely fashion, some are re-incarcerated, in essence, because of their initial incarceration. Then, others are left to resort to crime as a means of support, and still others are never rehabilitated due partly to the paucity of rehabilitation programs in prison. The Pew Center concluded that "the system designed to deter them from continued criminal behavior clearly is falling short."[30]

More than just a negligible return on investment, the incarceration-centered crime policy that chiefly ensnares blacks actually feeds the problem it purportedly solves. It jeopardizes public safety. Low employment and educational success rates are closely related to the high recidivism rates.[31] To the extent incarceration negatively affects the former, it necessarily increases the latter.

Fagan, West, and Holland state the case rather cogently:

Incarceration begets more incarceration, and incarceration also begets more crime, which in turn invites more aggressive enforcement, which then re-supplies incarceration. These dynamics spiral over time in a reciprocal dynamic that at some tipping point is likely to reach equilibrium.... It is, quite literally, a vicious cycle. The dynamic becomes self-sustaining and reinforcing, and continues even as externalities such as labor market dynamics or population structure undergo significant change, as well as in the face of declining crime rates and receding drug epidemics.[32]

The authors go on to specify the external mechanisms that contribute to and reinforce incarceration. They cite the declining economic fortunes of former inmates and the effects on neighborhoods where they tend to reside, resource and relationship strains on families of prisoners, which weaken the family's ability to supervise children, and voter disenfranchisement, which weakens the political economy of neighborhoods.[33]

In sum and substance, whether adjudged by way of a cost–benefit analysis or with a view toward public safety, the growing criminalization of black males and racial tracking in general are as counterproductive as they are unproductive.

Persistent racial disproportionalness and disparate treatment within the criminal justice system can be said to raise serious moral questions about America's level of active commitment to racial equality, fairness, and justice. Western details the many ways in which racial disparities in law enforcement rival racial inequalities in other critical areas of life, such as net worth, unemployment, infant mortality, and nonmarital childbirth.[34] Many of these are tied to the very kinds of deep divisions tackled by the black civil rights movement of the sixties. It is arguably the case that racial tracking rises to the level of a civil rights issue, even accepting criminality on the part of blacks as a contributing (and inexcusable) factor. As Loury notes,

> There could be no law, no civilization, without the imputation to particular persons of responsibility for their wrong acts. But the sum of a million cases, each one rightly judged on its merits to be individually fair, may nonetheless constitute a great historic wrong. The state does not only deal with individual cases. It also makes policies in the aggregate, and the consequences of these policies are more or less knowable.[35]

These consequences, as demonstrated here and elsewhere, are felt mainly by blacks.

Whether racial tracking is perceived by most American citizens as a matter of principle is separate and apart from the fact that it is a key feature of America's global image, and becoming more so. Within the larger international community, it is one of the ways the United States is distinguished from other countries. The United States claims less than 5 percent of the world's population, but fully 25 percent of the world's prison population, surpassing the former communist nation Russia. The American criminal justice system's treatment of blacks was considered grave enough to prompt Amnesty International, a human rights–monitoring organization, to declare the United States in violation of four international human rights treaties because of law enforcement improprieties rooted in racial and class inequality.[36] Moreover, in 1994, the United States ratified the International Convention on the Elimination of All Forms of Racial Discrimination (ICERD) treaty; it requires that all signatories comply with the anti–racial profiling provisions in it. The United Nation's oversight committee responded to the January 2009 report of the United States by officially expressing concern that the United States had failed to pass federal legislation to stop the practice of racial profiling.[37]

In conclusion, the racial divide in criminal law enforcement is appropriately treated as a public policy problem in that it yields macro-level, negative consequences on a continual basis for the American public – black and otherwise. The question that remains is why? Why has a public policy problem of this magnitude persisted for decades, unaddressed by the policy process? For answers to these questions, we turn to the public policy literature.

Basic Principles Policy Process Framework

There are several common threads that run through the major schools of thought on the primary drivers of public policymaking, and these threads contain insights on the political dynamics of racial tracking. I endeavor here to identify and articulate these threads. Like almost any effort to extrapolate generalizable principles, the following presentation of these threads stops short of capturing all of the particularities that occupy the richly complex research studies in the field. Importantly, however, it is sufficiently beyond abstraction that we can apply it to the study of race, crime, and justice and, in doing so, arrive at a more comprehensive understanding of this important policy subject. In what follows, I detail six observations made by the existing research on public policymaking. With a few exceptions, these are the six axioms that most works in the field already concede in varying degrees, either explicitly or implicitly. In addition to these six principles, I articulate a seventh principle reflected in the book's case study of race, crime and criminal justice politics. I use these seven research discoveries to construct a "basic principles policy process" framework.

By "principles" I mean the fundamental rules or laws by which the policy process has been shown to operate. As opposed to a set of exacting scientific theorems that neatly explain all-things-public policy, expounded here are certain elemental truths about the functioning of the process that emanate from the discoveries of major studies to date. No claim is made that every single tenet or every discovery of every work worth noting is articulated; rather, the central tenets of some of the most widely noted classic public policy works and the contemporary research seeded by these earlier works. The seven principles include what I term here (and not necessarily in order of importance): the principle of multidimensionality, the power player principle, the problem–process kinship principle, the politics principle, the systems principle, the opportunity principle, and the principle underscored by the present study of racial tracking, namely the public origins principle.

Principle of Multidimensionality. Perhaps the most basic "principle" of all is that of multidimensionality. It centers on the idea that the process has many moving parts. A single individual or entity does not dictate policy output. Nor is policy in a given area fully forged at a particular place or time. This rudimentary observation was established by the now defunct linear stages model, one of the more prominent original conceptions of the policy process. The model posited policy outcomes as the product of a multidimensional process. The main architects of the model – Lasswell, Jones, Anderson, and Brewer and de Leon[38] – conceived of policymaking as lodged in multiple steps or stages, with each stage succeeded by the one to follow in a linear fashion. Problem identification was followed by agenda-setting, then policy formulation, implementation, and, finally, feedback. Each stage enveloped its own set of concerns and personnel, and each operated relatively independent of one another.

Following widespread critique of the model as having severely limited applicability to actual policymaking,[39] the linear-stages model was largely abandoned by the mid-1980s as an instructive framework for either descriptive or explanatory purposes. Seldom were the stages in the linear model found to be as neatly distinct from one another as the model indicated. Rarely, if ever, did case studies show policy problems resolved within a singular policy cycle. Often, the same problem is addressed at multiple levels of government and by multiple institutions. In general, political science soon found the policy process to be anything but orderly, and in fact rather untidy. The linear-stages model is now of mostly heuristic value. It supplies a kind of universal language for theory-building, that is, a way for political scientists to think and empiricize in concrete terms about policymaking – its parts, participants, and modes of "processing" policy issues. While the linear-stages model is also of little value for explaining racial tracking, it is nonetheless noteworthy for purposes of this analysis in at least one important respect: implicit in its disaggregation of the policy process is the idea that the process is composed of many parts, that it involves many actors and sets of actors. Policymaking in the United States is decentralized, more or less.

Power Player Principle. Amid the multiplicity of participants in the decentralized policy process is a power vortex. Perhaps oddly, the policy process can be aptly described as a multicentric process that revolves around a center. Power is not evenly distributed. Notwithstanding the constitutional prerogative of every eligible U.S. citizen to cast an equal vote in elections and thereby exert some influence on governmental policy decisions, there are players in the game of policymaking that exert decisive influence. Everyone has a say, but some entities have a greater say in regard to policy output than others. This is the second principle operating within the policy process. True enough, there are tremendous differences among scholars as to which participants matter most. However, the common (and perhaps even obvious) theoretical conclusion articulated across the many theories of policy control is that of power consolidation, namely the idea that a measure of "greater" policy influence is actively exercised by someone. There is a key power player that effectively controls the on–off switch, so to speak.

Pluralism once described the policy process as largely the purview of pressure group competition, such that policies resulted from bargaining and compromises between participating groups.[40] Under that model – no longer considered descriptively accurate – power was widely distributed across groups. Conversely, elite theory locates the lion's share of policymaking in the hands of a powerful, privileged few. Sociologist C. Wright Mills and political scientists E. E. Schattschneider, Thomas Dye, G. William Domhoff, among others, argued a privileged few make the key decisions that end up affecting the mass of average citizens. The less important decisions are left for the less privileged to negotiate. In the work of Bachrach and Baratz and later also Ferguson's and others, the power elite are most impactful when dictating which issues will be addressed by the policy process and which will not.[41] The authors investigated the dynamics of what they termed "nondecision-making" and asserted that to the extent that a person or group – consciously or unconsciously – creates or reinforces barriers to the public airing of policy conflicts, that person or group has power.[42] Gaventa[43] expanded power elite theory to demonstrate there is also a mobilization bias in policymaking politics. Meanwhile, in sharp contrast with elite theory, others believe majority rule is the most basic rule of the policy process. Theorists from Anthony Downs to Benjamin Page, Robert Shapiro, and others offer empirical evidence proving the strength of the causal relationship between public policy outputs and majority opinion and also party positioning.[44] Taken as a whole, power theories are invariably anchored in the idea that something or someone is exercising primary control over the policy process – at some point and time.

Problem–Process Kinship Principle. A third axiom of policymaking pertains to the interconnectedness of policy problems and policy process: the manner in which the process operates is variable, and it varies partly in tandem with the nature and scope of the problem at issue. Not all policy concerns are the same, and consequently the same process will not emerge for all concerns. A different set of problems will actuate a different mix of participants and, in turn, a different set of politics and processes. Thus, it is important to consider the type of issues and concerns being addressed when attempting to understand the policy process. As a matter of principle, the nature of policy problems is an important piece of the puzzle of what the policy process tackles, how it operates, and what it produces. The idea that policy areas constitute arenas of power and relationships was first introduced by Theodore Lowi.[45] Lowi formulated a typology of policy issues, which has since been fine-tuned by other scholars.[46] The overarching point of Lowi's and other classification schemes is to illustrate that certain issue areas will stimulate political activism on the part of a larger or smaller scope of participants and power structures, depending on how much is perceived to be at stake in regard to a governmental policy, who is affected by the policy, and how they are affected. Under the original schema, redistributive policies involved a wider scope than regulatory policies, which in turn enveloped a wider and more contentious scope of politics than distributive policies.

As a general rule, issues with (or perceived to have) broad impact and consequences will amass greater interest and participation than the reverse. The more at stake, the more intense the interests and expectations of the participants. To return to the discussion of a moment ago regarding power, with the problem–process kinship principle now in hand, we can say that the locus of power will vary with the policy issue. In some policy areas, the "few" will be intensely organized and indulged, in others the interests of the masses will be piqued and eventually served. The distribution of power within the policy process is, according to a number of theories, a function of the problem–process nexus. Once you ascertain the perceived nature and scope of the problem at hand, you can better estimate the likely power relationships that will emerge. (In this regard, problem definition matters a great deal. More on this later.)

Politics Principle. The authoritative policy decisions of legislators, bureaucratic officials, judges, and other official policymakers do not always line up neatly with the policy problem such decisions are purportedly intended to redress. Consequently, the ideal of a policy process operating efficiently and earnestly and in a unidirectional fashion toward the goal of making society a better place is of modest value for understanding what actually occurs and why participants behave as they do. To be sure, some (often many) policy adoptions are motivated chiefly by an interest in achieving problem resolution. However, some (often many) are also driven chiefly by segmented interests that are disconnected from or only tangentially centered on problem resolution. Politically motivated behavior is an inherent feature of government policymaking. As a result, the process is as much a "political" policy process as it is a "problem-solving" policy process. Therefore, nailing down who is out to get what or whom – besides making the world a better place – is indispensable to grasping who gets what and why, and who does not.

Starting with David Mayhew's,[47] Richard Fenno's,[48] and Morris Fiorino's[49] classic works exposing the non-policy-related motives behind lawmakers' behavior, an impressive array of qualitative and quantitative studies to follow likewise reveal the effects of other putatively political factors. Among these are constituency-district interests, party identification and membership, ideology, monied interests, and so forth.[50] By necessity, reelection is the goal that every member of Congress must achieve in order to continue pursuit of any other goal within that body – be it political, policy-related, or otherwise. Of all the ancillary motives identified, then, it is a legislator's interest in being reelected that scholarly analyses of the legislative vote frequently uncover as a principal driver of legislative behavior, both on and off the floor of the legislature. Given that lawmakers and their policy decisions are not singularly geared toward responding to and fixing problems that arise in society, moreover, the policy process should be expected to sometimes fail to attend to what many consider major public problems and to sometimes stop short of fully resolving problems selected for resolution. Just when it will do one versus the other is something the "system principle" helps to unpack, which we take up next.

Systems Principle. The policy process is often considered analogous to biological processes, insofar as it is understood to have an evolutionary life course of its own. The whole is greater than the sum of its parts. It is, more precisely, an ecosystem with interconnecting and interacting parts, namely problems, participants, and policy subsystems. To the multidimensionality principle, then, we can add what I term a "systems principle." The latter captures the notion of the process, *as a whole*, reacting to or producing policy change in reaction to certain environmental stimuli while resisting or absorbing others. It is this systems-side of policymaking that partly accounts for the policy process' failure to ameliorate sometimes glaringly obvious and disadvantaging public policy problems.

Incremental theory tells us the most we should ever expect is for change to occur only gradually, by way of lots of small adjustments to what existed before and typically over the course of many years. Especially in democracies, "policy does not move in leaps and bounds."[51] Instead, the standard modus operandi is continuity and stability. In fact, for one of the originators of incrementalism,[52] Charles Lindblom, it is impossible to truly aim for, let alone achieve the loftier goal of rational, comprehensive reform. The operational effectiveness of the process is short-circuited by not only human motivations but also human limitations. A process that is dedicated through and through to problem solving requires weighing all possible policy alternatives, all important values, and then choosing the precise policy alternative that maximizes all of the important values. Bounded rationality theory cautions that, in essence, it is humanly impossible for lawmakers to undertake an all-knowing approach to problem solving. The result is shifts in attention (more so than informational inputs and environmental stimuli) partly drive shifts in policy outcomes.[53] Human shortcomings limit the rational undercurrents of policymaking. Further, there is too much disagreement about values and objectives among too many entities (citizens, elected officials, and public administrators) to realistically expect anything more than the "best they can do." It is this give and take among multiple actors that make major departures from existing policies highly improbable.

Amplifying the give-and-take aspects of policymaking, Fenno examined the relation between federal agency requests and appropriations. He found the decisions of the Appropriations Committee of the House of Representatives fit a similar pattern as that identified by Aaron Wildavsky. That is, the Committee's decisions "are mainly incremental – whether measured by the relation of budget estimates to appropriations or by the relation of appropriations to last year's appropriations."[54] Wildavsky and several others deemed budgetary processes excellent exemplars of incrementalism, as well as evidence of its roots in the competition between existing values and new values.[55] An agency budget is never developed from the ground up, with a reconsideration of all of the values and programs already agreed upon, against the full range of alternatives. Rather, the process begins from the prior year's budget (and its priorities), with attention given to a narrow range of increases or decreases (in furtherance of new priorities). For Wildavsky, incremental policy adoptions are rooted in consensual politics, wherein compromise carries the day.[56] For Hayes, the sources of incrementalism are found not only in the usual politicking that inheres in decision making or within the parameters of bounded rationality. As well, incrementalism is intentionally built into the design of the American governance structure. As James Madison's *Federalist No. 10* anticipated, the system of checks and balances, separated powers, federalism, bicameralism, multiple veto points, need for current majorities, and a myriad of other institutional impediments all "reinforce the tendencies toward inertia and incrementalism"[57] within policymaking.

In a large number of public policy studies, incrementalism is found to be spot-on in terms of explaining how the policy process operates most of the time and for much of policymaking but not in terms of accounting for how the process always works and in all situations.[58] According to punctuated-equilibrium theory, there are "bursts" of policy change. Meaning, there are instances of large-scale public policy changes that evidence occasional discontinuity, in contrast with the continuity theme of incrementalism. Under this theory, stability and status quo politics are not always and in every situation the rule of the day. Dramatic, even radical shifts in governmental policy are occasionally observed.

Developed by Frank G. Baumgartner and Bryan D. Jones in 1993[59] then elaborated further in subsequent studies,[60] the punctuation model accounts for both modes. Under ordinary circumstances, specialists and special interests control policy in ways that preserve the status quo. These "policy monopolies" or "policy subsystems" are aided by the fact that American political institutions (especially Congress) are structured in ways that already make change very difficult, as Hayes notes. During extraordinary times, nonetheless, broader systemic forces can disrupt the near monopoly that entrenched interests often have on the process, spur the mobilization needed to overcome political and institutional inertia, and eventually precipitate major policy change. The likelihood of mobilization is dependent partly on policy images or the way in which issues and problems are framed. Certain ways of characterizing an issue are more conducive to disruptions of policy subsystems and the dismantling of institutional impediments. Problem definition and public understandings of issues, then, set the stage for policymaking.

Understanding that responsiveness on the part of the policy process comes in more than just one form is also important for grasping the systems principle. On the one hand is knowing the proximal causes of formal policy adoption versus rejection, and on the other is ascertaining the circumstances that account for a policy problem being considered for formal adoption in the first place. Still another task is dissecting the choice to formally adopt one policy approach instead of other policy alternatives. The politics that lead policymakers to focus on one problem versus another are separate from the circumstances that lead them to prefer one or more policy options from among the range of available alternatives and separate still from the conditions under which formal policy adoption will actually occur. Using the policy literature as a backdrop, John W. Kingdon provides a clarification of the difference between agenda-setting and policy adoption. In doing so, he partly reconciles the two main schools of thought on the "systems principle." Kingdon notes "both gradualistic evolution and punctuated equilibrium seem to be at work in different parts of the process. The agenda changes suddenly and nonincrementally, which makes agenda-setting look like punctuated equilibrium. But the (policy) alternatives are developed gradually."[61]

In addition to operating as a whole and manifesting variegated forms of responsiveness (as a whole), under Kingdon's policymaking model the systems side of the policy process also entails multiple streams of activity, each with its own set of dynamics and center points. A refined variant of the less tidy garbage can model of choice,[62] Kingdon's multiple streams model identifies three largely independent processes. They include "streams" of problems, of policies, and of politics running through the political system. The "march of problems" concerns how people construct problems in accordance with their values and priorities. The second stream involves the development of policy proposals that are more or less viable, more or less consistent with existing values, and more or less controversial. The final stream, political process, comprises election outcomes, party control of national institutions and, most importantly, public opinion or national mood. Parallel processing is another term used at times to convey the idea that there is continual movement or "processing" within these streams and that the movement within each runs parallel to the processing in the next. Put simply, the three processes move simultaneously but on different platforms and in reaction to different stimuli.[63]

Opportunity Principle. According to the opportunity principle, the policy agenda will change suddenly and nonincrementally, and the policy process will subsequently shift into high gear, when conditions are ripe for it to do so. If and when things change, it is because a window of opportunity for change opens. A window of opportunity for major policy change will occur, moreover, when all of the processes operating within the policy process are acting on one accord, when they connect with one another to produce a simultaneous, joint "system" response. As Kingdon puts it,

While the items rising on a governmental agendas are set in the problems or political streams, the changes of items rising on a *decision* agenda – a list of items up for actual actions – are enhanced if all three streams are coupled together. Significant movement, in other words, is much more likely if problems, policy proposals, and politics are all coupled into a package.[64]

He adds that there is a takeoff point, meaning a point at which an idea "catches on."[65]

Alas, things do not just "take off" and change does not just happen on its own; someone has to make it happen. Policy entrepreneurs fulfill this "trigger" role; they take on the task of coupling the three streams. These individuals invest their time and resources in pushing certain problems, prompting important people to pay attention, as well as coupling solutions to problems and coupling problems and solutions to the right politics.[66] The key players within government that are most likely to "make something happen" on a national scale are the president, key members of Congress, and bureaucrats in the executive branch. Outside the government are the media, interest groups, political parties, and, of course, the general public. Although the U.S. Supreme Court's capacity as a key policy player is not parsed at length in the public policy literature, the judicial process literature amply demonstrates its potential as a major player in the policy process too, especially in regard to problem definition and as a principle-setter.[67]

Public Origins Principle. A seventh principle, which the present case study of racial tracking places in clearer perspective, is one that posits the public as the original center point of power in the policy process. I refer to it here as the "public origins principle." It envisages voters as the foundational power, that is to say the ultimate source of control and influence over policymaking. The rationale for it is concordant with that in James Madison's *Federalist No. 51*, in which he posits the people as the "primary control on the government," and *Federalist No. 49*, in which he describes the people as the "only legitimate fountain of power" and the "original authority." In a representative democracy voters elect officials, who in turn enact public policies. It logically follows, then, that voters have original control over the policy choices of those whom they elect and empower to make such choices. This is so regardless of the ebb and flow of electoral mobilization or the extent of public engagement and attentiveness. Meaning, irrespective of whether the electorate regularly exercises its power, in a democratic political system it is the electorate that possesses the ultimate wherewithal to empower or disempower elected officials, the policy subsystems they are a part of, and the policy choices forged by and within those subsystems. That the electorate chooses to not regularly exercise its power does not mean it does not have the power to do so. The public's wherewithal to stimulate policy change is constantly present, even if not constantly actuated.

While this study brings into sharper focus the primacy of public control and influence, there are strong hints of the idea that policy power rests in the hands of the masses in the policy studies discussed in the foregoing. All, in some way, explicitly or implicitly acknowledge that the public is at least potentially the final arbiter of policymaking. This is readily evident in the literature establishing reelection interests as the key driving force behind legislative behavior. Members of Congress follow the will of the public most notably on major issues. Early on Mayhew observed:

Congress in a peculiar way is an extraordinarily democratic body. If, on matters beyond the particular, congressmen are judged by positions rather than effects, then what kinds of laws are they likely to write? The answer is that they are much inclined to incorporate popular conceptions of instrumental rationality into the statute books.[68]

Even the U.S. Supreme Court – despite being twice removed from electoral processes – is not immune to public influence, as the extensive literature on the relation between public opinion and judicial output demonstrates.[69] The late Chief Justice William Rehnquist once remarked: Somewhere "out there" – beyond the walls of the courthouse – run currents and tides of public opinion which lap at the courthouse door.... Judges, so long as they are relatively normal human beings, can no more escape being influenced by public opinion in the long run than can people working at other jobs.... Judges need not "tremble before public opinion" in the same way that elected officials may, but it would be remarkable indeed if they were not influenced by ... currents of public opinion.[70]

The broad and considerable power of the public is implicit in several other works. For example, Gaventa's careful probe of elite theory and mobilization bias in the policy process arguably lends credence to the notion of a reservoir of latent power resting in the hands of the mass public, though at times stymied by the manipulation of a resourceful elite. Similarly, Bachrach and Baratz's claim of an elite constructing barriers to public airing of policy conflicts implies much the same, insofar as it concedes that public airing and engagement is pregnant with possibilities and consequences the elite wishes to avoid. Likewise, Ferguson's claim that candidates' dependence on campaign financiers predisposes candidates to avoid policy areas that challenge the status quo is a claim that is arguably perched atop the idea that candidates need campaign contributions in order to win over the votes of average citizens.

Moreover, Lowi-type schemas of policy and politics are similarly grounded on the premise that the scope of engagement on the part of the public matters. When the public is less engaged, the politics of policy subsystems and captured politics will prevail, and vice versa. The public is the principal power player that utilizes or concedes its power to others. In pinpointing the factors that contribute to an item rising on a decision agenda, finally, Kingdon states plainly: "perceived national mood and turnover of elected officials particularly affects agendas, while the balance of organized forces is more likely to affect the alternatives considered."[71]

I argue, further, that public consensus belies policy stasis. That is to say, the public permits certain conditions and problems to continue as is. Because, if the public were so inclined, it could utilize its power to change the existing state of affairs. Policy output or the lack thereof is fundamentally rooted either in the public's explicit endorsement of existing policies (and problems), in its tacit consent or endorsement of prevailing policies and conditions, or its failure to mobilize on behalf of policy change or reform. Empirical support for the conception of policy stasis as a byproduct of public consensus is found in studies of critical elections. Brady's work on the U.S. House of Representatives illustrates the linkage between critical elections (also known as realignments), political institutions, and public policy.[72] It shows major policy shifts typically follow major realignments among voters. Further, the policy paradigms that emerge anew after critical elections tend to maintain for a long period of time – until voters re-mobilize around a different set of values, priorities, and policies in response to major disturbances or crises. During the interim, a consensus for change either has not yet amassed or, as the case study of racial tracking in the remainder of the book shows, the existing majority consensus is supportive of or conducive to the existing status quo. In sum, much like incremental change, so too nonincremental change, new policy agendas, and the absence of policy change are all tied in various ways to public mood and preferences.

An argument that runs counter to the claim made here regarding the primacy of public power contends that public consensus or, more precisely, public endorsement of a given set of values and policy priorities is the result of indoctrination.[73] The public supports the prevailing approaches to problems and concerns, it is said, because the public is manipulated by a powerful elite and especially the elite-controlled media into believing the current state of affairs is what is best for the common good. The logic of this argument, however, is contradicted by research analyses proving a dynamic relationship between public opinion and environmental stimuli. Page and Shapiro present extensive evidence of a rational public, namely fifty years of time-series survey data that show the public maintains a stable set of values and fundamental beliefs over time. The stable belief frameworks, in turn, lead the public to not only maintain a stable set of policy preferences but also draw meaningful distinctions within certain policy areas based on its read of particularized circumstances.[74] As an example, while there is a stable distribution of public support for and opposition to abortion rights, there are also major distinctions drawn as to whether the reasons for an abortion are justifiable and these distinctions too remain stable over time. It would be a considerable feat for a small elite to control each of the public's reactions to the different justifications for an abortion and for the elite to exercise mass mind control in ways that produce a stable ranking of policy values over multiple decades.

Critically, public opinion and policy preferences shift in response to tangible changes in the sociopolitical environment. For example, support for women's rights increased as the number of women who worked outside the home increased during and following World War II. Support for school desegregation increased in connection with the black civil rights movement having exposed the downside of segregation. Growing support for gay rights in recent years corresponds with increased gay rights advocacy.[75] Inasmuch as the public reacts to tangible shifts in societal conditions and stimuli, public opinion and public consensus cannot be wholly attributed to mind control. Beside which, mind control theorists must also credit the powerful elite with generating the very mass mobilizations that often challenge and disrupt elite control. Finally, public access to massive amounts of information through internet sources and the sharply divergent viewpoints found there and in cable news make centralized control of the public mind even more infeasible in modern times.

In contrast with indoctrination theses, the present study of race, crime, and criminal justice policymaking shows that there is a broad consensus undergirding racial tracking and that the consensus is indeed a bona fide cross-racial *public* consensus among a majority of Americans.

Toward a Policy Process Theory of Racial Tracking

The basic principles policy process framework provides some guidance for our effort to better understand the persistence of racial tracking in the United States. It offers, more precisely, insight into the reasons why the policy process has failed to remedy the disparate treatment and overrepresentation of blacks within the criminal justice system. The framework theorizes racial tracking persists, ultimately, because major components of the policy process and the policy process as a whole actively enable it. To gauge how and the extent to which this is so, the remaining chapters highlight the fit between the main expectations derived from the framework and the research findings from the book's case study analysis of race, crime, and criminal justice policymaking. By way of introduction, I present here a brief overview of how the story of racial tracking detailed in the remainder of the book exemplifies the basic principles of the policy process.

To start, the systems principle tells us that we should expect to find a continuous "systems" response that maintains over a period of time and, specifically, for as long as racial tracking is observed. In other words, the major components and participants in the policy process likely function so as to capacitate racial tracking through repeated actions and enduring policy positions. Furthermore, they likely work in concert with one another. To fully understand the dynamics of race and criminal justice, then, we should embark on a longitudinal and cross-sectional analysis. Rather than focus on an isolated time period or a single set of actors and institutions as controlling, we should pay attention to the macro-level, longstanding patterns that racial justice outcomes may be part of and the degree of synchronicity across them. Pursuant to the systems principle, then, this study probes longstanding trends in order to ascertain the degree of correspondence over time and across the main forces known to operate in the policy process.

The problem–process kinship principle suggests that the way in which racial tracking is conceptualized within the larger national political arena is key. Is the phenomenon generally considered problematical, and to what degree? Whether its public imagery is fashioned in ways that connote a violation of basic American values and ideals or that signify a departure from societal norms will evoke more or less concern on the part of those who are not directly affected by the issue. The extent and nature of public involvement will be shaped also by the perceived stakes involved in blacks' overrepresentation and disparate treatment in the criminal justice system. The U.S. Supreme Court would seem the first place to look for an official statement on the problematical elements of racial tracking. This is owed to its institutional design as a guardian of the Constitution, its image as protector of minority rights, and its historic role in dismantling the racial caste system in the South. Accordingly, we examine how the Court reacted to racial influences in major criminal law cases over a period of time and, in particular, whether it deemed those influences impermissible from a constitutional-legal standpoint. We learn the Court did not define racial tracking in a way that was conducive to racial reform. Instead there was a multi-decade pattern of colorblind jurisprudence, wherein the Court consistently sidestepped, ignored, or dismissed the constitutional significance of racial influences in the criminal process. From the vantage point of this important institution, with all its moralizing force, racial tracking was not envisaged the kind of higher order problem suited to restorative justice.

Chapter 3 illustrates this colorblind approach to the black law enforcement experience through a detailed probe of Court rulings handed down from 1932 to 2005. Included among the criminal rights cases examined are roughly twenty-three key Sixth Amendment cases affecting the right to counsel, eighteen Fifth Amendment cases construing the right against self-incrimination, and twenty Eighth Amendment cases on the death penalty. The review of each case attends to the Court's official pronouncements as well as the sociopolitical circumstances from which the cases emerged. Case information was compiled from a variety of sources, such as the text of U.S. Supreme Court opinions, petitioner, respondent, and amicus briefs submitted to the Court, federal district and appellate court opinions, state court opinions, county and state court records, department of corrections files, criminal background checks, newspaper and magazine articles, databases and reports of governmental and nongovernmental organizations, and various secondary sources. In select cases, field, telephone, and electronic interviews of defense attorneys and prosecutors were also conducted. The purpose of this all inclusive approach to Court decision making is to help provide a fuller portrait of the intra- and extra-institutional factors to which the Court itself was also exposed. The findings from the analysis portray a Court that held steadfastly to a race neutral stance in the context of some of the most important major criminal law developments. Doing so has rendered the Court an unlikely avenue of racial justice reform.

In fact, the Court essentially construed racial tracking as more a matter of crime control than racial justice. Having done so, it laid the groundwork for expansion of the overall political scope of racial tracking beyond the interests of the racial minority population in the United States. Furthermore, given the "group-based and shifting patterns of conflict built into every regulatory issue, it is in most cases impossible for a Congressional committee, an administrative agency, a peak association governing board, or a social elite to contain all the participants long enough to establish a stable power elite."[76] Instead, for regulatory policies it is in the larger arena of Congress that the decisive bargains and decisions are made. Therefore, Congress is where this analysis next turns to understand the fate of racial justice in the policy process.

The opportunity principle prods us to consider what, if any, opportunities arose in Congress for racial reform of criminal justice to take off, that is to say, amass serious policy attention to or melioration of racial tracking. Are there instances in which the policy subsystems within Congress proved permeable to advocacy of this issue? We learn from the present case study that part of the answer to this question is "yes." Concerns about the racial divide in criminal justice did advance to a space on the government agenda, namely Congress. Chapter 4 presents an extended look at the steady stream of racial reform legislative proposals running through the process and their fate within the process. Reform advocates continually tried but generally failed to secure Congressional enactment of transformative racial justice measures. This conclusion is supported by the first in depth account of Congressional proceedings on the national racial justice legislative agenda covering a twenty-five-year period. It details the aims, provisions, sponsors, and procedural disposition of the roughly forty-five major policy proposals formally introduced in Congress between 1988 and 2012 and chiefly aimed at redressing the racial status quo in criminal justice. Legislative measures that targeted the police and investigation stage, the prosecution stage, adjudication and sentencing, and the prison stage of the process and also those aimed at the overall operational mode of the system are the centerpiece of the discussion. To fully illustrate the limited success of national racial justice initiatives, the analysis probes committee votes, hearings and reports; floor votes and debate remarks; as well as executive action and pronouncements. What becomes clear is that, with two almost-exceptions, everything from the weakest, bare-boned initiatives to the most aggressive legislative proposals failed to gain traction. Though the proposals contained much promise for remediation, enough to overcome the usual procedural obstacles to success, the racial justice agenda never took off within Congress.

The power player principle posits someone or something is most immediately responsible for driving the engine of racial tracking politics and steering it in ways that account for the missed opportunities, among other things. The racial justice agenda's failure was not a byproduct of invisible forces. There was a real, live culprit. When we expand our lens beyond the press for enactment of racial justice reforms from the late 1980s onward, we see more clearly the power player principle at work. We come to understand from Chapter 5 that the mainstream crime policy approach established and reinforced time and again by members of Congress from 1968 to 1994 had effectively foreclosed opportunities for the racial justice agenda to catch on. In other words, the prospects for policy adoptions that were specifically geared toward reforming the criminal justice system along racial lines were dimmed well before the reform effort was launched. It is also clear that law enforcement lobbies cannot be blamed for having forged or for that matter propelled the "get tough on crime" approach, even though they benefited tremendously. The march toward blisteringly punitive "law and order" policies was led, in chief, by members of Congress.

Chapter 5 probes modern national crime policymaking during the formative years of 1968–1994, with special attention to the plight of racial justice concerns within the traditional crime policy process. It examines key provisions in major national crime laws, Congressional floor and committee debate, votes and proceedings on the laws, inclusive of roughly forty sets of full committee and subcommittee hearings. The chapter also contains a multi-decade analysis of the congruence between crime policy expenditures and crime rates. We learn from the discussion that lawmakers were little concerned with the black law enforcement experience when fashioning modern anti-crime legislation. The seven omnibus crime laws that form the heart of modern federal policy on violent, property, and drug-related offenses afford an excellent window through which to observe the disposal of racial justice issues within mainstream crime policy proceedings. Five major policy trends are shown to have emerged by way of enactment of these mainstay crime laws. These trends constitute the definitive features of the existing "law and order" crime policy approach that lawmakers follow when crafting crime legislation. They include: federalization of criminal law, the shift to an incarceration-centered penal policy, increase in post-conviction punishments, diminution of the rights of the accused, and permanent enhancements to the enforcement infrastructure, as opposed to the prevention and rehabilitation infrastructure.

Three things in particular come to light upon examining Congress's decision to embark on this "law and order" strategy. First, the obstacles racial justice proponents faced when they pressed for passage of bills specifically aimed at racial tracking pale in comparison to the barriers encountered when they tried to interject their concerns into the mainstream crime policy process. Their failure was not for lack of trying. Second, the fact that development and implementation of modern "get tough" measures would magnify racially disparate criminal justice outcomes did not deter members of Congress from pursing them, with vigor. The conventional wisdom would have us believe that Republicans and conservatives are ultimately to blame, perhaps none more than President Ronald Reagan. The fact is, however, lawmakers voted almost unanimously for these bills – fully 99 percent in one instance. A third revelation is empirical data challenge the idea that law enforcement lobbies account for Congress's policy choices. Ultimately, the primary reason policymakers proceeded with little regard for the black law enforcement experience lay outside the scope of pressure politics and beyond the walls of Congress.

We are dissuaded by the politics principle from expecting there was a wholly sound informational base for Congressional lawmakers' embrace of the incarceration-centered crime strategies that helped deepen the racial divide in criminal justice. Meaning, aside from its unsuitable fit to the black law enforcement experience, we should not be surprised to find that the crime-fighting approach embraced by lawmakers also did not line up neatly with the scope and nature of violent crime. Therefore, to the extent the chosen solutions to crime were a mismatch to actual crime trends, the policy decisions behind both racial tracking and mainstream crime-fighting are properly understood as something other than information-driven behavior – just as the politics principle predicts. This is precisely what is proved by our probe of one of the major political influences on legislative behavior, in this case, party positioning on race, crime, and criminal justice. This study details how the two major political parties refashioned the political imagery of race, crime, and criminal justice policy. In a similar vein, racial justice advocates' failure to achieve a decisive legislative victory both in their push for racial reform and for racial safety valves likewise stemmed from something other than solution-oriented behavior.

The time-series analysis in Chapter 6 reveals critical shifts in the national politics of crime and punishment, shifts that effectively trumped concerns about the plight of blacks in the criminal justice system. It shows that prior to the late sixties, political strategies to resolve the race problem and the crime problem were in sync with one another, albeit briefly. Democratic and Republican policymakers alike acknowledged the interconnectedness of race and crime policymaking. But, the bipartisan race consciousness of the sixties was short-lived. Race and crime were soon decoupled, by way of four major developments. First politicians recast the challenge of crime control as a problem that concerned all Americans in equal measure, not one that disproportionately affected racial minorities. The victims' rights counterrevolution took the wind out of demands for fair and balanced treatment of the criminally accused, a good portion of whom were black. In place of blacks and the poor, women, the elderly, and children became the primary stakeholders in criminal justice policymaking. Finally, the dire predictions that fueled the War on Drugs further justified disregard for the negative effects of prison justice on black communities.

The result? Racial justice concerns were relegated to the sidelines of the politics of criminal justice, where they remain. The fact that statistical data on the geographic and demographic spread of crime showed racial concerns never ceased to figure prominently in the reality of crime and law enforcement did not deter policymakers from proceeding as if they had. Democrats and Republicans deracialized the crime policy arena and, thus, enormously expanded the scope of interests and stakes involved, even though crime itself continued to be unmistakably racialized. Once racial justice advocates began working in earnest in 1988 to moderate the racially disadvantageous fallout from the "law and order" agenda, they were treading against the tide of national crime politics that continually swelled from 1968 to 1994. To illustrate the thrust of the major national crime politics trends, the chapter presents a content analysis of party platforms and also presidential policy statements, speeches, and press conferences from 1964 to 2013. Coupled together with time-series data on criminal victimization, arrest, and imprisonment, the analysis brings to light the marked disconnect between the colorblind politics of crime and the racial impact of those politics.

The public origins principle points to the conclusion that all of the above could not have happened without the American public's tacit consent and endorsement. Absent public approval, Congressional lawmakers might well have assumed some other electorally profitable stance toward racial tracking and Supreme Court justices might well have taken the bold step of declaring racial tracking constitutionally impermissible. This is the conclusion to which the study's examination of public opinion also points. The analysis details a public mind-set that is generally supportive of a crime policy approach that is devoid of racial progressivism. More to the point, a majority of Americans neither believe nor endorse the notion that racial reform of criminal justice is a top priority as of now. In order to demonstrate the public understanding in this issue domain, Chapter 7 pursues three specific questions. What does the majority believe about the existence of racism and racial influences in American law enforcement? Second, how does public perception of the race problem in society at-large and in the criminal justice system in particular weigh against its perception of the crime problem? Third, what is the substance and nature of public policy preferences on both fronts? That is, to which end do most want lawmakers to invest their attention and energies – well-known racial disparities and improprieties in the justice system or other criminal justice policy matters? The answer to these questions is derived from a systematic look at roughly 150 indicators from cross-sectional attitudinal data stretching across 2000–2013. The data are drawn from several national survey sources, including the Pew Research Center, Gallup, Inc., the National Opinion Research Center, and the Bureau of Justice Statistics. Supplementing data from these sources are three original national panel surveys designed to probe in greater detail the specific questions of interests in this study.

The analysis reveals most Americans actually do not dispute the existence of racial improprieties in law enforcement, and most disapprove of such improprieties. However and importantly, racially disparate treatment, racial profiling, racialized imprisonment trends, and other aspects of the black law enforcement experience are not important enough to diminish the public's otherwise high regard for law enforcement, especially police officers. As far as a majority of Americans are concerned, blacks are partly to blame for their high arrest and incarceration rates. And, to the minimal extent the race problem is a matter of concern to the public, it is also believed to be on the mend. Meaning, the trajectory for the nation's enduring race problem is generally considered positive, whereas the nation's crime problem is headed in the wrong direction. As opposed to reforms that would make the system more racially neutral, then, most voters want their elected officials to prioritize the kind of reform that would make it tougher and more effective than it now is. The fact that the preponderant share and, in some cases, a majority of blacks also share many of these same beliefs tells us public attitudes in this sphere are symptomatic of more than just racist animus. They are deeply rooted.

There is a stream of expert policy knowledge on this subject available in the public domain, as scholarly studies have more than amply demonstrated the various pathways whereby racial tracking is traceable to societal forces. They have established in equally persuasive measure also that racial tracking can be meliorated by government intervention. The discussion in Chapter 8 contains an exhaustive account of the facts and information at the disposal of the public and policymakers. To my knowledge, the discussion in Chapter 8 contains the most comprehensive review of contemporary research data and analysis on the intersection of race and criminal justice in a single work to date. It synthesizes key findings from several disciplines, including political science, public policy, criminal law, criminology, sociology, psychology, economics, and media studies. The review demonstrates not only that there is a considerable wealth of cross-disciplinary empirical insight within reach. There is also a common theme across the four main schools of thought that are advanced across the disciplines. Racial theory, legal-processual theory, structural theory, and cultural theory are, in the main, on the same page. Taken as a whole, this body of scholarship tells us that macro-level forces are implicated and, thus, individuated factors alone are not determinative, neither with respect to overrepresentation nor maltreatment.

The message from across academe concerning the significant role and impact of societal influences scarcely makes its way into the public arena. Instead of the considerable empirical insight afforded by academic research, what gets transmitted to the public by mass media instead is what I term the "blacks-are-criminal" script. The script consists of a mostly negative portrait of blacks, it serves to reinforce racial stereotyping on the part of the public and, in the same stroke, also diminish support for racial reform of criminal justice. Ultimately, news media and mass media as a whole are consumer-driven industries. Thus, the script "sells" because it comports with public preferences on this front. The American tradition of individualist ideology essentially primes the public to reject structuralism as a general proposition and, as a consequence, favor the "blacks-are-criminal" script and the idea that blacks, rather than "the system," are in control of their own fate.

In conclusion, the same principles or forces that order the public policy process in other issue domains also order racial tracking. These principles enable us to better understand its persistence and, specifically, the lack of public policy reform. As to race and criminal justice studies that hone in on a particular time period, political party, or presidential administration – as opposed to the political system as a whole, this case study of the policy process offers what I hope is a useful additive. It urges a more concerted look at the role of the body politic and all of its constitutive parts, acting as a whole.

3

A Color-Blind Problem

U.S. Supreme Court and Racial Influences in Law Enforcement

The policy process framework tells us public imagery of a problem is key for understanding whether the process will respond to the problem. Problem-definition and framing help dictate also how the process is oriented. In the case of racial tracking, the U.S. Supreme Court is the most likely institution from which one might expect a clear and principled statement regarding its problematical elements, for a number of reasons. The Founders labeled the judiciary the guardian of constitutional liberties and protector of minority rights and interests. Alexander Bickel characterized the Supreme Court in particular as "the institution of our government" best equipped "to be the pronouncer and guardian of (enduring) values."[1] The modern Court played a pivotal role in articulating the constitutional and moral bases for the historic civil rights movement targeting racial inequality. The same court facilitated the criminal rights revolution of the sixties.

Quite apart from expectations, however, the reality is that the Court never regarded the persistent racial divide in American criminal justice as legally or ethically problematic. By way of a color-blind approach to adjudicating race-related challenges to law enforcement throughout its history, and especially from 1932 to 2005, the Supreme Court essentially ignored the deeply rooted systemic racial influences in law enforcement. It never really mattered to the Court that the black law enforcement experience is fundamentally distinctive from that of whites. Lani Guinier and Gerald Torres argue in *The Miner's Canary* that a more deliberate, progressive racial consciousness in America as a whole is a critical first step toward meaningful racial reform.[2] However, this principle-setting institution never raised a red flag regarding the persistent racial disparities in criminal process. True, there were occasions on which the Court struck down certain instances of deliberate discrimination by criminal justice actors,[3] but the notion that the criminal justice system itself is inherently flawed by racial difference or that race as a social and political construct is inextricably bound up in criminal process is an idea that failed to gain a foothold in federal criminal jurisprudence.

As tempting as it may be to isolate the source and locus of color-blindness to the judicial conservatism of recent courts (especially the Burger and Rehnquist Courts), an extended review of doctrinal developments points us in a different direction. Even as the infamously liberal Warren Court facilitated the broadest expansion of civil liberties in judicial history, and its successors generally abided within those expanded legal frameworks, all managed to avoid the task of confronting head-on, let alone uprooting, the race problem in criminal justice. The broader theoretical significance of the U.S. Supreme Court's longstanding tradition in this policy sphere is considerable. It supplied the groundwork for other policymaking institutions and political entities to be similarly indifferent to the racial dimensions of criminal process and, further, to also regard criminal justice outcomes as almost exclusively a crime-control issue, more so than a criminal justice issue.

This chapter illustrates how the Court repeatedly declined to construe racial differences in law enforcement in ways that engendered reform. Cole and Alexander perceptibly observe the recent weakening of Fourth Amendment protections in particular, most notably for black and poor suspects and defendants.[4] Their review of search and seizure cases compellingly illustrates the Burger-Rehnquist Court's nearly carte blanche permissiveness. The analysis in this chapter concentrates on the evidence of an extended color-blind approach on two major fronts. The first consists of death penalty cases in which litigants expressly alleged racial discrimination. The second front consists of major criminal law procedure cases in which the central legal questions pertained to the Fifth and Sixth Amendment rights of all criminally accused but race nonetheless loomed in the background. The analysis shows that in death penalty rulings extending back to 1932, the Court either sidestepped or explicitly rejected challenges to racially disparate outcomes in criminal process. Meanwhile, the racial markers present in many of the Fifth and Sixth Amendment criminal procedure rulings not only proved of little legal value to the Court, but seldom garnered even so much as judicial notice of their existence. That is to say, they were present and even glaringly obvious in the evidentiary record before the Court but were oftentimes dismissed – either explicitly or implicitly – as having no constitutional significance. As such, the Court would occasionally see race at work but not notice it.[5] Taken together, the decision making on both fronts signals the highest court in the nation was, in essence, disinclined from the early 1930s onward to red-flag the persistent racial influences in criminal justice.

The discussion begins with a brief description of the focus and rationale for the chapter's analysis. Then the Court's disposal of racial allegations in death penalty cases are examined. Following this is an in-depth look at racial influences in cases addressing the right to counsel and the right against self-incrimination.

Body of Evidence

The claim made here concerning the Court's longtime tradition of color-blind jurisprudence is grounded not in one or a few rulings but rather in a body of cases examined as a whole, stretching over several decades and ideological shifts within the Court.[6] The years following the Civil War, quite naturally, are of greatest interest.[7] Included among the criminal rights cases examined by the analysis are roughly twenty-three key Sixth Amendment cases affecting the right to counsel and eighteen Fifth Amendment cases construing the right against self-incrimination. Among the capital punishment cases, a total of twenty of the most noted cases are analyzed. The probe into each of the major cases is intended to be all-inclusive. Along with the Court's pronouncements, also taken into consideration is the larger sociopolitical context in which the cases emerged and in which the Court disposed of them. Thus, the text of the opinions and the final rulings as well as the circumstances of the cases is explored, inclusive of media attention, police investigation, trial court decisions, and the like. Special attention is paid to whether racial factors and influences are present.[8]

An underlying premise of the following critique of judicial behavior is that the Court is aware of the racial markers highlighted here, even though their opinions sometimes contain no explicit race-related remarks from the justices, and attorneys infrequently assert racial claims. It is an arguably sound premise for a number of reasons. First, the lack of explicit acknowledgment of racial influences does not signal justices' lack of awareness, nor that the influences are beyond justices' reach, nor that they are nonexistent, and it most certainly does not discount their disadvantaging impact on minorities. Further, the Court receives the entire certified record of the original lower court proceeding, which usually includes the original arrest warrants, criminal complaint, witness identifications, trial transcripts, and the like. These documents often reveal the kinds of racial indicators taken into account here. Also, the highly secretive judicial conferences (in which justices deliberate petitions for certiorari and the merits of cases) cover a much wider terrain than the official published record of cases, a fact confirmed by the conference notes recorded in justices' docket books.[9]

Perhaps most importantly, Supreme Court justices do not live in a vacuum. Well before cases reach the Court, national and local news coverage of the cases frequently disseminate physical descriptions, photographs or video footage of criminal defendants, and often more extensively in racially charged cases than in others.[10] Supreme Court justices follow the news, much like ordinary citizens. As the late Chief Justice William Rehnquist candidly remarked once: "The judges of any court of last resort, such as the Supreme Court ... go home at night and read the newspapers or watch ... television; they talk to their family and friends about current events."[11] Corroborating Rehnquist's account is a range of qualitative and quantitative works that establish empirical linkages between the institution and the larger public arena in which it is situated.[12]

Besides evidence they are likely aware of the circumstances surrounding the cases they take up, Supreme Court justices are also not precluded from taking those circumstances into consideration sua sponte when disposing of the cases. They have the legal authority to look beyond the scope of the official certified record formally presented to it. In a major affirmative action case, *Washington v. Davis* (1976),[13] the Court observed: "Although the petition for certiorari did not present this ground for reversal ... our Rule 40(1)(d)(2) provides that we 'may notice a plain error not presented' ... and this is an appropriate occasion to invoke the Rule." The so-called "plain error" in that case was the lower court had applied the wrong legal standard. The Court reversed on that basis and without prompting from either side.

The Court on Racial Disparities in Capital Sentencing

One would be hard-pressed to find more compelling evidence of the U.S. Supreme Court's indifference to the black law enforcement experience than that contained in death penalty rulings. It is in these cases that racial disproportionalness in law enforcement was before the Court in vivid ways and, consequently, those that offered the Court the most straightforward opportunities to redress it. A review of capital case rulings shows that the Court did just the opposite. It repeatedly upheld capital punishment, notwithstanding its disparate racial effects. It also flatly rejected race-based challenges to the statistical disparities and constructed barriers to future challenges. In addition, the Court's policy toward death penalty and race is one to which it held more firmly than its policy toward death penalty and certain other vulnerable population segments. This suggests it was not blind to disadvantage altogether but rather blind to racial disadvantage in particular.[14]

Despite telling statistics on its racialized use, the Supreme Court consistently upheld capital punishment. For much of the early postbellum period, blacks constituted the majority of prisoners executed under civil authority. The number steadily increased in the decades following the 1930s, when national government data became available. In 1930, blacks claimed 42 percent of executions; in 1940, they claimed 61 percent; in 1950, a total of 51 percent; then in 1960, as much as 63 percent of all executions in the United States.[15] As Chapter 1 indicated, more recent data reveal blacks continue to be overrepresented on death row.[16] Years of econometric studies show that when measured against other potential nonracial influences, race remains a major, statistically significant factor in regard to race-of-victim.[17]

Importantly, moreover, national civil rights organizations have very publicly and consistently criticized the uneven use of the death penalty. As early as 1919, in a study titled *Thirty Years of Lynching in the United States 1889–1919*, the National Association for the Advancement of Colored People reported data on the disturbing incidence of black lynchings in the South.[18] The campaign gained enough traction to be credited with partly motivating the introduction of anti-lynching bills in Congress. More recently, the Leadership Conference on Civil and Human Rights, an umbrella organization composed of more than 180 national organizations, did so as well. In a lengthy report titled "Justice on Trial," the Leadership Conference condemned the racial disparities in capital sentencing as "well documented" and "disturbing."[19]

The Court essentially turned a blind eye to this racially charged political and historical context for capital punishment and did so on a consistent basis. In fact, not until 1867 – almost eighty years after its first meeting in 1790 – did the Court even adjudicate legal claims under the Eighth Amendment's ban on cruel and unusual punishment. The first time it did, the Eighth Amendment was held inapplicable to states, namely in *Pervear v. Commonwealth* (1867).[20] Every challenge to follow over the next four decades was met with the same response: repeated validation of states' use of capital punishment.[21] At a time when racial disparities reached an all-time high and when the most racially liberal Court ever presided, death sentencing continued to be shielded. When blacks constituted fully 63 percent of all executions in the United States in 1960, it was the largest racial gap ever.[22]

The Warren Court did not endorse a single challenge to the constitutionality of capital punishment. The handful of death row appeals ruled upon favorably by that Court was not tied to the ultimate question of constitutionality but rather its particular application in select cases. In its first major death penalty ruling in *Trop v. Dulles* (1958),[23] the Warren Court held expatriation was cruel and unusual punishment but was careful to note: "Whatever the arguments may be against capital punishment ... and they are forceful ... in a day when it is still widely accepted, it cannot be said to violate the constitutional concept of cruelty." The Warren Court's last major death penalty ruling in *Witherspoon v. Illinois et al.* (1968)[24] stuck to the script. It invalidated the death sentence in the case but was even more resolved to assure the death penalty itself was left intact, asserting: "nothing we say today bears upon the power of a State to execute a defendant sentenced to death by a jury."

The first opportunity for the Court to address head-on racial disproportionalness in capital punishment came in 1972 and when it came, the Court did not stray from its tradition. All three cases comprising *Furman v. Georgia* (1972)[25] involved black male defendants. All were sentenced to death in the South, two for rape and one, William H. Furman, Jr., for murder. The *Furman* decision is often celebrated as a decisive victory for liberals because by invalidating the manner in which the death penalty operated, it effectively imposed a four-year moratorium on capital punishment. However, a post-*Furman* decision by the U.S. Supreme Court would clarify that the crux of *Furman* was to require that states put in place procedural mechanisms to ensure use of capital punishment by juries and judges was "suitably directed and limited so as to minimize the risk of *wholly* [emphasis added] arbitrary and capricious action."[26]

Important for present purposes is that not one of the justices in the celebrated *Furman* majority considered the death penalty's operation problematic because of the persistent statistical racial disparities linked to its use. In fact, the *Furman* majority offered little to no direct commentary on its racial dimensions, though the silence was not for lack of invitation. While the defense brief did not assert a racial claim per se, it came very close to the line. It noted at two separate points that all the jury knew of Furman was one half hour of his life on the morning of the crime, his age, and that he was black.[27] Beyond this, it stressed there was nothing in his case that distinguished it from the thousands of other murder offenses that did not receive death penalty.[28] The defense's invitation notwithstanding, racial unevenness was addressed forthrightly by only one justice in the majority, namely Justice William Douglas. Douglas did not believe the defendants in the case "were sentenced to death because they were black," but he nonetheless intimated a requirement of racial equity was implicit in the Constitution. Notably, in his view, outcomes were important, whether they were intentional or not. Determinative for Justice Douglas was that the manner in which the death penalty operated was *potentially* discriminatory. Capital punishment statutes, he said, were "pregnant with discrimination and discrimination is an ingredient not compatible with the idea of equal protection of the laws that is implicit in the ban on "cruel and unusual" punishments."

Racial discrimination was of minimal import to three of the remaining justices in the five-person majority. Justice William Brennan considered the death penalty cruel and unusual punishment under any circumstances, but at the same time he took the strongest position against capital punishment, Brennan assigned no meaningfulness to racial unevenness. His sole reference to race in *Furman* is contained in footnote 48 of his opinion, and it was intended to underscore his more central point about the lack of sufficient information in death sentencing proceedings. Meanwhile, Justice Stewart acknowledged the possibility race was a factor in the death sentences under review but no more than that – a possibility. He too did not find the racial factors in *Furman* decisive but chose to invalidate instead because the death penalty was, in his words, "wantonly and so freakishly imposed." En route to this conclusion, Stewart took note of the evidence put forth to demonstrate racialism and dismissed it, saying "racial discrimination has not been proved, and I put it to one side." Finally, Justice White, the fourth member of the *Furman* majority, also made no mention of the potential influence of race; rather, he was concerned the "death penalty is exacted with great infrequency."

Last in the *Furman* majority and the justice to whom most court observers would look for an unequivocal statement decrying the linkage between race and capital sentencing is Justice Thurgood Marshall. During his years on the bench, Marshall distinguished himself as a staunch defender of racial equality and one who was ever mindful of the perpetual effects of historic discrimination.[29] However, this was not the portrait of Marshall that emerged in *Furman*. Marshall joined Brennan in declaring capital punishment as inherently in violation of the Eighth Amendment. As to the significance of racial inequities, however, he was decidedly less forceful. Of the various considerations Marshall took into account, he weighted most heavily not race or racial differences but rather public opinion. A lack of public support for the practice was, in his view, chiefly decisive. He noted: "whether or not a punishment is cruel and unusual depends ... on whether people who were fully informed as to the purposes of the penalty and its liabilities would find the penalty shocking, unjust, and unacceptable."

Consequently, the point at which racial dynamics were treated as relevant by Marshall was in connection with the all-important premium he placed on public opinion. "Critical to an informed judgment on the morality of the death penalty," he argued, was the fact that it was used disproportionately against minorities and the poor. Marshall added: "I believe that the following facts would serve to convince even the most hesitant citizens to condemn death as a sanction: capital punishment is imposed discriminatorily against certain identifiable classes of people.... Indeed, a look at the bare statistics regarding executions is enough to betray much of the discrimination."

But for this statement, along with Justice Douglas's noted earlier, the *Furman* ruling may have temporarily suspended the death penalty but did not directly implicate it in the racially skewed makeup of death row.

A prelude to the outright dismissal of racial challenges to capital punishment by the Burger Court came in *Gregg v. Georgia* (1976),[30] in which Troy Leon Gregg, a white male, was the defendant. It was the first death penalty case following *Furman* and revision of death penalty laws in thirty-five states. The 7–2 majority in *Gregg* effectively lifted the de facto moratorium.[31] Most noteworthy for our purposes is that, in defending the Georgia statute against the claim it was arbitrary, *Gregg* directly mentioned race merely as an aside to a larger point. Describing the report that trial judges in Georgia were required to submit to the state's supreme court, the Court observed the report contained the following: "responses to detailed questions concerning the quality of the defendant's representation, whether race played a role in the trial" and whether the trial judge questioned the defendant's guilt or sentence.

There was no on-point discussion of race at all in *Gregg*, nor of the evidence trial judges in Georgia were required to consider to determine whether race played a role. Neither of the dissents authored by Justices Brennan and Marshall so much as broached the subject. Where the issue of discrimination was addressed in the ruling, it was only in connection with the Court's defense of the new procedural mechanisms added to Georgia's capital punishment law, as opposed to the racialized pattern of capital sentencing in the state. As to the Court's position on discrimination in capital sentencing, Justices White and Rehnquist and Chief Justice Burger criticized petitioner's claim in *Gregg* as an "indictment of our entire system of justice" and one that did not recognize "mistakes will be made and discriminations will occur."

The infamous *McCleskey v. Kemp* (1987) appeal placed the issue of racial disproportionalness and discrimination in capital punishment squarely before the Court.[32] Although as many as eighteen legal issues were articulated in McCleskey's petition, the Court opted to focus only on "whether a complex statistical study that indicates a risk that racial considerations enter into capital sentencing determinations" proved McCleskey's death sentence was unconstitutional under the Eighth or Fourteenth Amendment. At the center of the case was Warren McCleskey, a black man, convicted of murdering a white police officer during an armed robbery, and sentenced to death. To support his discrimination claim, McCleskey presented a statistical study by Professors David C. Baldus, Charles Pulaski, and George Woodworth. Known as "the Baldus Study," it examined more than 2,000 murder cases that occurred in Georgia during the 1970s. The study revealed disparity in the imposition of the death penalty based on the race of the victim and, to a lesser extent, the race of the defendant. A total of 230 variables that could have explained the disparities on nonracial grounds were taken into account in the study's regression analysis. Even after taking into account thirty-nine of the more pertinent nonracial variables, it found defendants charged with killing white victims were 4.3 times more likely to receive a death sentence than those killing black victims.

Rejecting McCleskey's equal protection claim, the 5–4 majority in *McCleskey* imposed the Fourteenth Amendment intent standard and ruled McCleskey had the burden of proving "the existence of purposeful discrimination" and, more, that it "had a discriminatory effect" on him in particular. Writing for the Court, Justice Powell clarified that in this context "discriminatory purpose" meant the state legislature had adopted or maintained the capital punishment statute "because of" and not merely "in spite of" its racial effects. Acknowledging that in certain other contexts[33] it had "accepted statistics as proof of intent to discriminate," the Court distinguished those from *McCleskey* because, in them, "the statistics relate to fewer entities, and fewer variables are relevant," or the decision maker had an opportunity to explain the statistical disparity, neither of which was practicable in this instance. Crucially, according to the Opinion, McCleskey's statistical proffer represented a challenge to the all-important concept of discretionary judgment. It reasoned "because discretion is essential to the criminal justice process, we would demand exceptionally clear proof before we would infer that the discretion has been abused," which apparently the Baldus Study was not. McCleskey's Eighth Amendment claim was rejected too, because the Court found "numerous features" of the Georgia statute had met the concerns articulated in *Furman*.

Several additional aspects of *McCleskey* are noteworthy. First, the ruling did not dispute the accuracy of the Baldus Study and whether racial influences had a bearing on death sentencing, even though the district court dismissed the findings altogether. What was rejected in *McCleskey* instead was the assertion race was a factor specifically in McCleskey's case. *McCleskey* actually conceded, "the Baldus study demonstrates that black persons are a distinct group that are singled out for different treatment in the Georgia capital sentencing system." Crucially, moreover, the justices went further to say "disparities in sentencing are an inevitable part of our criminal justice system," and "there is, of course, some risk of racial prejudice influencing a jury's decision in a criminal case. There are similar risks that other kinds of prejudice will influence other criminal trials." The question to be considered, thus, was that of "at what point that risk becomes constitutionally unacceptable." The Constitution did not require the elimination of "any demonstrable disparity that correlates with a potentially irrelevant factor." As such, *McCleskey* not only recognized but deemed permissible racial disproportionalness as well as "some" racial discrimination in capital sentencing under the U.S. Constitution.

For the first time ever, the dissents articulated coherent constitutional frameworks that denounced racially disparate capital sentencing. A common theme across the dissenting opinions was that the racial disparities highlighted in the Baldus Study established a "constitutionally intolerable level of racially based discrimination." Both Brennan and Blackmun's dissents made much of the history of dual criminal laws, but their strongly worded dissents would come well after capital sentencing had regained its political currency over the preceding fifteen years. Further weakening their practical impact, two of the four dissenters (Blackmun and Stevens) actually preferred to reverse and remand. They wanted the lower courts to "decide whether the Baldus study is valid" and "whether the particular facts of McCleskey's crime and his background" placed the case "within the range of cases that present an unacceptable risk that race played a decisive role in McCleskey's sentencing."

On the one hand, *McCleskey* is widely considered the pivotal case in which the Rehnquist Court dealt a huge blow to ongoing efforts to redress racial inequality in capital sentencing.[34] There can be little question that *McCleskey* was a departure from earlier death penalty rulings, insofar as it addressed race-based challenges head-on and expressly rejected those challenges, their rationale, and their evidence. On the other hand, it could be said *McCleskey* did little more than make explicit what had been implicit all along in prior Supreme Court death penalty rulings, namely that it did not matter that blacks were overrepresented on death row. Three considerations point to this conclusion. First, the racial disproportionalness in capital sentencing was well-known in the decades leading up to *McCleskey*, when the Court endorsed capital punishment time and time again. Secondly, the specter of race hovered in the backdrop of the 1972 *Furman* decision, as indicated earlier. Finally, Warren McCleskey's appeal had been rejected fully six times before the Court agreed to take the case. It was rejected twice by superior courts in Georgia, twice by the Georgia Supreme Court, and twice by the U.S. Supreme Court in 1980 and again in 1981. Apparently, then, the Court was just as underwhelmed by the evidentiary record in *McCleskey* as in earlier cases and used the case as a vehicle to make as much explicit.

New in *McCleskey* was the decision to set a virtually impossible evidentiary threshold for future race-based challenge to capital punishment. In fact, it could be said that extension of the intent standard to the Court's assessment of appeals alleging cruel and unusual punishment was the real fait accompli of *McCleskey*. The dissent made as much clear and proffered a compelling and detailed case law analysis showing the Court had never applied the intent standard to Eighth Amendment cases prior to *McCleskey*. By setting such a nearly impossible standard the Court essentially shielded the death penalty from race discrimination challenges for years, perhaps even decades to come.

The political and legal significance of the U.S. Supreme Court's position on race and the death penalty becomes clearer when placed side-by-side with its stance on the use of the death penalty against other vulnerable or otherwise marginalized population segments. Reversing a longstanding precedent, *Thompson v. Oklahoma* (1988)[35] prohibited the execution of convicts who were under the age of sixteen at the time of the crime. And reversing *Stanford v. Connecticut* (1989),[36] *Roper v. Simmons* (2005)[37] forbade imposition of the death penalty on offenders under eighteen.

Finally, *Atkins v. Virginia* (2002)[38] declared execution of the mentally retarded cruel and unusual punishment, overturning *Penry v. Lynaugh* (1989).[39] In essence, although the Court was inclined to endorse certain challenges that call into question states' use of capital sentencing against large population segments considered vulnerable on various grounds, it consistently declined to do so in regard to the traditionally marginalized racial and ethnic minority groups overrepresented on death row.

Race, the Right to Counsel, and Suspect Criminal Process

The same indifference exhibited by the U.S. Supreme Court in death penalty rulings is observed also in a series of major rulings on the Fifth Amendment right to counsel and the Sixth Amendment right against self-incrimination. In both, the Court ignored oftentimes glaring instances of racial discrimination in law enforcement. The racial dimensions of these other criminal rights cases are not as neatly articulated, quantified, and packaged for the Court as they were in the *McCleskey* Baldus Study, but they are no less ominous. In some ways they are more concerning because they put a human face on the "risk of racial prejudice" alluded to in *McCleskey* and *Furman*. They help to depict the racialized and sometimes brutal tactics utilized by law enforcement officials, how those tactics unfolded in the context of individual cases and, critically, how they ultimately impacted the lives of black citizens, defendants, and convicts. The Court's line of right-to-counsel decisions actually originated partly in a case in which the specter of race was more obvious than in any other in Court history, namely *Powell v. Alabama* (1932).[40] In fact, Klarman has argued that modern criminal procedure as a whole originated in cases like *Powell* and others in which the South's treatment of black defendants was on display.[41] *Powell* concerned the capital sentencing in 1931 of seven black male teenagers, ages fourteen to nineteen, for the rape of two white teenage girls on a freight train en route to Scottsboro, Alabama. Their death sentence came at the conclusion of three separate, one-day jury trials – all the culmination of a series of highly racially charged incidents. The defense brief fully detailed these facts, all of which went unchallenged. A message was sent to a "sheriff posse" by wire "to get every negro [sic] off of the train."[42] The rape allegations came well after-the-fact. The next day's local newspaper reported "a great crowd" and a "threatening crowd" gathered at the county jail.[43] Although the population of Scottsboro was roughly

2,500, the crowd outside the courtroom was estimated at 10,000.[44] The mayor and other local leaders "plead for peace and to let the law take its course."[45] The sheriff requested that the governor of Alabama deploy the National Guard, and militia were required to "assist in safeguarding the prisoners ... from beginning to end."[46] Of the three legal claims articulated by the defense, two were that defendants were denied an impartial trial and the right to counsel. The other was that defendants were deprived of Fourteenth Amendment rights through the statutory exclusion of blacks from southern juries. In fact, repeated mention of race was made throughout the petitioners' brief.

The Hughes Court not only rejected the defense's racial discrimination claim; it altogether disregarded the intensely racial elements of the case that propelled the case to national notoriety in the first place. Repeated reference to the defendants' race was made throughout the Court's opinion, but there was no judicial notice of it at all. The seven references to race were proffered solely in connection with the Court's effort to distinguish the Scottsboro defendants from others involved in the precipitating incident.[47] As well, at the same time that it was noted the attitude of the community was one of "great hostility," the Court downplayed it and concluded it did not "sufficiently appear that the defendants were threatened with, or that they were actually in danger of, mob violence." As to the Fourteenth Amendment discrimination claim, that was promptly disposed of at the outset and without explanation, with the justices stating only: "The only one of the assignments which we will consider is the second, in respect of the denial of counsel." Finding the defendants were denied effective counsel (appointed the day of the trial), the crux of the holding rested chiefly on the defendant's limited intellectual capacity to defend themselves. It underscored they were "ignorant and illiterate," not that they were black, or that the state militia escorted them throughout the trial, or that their arrest and prosecution fit the well-known pattern of discriminatory law enforcement in the Jim Crow South. In essence, the fact that their arrest, prosecution, and conviction were racially tainted was ultimately irrelevant to the Court.

Under the leadership of Chief Justices Hughes, Stone, and Vinson, the Court continued to sidestep the racial subtext in almost all of the right-to-counsel cases to immediately follow *Powell*. Consider, to start, those in which the basic framework of the right was constructed. Southern biases came into play in *Johnson v. Zerbst* (1938),[48] which extended the right to counsel to all federal criminal proceedings and required an intelligent waiver of that right. Labeling the lead defendant a "hoodlum," the prosecution pursued what was, at bottom, a southern strategy within a legal proceeding in that it appealed to the regional loyalties and sympathies of the trial court. In turn, Johnson, a white man enlisted in the Marines and serving in South Carolina, considered it beneficial to tout his southern roots. Both strategies were played out before a South Carolina jury and at a time when racial segregation was a central feature of southern life. For its part, the Court offered no racial commentary of any kind. This is noteworthy for our purposes because *Johnson* was expressly grounded partly in *Powell*, which supplied the precedential groundwork for the final judgment in *Johnson*.

Two subsequent rulings also drew specifically on *Powell* but did so without alluding to the racially charged aspects of *Powell*. Nor did the litigant briefs. The silence on both ends speaks volumes about the decoupling of race and criminal procedure, because both cases involved efforts to distinguish the facts in these cases from those in *Powell*. The final decision in both underscored the limited nature of the counsel guarantee. Thus, both were a virtual invitation for the Court and the prosecution especially to make much of the fact that the *Powell* defendants were uniquely situated precisely because of the racially charged nature of their prosecution and conviction. *Bute v. Illinois* (1948)[49] differentiated *Powell* as among the "extreme cases [that] have well illustrated the kind of service to the cause of justice which can be rendered by this Court in thus giving effect" to due process. Meanwhile, when reflecting on *Powell*, the defense brief noted only: "the young and the illiterate are not the only defendants who may require legal assistance."[50] It too focused squarely on intellectual capacity. Referring again to *Powell*, it emphasized: "feeble-mindedness, illiteracy, or the like."[51] Similarly, the State of Illinois brief emphasized the importance of focusing on "the particular facts and circumstances surrounding cases" when invoking the Sixth Amendment.[52]

In *Betts v. Brady* (1942)[53] as well, the Court stopped short of intimating race had anything to do with the judgment in *Powell* or the discriminatory circumstances that gave rise to it. The closest *Betts* came to such an acknowledgment was its description of the defendants in *Powell*: "ignorant and friendless negro [sic] youths, strangers in the community, without friends or means to obtain counsel, were hurried to trial for a capital offense." *Betts* is generally regarded as controversial because it declared "the Sixth Amendment of the national constitution applies only to federal courts."

By the time the U.S. Supreme Court rendered its groundbreaking right-to-counsel decision in 1963 in *Gideon v. Wainwright*,[54] race had become the proverbial elephant in the courtroom. Over time, the institution had managed to decouple Sixth Amendment adjudication from its racial roots in *Powell*. *Gideon* expressly overruled *Betts*, and held the right to counsel applicable to state proceedings. But, even as the Warren Court itself acknowledged the historic significance of *Gideon* and that it evolved directly out of *Powell*, and even as it clarified *Powell* was limited to "the particular facts and circumstances of that case," the opinion made no mention of the racial elements of *Powell* – this time not even the race of the defendants. As well, Justice John Marshall Harlan's concurring opinion detailed what he termed the "particular facts" in *Powell*, but it was a race-neutral account of the facts. He described the case as follows: "In 1932, in *Powell v. Alabama* ... this Court declared that under the particular facts there presented – 'the ignorance and illiteracy of the defendants, their youth, the circumstances of public hostility ... and above all that they stood in deadly peril of their lives' – the state court had a duty to assign counsel."

One could argue that the facts in these cases did not lend themselves readily to a more forthcoming statement about race, notwithstanding the racialized jurisprudential roots of *Bute*, *Betts*, and *Gideon* and the practical role these roots (quietly) played in helping to lay the foundation for a national right to counsel. The defendants in these three cases were all white. None of the cases had the trappings of traditional southern bias, having been adjudicated in Illinois, Maryland, and Florida, respectively. Nor were there any other obvious signs of racial influences bearing on the prosecution or adjudication of the defendants. The same cannot be said of the remaining right-to-counsel cases, in which the Court accomplished several things. Among these, it established policy concerning the waiver of right to counsel; what constitutes a "critical stage"; court-imposed limitations on defense counsel actions and on attorney–client interaction; the applicability of the right across offense types; and, finally, constitutional remedies for Sixth Amendment violations.

At the same time the ruling was used to strengthen the right to counsel, the Warren Court barely took notice of the glaring prejudicial aspects of *Moore v. Michigan* (1957).[55] The Opinion described Willie Moore as "a Negro then 17 years old and with only a seventh-grade education" convicted of murdering "an elderly white lady." It further noted that while in police custody the county sheriff pressured Moore into waiving his right to counsel and confessing to the crime, all under the threat of mob violence, in nearly all-white Kalamazoo County, Michigan. Additionally, the trial judge claimed to have also obtained a detailed confession from

Moore during a five–ten minute conversation with Moore in his private chambers, off the record. During trial, the same judge labeled the crime as "the most pronounced case of sadism in the criminal annals of this county,"[56] a descriptor consistent with an extended history of criminal justice actors labeling and associating black suspects with the most extreme forms of violence and dangerousness.[57]

Meanwhile, the defense brief went to some lengths to connote a connection between the racial dimensions of *Moore* and those of *Powell*. As to the threat of lynching, it noted: "Testimony by the Respondent and by various officers of the Sheriff's department and the Prosecuting Attorney's staff shows that there was high tension in the community" and was warned the Sheriff could not do anything to protect him.[58] It added: "Willie B. Moore is a colored man and was seventeen (17) years of age at the time of his sentence.... He had a seventh grade education.... He was without the assistance of counsel for his defense, was without the aid or assistance of friends or relatives."[59] Again later: "When Willie B. Moore was arraigned and sentenced, he was seventeen years of age. He was a colored man and had been born in Arkansas.... He had a sixth grade education."[60] Finally: "In *Powell v. Alabama* ... the Defendants were young, ignorant, illiterate and were without the benefit of friends or counsel. Such a background had this Respondent, and the United States Supreme Court held that such a background must be considered in reference to due process."[61]

Despite the apparent facts of the case as well as invitations in the defense brief, the Warren Court opted to not comment on any possible linkage between the Sixth Amendment issues at hand and Moore's race. It held that Moore's right to counsel was violated, that any waiver must constitute an intelligent waiver, and that it is the judge's responsibility to ensure the right is intelligently and competently waived. The extent of its commentary on race consisted of the following and nothing more: "We believe that the expectation of mob violence, planted by the Sheriff in the mind of this then 17-year-old Negro youth, raises an inference of the fact that his refusal of counsel was motivated to a significant extent by the desire to be removed from the Kalamazoo jail at the earliest possible moment." It also offered the following: "The Sheriff's statement must be evaluated for its effect upon the capacity of this 17-year-old Negro youth of limited education and mental capacity to make an intelligent, understanding waiver of constitutional rights of supreme importance to him in his situation."

Carnley v. Cochran (1962)[62] brought the Warren Court face-to-face with just how deeply entrenched the racial caste system in the South's criminal justice system remained almost a decade after its pronouncement in *Brown v. Board of Education* (1954),[63] and, once again, the Court barely blinked. Willard and Pearl Carnley, a white couple, were charged with incestuous intercourse with their thirteen-year-old daughter, convicted under the Florida Child Molester Act, and sentenced to up to twenty years in prison. Among other things, the Florida act authorized state trial judges to commit convicted defendants to a state hospital. Reiterating its holding in *Moore* regarding an intelligent waiver, the Court detailed several provisions of the act in footnote 4 of its opinion. There it noted the act required that a defendant be committed either to prison or to "the hospital or state institution to which he would be sent as provided by law because of his age or *color* [emphasis added]." That the 1951 Act in question mandated racial segregation did not elicit a single remark from the Court throughout its entire opinion. This, even though the act was amended by the Florida legislature in 1953, 1955, and again in 1957, and none of these amendments revised the segregation provision.[64] Also unremarkable to the Court was that the Supreme Court of Florida reviewed the act for constitutionality and left intact the segregation provisions some three years following *Brown*. Finally, the fact that the segregation provisions of the act described by the Court were of such little importance as to be placed in a footnote, rather than the text of the opinion, further illustrates the point advanced here: it remained below the Court's radar.

National media began to highlight with greater frequency the racially suspect jury verdicts emerging out of the South as early as 1957, around the same time the civil rights protests in the region began to gain greater national and international attention. The Warren Court, however, did not follow suit. In denoting the stage in criminal process at which legal representation is critical, it remained obliviously focused on the Sixth Amendment claim in *Hamilton v. Alabama* (1961) made by attorneys Thurgood Marshall, Jack Greenberg, and James Nabrit.[65] In *Hamilton*, an all-white jury in Birmingham, Alabama, sentenced Charles Clarence Hamilton, a black man, to death in the electric chair. His crime, according to the state court opinions, was "breaking and entering a dwelling at night with intent to ravish."[66] Basically, Hamilton was sentenced to die for intending to rape a white woman. Court records described the intended victim was a woman of "Italian birth." According to a *Time*

Magazine article, it took the jury just over an hour to reach its verdict. The *Time* article also highlighted growing racial conflict across the South and the starkly different jury verdicts rendered in connection with the conflict. To illustrate, it compared Hamilton's case to another adjudicated in Longview, Texas, around the same time. The Texas case involved a twenty-two-year old white man's drive-by shooting and murder of a black teenager and the critical wounding of two other black teenage girls. His official defense: he did not intend to murder but simply to "scare somebody and keep the niggers and the whites from going to school together."[67] The defense attorney appealed to the jury to "call it a bad day and let the boy go on in life."[68] For its part, the U.S. Supreme Court concluded in *Hamilton* the defendant was entitled to counsel at arraignment because it is a critical stage but was silent on the racial dynamics of the case brought before it as well as the jury verdict's divergence from the white legal norm in the South.

The case in which the Warren Court extended the concept of "critical stage" to include juvenile proceedings elicited a number of race-related observations by the justices, but none ascribing them any substantive legal importance. The defendant in *In re Gault* (1967)[69] was a fifteen-year-old white male sentenced to up to six years confinement in a juvenile detention for making lewd phone calls. Upon stressing the unique vulnerability of juvenile defendants, the Court quoted from the opinion of an earlier case that involved a fifteen-year-old black male convicted of murder, based on a forced confession.[70] A passage from the *Gault* Opinion notes: "What transpired would make us pause for careful inquiry if a mature man were involved. And when, as here, a mere child – an easy victim of the law – is before us, special care in scrutinizing the record must be used. Age 15 is a tender and difficult age for a boy of any race." Interestingly, one could conclude the idea that race could be a factor is imbedded in this reasoning, but it is certainly not an idea the Court chose to make explicit.

In a case containing all of the usual telltale signs of a racialized criminal investigation and prosecution, the Warren Court settled on what racial progressives would consider the right fix for the case at hand but a wrong reaction to the deeper systemic racial problems manifest in the case. *Coleman v. Alabama* (1970)[71] involved two black male defendants, John Henry Coleman and Otis Stephens, convicted and sentenced in Birmingham, Alabama, to twenty years in prison for assault of a white couple. Intense local media coverage detailed the assault and ran descriptions of the black male assailants for three months following the July

21, 1966, incident. This led to what the defense brief described as a "tremendous manhunt" for three black assailants in addition to several local fund drives for the victim.[72] The enormous local media coverage of the incident and the associated racial tensions were picked up also by national news media. A *New York Times* article would later report not simply that the right to counsel was bolstered in *Coleman* but, more precisely, "the Court overturned the 20-year prison terms of two Negroes from Birmingham, Alabama – John Henry Coleman and Otis Stephens, who were convicted of shooting a couple during a robbery attempt."[73]

The process by which the black defendants in *Coleman* were identified exemplified the kind of problems researchers have shown to be uniquely disadvantaging for nonwhites, namely those associated with cross-racial witness victim identification and overly zealous police investigation tactics.[74] Owens and Snyder provide an in-depth case study account of what they term the "any four black men will do" phenomenon, whereby law enforcement officials scapegoat minority defendants in order to reassure the public in the wake of a major crime.[75] Only after one of the defendants in *Coleman* "was singled out by the officers to step forward and adjust his hat back and forward on his head" did the injured victim identify Coleman and Stephens as his assailants, some two months after the crime.[76] Eight months later at trial, the victim claimed to have seen Coleman "face to face," "looked into his face" and "got a real good look at him," testimony that sharply contradicted two previous accounts he initially gave. According to the Court's opinion, "on neither occasion was Reynolds able to provide much information about his assailants." Further, the defense brief noted Reynolds initially stated "he didn't believe he could identify his assailants" and his wife stated she "definitely" could not identify the assailants.[77] The police detective also testified Reynolds "did not identify any of his assailants from mug shots." Stressed by the Court was that Reynolds "gave a vague description – that the attackers were "young, black males, close to the same age and height." Critical for our purposes is that, in the sentence to follow, the Court itself highlighted the inconsistency: "Petitioners are both Negro; but Stephens was 18 and 6'2", and Coleman, 28 and 5'4 ½"." This led the justices to conclude simply that the particular circumstances in *Coleman* demonstrated the importance of counsel at preliminary hearings, not that such circumstances more often involve minorities in particular.

Strangely, three years earlier in a case involving a white defendant (*U.S. v. Wade*) and post-indictment lineups,[78] the justices indirectly acknowledged the research that proved the unique vulnerability of racial minorities in cross-racial identifications. The oddity is that, in *Coleman*, the Court essentially redressed the problem in the instant case but declined to acknowledge its deeper roots when doing so might have mattered more, both for the black litigants and others similarly situated. The opinion in *Wade* detailed an example intended to illustrate how racial minorities can be surreptitiously singled out by police officers in lineups. Without any prompting from defense counsel and drawing instead upon scholarly studies documenting the problems associated with interracial witness identification, *Wade* states: "In a Canadian case ... the defendant had been picked out of a line-up of six men, of which he was the only Oriental." The defendant, Billy Joe Wade, was white. Eustace, Texas, the town in which he was convicted, was all-white. The witnesses identifying Wade and his co-conspirators in a lineup were also white. Yet, in this otherwise nonracial case, the Warren Court took time to note the potential for race to infect witness identifications en route to finding that the right to counsel is guaranteed in post-indictment police lineups.

In *Kirby v. Illinois* (1972)[79] the Burger Court not only continued the longstanding pattern of sidestepping racial influences in criminal justice. It also reached what civil rights advocates considered a wrong conclusion in regard to police investigations and the right to counsel. More, it did so at a time in modern crime politics when judicial intervention on behalf of minority rights was arguably most needed. Among the policy issues imbedded in the legal questions in *Kirby* were questionable police tactics and also a phenomenon that would later become known as "racial profiling." The case itself emerged against the backdrop of tremendous racial and sociopolitical transition in the American inner city and also rising crime rates. Many of the major cities outside the South experienced the devastation of the sixties race riots. The 1968 Kerner Commission Report specifically identified police misconduct and discrimination in the affected cities as one of the primary causes of the riots.[80] What nonetheless followed in the wake of the riots was a marked increase in public support for more stringent "law and order." Aggressive policing tactics became the rule of the day in many of these cities, though increasingly criticized by civil rights leaders and organizations.[81] Perhaps none provoked more ire than Chicago Mayor Richard M. Daley, Sr.'s now infamous order for Chicago police to shoot to kill and maim rioters in the aftermath of Dr. Martin Luther King's assassination in January 1968.

Against this volatile backdrop, on February 21, 1968, the defense brief intimated the two black defendants in *Kirby* were the targets of racial profiling. It asserted the victim's "identification was patently arranged by the police."[82] Thomas Kirby and Ralph R. Bean were stopped by Chicago police, searched, and taken to a police station where they were identified by a robbery victim. Kirby and Bean were later sentenced to five to twelve years in prison for robbery, based largely on the victim's identification. At trial, the police claimed their initial stop of Kirby was a case of mistaken identity and that they mistook him for another suspect (Alphonso Hampton) whose picture and description were on a police bulletin. However, the opinion of the Appellate Court of Illinois highlighted the discrepancy in the police officers' testimony pertaining to physical descriptions of Kirby versus Hampton. Despite this, and in no less than a footnote (footnote 1), the Burger Court resolved: "The legitimacy of this stop and the subsequent arrest is not before us." It proceeded to declare also the right to counsel is not guaranteed in pre-indictment, face-to-face lineups.

The pattern of color-blind jurisprudence, now conjoined with judicial conservatism, would continue in *U.S. v. Ash* (1973).[83] *Ash* also involved the questionable identification of a black male defendant. At the center of the case was an armed bank robbery by two masked males, which lasted less than four minutes. Immediately afterward "none of the four identification witnesses was able to give the police a description of the gunman's facial characteristics."[84] Five months later, the witnesses were "showed five black-and-white mug shots of Negro males of generally the same age, height, and weight, one of which was of Ash."[85] All made what even the Supreme Court conceded were "uncertain identifications of Ash's picture." Shortly before trial, which came almost three years after the crime, the same witnesses were showed five color photographs whereupon only three identified Ash and none selected Bailey. At trial, these three were "unwilling to state they were certain of their identifications."[86] The fourth identified Ash and Bailey at trial but had previously failed to do so during the color photographic lineup and instead identified another man as one of the robbers. The Court upheld Ash's conviction. As well, it held the Sixth Amendment did not bar the admission of post-indictment identifications made on the basis of photographic lineups and in the absence of defense counsel.

Oddly, then, juxtapose this with *U.S. v. Wade* (1967), in which the Warren Court of its own accord cited research on the compromised reliability of cross-racial identifications, when it did not matter for the litigant, and then proceeded to enlarge the right to counsel. In *U.S. v. Ash* (1973), the Burger Court highlighted the questionable nature of the identification of the black defendant in *Ash* but then proceeded to limit the right to counsel, when it arguably did matter for the litigant. Important for our purposes, moreover, is that neither Court addressed head-on the deeper underlying issues highlighted by researchers when it mattered, insofar as the country as a whole was on its way to abandoning the sixties civil rights agenda and its concern for minority rights.

Moving now to the series of major rulings that delineated a trial judge's authority over attorney–client interaction, we observe the same pattern as that found in its rulings on the counsel waiver and the definition of a critical stage. The Court's first ruling on the power to deny counsel requests for preparation time likewise overlooked several conspicuous racial markers in the case. The defendant in *Avery v. Alabama* (1940)[87] was a black man. Lonnie Avery was arrested more than six years after the crime and convicted by a state mandated all-white jury of murder in Bibb County, Alabama, a rural county with a predominantly white population of fewer than 1,000. Following a brief, one-day trial, he was sentenced to death.[88] On January 2, 1940, the Hughes Court rejected defense counsel's claim that the trial judge's decision to deny a continuance and to set the date for trial only three days following arraignment infringed on Avery's right to effective counsel. With virtually no acknowledgment of the unusual circumstances surrounding the case, the Court ruled the trial was fairly conducted. This even as the defense brief invoked race and stressed: "The defendant, your petitioner, is a negro [sic]. He is ignorant and illiterate and probably insane. His mind appears to a layman as being feeble. He is unable to read or write," in an apparent attempt to link the case to *Powell*.[89]

The two main cases that addressed trial judges' authority to limit attorney–client communication expose a criminal jurisprudence that reacted differently to cases raising similar legal questions, with a key difference between them being the defendants' race. The white male defendant in the first case, John A. Geders, was prohibited by the trial judge from consulting with his attorney during a seventeen-hour overnight trial recess. Geders, along with eight co-conspirators, was convicted of conspiracy to fly 1,000 pounds of marijuana from Colombia into the United States in a rented plane. The Burger Court unanimously reversed in *Geders v. U.S.* (1976),[90] stating a client would ordinarily consult with an attorney overnight. In marked contrast to this ruling is the Court's disposal of an appeal by a black male defendant in *Perry v. Leeke* (1989).[91] Donald Ray Perry was convicted of kidnapping, raping, and murdering a white woman in 1981 in South Carolina, and sentenced to lifetime imprisonment. He was barred from consulting his attorney during a fifteen-minute trial recess.

There was evidence before the justices that Perry was "mildly retarded," that he was a nonviolent person who could be easily influenced by others, that he was declared incompetent to stand trial by the South Carolina State Mental Hospital, and was committed shortly after his arrest.[92] In addition, trial testimony from Perry implicated a white male. He testified: "Duke-Dog got out of the car and he told me, say, nigger, you better follow me and you better do what I say do or else I'm gonna take you out."[93] Nonetheless, the Rehnquist Court 6–3 majority reached a conclusion in *Perry* that was markedly different from that in *Geders*. It held that defendants have no right to such consultation. This included mildly retarded, black males subject to manipulation by others, in this case, white males.

A similar set of discrepant results are found in the Burger Court rulings on the applicability of Sixth Amendment rights across offense types. A liberal construction prevailed in *Argersinger v. Hamlin* (1972) involving a white defendant.[94] There, following a complaint from a neighborhood resident, door-to-door salesman John Richard Argersinger, a white male, was stopped by police, then arrested and charged with carrying a concealed weapon – a misdemeanor. He was subsequently convicted and sentenced to ninety days in jail. The Burger Court reversed, holding the right to counsel is guaranteed regardless of whether the offense is a misdemeanor or felony. Virtually the same question of whether the right to counsel is guaranteed in all criminal proceedings met a more conservative response from nearly the same Court composition[95] in *Scott v. Illinois* (1979),[96] which involved a fifty-two-year-old black male defendant, Aubrey Scott. In Scott's case the Burger Court decided he was not entitled to counsel, as a prison sentence was not imposed, notwithstanding the fact that the applicable state statute authorized it. Scott was accused of stealing a $12.95 attaché case and an address book from a F. W. Woolworth store. As opposed to the counter clerk who assisted Scott during the time of his visit to the store, the sole prosecution witness against Scott was the store's white security guard. Following a bench trial in Chicago, Illinois, Scott was convicted of theft.

Last, *U.S. v. Morrison* (1981)[97] was a case in which federal law enforcement agents engaged in race-baiting and it served as the platform on which the Burger Court limited the recourse available to criminal defendants denied the right to counsel. The case involved a mix of the problems researchers have shown to plague drug crime investigations and prosecutions, namely they disproportionately target racial minorities.[98] A year before *Morrison*, an ACLU amicus brief (submitted in a case discussed in the next subsection) provided the Court evidence of the racially suspect drug courier profile used by law enforcement officials in drug investigations. In *Morrison*, the Federal Drug Enforcement Administration (DEA) agents twice interviewed Hazel Morrison, a black woman, without her counsel-of-record's knowledge or permission. In an effort to pressure her to submit to questioning, the agents "warned the trial judge in her case was the "worse SOB in the federal courts," that he "hates black people," and that her "goddamn ass (was) going to jail," according to state court records. The agents also made disparaging remarks about her attorney, Salvatore J. Cucinotta. Morrison was indicted on June 28, 1978, of two counts of distributing heroin and later accepted a conditional plea imposing five years in prison.[99] On review, the Supreme Court held that, even if the Sixth Amendment violation was deliberate, there was no evidence the violation adversely impacted her case.

In sum, starting with its 1932 *Powell v. Alabama* decision, the Sixth Amendment right-to-counsel cases reviewed by the Court were replete with elements that systematically worked to the disadvantage of black and minority defendants. Despite this, the Court largely rendered its decisions as if those elements were nonexistent. Where it indirectly alluded to them, it stopped far short of assigning them any judicial or legal importance. In effect, the Court proceeded from one case to the next, seeing race but not really noticing it.

Race, Fifth Amendment Rights and Suspect Police Strategies

Fifth Amendment rulings construing the privilege against self-incrimination supply additional evidence of the Supreme Court's longstanding tendency to overlook the racial dimensions of law enforcement. These cases help to expose the use of heavy-handed investigatory tactics against racial and ethnic minorities and the Court's role in shielding and, in some instances, tacitly condoning their usage. In what follows, I highlight the racial elements of each of these cases and describe the Court's response, or the lack thereof. The major cases may be divided into several categories, namely those: establishing the Court's authority to adjudicate the right; determining applicability of the right to states; delineating the procedural safeguards for protecting the right; detailing the circumstances and criminal offenses to which it applies; and articulating exceptions to the privilege.

As in the right-to-counsel rulings, also in this sphere the Court's work began in earnest with a highly racially charged case. The privilege against self-incrimination was used to invalidate a federal prosecution in 1897,[100] held inapplicable to states in 1908,[101] then enormously expanded both in terms of reach and substance. *Brown v. Mississippi* (1936)[102] in many ways marks the starting point of this trend. In *Brown*, the Hughes Court took great pains to detail at length the racial brutality involved in the case yet attribute no legal weight to it at all. This is a perfect illustration of how the Court regularly saw racism in law enforcement (quite literally in this instance) but again without noticing it now four years after *Powell*. The three black male defendants in *Brown* were indicted on April 4, 1934, for the March 30, 1934, murder of a white planter, tried on April 5, 1934, and convicted and sentenced to death the following day, April 6, 1934, less than six days after the crime. Following the lead of petitioners' brief, which described the defendants as "ignorant, illiterate 'cornfield' negroes [sic],"[103] the Court likewise labeled the defendants "all ignorant Negroes."

Recounting the experience of defendant Yank Ellington, the final decision reported that on the night of his arrest,

a number of white men ... seized him and, with the participation of the deputy, they hanged him by a rope to the limb of a tree, and, having let him down, they hung him again, and when he was let down the second time, and he still protested his innocence, he was tied to a tree and whipped, and still declining to accede to the demands that he confess, he was finally released and he returned with some difficulty to his home, suffering intense pain and agony. The record of the testimony shows that the signs of the rope on his neck were plainly visible during the so-called trial.

The Opinion continued, describing how two days later the defendant was again taken into custody and "severely whipped," along with his two co-defendants, Ed Brown and Henry Shields. The latter were made to strip and "were laid over chairs and their backs were cut to pieces with a leather strap with buckles on it."[104] The Opinion explained that, when asked during his testimony at trial how severely Ellington was whipped, the deputy sheriff replied: "not too much for a negro [sic]." Finding Kemper County, Mississippi, sheriffs had used "extreme brutality"[105] to extort defendants' confessions, the Court remarked the trial transcript "reads more like pages torn from some medieval account than a record made within the confines of a modern civilization." In the end and notwithstanding the apparently discriminatory aspects of the case, the final decision of the Court simply reversed defendants' convictions, and said nothing of the unmistakably racialized nature of their treatment. Almost two decades would pass before the Court made state proceedings subject to Fifth Amendment protections in 1964.[106] *Brown* was initial proof to the Court that, during the interim, it was blacks and minorities in the South who would be uniquely vulnerable to the lack of such protections.

In *Adamson v. California* (1947),[107] despite defense counsel repeatedly raising "the flag" of racial impropriety, so to speak, the Court responded with its usual marked silence. The defendant, Admiral Dewey Adamson, was a young black male charged, convicted, and sentenced to death for the July 23, 1944, murder of a white woman in Los Angeles.[108] Defendant's brief repeatedly invoked race, alluding at multiple points to the fact that the defendant was black. The statement of facts section of the brief noted he was "a poor negro [sic]" whose victim was a white woman.[109] The section articulating the legal questions at hand again noted he was "a poor negro [sic], and not shown to have been in any way connected with the deceased."[110] In multiple other sections, the brief emphasizes the absence of any "colored" persons in the vicinity of the crime. More, he was "a poor negro [sic]" denied a fair trial in violation of the Fourteenth Amendment.[111]

Perhaps most unusual is Justice Black's dissent, which contained a lengthy treatise detailing Congressional debate and proceedings on the Fourteenth Amendment. In it, Black presented a history of various forms of extreme racial discrimination practiced against blacks in the South and elsewhere. That history, he noted, is what led to the introduction and adoption of the amendment. However, even though Justice Black's review might be construed as responsive to the defense's claim of a Fourteenth Amendment violation, the body of his opinion was itself entirely devoid of any discussion of racial influences in the instant case or in general. In fact, the treatise on Fourteenth Amendment history was inserted in an appendix to Black's opinion. For its part, the Vinson Court too was detached from the familiar racial script in *Adamson* and unmoved by the defense's legal claim as well. *Adamson* held "the clause of the Fifth Amendment protecting a person against being compelled to be a witness against himself" inapplicable to states.

"Foreign-born" was a prominent part of the description the Warren Court used when referring to the defendant in *Spano v. New York* (1959). Vincent Joseph Spano was convicted of first degree murder and sentenced to die in the electric chair, due largely to a confession obtained following all-night questioning by as many as fifteen police and prosecutors. The Court's opinion made repeated mention of the defendant's ethnicity. This is noteworthy partly because it was unprompted, as neither the opinion of the New York Court of Appeals nor the lone dissent there contained any reference to the defendant's ethnicity. Thus, the Court's reference to it gives the impression that it mattered – that the Court was aware of its practical relevance – but without exactly saying so.[112] Writing for the Court, Chief Justice Warren began as follows: "The State's evidence reveals the following: Petitioner Vincent Joseph Spano is a derivative citizen of this country, having been born in Messina, Italy." Again later, where Warren details the extensive questioning to which Spano was subject, he again began by noting: "Petitioner was a foreign-born young man of 25 with no past history of law violation or of subjection to official interrogation ..." The first line of the case syllabus opened with the description: "After petitioner, a foreign-born young man of 25 with a junior high school education and no previous criminal record." Notwithstanding the Opinion's multiple references to Spano's foreign birth, however, when passing upon his mental fitness for interrogation in the absence of counsel, Warren highlighted instead the defendant's and his mother's history of emotional and mental instability. It was largely on this basis, rather than the defendant's foreignness, that the Court concluded his confession was involuntarily obtained in violation of the Fifth Amendment.

The two main cases in which the Court began the task of detailing the procedural safeguards required under the Fifth Amendment both involved minority defendants and strong hints of racially tainted behavior on the part of police investigators. The Hispanic heritage of the defendant in *Escobedo v. Illinois* (1964) was front-and-center during the police investigation, again at trial, and again on appeal to the Supreme Court.[113] The interrogation tactics used to elicit incriminating statements from the defendant, Danny Escobedo, were blatantly formulated on the basis of racial-ethnic considerations. Although Escobedo was fluent in English, the Hispanic officer[114] assigned to interrogate Escobedo set out to exploit his Hispanic heritage. The trial court, Illinois Supreme Court, defendant's brief, and U.S. Supreme Court each separately acknowledged that, during interrogation, the officer made several false promises to the defendant, all in Spanish.[115] The promises were made contingent upon Escobedo identifying a Benedict DiGerlando as the shooter. Notably, according to the Illinois Supreme Court and the defendant's brief, the officer also stated: "Benny is Italian and there is no use in a Mexican going down for an Italian."[116]

Escobedo's ethnicity figured prominently in the Warren Court's illustration of the high-pressured nature of the interrogation. The Opinion highlighted the fact that the defendant was "a 22-year-old of Mexican extraction with no record of previous experience with the police." It went on to state that one of the "critical circumstances" distinguishing *Escobedo* from an earlier case was "that petitioner there, but not here, was a well educated man who had studied criminal law while attending law school for a year." Moreover, given that no other portion of the opinion alludes to Escobedo's educational background and training, the Court's reference in this context to Escobedo's Mexican heritage is best understood as having drawn a connection between Escobedo's foreign origins, his ability to comprehend aspects of the interrogation, and the voluntary nature of his confession. Such an understanding is further warranted by the fact that the Illinois Supreme Court's opinion went to great lengths to dispel the notion that Escobedo was of "subnormal intelligence." It went so far as to highlight that the trial judge had remarked "I was impressed with this defendant's intelligence. I don't know how old he is, but he certainly is not ignorant by a long stretch."[117] For news media too, Escobedo's ethnicity was pertinent. A June 23, 1964, *New York Times* article reporting on Escobedo's overturned conviction noted: "It was also shown that no one had advised Escobedo, a 22-year old man of Mexican extraction of his constitutional right to remain silent."[118] Warren essentially relied on the vulnerability of defendant's foreign status in *Escobedo* but without acknowledging he did so.

The landmark *Miranda v. Arizona* (1966)[119] ruling brought the Court the closest it ever came to assigning legal value to racial influences; still, it did not cross its traditional line of silence. Of the four appeals decided in *Miranda*, racial and ethnic minorities were at the center of the two that involved the most serious charges. A Mexican male, Ernesto Miranda, was convicted of kidnapping and rape in Phoenix, Arizona, and sentenced to twenty to thirty years imprisonment. Roy Allen Stewart, a black male, was found guilty of robbery and first degree murder in Los Angeles, California and sentenced to death. Perhaps the most striking aspect of each of these cases was that the Warren Court's repeated references to race occurred without any prodding. Neither state court opinion took notice of the defendants' racial or ethnic background. In fact, there is no reference at all to Miranda's ethnicity in the state court opinions. The only reference to Stewart's race in the lower court's opinion was indirect, as follows: "Mrs. Wells, who suffered a fractured jaw, said that the culprit was a "colored man," but she was unable to identify him." Also, neither of the petitioners' briefs highlighted defendants' racial and ethnic background, apart from witness descriptions in the Stewart case. In the two places where Miranda's brief describes him, it notes only that he was "a poorly educated, mentally abnormal, indigent defendant"[120] and that he was "an indigent, (who) was 23 years old at the time of the interrogation."[121]

In sharp contrast to the litigant briefs and state court opinions, Chief Justice Warren's writing took what I will term a seemingly more "race subconscious" approach. In explaining why it regarded the defendant's statements as involuntary, Warren highlighted but did not elaborate the racial markers in the case, as follows:

The potentiality for compulsion is forcefully apparent ... in Miranda, where the indigent Mexican defendant was a seriously disturbed individual with pronounced sexual fantasies, and in Stewart, in which the defendant was an indigent Los Angeles Negro who had dropped out of school in the sixth grade. To be sure, the records do not evince overt physical coercion or patent psychological ploys. The fact remains that in none of these cases did the officers undertake to afford appropriate safeguards at the outset of the interrogation to insure that the statements were truly the product of free choice.

The Court's references to racial background were not confined to the instant case but were included also in its review of prior cases in footnotes 24 and 53. To help illustrate how interrogation procedures may give rise to false confessions, Warren's Opinion cited a 1964 New York example in which "a Negro of limited intelligence confessed to two brutal murders and a rape which he had not committed." To support another of its claims – that the five-day detention of four persons at Stewart's house at the time of his arrest – was not an isolated incident, again the Court cited an example involving black persons in Washington, DC, in 1958, as follows: "Seeking three 'stocky' young Negroes who had robbed a restaurant, police rounded up 90 persons of that general description. Sixty-three were held overnight before being released for lack of evidence. A man not among the 90 arrested was ultimately charged with the crime." Though Warren made numerous references to the race and ethnicity of the defendants in *Miranda*, he left race entirely to the side in disposing of the claimants Fifth Amendment challenge and rendering the groundbreaking judgment imposing the now infamous "*Miranda* warnings."

The question of when *Miranda* warnings must be given was addressed in several cases[122] to follow, two of which were borne of racialized events, yet the sole issue to which the Court directed its attention was how to define "custody." In *Orozco v. Texas* (1969),[123] the Mexican defendant, Reyes Arias Orozco, was tried and convicted of murder with malice by a Texas jury and sentenced to ten years in prison. According to the Texas Court of Criminal Appeals, the white male victim "beat appellant about the face with his hands and called him "Mexican grease."[124] The assault occurred moments after the victim had propositioned Orozco's female friend at a restaurant, where all three crossed paths for the first time. During trial, the arresting officer, Patrolman J. W. Johnson, repeatedly referred to Orozco and his friend, Hosea Miramontes, as "boys."[125] When asked "was there any witnesses to the shooting. Was James Ishcomer one of the men that was out there?" Johnson recounted only the witnesses ethnicity, replying: "Yes, sir, the Indian."[126] The only issue of note for the Supreme Court was that the defendant was entitled to *Miranda* protections, even though his detention occurred outside the police station.

The racial profiling documented in some detail in *U.S. v. Mendenhall* (1980)[127] was deemed by the Burger Court as not "irrelevant, but ultimately not decisive." Consequently, it had no legal bearing on the Court's final judgment, even as the Court acknowledged its existence. *Mendenhall* rendered the Court's most exacting definition of "custody" to date and did so in the context of circumstances that could be said to have demanded greater judicial scrutiny in the instant case as well as many others to come. At the center of the case was a twenty-two-year old black female, Sylvia Mendenhall, who was stopped, searched and questioned by two white agents of the Drug Enforcement Administration (DEA) immediately upon arriving at the Detroit Metropolitan Airport. According to the agents, she "fit the so-called 'drug courier profile.'"[128] Subsequently accompanied by both agents to the DEA airport office, Mendenhall was then asked by a third female officer to disrobe. At trial, the defense challenged introduction of the criminal evidence obtained, arguing she was not properly *Miranda*-ized. The Court rejected the challenge and found Mendenhall had not been "seized" and was free to go, even though the agents failed to inform her she was free to leave. Critical for present purposes is, in reaching this conclusion, Justice Stewart acknowledged that race may have been relevant during the incident but was not decisive as far as the case was concerned. Writing for the Court, he stated:

It is argued that the incident would reasonably have appeared coercive to the respondent, who was 22 years old and had not been graduated from high school. It is additionally suggested that the respondent, a female and a Negro, may have felt unusually threatened by the officers, who were white males. While these factors were not irrelevant ... neither were they decisive.

Instead of the defense brief, the Court's racial commentary was prompted by the amicus briefs submitted by the American Civil Liberties Union (ACLU) and the National Legal Aid and Defender Association. The text of the defense brief made no claims about racial profiling, although it used footnotes to make a general allegation about law enforcement's racially biased use of drug courier profiles. In footnote 24, the brief notes "agents involved in searches at other airports have testified that their courier profiles, included, inter alia, "passengers of Hispanic origin (especially Mexicans)."[129] In footnote 26, the brief again mentions reliance on "the Mexican ancestry factor."[130] One could read into defense counsel's reticence a growing lack of faith in the Court's regard for racial impropriety in the wake of decades of indifference.

Meanwhile, extensive involvement in *Mendenhall* on the part of several national organizations might have otherwise served as a cue to the Court regarding the scope of the racial profiling problem in the United States. Growing use of a drug courier profile compelled organizations such as the National Legal Aid and Defender Association to present evidence to the Court that showed the courier profile disproportionately impacted minorities, Hispanics especially. The more forceful objection to the racial profiling pattern was lodged by the American Civil Liberties Union. The ACLU's brief made much of the fact that "all that the agents knew of respondent when they fixed their attention on her was that she was young, black, a woman, and was last to leave a plane from Los Angeles."[131] In the opening section, it recounted a *New York Times* article on the crime-fighting strategy of the South African apartheid regime in 1966, a strategy the article claimed was designed "to treat every black man as a criminal suspect."[132] Throughout the brief, repeated mention was made of Mendenhall's race. Finally, attacking the drug courier profile head-on, the ACLU brief noted: "A particular DEA agent may stop only the blacks and hispanies [sic] who meet the profile.... Discrimination made possible by the 'chameleon-like' nature of the drug courier profile and the discretionary manner in which it is applied, is precisely what the Fourth Amendment was designed to prevent."[133] The Court disagreed. This time, it said so. It rejected the ACLU's evidence of widespread racial profiling. It did so upon a determination that it was not "irrelevant" yet "not decisive."

Estelle v. Smith (1981)[134] emerged from a series of local and national events that had all the trappings of a typical modern American crime story featuring a dangerous black male, and it inspired the usual nonresponsiveness of the Supreme Court in this sphere. Local newspapers ran articles with menacing-looking pictures of the black male defendant, Ernest Benjamin Smith.[135] Widespread use of the imagery in this case fit what several studies prove is a pattern, wherein media depictions of lawlessness are subliminally associated with blackness.[136] Owners of the store in which the incident occurred (now a subsidiary of Dean Foods Corporation) launched a program that as of 2010 awarded up to $1.5 million dollars as a reward to crime tipsters.[137] As for the record before the Court, the defense brief honed in on the defendant's race in its opening line: "Respondent Ernest Benjamin Smith, Jr., a black American, was convicted and sentenced to die as a result of a convenience store robbery in Dallas, Texas.... Mr. Smith himself did not fire a shot."[138] Following a ninety-minute, court-ordered psychiatric examination, Dr. James Grigson labeled Ernest Benjamin Smith a "a very severe sociopath" and concluded "there is no treatment, no medicine ... that in any way at all modifies or changes this behavior."[139] It too was consistent with research establishing a widespread tendency for criminal justice actors to reserve the most damning and demeaning criminal descriptions for black suspects.[140] The doctor's testimony was the key evidence leading to Smith's death sentence. The Supreme Court ruled the confession inadmissible simply because Smith was not advised of his right to remain silent prior to the examination.

Edwards v. Arizona (1981)[141] offers the most telling insight into the post–Warren Court shift toward an even more resolute race-neutral stance, along with a separate case, *Michigan v. Mosley* (1975).[142] Both supplied the occasions on which the Court further clarified (meaning in this instance, restricted) the circumstances to which *Miranda* warnings applied. Both involved black defendants. Robert Edwards, a twenty-four-year old black male, was charged with murder, burglary, and robbery in Tucson, Arizona, then convicted and sentenced to death. When he requested an attorney, police officers connected him by telephone to the county's prosecuting attorney. Instead of appellant's brief, it was actually Arizona's brief that exposes the racial dimensions of the case. The defense brief noted: "Edwards, a twenty-four year old indigent black, was arrested on January 19, 1976, under authority of a criminal complaint and an arrest warrant charging him with murder, burglary and robbery."[143] However, the government's brief went beyond this and commented on the defendant's race at multiple points. In the first, it recounted: "Edwards "said that he was placed in solitary with a 'brother' named Al J. Carter."[144] It again noted: "Edwards also refered [sic] to the officer who arrested him as a 'brother.'"[145] Further: "It appears therefore that he uses this term to describe fellow blacks, and not necessarily as a term of friendship."[146] Finally, in what appears to have been a display of racially charged sarcasm, the government brief disputed Edwards's claim that he was placed in solitary confinement and, thus, did not make a voluntary statement. It clarified: "petitioner was not in 'solitary' as such, he was with a 'brother' named Al J. Carter."[147]

The Court not only sidestepped the racial innuendo altogether. But, it seemed bent on dispelling the notion that the black defendant in the case was at any disadvantage. As such, *Edwards* evinced a Court disinclined to attribute, even implicitly, any meaning to the fact that Edwards was an indigent black man confronted and physically confined by multiple white police officers, or to leave the door open for others to do so. This, as the defense brief tried to open the door for the Court to do otherwise, claiming: "Coercion need not take the physical form of the rack, the rubber hose or the blackjack. Spirit and mind may be as effectively twisted to an interrogator's will as may the body."[148] Instead, the Court concluded: "we do not hold or imply that Edwards was powerless to countermand his election" to make incriminating statements "prior to his having access to counsel."

Fare v. Michael (1979)[149] reflected the Supreme Court's tacit endorsement of what researchers argue is a tendency on the part of criminal justice officials to react differently toward black and white juvenile offenders. Bridges and Steen prove, more precisely, that officials' perceptions of juvenile offenders influence their classification, assessment, and final recommendation for punishment in ways that vary partly along racial lines.[150] The defendant in *Fare*, a 16 ½-year-old minority male, was convicted of murdering a white male in Van Nuys, California and committed to the California Youth Authority as a ward of the court. His conviction was based chiefly on a confession made during police questioning in the absence of counsel.[151] The final ruling in *Fare* dealt with the counsel request requirement under the *Miranda* rule, but a key element of the prosecution's strategy was to depict Michael C. as street savvy, despite his young age. The California Court of Appeals stressed the admission of a confession did not depend on age alone but a combination of the defendant's age plus his "intelligence, education, experience, and ability to comprehend the meaning and effect of his statement."[152] The Burger Court agreed with the trial court's characterization of the minority teenager in *Fare* as "not being a young naive individual with no experience with the courts." It further concluded that "no special factors indicate that respondent was unable to understand the nature of his actions. He was a 16 1/2-year-old juvenile with considerable experience with the police. He had a record of several arrests. He had served time in a youth camp, and he had been on probation for several years."

Also present in *Fare* was the well-studied racial difference in public confidence and trust in law enforcement, a phenomenon the Court overlooked as well. The exchange between defendant Michael C. and police interrogators manifests what researchers describe as persistently lower levels of trust in police officers on the part of minority teenagers.[153] The police asked the teenager in *Fare* whether he wished to waive his right to have an attorney present, and in direct response Fare asked: "Can I have my probation officer here?"[154] When advised he could have an attorney but not his probation officer, Michael C. responded by asking, "How I know you guys won't pull no police officer in and tell me he's an attorney?"[155] Shortly after, there is a pause in the recording of the interrogation, followed by "crying," then Michael's confession.[156] In view of the Court, this constituted a knowing and intelligent waiver – his young age, mistrust, and minority status notwithstanding.

The timing of the arrest of the defendant in *Harris v. New York* (1971)[157] coincided with the early phases of a law enforcement–heavy national anti-crime strategy, one disproportionately executed in black neighborhoods. In *Harris* and several subsequent rulings[158] the Burger Court would effectively defer to the strategy, enabling it to snowball in ways that would eventually prove devastating chiefly for blacks. At the center of *Harris* was a black male defendant, Viven Harris. He was convicted by a jury and sentenced to a six to eight year prison term for "feloniously selling a narcotic drug" to two undercover narcotics detectives in mostly white New Rochelle, New York. Harris had actually attempted to sell two bags of baking powder at six dollars each.[159] His arrest was part of an undercover sting that focused on what prosecutors deemed a "small group of dealers in and users of narcotics who inhabited" the vicinity of North Avenue in New Rochelle,[160] an area in the town known for drug trafficking area.[161] At issue in the Supreme Court case was an incriminating statement taken from Harris at the county courthouse in the presence of three assistant district attorneys, two other law enforcement officers, and the district attorney's stenographer. The statement was taken without adequate Miranda warnings, then used during trial to impeach Harris's credibility.[162] A law review article authored by Alan M. Dershowitz and John Hart Ely characterized Harris as nothing more than a "little guy in the great scheme of things."[163] The defense described him as "23 years old with a tenth grade education ... indigent, (and) addicted."[164] But his classification by prosecutors as a felonious drug dealer was sufficient for the Court to carve out an exception to *Miranda* and, in doing so, help lay the legal foundation for a drug war that would claim millions of minority and poor casualties.

Finally, moreover, two classic texts in critical legal theory underscore the Court's careful exercise of its highly tenuous power over the course of history, particularly in cases involving controversial issues such as race. Robert G. McCloskey averred the Court's history establishes "over and over" that "the Court seldom strayed very far from the mainstreams of American life and seldom overestimated its own power resources."[165] The same history, according to McCloskey, "has repeatedly attested, the members of the Supreme Court are children of their times."[166] Chiefly concerned with the exercise of judicial review, Alexander Bickel offered a similar perspective in a slightly different light. He asserted the Court exercises a triune function: "it checks, it legitimates, or it does neither."[167] The matter of which action it will choose when confronted by perennial problems such as race is largely a function of mainstream politics. Bickel's analysis of the segregation cases led him to conclude that "over time, as a problem is lived with, the Court does not work in isolation to divine the answer that is right…. When at last the Court decides … the answer is likely to be a proposition to which widespread acceptance may fairly be attributed."[168] Thus, when faced with a problem or proposed solution that lacks widespread acceptance, the Court will stay its hand and do so through resort to technicalities, jurisdictional claims, and other legalistic methods of avoidance.

Dickerson v. U.S. (2000)[169] represents just such a case, in which the Court "stayed its hand" with respect to racialized criminal justice. *Dickerson* manifested the continuing dynamic interplay between race and modern criminal justice in a rather compelling fashion. At issue in the case was the Omnibus Crime Control and Safe Streets Act adopted by Congress in 1968. Among other things, the act sought to overturn the landmark *Miranda v. Arizona* (1966) Supreme Court ruling that imposed certain procedural safeguards to protect Fifth Amendment rights. Enactment of the bill came at precisely the time when the country took a rightward turn toward racial conservatism on several fronts, most vividly on the crime policy front.[170] The race riots of the late sixties, emergence of the black power movement, and white flight from the inner city coincided with a precipitous decline in the saliency of race and racial progressivism.[171] Rising crime rates were seized on by self-proclaimed segregationist and presidential hopeful George Wallace. They were leveraged as well in the "law and order" agenda of candidate Richard M. Nixon. Then and now, both candidates' emphasis on crime-fighting was viewed as partly racially motivated – a roundabout way of engaging in the usual anti-minority bigotry, this time through more politically palatable means: crime-fighting.[172]

Congress's enactment of the 1968 crime bill was also seen as in part racially motivated, as it conferred enormous powers on law enforcement, with the mostly black participants in the race riots as the bill's main target.[173] More than three decades after-the-fact, the concerns relating to *Miranda*, rollout of the law and order agenda, criminal rights and the like were just as politically ripe as they were in 1968. As many as thirty amicus briefs were submitted to the Court by various parties, including national law enforcement and civil liberties organizations. Several briefs were from nationally prominent conservatives. Included among the latter were Senator Trent Lott, who during the 1990s spoke admiringly of the Segregation Party platform headed by Strom Thurmond during the 1940s. Strom Thurmond too added his name to the list of those urging the Court to affirm the 1968 legislative reversal of *Miranda*.

The thirty-four-year-old black male defendant at the center of *Dickerson* faced more than fifty years in prison for aiding the actual offender in a bank robbery in Alexandria, Virginia. Charles Thomas Dickerson's appeal challenged admission of statements he made during custodial interrogation, before receiving warnings required by *Miranda*. In an opinion for the Court delivered by Chief Justice Rehnquist, the justices held that the Court and not Congress has the final say over the admissibility of statements made during custodial interrogation in federal and state courts. In short, a jurisdictional claim was the central focus of the *Dickerson* ruling and not the tremendous racial and political transition that came to a head in the case. It was, to borrow the words of Bickel, the means by which the Court again declined to "check" the crime-fighting strategy that snowballed over the years into a strategy that disproportionally ensnared blacks and other racial minorities. According to the reasoning offered by Stroup, the outcome was not by chance. Rather, like the Court's rejection of the statistical proffer in *McCleskey*, the ruling in *Dickerson* emerged within a social, political, and legal context that featured a federal retreat from the promise to undo the continuing taint of racial discrimination in U.S. society.[174] The U.S. Supreme Court followed suit.

No Problem

In conclusion, the preceding analysis illustrates that, throughout its history, a primary moralizing institution within American national governance consistently looked askance at racial influences in criminal justice. It shows that from 1932 to 2005, the U.S. Supreme Court followed a color-blind approach to criminal jurisprudence. This is just as true for the

Warren Court as it is for that liberal court's predecessors and successors. True, the Burger and Rehnquist Courts were in many ways more definitively blind to the role of race, but their basic orientation was part and parcel of a much larger historic pattern. The institutional posture of the Court during the entire period in focus was one of avoiding racial improprieties on this front – whether they were squarely before the Court, hovering ominously over the case, or only remotely relevant to the litigant's claim. Racial tracking never carried much legal weight.

The institution's indifference to the role of race in criminal justice carries enormous consequences for American government and society at large, as the Court's failure to act arguably permitted the problem to continue largely unchecked. In fact, the dissents in *McCleskey* virtually stated as much. Justice Blackmun commented about the defendant: "If a grant of relief to him were to lead to a closer examination of the effects of racial considerations throughout the criminal justice system, the system, and hence society, might benefit." He continued with a more forceful commentary on the history of race and criminal justice, saying "we cannot pretend that in three decades we have completely escaped the grip of a historical legacy spanning centuries. Warren McCleskey's evidence confronts us with the subtle and persistent influence of the past." Indeed, both Justice Brennan and Justice Blackmun's opinions placed great weight on the history of dual criminal laws, noting that its genesis was traceable to the early post-Civil War period and that the "legislative history of the Fourteenth Amendment reminds us that discriminatory enforcement of states' criminal laws was a matter of great concern for the drafters." Yet, for the majority of U.S. Supreme Court justices from that time onward, the duality of criminal law enforcement was not a problem, certainly not one for the institution to solve.

The Court thus left to lawmakers the task of addressing the race problem in criminal justice. We turn next to a look inside Congress to assess lawmakers' response to racial tracking, or the lack thereof.

4

Opportunities for Change

The Racial Justice Agenda in Congress

Racial tracking made it to the governmental agenda but did not make it to the decision agenda in Congress. More precisely, racial justice advocates repeatedly tried but failed to create a window of opportunity for redress of racial tracking in the criminal process. Their push for enactment of corrective federal legislation continually faltered as a result. The lack of success is not readily attributable to a lack of viable policy options. For a quarter century, proponents of racial justice put forward a legislative agenda composed of a wide and varied range of options from which prospective supporters could choose as a way to commit either tangible or symbolic support to racial reform of criminal justice. Despite this, everything from the weak, narrowly construed, and economical measures to the more aggressive, wide-reaching, and costly proposals met the same fate. It mattered little whether the issue at hand was that of which stage of the criminal process to tackle, which requirements and prohibitions to put in place, or how to enforce the bills.

It would be a mistake also to blame the demise of the Congressional racial justice agenda on the usual institutional and political impediments to policy reform. Besides the substance of policy options, the other factors that typically play a major role in dooming legislative initiatives launched in Congress also did not figure largely in the agenda's downfall. Informational deficiencies, regional and partisan polarization, inadequate parliamentary skill, intense opposition, and little known sponsors were not determinative. Ultimately, it was the most decisive of the "usual culprits" that sealed the agenda's fate. Reformers continually fell far short of the votes needed to move the bills through the formal legislative process.

What follows is an in-depth look at the substantive elements of the racial justice agenda and its failure to "take off" in Congress between 1988 and 2012.[1] The window of opportunity potentially forged by racial justice advocates was all but foreclosed. The discussion begins with a description of the policy proposals composing the racial justice agenda, namely the goals, targets, and enforcement mechanisms encompassed by the proposals. Next it gives an account of how the racial justice agenda fared in the formal legislative process. Last is an explanation of how the standard drivers behind legislative outcomes came into play.

Smorgasbord: Policy Alternatives and the Racial Justice Agenda in Congress

The policy goals of the Congressional racial justice agenda were to reduce existing racial disparities in criminal law enforcement and to thwart systemic racial influences in the criminal justice system. Advocates were motivated by the belief that federal government action in this policy sphere was imperative. Though more than thirty states and localities had enacted anti–racial profiling policies, a national solution was considered key to resolving what was fundamentally a national problem. The U.S. Constitution demanded as much, not the least of which because the Fourteenth Amendment guarantees every American citizen equal protection of the laws. Accordingly, the express purpose of the majority of racial justice measures introduced in Congress between 1988 and 2012 was "to enforce the constitutional right to equal protection of the laws."[2]

Taken as a whole, the reform agenda supplied a way for members of Congress to tackle the racial dynamics of every major stage of the criminal process, from the police investigation and prosecution to the court and imprisonment phases of the process. Comprehensive measures that targeted the basic operational mode of the criminal justice system also formed part of the agenda. As to its substantive provisions, certain components of the agenda consisted of official denouncements of racialized law enforcement; others entailed more aggressive prohibitions; still others imposed a variety of requirements and regulations imposed on state and local law enforcement agencies. Just as variegated as the substantive provisions were the implementation methods proposed. They ranged from judicial enforcement, to grant incentives, to federal funds cut-off provisions, to criminal prosecution and more. In sum and substance, the agenda presented a significant number and variety of viable opportunities for prospective supporters in Congress to join the effort. At the same time the agenda was purposely designed to have a broad appeal, it was also poised to effectuate change in regard to several important aspects of the black law enforcement experience.

The black experience during encounters with police officers received more attention from racial justice advocates than any other aspect of the black law enforcement experience during the period in focus. The national racial justice agenda was launched in earnest in 1997 following widely publicized allegations of racial profiling by police, allegations which appeared to have been corroborated in a number of ways. Although the first major racial justice proposal was introduced in 1988, not until the late 1990s was there a steady stream of legislative initiative put forth, almost annually. Black news media outlets such as *Jet*, *Ebony*, and *Essence* magazine had long reported on claims of racialized policing.[3] Mainstream media coverage came in the wake of several controversial incidents.[4] They included a 1992 incident in which Oneonta, New York, police stopped and questioned more than 200 young black men in the town based on an elderly white woman's claim to have been robbed by a black man (with a cut on his hand). Many were rounded up after the State University of New York at Oneonta supplied the names of all of its black male students to local police. The Court of Appeals for the Second Circuit corroborated plaintiffs' account of events but also validated the police strategy (because the description on which they relied noted a cut on the suspect's hand).[5] Moreover, it was also during the 1990s that widespread allegations of racial profiling were lodged against the Maryland State Police and New Jersey State Police, allegations which were supported with statistical data in a lawsuit filed by the American Civil Liberties Union and the Maryland chapter of the National Association for the Advancement of Colored People on behalf of eleven black motorists. The data showed the overwhelming majority of drivers stopped by Maryland troopers on Interstate 95 were black and Hispanic.

New York Times contributor Jeffrey Goldberg further grounded the allegations and statistical evidence by way of up-close and personal observations from drive-along he took part in as background research. Goldberg's 1999 article detailed the fallout that occurred when New Jersey State Police superintendent stated: "Today, with this drug problem, the drug problem is cocaine or marijuana. It is most likely a minority group that's involved with that."[6] The article further quoted a Maryland officer to have said: "Some blacks, I just get the sense off them that they're wild.... I mean, you can tell. I have what you might call a profile."[7] Further validation of racial profiling allegations came from a U.S. Department of

Justice investigation into complaints of racial profiling by state troopers on the New Jersey Turnpike, which resulted in the state police agreeing to a consent decree that mandated new state policies to prevent racial profiling.[8] Federal law enforcement racial improprieties were spotlighted during the 1990s as well, especially those of the U.S. Drug Enforcement Administration (DEA). It was criticized for "Operation Pipeline," a DEA-run drug program that trained state and local police to use a drug courier profile when attempting to interrupt the flow of drugs along Interstate-95, from Florida to the Northeast. Among the "key characteristics" identified by the program was a suspect's race.

The high-profile incidents, lawsuits and studies that garnered national media attention during the 1990s were a launching pad for the many Congressional legislative initiatives introduced thereafter.[9] When Representative John Conyers first addressed racial profiling at length in Congress in 1997, he said: "There are virtually no African-American males – including Congressmen, actors, athletes, and office workers – who have not been stopped at one time or another for an alleged traffic violation, namely driving while black."[10] Senator Russell Feingold went further and asserted in 2001, "skin color alone still makes too many Americans more likely to be a suspect, more likely to be stopped, more likely to be searched, more likely to be arrested, and more likely to be imprisoned."[11] Accordingly, reformers offered multiple anti–racial profiling measures, which can be categorized into four types. The first type did little more than officially register Congress's disapproval and its sense that something should be done about it. An example is the resolution sponsored by Representative Chris Bell in 2004.[12] The Bell resolution declared racial profiling was "a real and measurable phenomenon" and that it was wrong, ineffective, harmful, and damaging to the criminal justice system. It also resolved Congress and the states should enact legislation to ban the practice and require all law enforcement agencies to take steps to prevent the practice. That is all the resolution did, as is customary for formal resolutions. It was, for all practical purposes, a paper tiger.

The second type of racial profiling proposal was equally insubstantial and mostly called for information-gathering. The Traffic Stops Statistics Study Act, first introduced by Conyers in 1997, then again in 1999 with Senator Frank Lautenberg, focused on police traffic investigations.[13] The Act called for a study to help lawmakers ascertain whether racial profiling actually occurred. The 1997 version of the Traffic Study Act reported by the House Judiciary Committee directed the U.S. attorney general to conduct a study of stops for routine traffic violations. Several factors were to be taken into consideration, including: the number of individuals stopped, their race and ethnicity, the reason for the stop, whether a search was conducted and why, whether a citation or arrest resulted, whether and what contraband was discovered, and the "benefit of traffic stops with regard to the interdiction of drugs."[14] Besides the fact that it merely required data collection, the bill reported out of the House committee was wanting in two other respects. It did not require agency participation and it expressly prohibited use of data collected under the act in "any legal or administrative proceeding to establish an inference of discrimination on the basis of particular identifying characteristics."[15] In essence, the data were for legislators' use, not for use by victims of racial profiling.

A third type of anti–racial profiling measure was only minimally more robust than the first two types. The 2002 version of Senator George Voinovich's Uniting Neighborhoods and Individuals to Eliminate Racial Profiling Act (UNITE Act) directed the U.S. attorney general to establish an education and awareness program on racial profiling and its negative effects. The program was to be offered to state and local law enforcement agencies at regional centers. Additionally the U.S. Department of Justice was required to assist agencies that "would most benefit from the education program" in their efforts to implement a racial profiling prevention plan.[16] Here again, actual agency participation was not mandated, nor were any criteria specifying which agencies "would most benefit." It was, at bottom, then, a sensitivity-training proposal.

It bears emphasizing neither the anti–racial profiling resolutions that merely condemned the practice, nor those that called for compilation of racial profiling data and information, nor the sensitivity-training measures set out to actually do anything of note. The proposals left the racial status quo undisturbed and police officers free to carry on as usual. Ironically, it is precisely these features that also made the bills the most palatable of all those composing the racial justice agenda. Who could reasonably object to taking a stand against racial discrimination, as called for in Bell's resolution? And who would take issue with the Traffic Study Acts' goal of merely establishing to the satisfaction of doubting minds that racial influences in the administration of criminal justice were not imaginary? And who would stand in the way of law enforcement agencies at least having access to anti–racial profiling resources, should they choose entirely of their own accord to take advantage of them? As a practical matter, these measures afforded the membership an easy way to commit symbolic support to the cause of racial justice, if nothing else.

A fourth type of anti–racial profiling legislation advanced by racial justice proponents entailed a Catch-22. This type was more promising in terms of its potential to bring about real-life change but less so in terms of its prospects for eventually winning Congressional approval. In other words, where the broader sociopolitical environment outside Congress was concerned, these robust bills stood to meaningfully improve the lot of racial minorities. Yet, these same measures could also provoke a terse reaction from the law enforcement community. Similarly, they offered members of Congress the choice of resolving a longstanding problem of national proportions while simultaneously intruding in a policy area traditionally superintended by states. Notwithstanding the dilemmas these more progressive reform bills posed, their inclusion alongside the aforementioned weaker types of policy measures further diversified the Congressional racial justice policy portfolio. As such, they widened even more the range of legislative options at the disposal of prospective supporters.

The critical distinction between the strong and weak anti–racial profiling measures is that the former actually did something beyond mere pronouncements, information-gathering, and training. They banned racial profiling and did so in unequivocal terms. All twelve End Racial Profiling Acts (ERPAs) introduced between 2001 and 2011 by Representative Conyers and Senators Feingold and Cardin provided: "No law enforcement agent or law enforcement agency shall engage in racial profiling."[17] That the ERPAs were chiefly focused on the investigatory stage of the criminal process – despite their extensive provisions – is reflected in the bills' lengthy exposition of what constitutes "racial profiling." The 2011 version defined it as "the practice of a law enforcement agent or agency relying, to any degree, on race, ethnicity, national origin, gender, or religion in selecting which individual to subject to routine or spontaneous investigatory activities or in deciding upon the scope and substance of law enforcement activity following the initial investigatory activity."[18] Significantly, "routine or spontaneous investigatory activities" consisted of the following policing activities: interviews; traffic stops; pedestrian stops; frisks and other types of body searches; consensual or nonconsensual searches of the persons, property, or possessions (including vehicles) of individuals using any form of public or private transportation, including motorists and pedestrians.

There was more. The bills also mandated that federal and state law enforcement agencies maintain policies to eliminate racial profiling as well as any existing practices that permit or encourage racial profiling. Agency policies were to include an official ban on racial profiling. Administrative complaint procedures were required too, as were racial profiling training, data collection, and formal disciplinary procedures. Alongside the requirements imposed on state and local agencies was a list of responsibilities delegated to the U.S. attorney general and various other federal entities. A final feature of the ERPAs and other strong anti–racial profiling measures at least aimed to make the bills more amenable to outside law enforcement groups. Nearly all qualified the implicit critique of law enforcement. Sponsors' floor remarks and the text of bills were careful to praise law enforcement and point out that, to the extent that racial profiling was real, it was the making of only a tiny percentage of officers. The point about the isolated nature of policing improprieties was underscored over and over again. The text of the 2001 version noted: "The vast majority of law enforcement agents nationwide discharge their duties professionally, without bias, and protect the safety of their communities."[19]

As if to appease the law enforcement community, again in 2004, Feingold clarified the "bill should not be misinterpreted as a criticism of those who put their lives on the line for the rest of us every day."[20] The point was made again in 2005 by Feingold,[21] in 2007 and 2010 by Conyers,[22] and in 2011 by Senator Cardin.[23] Notably, racial profiling was regularly defined in a way that made clear certain circumstances justified the use of race in police investigations. The 2011 ERPA bill defined racial profiling as having occurred "except when there is trustworthy information, relevant to the locality and timeframe, that links a person of a particular race ... to an identified criminal incident or scheme."[24] Last, data collection provisions expressly prohibited public release of the identity of individual police officers. Thus, the anti–racial profiling provisions targeting illicit police behavior also shielded police misdeeds from public exposure and scrutiny.

In addition to the police arrest and investigation stage, moreover, proponents set out to ameliorate racial patterns at the prosecution stage of the criminal process. The list of choices as to exactly what to tackle at this stage was not as elaborated as that pertaining to the investigation stage. The prosecution-related initiatives were narrower in scope, in that they highlighted the need for remediation mostly in connection with one problem area, namely drug prosecutions. The many other red flags raised over the years by law enforcement critics, such as those related to imbalance in formal charging, bias in leniency, questionable discovery tactics, discriminatory use of peremptory strikes and so on, went largely unaddressed during the period in focus. This is not to say proponents were entirely inattentive to the extensive and varied nature of racial differences at the prosecution stage but rather they chose to concentrate their efforts on a fraction of the problems manifest at this juncture over the years. Still, although this more measured strategy centered on a limited set of concerns, federal drug prosecutions happened to also be among the more controversial practices. They had already grabbed the national spotlight and, as a result, portended better prospects for building a Congressional consensus around drug prosecutions than did the other, less visible prosecutorial improprieties, such as racialized peremptory challenges.

Like the anti–racial profiling measures, these too stemmed from racially charged incidents that had captured the public's attention (momentarily). A 2009 CBS *60 Minutes* news report revealed that the work of an undercover narcotics officer, Tom Coleman, led to the arrest of forty-six people in 1999 on drug-related charges in Tulia, Texas, a small farm town of fewer than 5,000.[25] Almost all of those arrested were black and, together, accounted for about 13 percent of the town's adult black population, where Coleman concentrated much of his efforts. The *60 Minutes* report noted Coleman acknowledged that, besides having no prior undercover experience when he was hired by the town's sheriff, during the time he was undercover, he wore no wire, had no partner to corroborate his testimony, collected no fingerprint evidence, and had no surveillance video or still images to prove guilt. Coleman himself also purportedly had a history of racial impropriety. Yet the defendants, many with no prior criminal history, were sentenced to prison terms of between 20 and 341 years, based in many instances solely on Coleman's perjured testimony. A similar incident occurred in Hearne, Texas, where the informant reportedly added baking soda to narcotics recovered as evidence in one of the cases, according to Congresswoman Sheila Jackson Lee.[26] The Tulia defendants were later pardoned by Texas Governor Rick Perry, but only after having served as much as four years in prison. The district attorney of Robertson County, in Hearne, Texas, later offered to settle a lawsuit brought on behalf of the black defendants by the American Civil Liberties Union.[27]

Congresswoman Maxine Waters underscored the tremendous power given to prosecutors by determinate sentencing laws. Waters expressed the need for federal legislation to correct the racially disproportional use of prosecutors' virtually unchecked power. Her 2004 bill proposal noted "prosecutors, not judges, have the discretion to reduce a charge, accept or deny a plea bargain, reward or deny a defendant's substantial assistance or cooperation in the prosecution of someone else, and ultimately, to determine the final sentence of the defendant."[28] It also observed the widely criticized disparity in drug sentencing stems not so much from judicial discretion as from prosecutorial discretion. Accordingly, the Waters initiative sought to impose federal restrictions on the prosecution of drug-related offenses by requiring prior approval from the U.S. attorney general for federal prosecution of an offense under the Controlled Substances Act, as amended (a.k.a. the Controlled Substances Import and Export and Comprehensive Drug Abuse Prevention and Control Act of 1970).

A more direct attack on the prosecution stage came in a series of acts introduced by Representative Sheila Jackson Lee in 2005, 2007, and 2009. Each was titled the "No More Tulias: Drug Enforcement Evidentiary Standards Improvement Act." Citing similarly disturbing anti-drug task force incidents in Alabama, Arkansas, Georgia, Massachusetts, New York, Ohio, and Wisconsin, Representative Lee asserted such abuses were widespread and tied specifically to abuse of prosecutorial discretion. In floor remarks, Congressman Lloyd Doggett likewise claimed that "what happened in Tulia was ... not an isolated example" and that the Tulia and Hearne incidents were simply "two instances that are publicly known in Texas of prosecutorial abuse concerning the investigation and enforcement of our drug laws."[29] He continued: "they were really outrageous examples – so outrageous that a Republican Governor pardoned all the people involved in the Tulia incident."[30] Lee's "No More Tulias" bills were expressly designed to force law enforcement agencies "to acknowledge that it is unfair to discriminate and prosecute one race, one community, one city, one rural area."[31] Together, the two main requirements of the Lee initiatives represented both ends of the racial justice agenda.

On the more aggressive end was a provision that, if enacted, would have restructured a substantial portion of prosecutions and convictions throughout the country. Section 3 established evidence thresholds for drug-related convictions and also mandated enactment of state laws that would require evidence to corroborate a law enforcement officer's testimony. The section was intended to directly influence prosecutors' decisions as to whether there was sufficient, untainted evidence to press formal drug charges against an individual. Lee reasoned, if there was insufficient evidence to convict, then there was insufficient evidence to charge. Representing the other extreme of the racial justice agenda was a provision that required information-gathering at the sentencing stage. It stood to have no real-life impact at all, at least not immediately. Section 4 mandated collection of data on the racial distribution of charges brought by prosecutors; the nature of the criminal law specified in the charges made; and the city or law enforcement jurisdiction in which the charge was made.

Although many progressives in Congress made much of alleged abuses of prosecutorial discretion, it was actually racial unevenness in sentencing that ranked alongside racial profiling as one of the two prime targets of reformers. Notwithstanding, there were almost as many bills related to court behavior as to police officer behavior; here again advocates honed in on a narrow set of substantive concerns. Instead of confronting the many ways in which court treatment of blacks has been said to diverge from that of whites, proponents concentrated their efforts almost entirely on the crack-cocaine disparity and capital punishment. Even of the many sentencing-related issues highlighted over the years, only a handful were targeted. Even so, the introduction of nearly a dozen legislative routes to reforming racialized court sentencing meant prospective supporters had some room to maneuver, even within these limited parameters.

Racial justice advocates primarily blamed federal sentencing laws for the marked disparities observed in connection with punishment of crack cocaine versus powder cocaine offenses. To put a human face on the problem, Senator Richard Durbin of Illinois recounted the story of Eugenia Jennings, a mother of three young children who was sentenced to twenty-two years in prison for selling the equivalent of six sugar cubes of crack cocaine.[32] The disparity Durbin and others sought to revise was actually more akin to a gulf, one that emerged in the wake of enactment of the Anti-Drug Abuse Act of 1986. Under this law, infractions involving at least five grams of crack cocaine versus those involving at least 500 grams of powder cocaine were both subject to a mandatory prison sentence. Because it took 100 times more powder cocaine than crack cocaine to trigger a prison sentence, the penalty structure came to be known as the "100-to-1 drug quantity ratio."[33] Later, the 1988 Anti-Drug Abuse Act legislated a mandatory minimum prison sentence for simple possession of crack cocaine, a move that made it the only federal mandatory minimum for a first offense of simple possession of a controlled substance. According to the U.S. Sentencing Commission, the result of these mandatory minimums was that the average sentence for federal crack cocaine offenders was 122 months compared to an average sentence of 85 months for federal powder cocaine offenders as of 2006. It would be difficult to overstate the impact of the 100-to-1 sentencing structure on black and other racial minority defendants. It was enormous, as blacks constituted the vast majority of individuals charged with crack distribution in the federal system. The percentage was as high as 82 percent in 2006.[34]

Proponents of racial justice endeavored to correct this imbalance. At least eleven major sentencing reform bills were introduced between 2004 and 2009.[35] They ranged from weak to strong. Representative Maxine Waters's Justice in Sentencing of 2004[36] was the most aggressive of all. Instead of simply equalizing drug sentencing, Waters's bill aimed to altogether eliminate mandatory minimum prison terms. From 2006 onward, lawmakers introduced more moderate measures that sought to equalize, rather than completely eliminate mandatory drug sentences. Leading this pack was Senator Jeff Sessions's Drug Sentencing Reform Act of 2006, which decreased the mandatory minimum sentencing thresholds for powder cocaine and increased thresholds for crack cocaine.[37]

The sentencing reform effort culminated in late 2009, with the introduction of the Fair Sentencing Act in the Senate by Richard Durbin in October 2009 and in the House by Lee in January 2009.[38] While admitting on the floor of the Senate that many of the same lawmakers supporting the Fair Sentencing Act of 2010 were responsible for enacting the Anti-Drug Abuse Act of 1986, which the 2010 act sought to revise, Durbin also expressed his own personal regret for having done so. He openly acknowledged the racial problems that emerged unexpectedly in the wake of the 1986 act. He said the act "took its toll primarily in the African-American community. It resulted in the incarceration of thousands of people because of this heavy sentencing disparity and a belief in the African-American community that it was fundamentally unfair."[39] The initial version of the Fair Sentencing Act of 2010 introduced by Durbin and Lee actually set out to eliminate altogether the sentencing disparity by establishing the same sentences for crack and powder cocaine offenses. In addition to setting a one-to-one ratio between crack and powder cocaine sentences, the initial Durbin–Lee bill also voided the five-year mandatory minimum prison term for first-time possession of crack cocaine. The rest of the ten major sentencing reform proposals introduced in Congress over the years were structured along similar lines.

Meanwhile, taking aim at the longest running national controversy in race and punishment was a bill introduced in 1988 in the House by Congressman John Conyers.[40] Conyers's 1988 proposal sought to reverse the 1987 U.S. Supreme Court *McCleskey v. Kemp* ruling, which rejected statistical disparities in capital sentencing as evidence of constitutional impropriety under the Eighth and Fourteenth Amendments. The 1988 measure prohibited the imposition or carrying out of death sentences in a racially disproportionate matter; it targeted racial disproportionalness both with respect to defendants as well as victims. As well, the bill laid out a set of requirements for a *prima facie* showing of racial disproportionalness and permitted states to rebut by showing that nonracial factors explain the disparities. Finally, under Conyers's proposal, death penalty states were required to collect and maintain data on all cases of death-eligible crimes and to appoint counsel for indigent defendants. Further, it barred state courts from disposing of claims under the Act absent these data, and it made the bill's provisions retroactive. Taken together, these provisions meant Conyers's bill would potentially correct existing disparities and prevent further perpetuation of racial differences.

As compared to other aspects of the black law enforcement experience, racial justice advocates devoted far less time and energy to improving the lot of blacks already behind bars. The most noteworthy exceptions are three pieces of legislation introduced by Representative John Conyers. Although Conyers's introductory statement made reference to the Amadou Diallo shooting and the Abner Louima assault upon introducing one of the measures,[41] the bill itself dealt with the more disturbing aspects of the prison experience, namely sexual assault and death. The Law Enforcement Trust and Integrity Act of 2000 increased criminal penalties for sexual abuse offenses in federal prisons.[42] This 2000 version, plus earlier versions of the bill, also mandated data on the racial characteristics and "death of any person who is in the process of arrest, has been arrested, has been incarcerated or is en route to be incarcerated at any municipal or county jail, State prison, or other State or local correctional facility."[43] A provision requiring information on the medical treatment given to or withheld from persons in custody was added to the second version.[44]

The political attractiveness of these initiatives was that they essentially duplicated laws and practices already in place. The Centers for Disease Control already tracked custody-related deaths. And a provision that amended the Violent Crime Control and Law Enforcement Act of 1994 to stipulate data collection on deaths in custody was already making headway within the House Judiciary's Committee's Subcommittee on Crime and would eventually become law.[45] Even the criminal penalties imposed by Conyers' Law Enforcement Integrity Acts mirrored penalties for offenses already included in the U.S. Criminal Code. In short, the prison-related components of the racial justice agenda were not much of a stretch from crime policies already in place. As a practical matter, all that really set the Conyers measures apart is they explicitly linked prison reporting to the racial justice cause, in that he was one of the most ardent longtime champions of the cause and he understood any reform of the prison experience would necessarily impact blacks more than other groups.

Complementing the aforementioned array of proposals that focused on individual stages of the criminal process were those with the more ambitious goal of institutional reform. Within this group too were those that skimmed the surface and those that dug much deeper. An example of the softer approach is a series of Justice Integrity Acts first introduced in July 2008 by then-vice presidential candidate Senator Joseph Biden and also Representative Steven Cohen. Introduced again in 2009 by Cohen along with Senator Benjamin Cardin,[46] the Biden–Cohen–Cardin proposals were essentially information-gathering measures. The main difference between these and the Traffic Study Acts discussed earlier was that the Traffic Acts sought to ascertain whether there was a problem, whereas the Justice Integrity Acts were based on the belief a problem did in fact exist. They aimed to uncover the root cause of "unwarranted racial and ethnic disparities." Under a pilot program envisioned in the Biden–Cohen–Cardin proposals, the U.S. Justice Department the Attorney General would identify ten U.S. districts. Within each district, an advisory group would be created and composed of federal and state prosecutors and defenders, private defense counsel, federal and state judges, correctional officers, victims' rights representatives, civil rights organizations, business representatives and faith-based organizations engaged in criminal justice work. The advisory groups would each collect data, study causes, and submit a final report to the attorney general who would then submit a summary report to Congress.

Although weak in the sense that the acts effectively provided for the formation of committees to study the underlying causes of racially uneven criminal justice outcomes, the Biden–Cohen–Cardin initiatives nonetheless proceeded from the premise that the system *in toto* was in need of legislative attention. Also, while the Traffic Study Acts were mainly concerned with racial profiling at the police stage, the Justice Acts addressed the overall law enforcement apparatus. Biden said the 2008 Justice Act was the final product of "studies, reports, and case law from the last several years (that) have documented racial disparities during many of the stages of the criminal justice system – law enforcement contact with a suspect, arrest, charging, plea bargaining, jury selection, and sentencing."[47] He honed in on prison statistics, but quickly added:

These numbers, and studies and reports ... show similar disparities during other stages of the criminal justice process, engender a crisis of public trust in the integrity of our criminal justice system and raise the possibilities that we are failing to make good on the constitutional promise of equal protection.[48]

The more aggressive institutional reform proposals aimed to revamp the operations side of law enforcement. Representative John Conyers described his Law Enforcement Trust and Integrity Acts as constituting a "new approach to the dilemma of police misconduct" that focuses not on "episodic incidents" but "targets hiring and management protocols much farther up the chain of causation."[49] In essence, they stemmed from the belief that individual law enforcement agents' behavior is a reflection of agency culture, procedures, and management. Conyers also noted his measures did more than offer money to law enforcement agencies "without any selection criteria or performance benchmarks."[50] The three Law Enforcement Trust and Integrity Acts he introduced in 1999 and twice in 2000 required the U.S. attorney general to recommend areas for the development of national standards for the accreditation of law enforcement agencies. The political significance of this particular provision is that it would have thrust the Justice Department into an area normally superintended by a nongovernmental credentialing agency, the Commission on Accreditation of Law Enforcement Agencies (CALEA).[51] Crucially, Conyers's Trust and Integrity Acts also made it a federal crime to "subject, or attempt to subject, any person to force exceeding that which is reasonably necessary to carry out a legitimate law enforcement duty."[52]

In summary, besides a selection of policy options for tackling individual facets of the criminal justice system, racial justice proponents also introduced a mix of initiatives geared toward system-wide reform.

Reformers did not stray too far from the beaten path in deciding which enforcement methods to utilize. This more conservative legislative strategy potentially improved their chances of bypassing a common sticking point in Congressional policy proceedings in general, which is that of how to implement a bill. For the most part they relied on the standard routes used for policy implementation. But even in sticking to these traditional routes, racial justice advocates nonetheless managed to tender an assortment of options from which members at large could choose in order to settle what are really the most decisive issues in any policy proceeding. Who would be affected by the bills, in what ways, and to what benefit or cost were ultimately questions that had to do with whether and how any enacted proposals would alter the racial status quo in the criminal justice system. How advocates broached these concerns necessarily dictated whether and to what extent legislative reforms would succeed in actually changing the reality of race and law enforcement in the United States.

Four types of enforcement mechanisms were incorporated across the various initiatives composing the racial justice agenda. Judicial enforcement was the preferred approach to implementation of federal civil rights laws enacted during 1957–1992 to combat discrimination in education, employment, housing, and public accommodations.[53] Court enforcement was likewise the choice of Congressional racial justice advocates in their fight against racial unevenness in criminal justice during 1988–2012. Civil action was authorized by the bulk of racial justice proposals, especially those that targeted police misconduct and prison management. The right to file a civil lawsuit in state or federal court was given to aggrieved individuals and to the U.S. attorney general by the Law Enforcement Integrity Acts and Conyers–Feingold–Cardin anti–racial profiling proposals measures. Courts, in turn, were empowered to provide declaratory or injunctive relief.

Certain of the measures designated administrative agencies as the primary enforcement mechanism. The two Racial Profiling Prohibition Acts introduced in 2001 and a Racial Profiling Prevention Act introduced in 2012 by Representative Eleanor Holmes–Norton authorized the U.S. secretary of transportation to carry out key provisions.[54] Meanwhile, enforcement of the various sentencing reform proposals was entrusted to the U.S. Sentencing Commission, established in 1984 to develop guidelines for federal judges to follow in applying federal sentencing laws in individual cases, as well as make recommendations to Congress regarding sentencing laws. The administrative enforcement mechanism of choice for racial justice advocates was the U.S. attorney general (AG). Under the ERPAs, it was the AG that would devise and superintend everything from data collection and administrative complaint regulations to the criteria for funds cutoff to which cases to litigate in court, which grants to award, and more. Under the Justice Integrity Acts, the AG decided which states would be awarded pilot programs. The Justice in Sentencing Act of 2004 required prior written approval of the AG for cocaine-related prosecutions, and the Law Enforcement Trust and Integrity Acts required AG approval for prosecution of police officers under the acts.

Added to oftentimes carefully constructed lists of AG authorities was a blanket provision that required compliance with "such other regulations as the Attorney General determines are necessary to implement this Act."[55] Construing such a large role for the U.S. attorney general arguably made the racial justice agenda that much easier to sell to lawmakers, partly because it helped to ensure the measures were readily adaptable to the particularized circumstances of state and local law enforcement agencies. It also increased the likelihood that enforcement would be responsive to shifts in the sociopolitical environment, as enforcement of the measures would change in concert with changes in presidential administration. To this extent, then, reformers effectively de-politicized elements of the racial justice agenda by linking enforcement to broader shifts in national presidential politics. Bipartisanship was effectively folded into the bills. Republican administrations could be expected to enforce the bills in line with their ideological preferences, as could Democratic administrations – all contingent upon national voting trends.

Additionally, Congress's purse strings were used to secure compliance on the part of states and law enforcement agencies. Positive financial incentives were instituted; so were financial penalties; and sometimes a mix of the two was folded into a single bill. The "carrot" aspects of this "carrot-and-stick" approach ran the gamut and were variously packaged as resource funding, development grants, demonstration projects, and the like. Senator Voinovich's Uniting Neighborhoods and Individuals to Eliminate Racial Profiling Act (UNITE Act) of 2004 awarded grants to agencies to assist them in developing programs to eliminate racial profiling. The 2000 Traffic Stops Statistics Study Act awarded funds to agencies that agreed to collect data as prescribed in the act. The ERPAs awarded grants to help agencies develop and implement best practices, specifically purposed to ensure racially neutral law enforcement. To promote the use of disciplinary action against officers, the ERPAs also awarded grants specifically for (1) purchasing equipment that would "help identify officers or units of officers engaged in or at risk of racial profiling or other misconduct" and for (2) establishing management systems to hold supervisors accountable for subordinates' conduct.[56] The Law Enforcement Trust and Integrity Acts also awarded funds for agencies to improve overall management and operations. The more fiscally conservative incentives involved demonstration and pilot programs that either awarded funds to a limited number of states on a competitive basis or set a cap on the total amount of funds that could be disbursed. For example, the data collection demonstration project authorized by the Feingold-Conyers measures in 2005 and later years appropriated a total of $5.5 million dollars to a total of five states. In 2012

Representative Eleanor Holmes-Norton introduced the Racial Profiling Prevention Act, which awarded grants to states that adopted anti–racial profiling laws.[57]

A range of more forceful funding-related measures were also put forth. Several bills contained funds cutoff provisions that, in effect, attached strings to monies awarded to states and to law enforcement agencies through a number of federal programs already in place. To the formulas and criteria used by these existing programs, racial justice proponents added further stipulations. Importantly, however, the issue of which programs to target, what percentage of funds to restrict or deny, for how long, under what conditions, and so on was left open. Among the possibilities was a key source of federal law enforcement funding, namely the Edward Byrnes Memorial Justice Assistance Program administered by the Department of Justice's Bureau of Justice Assistance. Byrnes programing was the logical place to start in attempting to apply financial pressure to law enforcement agencies. The Byrnes budget was large enough that lawmakers had some wiggle room in which to make noncompliance either more' or less costly. The authorizing statute set the Byrnes budget at $1.1 billion annually, although actual funding had hovered around $500 million according to a report of the National Center for Justice Planning.[58] In 2009 the American Recovery and Reinvestment Act (Recovery Act) gave it a one-time boost of $2 billion. Even amid severe budget cuts in Fiscal Year 2012, nearly $300 million was appropriated by Congress to the program. Not only was it a huge source of funding for law enforcement agencies, it was also one upon which agencies relied regularly. In Fiscal Year 2011, the Bureau of Justice processed more than $368 million federal dollars following 1,348 applications from local governments and 56 applications from state and territorial governments.[59]

One of racial justice advocates' more aggressive approaches to Byrnes funding was incorporated in Congresswoman Lee's "No More Tulias" proposals. They altogether prohibited federal funding to states under the Byrne Grant Program or any other law enforcement assistance program of the Department of Justice unless and until the state was found to be in compliance with the bills. The ERPAs required Byrnes applicants to pre-certify the agency met the requirements of the acts, as a condition for receiving funds. A second source of federal law enforcement funding presented still more enforcement options. It too had a sizeable budget. The "Cops on the Beat" Hiring Program was allocated an initial budget of $8.8 billion when first established by the Clinton administration in 1994, it underwent funding cuts in some of the years to follow but received a $1 billion appropriation in 2009 under the Recovery Act.[60] For Fiscal Year 2011, Cops on the Beat was appropriated more than $243 million to help agencies hire new officers.[61] All of the ERPAs included a funds cutoff provision that was tied to the "Cops on the Beat" program administered through the Department of Justice.

A third funding program constituted one of the largest sources of federal monies for states but actually yielded fewer racial justice enforcement scenarios. The funding pertained to transportation and highways and, consequently, was useful almost exclusively in connection with anti–racial profiling initiatives. First initiated in 1916, the federal infrastructure development program was substantially modified in 2005 by a multi-year reauthorization act, the Safe, Accountable, Flexible, Efficient Transportation Equity Act: A Legacy for Users (SAFETEA-LU).[62] The first of the bill's eleven titles provided federal aid to highway construction, management, and development. For this title alone, Congress appropriated an annual average of $40 billion during Fiscal Years 2005 through 2009. According to the conference committee report accompanying the infrastructure bill that originated in the House (H.R. 3), the Congressional Budget Office estimated discretionary outlays would sum to about $214 billion over the entire period covered by the act.[63] From a reformist perspective, the measure was potentially a mother lode. Accordingly, each of the Racial Profiling Prohibition Acts sponsored by Representative Norton directed the secretary of transportation to withhold between 5 and 10 percent of federal highway aid apportionments for a state that failed to adopt and enforce standards prohibiting the use of racial profiling on federal-aid highways.

Because contemporary attempts to assert federal influence over state and local matters often converge on the Congressional appropriations process (a phenomenon known as "regulated federalism"),[64] moreover, the racial justice agenda was very much in step with existing policy norms. Further, proponents' "carrot and stick" approach gave prospective Congressional supporters a number of ways to finesse real-life reform so as to suit their own political purposes, especially the financial incentives. The incentives potentially made it easier to sell the bills to lawmakers' home districts because they could just as easily be packaged as pork barreling, an enduring feature of electoral success.[65] What is more, they could do so in service of a loftier goal that went well beyond simply bringing home the bacon, so to speak. Even for fiscal conservatives, there was room to negotiate and guard against lengthening the list of increasingly unpopular unfunded federal mandates.[66] Whereas Senator Voinovich's

Racial Profiling Education and Awareness Act of 2002 contained a blank appropriations title that awarded "such sums as are necessary to carry out" the act,[67] the Biden–Cohen–Cardin Justice Integrity Acts was more cost-conscious and set specific expenditure levels (initially a $3 million dollar maximum), as did other spending-conscious bills.

Taken as a whole, the racial justice agenda of 1988–2012 included so many policy configurations and tendered members of Congress so many ways to address racial tracking in criminal justice that one is hard-pressed to find fault in the substantive elements of the advocacy strategy. To borrow a phrase, reformers bent over backward to secure some form of federal intervention on this front – by any means necessary.

Demise of the Racial Justice Agenda

The racial justice agenda almost always failed to gain traction in the formal legislative process in Congress, despite more than two decades of sponsorship and numerous policy configurations. Of the forty-five measures examined here, only two were enacted, one of which can scarcely be considered a resounding success and the other, a circumspect victory at best. A third made some headway toward passage. Aside from these, none of the stand-alone proposals examined even so much as advanced to a floor debate in the House or Senate – neither those that targeted the police investigation, prosecution, court, or imprisonment phases of the criminal process. This was the fate of the mildest and the most aggressive bills and all those in between. The one major bill proposal that did pass both chambers was the Fair Sentencing Act of 2010. Introduced by Congresswoman Lee and Senator Durbin in 2009, it was adopted by unanimous consent in the Senate on March 17, 2010, by voice vote in the House on July 28, 2010, and signed into law by President Barack Obama on August 3, 2010.[68] The Fair Sentencing Act eliminated the five-year minimum prison sentence mandate for first-time crack cocaine offenders and reduced the disparity in sentencing for crack versus powder cocaine offenses. The latter was accomplished by raising the mandatory imprisonment trigger amount for crack cocaine offenses from 5 grams to 28 grams. The trigger quantity for powder cocaine remained at 500 grams. The sentencing disparity was thereby reduced from 100-to-1 to 18-to-1.

Although enactment of the Fair Sentencing Act constituted an official win for advocates of race reform, there are six important caveats worth noting. One, the new law did not eliminate the disparity, as lead sponsors Senator Durbin and Congresswoman Lee had initially sought. Two, the law instituted a corrective to the racial impact of sentencing in an important area but without language in the text that expressly acknowledged Congress's intent to combat racial influences per se, as did many other racial justice proposals. As such, Congressional adoption of the bill proceeded without official acknowledgment of systemic racial influences in criminal law enforcement. Third, the provisions of the bill were not made retroactive, arguably leaving intact the gross disparities in imprisonment that followed in the wake of the Anti-Drug Abuse Acts of 1986 and 1988. The Sentencing Commission would later, on June 30, 2011, amend its guidelines to make the 2010 statutory provisions retroactive, but not automatically and only for crack offenses by way of a judge's ruling following a motion submitted by defense counsel and subject to challenge by a prosecutor.[69] Fourth, sections 5 and 6 of the law actually increased penalties for a lengthy list of drug-related offenses, which meant the bill was as much a victory for punishment advocates as for reform advocates. Relatedly and importantly, the bill left untouched the many other concerns that have emerged over the years in connection with criminal court decision making, beyond crack-cocaine sentencing.

Yet another caveat to the 2010 legislative "victory," is the bill's success in Congress is partly attributable to the more than fifteen years of hard work put in by the U.S. Sentencing Commission, an independent agency within the judicial branch. Senator Durbin remarked on the Senate floor that the Commission had been "urging Congress to act for 15 years" and that it "repeatedly recommended that Congress take two important steps," namely to reduce the sentencing disparity and eliminate the mandatory minimum penalty of imprisonment for simple possession of crack cocaine.[70] It was the Commission that laid the foundation and, one might add, increased the pressure on Congress to act. The Commission led the way by promulgating new guidelines as early as 1995, guidelines that would have done more to equalize sentencing. It is arguable, then, the victory was most immediately a Commission victory and only secondarily a legislative victory.

Proof that the Commission, more so than Congress, sowed the seeds of the 2010 enactment is that Congress's initial response to the revised 1995 Commission guidelines was to reject them by way of passage of S. 1254, signed into law by President Bill Clinton. Leading the charge against the Commission's 1995 amendment to the guidelines was Senator Spencer Abraham, chief sponsor of S. 1254, officially titled "A Bill to Disapprove of Amendments to the Federal Sentencing Guidelines Relating to Lowering of Crack Sentences." In his introductory remarks, Abraham rehearsed many of the usual alarmist messages about crack cocaine voiced over the years. Crack was associated with violence to a greater extent than powder cocaine. Crack had devastating pharmacological effects and produced more medical emergencies. Crack was sold in smaller and cheaper quantities, was more readily and widely available and, as a result, "easier for small kids to get and use."[71] Following its 1995 recommendations, the Commission would again present the issue to Congress in 1997, in 2002, and again in 2007, at which point it embarked on a relatively creative strategy of its own. Instead of simply waiting to amend the statutory minimums, the Commission attempted to initiate change on its own by altering the formulas it had previously devised to implement federal mandatory sentencing laws. The Commission concluded in 2007 that its own guidelines had contributed to the problems associated with the 100-to-1 drug quantity ratio. Having reached this conclusion, it modified the guideline ranges to *include* mandatory minimum penalties, rather than *exceed* the minimum penalties. The new Commission guidelines took effect in November 2007 and assigned a base offense level of 24 to the 5-gram triggering quantity for crack cocaine that was in effect at the time (i.e., 5 grams of crack). The base offense level of 24 translated to fifty-one to sixty-three months imprisonment.[72]

In contrast, the law passed by Congress in 2010 resulted in the trigger quantity for crack cocaine being set at a higher base offense level of 26, which corresponded to a higher sentencing range of sixty-three to seventy-eight months.[73] In essence, then, Congress's action in 2010 effectively increased the minimum prison sentence for crack cocaine above the range put in place by the Commission in 2007. Thus, passage of the Fair Sentencing Act of 2010 is appropriately characterized as less than a resounding victory for racial reform. It did not improve upon but actually moved backward from the Commission's 2007 recommendations. In reality, the new 18-to-1 ratio put in place by the 2010 Act was just shy of the 20-to-1 ratio President Ronald Reagan had initially asked Congress to institute in 1986, before Congress opted instead for a 100-to-1 ratio.[74]

Still, in strictly legislative terms, the 2010 act was a win; it was enacted into law.

The only other racial justice measure within the scope of this analysis and enacted into law was a minor provision appended to a massive infrastructure bill. Adoption of this particular provision constitutes, at most, a tiny victory. An anti–racial profiling grant program titled "Grant Program to Prohibit Racial Profiling" was added as Section 1906 to the Safe, Accountable, Flexible, Efficient Transportation Equity Act: A Legacy for Users (SAFETEA-LU), which was passed by Congress and signed into law by President George Bush in 2005. Section 1906 of Title I authorized appropriations for federal aid to highways and directed the secretary of transportation to make grants to states that adopted laws prohibiting racial profiling in the enforcement of state laws on federal-aid highways. Under SAFETEA-LU, states were required to also maintain data on traffic stops conducted on federal-aid highways and "provide assurances satisfactory to the Secretary that the State is undertaking activities to comply with the requirements" of the program.[75] No specifics were detailed in the bill as to the substantive content of said "assurances."

Compounding the lack of specificity with respect to the requirements and prohibitions of the grant program was the paltry funding allocated to it by Congress. Only $7.5 million was set aside, for all fifty states, for each of Fiscal Years 2005 through 2009. This, out of a bill that authorized a total of $40 billion annually for Title I alone and well more than $200 billion for the entire law. Further, the amount of each grant was capped at a mere 5 percent of the total amount states received under Title I, which necessarily meant its likely impact on total federal highway funding for states was minuscule. No state could receive a grant for more than two fiscal years, which meant states would be free thereafter to abandon anti–racial profiling policies or, at the very least, would have less incentive to continue enforcing them. These drawbacks notwithstanding, the grant program was a step toward the bigger goal pursued for several years by Congresswoman Eleanor Holmes-Norton's Racial Prohibition Acts. These proposals had mandated a cutoff of 5–10 percent of all federal-aid highways for noncompliant states, as opposed to a limited incentive grant program. That the anti–racial profiling grant program was but a small step was noted as such by Norton upon her reintroduction of the provision in 2012. There, she said of her 2005 feat: "the grant program was just a small piece of the very large SAFETE-LU bill"; she also stated fewer than half of states ultimately participated in the program during 2005 to 2009.[76]

It seems, then, advocates could not pay a majority of states to adopt anti–racial profiling laws. Federal funding for the "Grant Program to Prohibit Racial Profiling" was not renewed by the Moving Ahead for Progress in the 21st Century Act (MAP-21), the next massive multi-year highway authorization enacted following the 2005 act.[77]

Virtually all of the remaining major racial reform initiatives put forth in Congress between 1988 and 2012 were never taken up on the floor of either chamber for debate and were essentially relegated to the dustbin.

Moreover, all of these "dustbin" measures failed to get past the committee stage, except three. The first ever racial justice measure reported out of committee was Representative John Conyers' Traffic Stops Statistics Study Act of 1998. It was passed by the House in a voice vote on March 24, 1998, over a year after it was introduced on January 7, 1997, but was never taken up in the Senate. Another was the 2000 version of Conyers' Traffic Stops Statistics Study Act, introduced in the House on March 15, 1999. It was placed on the House calendar on March 13, 2000, but never taken up on the House floor. Representative Lee's Drug Law Enforcement Evidentiary Standards Improvement Act of 2005, the third and final measure, did not actually go through committee at all but came to the floor in the form of a rider amendment on June 16, 2005. It was promptly voted down in a voice vote.

The road to passage of the racial justice agenda was blocked from the very start of the process. Committees proved to be advocates' most formidable procedural challenge – a virtual graveyard for racial justice measures in much the same way they once were for civil rights proposals during the 1940s through 1960s.[78] Seldom was action of any kind taken on racial justice measures while under committee charge. Almost a dozen measures were never even referred to a subcommittee, where the bulk of legislative work is ordinarily done, especially in the House.[79] Committee hearings were held on only five occasions, not including the 1998 Traffic Study Act adopted in the House, which went straight to committee markup. Normally, the fact that the racial justice proposals languished in committee would mean little more than they met the same fate as the vast majority of bills introduced in Congress. Congressional committees exercise their "gatekeeping" power and block as many as 90 percent of bills from reaching the floor.[80] Except, official co-sponsors of the racial reform bills numbered as many as 50 members on a few occasions and in one instance as many as 127, something that sets these three apart from the bulk of bills that die in committee for lack of active support. At times, there was a sizeable coalition of members at least interested in debating the merits of the bills.

Also in the Senate, where parliamentary rules all but guarantee an opportunity for debate even on the least popular measures because policy control is widely disbursed across individual members,[81] none of the chamber's powerful parliamentary rules were used to move the justice agenda forward. Oddly, the House – with all of its cumbersome procedures – proved more amenable to floor action than the Senate. The only dustbin measures that received any floor attention at all in Congress were those offered in the House. At the same time, four of the five

Congressional committee hearings were held on the Senate side. But hearings were about as far as the bills progressed in the Senate. In sum, the racial justice agenda stood as small a chance of overcoming procedural obstacles in the Senate as in the House.

Racial Justice and the Usual Culprits of Congressional Stalemate

The demise of the racial justice agenda in Congress cannot be pinned chiefly on the usual culprits of policy defeat. As much is revealed by a look at how the standard drivers of legislative decision making came into play in Congressional proceedings on the agenda.[82] Many of these were actually favorably aligned with the push for criminal justice reform. To start with, members of Congress were provided a solid informational base upon which to justify legislative action. Proponents assembled an extensive array of data to demonstrate the black law enforcement experience in many quarters was a *bona fide* public policy problem. Often, these data were detailed in the actual text of the bill proposals, a move that partly compensated for the lack of committee hearings and consideration. Federal district and appellate court rulings contained legal evidence. Expert testimony at committee hearings and also research reports by scholars, government agencies, think tanks and advocacy organizations proffered empirical evidence.

As an example, the Reasonable Search Standards Act, introduced by Senator Richard Durbin, was argued necessary in light of a study by the U.S. Government Accountability Office (GAO), conducted at Durbin's request. The study examined personal search data from the U.S. Customs Service database for fiscal years 1997 and 1998, encompassing 102,000 arriving international passengers subjected to some form of personal search.[83] Additional insight was offered by a separate 2000 GAO report commissioned by then Congressional Black Caucus Chairman James Clyburn. It detailed the findings of three social science analyses of racial profiling of motorists, an American Civil Liberties study, and a New Jersey Attorney General Office report on motorists stopped on the New Jersey Turnpike. The GAO presented these studies together with other available federal, state, and local data on motorist stops.[84] Many of the remaining racial justice bills detailed the findings of various research studies as well.

Another benefit working on behalf of the racial justice agenda was cross-regional advocacy, something that debunked possible claims the legislation targeted only certain cities or states. Potential supporters could credibly claim to be part of a broad-based progressive movement, as sponsors and co-sponsors of the agenda represented districts and states throughout the country. A case in point is the ERPA of 2001. All ten of the standard regional designations used by the Office of Management and Budget for federal programs were represented by the bill's ninety-five co-sponsors. The representatives from Region I included elected officials from Connecticut, Massachusetts, as well as Vermont – the state with the smallest minority population. From Region II were representatives of states such as New York and also New Jersey, home of the infamous New Jersey Turnpike controversy. Virginia and Pennsylvania's congressmen were among those from Region III, Mississippi and Tennessee from Region IV, and Wisconsin, Michigan, and Indiana from Region V. States in the Deep South, such as Texas and Louisiana, along with Missouri represented Regions VI and VII. Among the remaining three remaining regions were House representatives from Utah, Colorado, Arizona, Hawaii, as well as California, Oregon, Alaska, and even Hawaii. In short, the broad spectrum of active supporters made the effort a genuinely national reform effort.

The divisive partisanship characteristic of contemporary Congresses also did not doom the agenda. Racial justice measures were just as unsuccessful under Democrat-controlled Congresses as under Republican control.[85] On the flip side, bipartisan advocacy was not uncommon. Although the list of official sponsors and co-sponsors was most often composed of Democrats, there were multiple occasions when Republican legislators took the lead. For example, Republican Senator George Voinovich introduced the Uniting Neighborhoods and Individuals to Eliminate Racial Profiling Act of 2002 and 2004. During his introductory remarks, he spoke at length about several anti–racial profiling initiatives he himself had previously spearheaded, as mayor of Cleveland and as governor of Ohio.[86] In both 2006 and in 2007, Republican Senator Jeff Sessions was the first to introduce measures to reduce the 100-to-1 crack versus powder cocaine sentencing disparity. Democratic leader Senator Richard Durbin described Sessions as "a leader in calling for reform of crack/powder sentencing policy."[87] Republican Senator Orrin Hatch sponsored the Fairness in Drug Sentencing Act of 2007 and Republican Congressman Roscoe Bartlett introduced the Powder-Crack Cocaine Penalty Equalization Act of 2007. In offering his measure, Hatch made clear he agreed with the Sentencing Commission's conclusion that the 100-to-1 sentencing disparity was "unjustifiable" and "exaggerated the relative harmfulness of crack."[88] Just prior to passage of the Fair Sentencing Act of 2010, co-sponsor Senator Durbin revealed there was "a bipartisan consensus that current cocaine sentencing laws are unjust" and that "Democrats and Republicans have come together to address the issue in a bipartisan way."[89]

To the extent that the considerable power vested in Congressional committee chairs was used on behalf of the racial justice agenda, it was often used on a bipartisan basis. The House Judiciary Committee was chaired by Republican Henry Hyde when the first racial justice measure ever reported out of committee advanced to the floor. Hyde personally worked behind the scenes to solicit favorable input from the Office of Management and Budget, which input ultimately eased concerns about the likely financial impact of the Traffic Statistics Study Act of 1998 on state law enforcement budgets. Conyers would later acknowledge the Judiciary Committee's approval of the 1998 measure was done on a "bipartisan basis."[90] Hearings on a later version of the Traffic Study bill before the Senate Subcommittee on the Constitution in March 2000 were chaired by then–Republican Senator John Ashcroft. In his opening remarks, Ashcroft called for expansion of the list of data to be collected and concluded: "regardless of the prevalence of racial profiling, the mere fact that these allegations exist troubles me greatly."[91] Following the hearing, Ashcroft reportedly said his thinking on the issue was influenced by moving testimony given by victims of racial profiling.[92]

Insider strategies were used also. As a member of the House Committee on Transportation and Infrastructure, Congresswoman Eleanor Holmes-Norton worked from within the committee to attach her 2005 anti–racial profiling mandate initiative to a massive federal highway aid bill, the Safe, Accountable, Flexible, Efficient Transportation Equity Act: A Legacy for Users.[93] Then, when appointed as one of the House managers to the conference committee that ironed out differences between the House and Senate versions of the bill, Norton continued to press for inclusion of a stipulation that required states to implement anti–racial profiling laws or risk loss of federal aid funds. Pressing alongside her on the conference committee were several other "insiders" who were also active sponsors and/or co-sponsors of racial justice measures over the years, including fellow House conferee John Conyers and Senate conferees Barack Obama, Hillary Clinton, George Voinovich, Jim Jeffords, and Frank Lautenberg.[94]

Advocates' procedural maneuvers suggest they were not lacking in parliamentary skill either. Several tactics were used to confront committee inertia. Referral of the bills was always made to committees on which bill sponsors were either ranking or long-serving members. For instance, the House Judiciary Committee was entrusted with all of the ERPAs sponsored in the House by Congressman John Conyers. It was the best platform for Conyers, who was the committee's longest serving member, having first been appointed in 1965, and who served as chair in the 110th and 111th Congresses and as ranking member in the 112th. Moreover, multiple referral was used on several occasions in an attempt to preempt committee inaction. The 2007 and 2010 ERPAs were referred to two of the Judiciary Committee's subcommittees, the Subcommittee on the Constitution and the Subcommittee on Crime. So were several of the earlier versions of the sentencing reform proposals, including the 2007 House versions introduced by Representatives Roscoe, Rangel, and Lee. Sequential referral was also utilized, such as in the case of the 2004 Justice in Sentencing Act sponsored by Congresswoman Waters. It was referred, first, to the Judiciary Committee, then to the Energy Committee for a stipulated period of time.

Proponents even went so far as to buck standard protocol for floor proceedings. Congresswoman Sheila Jackson Lee did so by offering the "Jackson Lee Amendment" on June 16, 2005, during House consideration of an unrelated appropriations bill to fund the Departments of State and Justice and other agencies. She explained her amendment helped to "protect against the racial imbalance of the prosecutions of African Americans and other minorities" under the Byrnes grant process.[95] One day prior, the leadership had arranged for Lee to control five minutes of floor debate in order to offer an amendment to the appropriations bill. However, the amendment Lee actually presented was different from that previously cleared by the leadership. The following statement from floor manager Congressman Frank Wolf, which went unchallenged, helps to illustrate as much: "Mr. Chairman, this is a different amendment than was printed in the Record. I am not even sure that it addresses the same issue."[96] Following a terse exchange with both Lee and Congresswoman Waters, Wolf again noted: "The amendment was changed. In fact, the title was there and then the amendment changed."[97]

Although advocates pushed hard to move the bills through the parliamentary stages of the policy process, they did not exactly drive a hard bargain with respect to the bills' substantive provisions. Sponsors provided ample opportunity for members in both chambers to negotiate and reach an amenable compromise regarding the requirements, prohibitions, and enforcement provisions within the proposals. Proposals were continually adjusted and readjusted to make them more palatable to would-be supporters. The series of ERPAs was a veritable smorgasbord of compromise opportunities. They were the most comprehensive anti–racial profiling bills, encompassing all of the main provisions of both the weak as well as the stronger proposals (e.g., data collection, training, and monitoring). Sponsors made a number of concessions to bolster the appeal of the ERPAs in particular. Initially, under the proposals, agencies were permitted to develop their own administrative complaint procedures. Then in 2005 and 2007, the revised proposals mandated participation in a complex complaint procedure crafted by Congress and the attorney general. But afterward, proponents reverted to the original, more lenient approach, which left it to agencies to decide how to handle complaints.

Additional evidence of a willingness to play politics was advocates' abandonment of one of the more controversial provisions in the ERPAs, namely the 2001 and 2004 versions' requirement that agencies develop "procedures to discipline law enforcement agents who engage in racial profiling."[98] In 2005 and 2007, this stipulation was changed to specify only that agencies take "appropriate action" and "corrective action" respectively. In 2010 and 2011, the disciplinary provision was deleted entirely. Finally, and perhaps most significantly, the bare-bone measures advanced by the House Judiciary Committee in 1998 and also Congressman Bell in 2004 say much about the lengths to which proponents were willing to go in order to get *something* passed, even if that amounted to something as small as data-gathering or an official Congressional rebuke of racial profiling.

Yet another benefit working on behalf of the racial justice agenda was the celebrity status of some of its official sponsors. Almost all of the bills secured endorsements from some of the most high profile politicians in Washington. This helped to separate the race reform proposals from the thousands of bills introduced and then passed over each year because of sheer obscurity. A sizeable portion of the list of sponsors of several bills was a veritable who's who of power brokers at the time the bills were under consideration. Among Senate notables co-sponsoring the Traffic Stops Statistics Study Act of 2000 were former Democratic Party presidential candidate Senator Edward Kennedy. Also, in floor remarks on the ERPA of 2001, Senator Feingold said "minutes after Senators (John) Corzine and (Hilary) Clinton were sworn in," they inquired about ways they could actively support the bill.[99] On the list of official sponsors of the 2005 ERPA were former Democratic presidential nominee Senator John Kerry as well as future President and then-Senator Barack Obama. Future Speaker of the House Nancy Pelosi signed on as co-sponsor of the 1988 death penalty bill introduced by Representative Conyers, one of the first serious measures advanced by reformers. And as late as 2011, the racial justice agenda continued to land major endorsements, securing co-sponsorship from Senate Majority Leader Harry Reid and Majority Whip Richard Durbin.

Black lawmakers overwhelmingly endorsed the measures. A total of thirty-one of the forty-three members of the 112th Congressional Black Caucus (CBC) were among co-sponsors of the ERPA of 2011. In fact, leading the charge on the House side was one of the Caucus's founding members, who happened to also be the second longest serving member in the House of Representatives, John Conyers. Caucus founders William Lacy Clay and Charles Rangel also joined the effort, as did three of its executive leaders: Representatives G. K. Butterfield, Second Vice Chair; Yvette Clarke, Secretary; and Andre Carson, Whip. Rounding out the list of Congressional Black Caucus lawmakers officially backing the measure were many nationally prominent members, such as Congressmen Elijah Cummings of Maryland, Alcee Hastings of Florida, Jesse L. Jackson, Jr. of Illinois, and John Lewis of Georgia.

There was a wide variety of outside groups that lined up behind the criminal justice measures. Just as the bills were not sponsored exclusively by black lawmakers, so they were also not aimed exclusively at blacks or other racial minority groups. Expansion of the agenda over time to envelope a range of traditionally marginalized groups as beneficiaries, in turn, helped broaden the political base of outside support. The first Traffic Study Act introduced by Conyers in January 1997 focused only on the racial and ethnic characteristics of individuals targeted by law enforcement,[100] but the 2011 ERPA, sponsored by Senator Benjamin Cardin and Conyers, extended targeted protection to other demographic groups, as did some of the earlier versions. The ERPAs delineated protections on the basis of race, ethnicity, national origin, gender, and religion.[101] Senator Durbin's Reasonable Search Standards Act was aimed at profiling by the U.S. Customs Service also on the basis of sexual orientation.[102] National organizations representing a variety of interest groups, in turn, publicly supported the bills. A large number of left-leaning civil rights organizations submitted letters of support, testified at committee hearings, and utilized their own platforms to advocate on behalf of the bills. An umbrella lobby group composed of more than 200 separate national organizations, the Leadership Conference on Civil and Human Rights, was one of the more vocal outside supporters. A letter submitted by the Leadership Conference in support of the 2011 ERPA was undersigned by eighty-five national organizations and thirty-six state and local organizations. Included among the undersigned were the American Civil Liberties Union, Human Rights Watch, the National Association for the Advancement of Colored People, the National Association of Criminal Defense Lawyers, and the National Education Association, to name a few.

There are no clear indications that outside law enforcement lobbies poured a great deal of energy into impeding Congressional action on the racial justice agenda. In the next chapter, we observe more closely their role in prodding lawmakers to enact heavily punitive anti-crime policies, which enactments stood to worsen the black law enforcement experience. As to their mobilization in Congressional proceedings chiefly geared toward racial reform of criminal justice, however, the law enforcement sector was, to some extent, split. Organizations representing police brass and minority law officers went on record in favor of racial justice measures. Lobbies representing rank-and-file police officers tended to oppose the bills, such as the Fraternal Order of Police and the National Troopers Coalition. Vice President of the Fraternal Order of Police (FOP) Steve Young did so in testimony before the Judiciary Committee in 2001. Speaking on behalf of the FOP's nearly 300,000 police officers, Young said: "The so-called practice of racial profiling is being hyped by activists, the media and others with political agenda (sic) who presuppose that a man or a woman in a police officer's uniform is inclined to be racially biased. This is just not so."[103]

The single most influential outside force supportive of the underlying principles of the racial justice agenda was the office of the president. We learn more in the next two chapters about presidents' vigorous support of the stringent "law and order" enactments that served to exacerbate the racial divide in criminal justice. However, at least in the context of racial justice policy proceedings, however, every president from the time the racial justice reform effort in Congress launched in 1988 through 2012 lent either symbolic support, specific legislative endorsement, or other forms of presidential leadership. Not all elements of the reform agenda won a presidential nod, nor did presidents support the cause in equal measure. However and importantly, Republican and Democrat presidents alike publicly condemned racial profiling in unequivocal terms. Inasmuch as racial profiling was a centerpiece of the racial justice agenda, it is safe to say the agenda did not suffer from a deficit of presidential support. More generally, the bills were not a casualty of executive opposition.

President Bill Clinton issued a Memorandum on Fairness in Law Enforcement in June 1999.[104] The memo directed federal law enforcement agencies to design and implement a system to collect and report statistics relating to race, ethnicity, and gender for law enforcement activities. The activities were to include both traffic and pedestrian stops, interviews of entrants to the United States, voluntary and involuntary searches as well as prosecutions by U.S. attorneys. The data collection requirement was considered a means to "begin addressing the problem of racial profiling" on the part of federal law enforcement agencies."[105] The memo also directed the U.S. Justice Department to analyze the data and recommend ways to improve the fair administration of federal law enforcement activities. The same day the memo was issued, President Clinton remarked at a roundtable discussion: "We must stop the morally indefensible, deeply corrosive practice of racial profiling.... It is wrong; it is destructive; and it must stop."[106]

There was more concrete executive action against racial profiling during President George W. Bush's tenure in office than in any other. President Bush issued a Memorandum on Racial Profiling in February 2001 directing the attorney general to review the use of race by federal law enforcement authorities in conducting stops, searches, and other investigative procedures. The memo added that the AG was to work with Congress as well as federal, state and local law enforcement to assess the extent of the problem and make "recommendations for the improvement of the just and equal administration of our Nation's Laws."[107] Bush announced the directive in an address before a Joint Session of Congress in 2001. There, he said of racial profiling: "It's wrong, and we will end it in America."[108] Additionally, during his confirmation hearing then-attorney general nominee and former Senator John Ashcroft stated: "I think racial profiling is wrong. I think it's unconstitutional. I think it violates the 14th Amendment. I think most of the men and women in our law enforcement are good people trying to enforce the law. I think we all share that view. But we owe it to provide them with guidance to ensure that racial profiling does not happen."[109] Later, as attorney general for the Bush administration, Ashcroft wrote Congress to say the Traffic Study bill that was under consideration in the House was "an excellent starting place for such an enterprise."[110]

Acting on President Bush's directive, the Department of Justice issued in 2003 the first ever federal policy guidance to ensure an end to racial profiling in federal law enforcement.[111] For the roughly seventy federal agencies with police powers, the guidelines specified:

In making routine or spontaneous law enforcement decisions, such as ordinary traffic stops, Federal law enforcement officers may not use race or ethnicity to any degree, except that officers may rely on race and ethnicity in a specific suspect description. This prohibition applies even where the use of race or ethnicity might otherwise be lawful.[112]

Although a number of civil rights organizations complained the guidelines did not go far enough to actually ban racial profiling and contained too many loopholes,[113] the guidelines did expressly criticize the practice at length and deemed it an "invidious use of race," ineffective, harmful, and costly. The guidelines and, in this instance, the Bush administration did more than Congress was apparently willing or able to do. Finally, earlier in 2001, the Justice Department launched the Reducing Racial Profiling initiative to help police agencies reduce racial profiling. Under the project, the COPS Office funded twenty-one sites at approximately $200,000 each.[114] When introducing the Reasonable Search Standards Act in April 2001, Senator Durbin commended President Bush and Attorney General John Ashcroft for having designated racial profiling a high priority for the Administration and asserted: "We applaud their commitment to this important issue."[115]

President Barack Obama signed into law the only major racial justice measure adopted by Congress during the period in focus, the Fair Sentencing Act of 2010. President Obama's sense that there was a problem in criminal justice was apparent well before his succession to the White House. Senator John Corzine said in floor remarks on the 2005 ERPA that then-Senator Obama had been "a constant champion of efforts to combat racial profiling."[116]

Senator Obama took the lead in writing one of the Nation's most innovative pieces of legislation on the collection of racial profiling data when he was in the Illinois State Senate, and he has been equally committed to the issue since joining the U.S. Senate. Both Senators Feingold and Obama have worked tirelessly to make the bill we are introducing today a reality.[117]

In 2008, President-Elect Barack Obama pledged that, upon assuming office, he would pursue the "Obama–Biden Plan" to, among other things, "ban racial profiling by federal law enforcement agencies and provide federal incentives to state and local police departments to prohibit the practice."[118]

As president, Obama has used his office's considerable media capital to validate the decades-old claim of pervasive racial profiling. He did so in remarks about two highly publicized incidents. The first involved a black male Harvard University professor, the other a black male teenager in Florida. Professor Henry Louis Gates was handcuffed and arrested for disorderly conduct following a verbal altercation Gates had with a local police officer on the front porch of Gates's home in 2009. When asked at a news conference to comment on the Gates incident and what it signified about race relations in America, President Obama said:

The fact of the matter is, is that this still haunts us. And even when there are honest misunderstandings, the fact that blacks and Hispanics are picked up more frequently and oftentimes for no cause casts suspicion even when there is good cause. And that's why I think the more that we're working with local law enforcement to improve policing techniques so that we're eliminating potential bias, the safer everybody is going to be.[119]

The death of an unarmed sixteen-year-old black teenager, Trayvon Martin, and the acquittal of his white assailant were the occasions on which President Obama spoke at length about the widespread practice of racial profiling. Following the "not guilty" verdict in the 2013 trial of Florida neighborhood watch patrolman George Zimmerman, President Obama remarked: "Trayvon Martin could have been me 35 years ago." He stated, further:

There are very few African American men in this country who haven't had the experience of being followed when they were shopping in a department store. That includes me. There are very few African American men who haven't had the experience of walking across the street and hearing the locks click on the doors of cars. That happens to me, at least before I was a Senator. There are very few African Americans who haven't had the experience of getting on an elevator and a woman clutching her purse nervously and holding her breath until she had a chance to get off. That happens often.[120]

Shortly after the initial February 26, 1012, fatal shooting of Martin[121] and the local police department's failure to fully investigate the shooting, Obama offered a reflection at a March 23, 2012, news conference. He pointed squarely at the broader context in which the Martin tragedy occurred and, in doing so, underscored the fact that it was symptomatic of a much deeper problem with race, crime, and justice in the United States. The president said:

I think every parent in America should be able to understand why it is absolutely imperative that we investigate every aspect of this and that everybody pulls together – Federal, State, and Local – to figure out exactly how this tragedy happened.... I think all of us have to do some soul searching to figure out how does something like this happen. And that means that we examine the laws and the context for what happened, as well as the specifics of the incident.[122]

President Obama's tenure in office marked the third presidential administration to signal to lawmakers and to the public that there was a systemic race problem in the criminal justice system. Thus, presidential indifference and opposition did not figure largely in the fate of the Congressional racial justice agenda.

The bottom line as to why the agenda made little headway in the Congressional legislative process is that a majority of members in both chambers chose to not vote for the agenda. Though sponsorship alone does not tell the whole story behind a bill's advocacy, it does say something about proponents' limited success in mobilizing the consensus and votes needed to facilitate its succession from committee consideration to floor adoption. In this case, efforts to bring more lawmakers on board proved futile often from start to finish. Earlier in the discussion it was noted there were more than a few occasions on which official co-sponsors of racial justice measures numbered in excess of fifty representatives. But, there were a total of only eight such instances. Of the roughly forty-five major initiatives advanced in the House and Senate, fourteen were co-sponsored by three or fewer members in each chamber, many of the others by fewer than a dozen. The most the agenda ever secured in the way of official endorsements was 127 co-sponsors in 2004. And while this represents, theoretically, 62 percent of all Democrat seats in the House for the 108th Congress, it constitutes only 29 percent of the overall House membership. This is a meager number, given that passage in Congress calls for a "yea" vote from 51 percent of the 435 voting members of the House, plus often 60 percent of the Senate membership in the age of cloturitis.

Conclusion

A central point of the preceding analysis is that the Congressional racial justice agenda was not a casualty of the strategic factors that normally impede legislative success. Proponents approached their mission with such a degree of open-mindedness that a mere pronouncement against racialized law enforcement was a suitable policy advancement. In doing so, would-be supporters were given relatively low-risk means of adding their name to the otherwise short list of lawmakers who continuously fought to improve the black law enforcement experience. Put bluntly, paying lip service to the cause was included among the many policy options advocates put forth. Of course, their end goal was to accomplish much more – much more than lip service and much more than the victories to which they eventually lay claim.

Of the two reform measures that were adopted in 2005 and 2010, the first essentially paid (or at least tried to pay) states to adopt laws prohibiting racial profiling on federal-aid highways. But it lacked detailed requirements as to what the laws must stipulate, and it paid only small sums of money to incentivize state action. Hardly enough money to spur widespread reform of state and local law enforcement operations. The other policy "reform" effectively extended the mandatory sentence prison term beyond what the U.S. Sentencing Commission had initially prescribed. To put it bluntly, the Fair Sentencing Act adopted by Congress in 2010 scaled back the more progressive reform put in place by the Sentencing Commission in 2007. It was a step backward from the change that would have been wrought had Congress not substituted its own policy for the administrative policy already put in place by the Commission.

Congressional lawmakers cannot credibly claim to have lacked systematic evidence concerning the problematic nature of the black law enforcement experience, or that they did not know. Nor can regionalism, parochialism, partisan polarization, limited parliamentary skill, failure to compromise, intense anti-reform lobbying, or presidential opposition help explain the agenda's undoing. Indeed, Presidents Bill Clinton, George W. Bush, and Barack Obama all lent the enormous weight of the office of the presidency to the basic principles of the racial justice reform effort underway in Congress, either through public endorsement, legislative leadership, or through independent executive action.

The racial justice agenda foundered in the formal process, quite simply, because members of Congress chose not to vote in support of it. The fundamental question, then, is: why?

In the next chapter, we learn that the rest of the membership did not support the agenda for reasons that lay well beyond the scope of the usual sources of Congressional inertia. Lawmakers were unwilling to deviate from the core thrust of criminal justice policymaking. They chose, instead, to stick to the criminal justice play book written in earlier mainstream crime policy proceedings of 1968–1994, a playbook firmly affixed in the policy landscape well before the launch of the national racial justice agenda in earnest in 1997. The crime-fighting play approach they followed, moreover, accorded the racial justice agenda far less political weight and significance than the "law and order" agenda. It continues to do so. According to the crime-fighting approach, racial tracking is a lamentable but unavoidable (and tolerable) consequence of getting tough on crime and saving America from utter destruction at the hands of drug peddlers, drug users, and violent criminals. Blacks' disparate treatment and overrepresentation in the criminal justice system is, in essence, collateral damage in not only the War on Drugs but in the fight against crime generally.

The end result of this basic policy position is that, just as racial justice advocates were generally unsuccessful in nudging open a doorway to racial change in the criminal justice system, they were thwarted also in earlier attempts to preemptively minimize the chance that modern anti-crime would further exacerbate those differences. Ultimately, it was this broader, deeply rooted anti-crime policy orientation that foreclosed the opportunity for lawmakers to commit to the racial justice agenda or, for that matter, to any other race-conscious criminal justice policies. In a manner of speaking, the fight on behalf of the Congressional racial justice agenda was over before it began. The playbook lawmakers would follow had already been written.

5

Congress as Power Player

Racial Justice versus "Law and Order"

Members of Congress dimmed the prospects for adoption of policies aimed at dismantling racial tracking well before such policies were proposed from 1988 onward. In effect, lawmakers preemptively sealed the fate of the racial justice agenda in ways that ensured it would never take off in the House or Senate. They did so by committing to a colorblind approach to public safety, one that remains today the gold standard of crime-fighting. This chapter offers a close-up look at modern national policymaking during the formative years of 1968 to 1994. It demonstrates that not only were crime policymakers scarcely interested in reducing then-existent racial disparities in criminal justice; they were even less interested in ensuring the newly enacted "get tough" laws did not further exacerbate the disparities. In the context of these proceedings too, racial justice concerns were rejected. Vigorously and nearly unanimously, federal lawmakers embraced instead a long-term, incarceration-centered approach to crime-fighting that carried disastrous racial consequences, and they did so over the course of multiple decades, numerous votes, and several power shifts.

The question of note is why? What were their motivations, and, more directly, were they motivated by the kind of interest group pressure politics that so often prevail in Congressional decision making? The answer to the latter is "no." It is true the "law and order" approach embraced by Congress was precisely what law enforcement lobbies sought. But the drumbeat from advocates of racial justice and crime prevention was much louder. Ultimately, the primary reason policymakers proceeded with little regard for the black law enforcement experience lay well beyond the walls of Congress.

136

The omnibus laws that form the heart of modern national crime policy on violent, property, and drug-related offenses afford an excellent window through which to observe lawmakers' regard for racial justice within the mainstream crime policy process. Included among these seven laws are the Omnibus Crime Control and Safe Streets Act of 1968; Comprehensive Drug Abuse Prevention and Control Act of 1970; Sentencing Reform Act of 1984; Anti-Drug Abuse Acts of 1986 and 1988; Crime Control Act of 1990; and Violent Crime Control and Law Enforcement Act of 1994.[1] The analysis details the five anti-crime policy trends and strategies imbedded within these mainstay crime laws.[2] Among these are: federalization of criminal law, an incarceration-centered penal policy, increased post-prison and post-conviction punishments, diminution of the rights of the accused, and permanent enhancements to the enforcement infrastructure over the prevention and treatment infrastructure.

These trends constitute the core features of the "law and order" approach to crime-fighting that was formulated during 1968–1994, continues to dominate today, and contributes to the persistence of racial tracking. In addition to an in-depth examination of Congressional floor and committee debate and proceedings on these foundational laws, this chapter also provides a detailed account of how legislators reacted to (or, more aptly, dismissed) racial justice concerns, particularly when such concerns stood to temper the all-out press for a stringent anti-crime strategy.[3] I begin with a layout of how racial justice initiatives were repeatedly rebuffed within the mainstream crime policy process in Congress. Then, I present the development and implementation of the five main features of American crime policy. Following this, I turn to a discussion of the more immediate forces driving lawmakers' policy choices.

Just Say No: Racial Justice in the Mainstream Crime Policy Process

Congress continually rebuffed the many red flags raised by racial justice advocates during its march toward an incarceration policy. The anti-crime strategy launched in 1968 signaled as well a retreat from the racial progressivism of the 1950s and 1960s. Up until 1968, a majority of federal lawmakers were dedicated to combating de jure and de facto discrimination. They took extraordinary steps to enact the landmark Civil Rights Act of 1964, the Voting Rights Act of 1965, and the Federal Equal Housing Act of 1968. However, with the advent of the race riots of the late 1960s and increased crime concerns came a marked shift in policy priorities, especially in regard to race. The 1968 Kerner Commission report highlighted a deepening racial division throughout the country as the genesis of the race riots. The Commission pinpointed encounters with law enforcement as the precipitating spark in almost half of the disorders. In essence, the Kerner Report brought into sharper focus the dynamic interplay between race and criminal law enforcement in the United States. It also cited socioeconomic reforms and improved community relations as the best approach to riot prevention. Despite revelation of these findings and recommendations in February 1968 – that law enforcement was part of the problem that led to past race riots – federal lawmakers turned only several months later to an almost exclusively enforcement-centered strategy as the primary route to preventing future race riots.

The first of the major modern anti-crime laws, the 1968 Omnibus Crime Control and Safe Streets Enforcement Act, signified very early on what would become Congress's standard reaction to the racialized aspects of law enforcement. A main target of the 1968 crime bill was the string of sixties race riots. It authorized federal grants to state and local law enforcement agencies for the express purpose of combating civil disorders and organized crime, as against the other types of crimes also on the rise during the late 1960s. So that there would be no confusion about lawmakers' primary target, they wrote in the bill in unequivocal terms: "In making grants under this part ... the Administration... shall give special emphasis ... to programs and projects dealing with the prevention, detection, and control of organized crime and of riots and other violent civil disorders." In addition, expansion of the U.S. attorney general's authority to use wiretapping was also explicitly linked by members of Congress to the race riots, though opposed by the Johnson administration and civil liberties groups. The wiretapping provision in section 2516 actually placed riots on a par with treason and espionage.

Two votes speak volumes about the negligible amount of concern Congress had for how the 1968 crime bill might disproportionately handicap racial minorities. First, members voted for a provision to disqualify persons convicted of rioting from federal employment for five years but did not do so for other crimes. A great deal of latitude was allotted for federal agencies' use of the disqualification provision. Agencies were not confined to rejecting an applicant solely on the basis of a court determination but could do so based on their own conclusion as to whether a conviction was in "furtherance" of a riot. Critically, the Kerner Commission recommendation to proactively diversify the pool of police officers was rejected. Adopted instead was a provision that prohibited any effort to require that law enforcement agencies achieve racial balance. Title I provided:

Nothing contained in this title shall be construed to authorize the Administration (1) to require, or condition the availability or amount of a grant upon, the adoption by an applicant or grantee under this title of a percentage ratio, quota system, or other program to achieve racial balance or to eliminate racial imbalance in any law enforcement agency, or (2) to deny or discontinue a grant because of the refusal of an applicant or grantee under this title to adopt such a ratio, system, or other program.

In short, lawmakers were little concerned about the lack of diversity but very concerned about certain efforts to promote diversity. A final powerful sign of the times on this policy front is that the bill was signed into law by President Lyndon B. Johnson, the same president who aggressively spearheaded civil rights legislative reform over the previous decade as Senate majority leader and then as president.

The overwhelming majority of Congress members again opposed efforts to proactively diversify state and local law enforcement agencies in the next major crime policy proceeding, which culminated in the passage of the 1984 Criminal Justice Act Revision. Fully 99 percent of senators and nearly 80 percent of House members voted to prohibit use of the emergency federal assistance authorized under the act so as "to deny or discontinue such assistance upon the failure of such applicant to adopt, a percentage ratio, quota system, or other program to achieve racial balance in any criminal justice agency."[4] But, at the same time that lawmakers took definitive steps to block certain diversity measures, they offered little more than symbolic support to the basic principle of nondiscrimination. Meanwhile, reformers mustered out of the 1984 proceedings a prohibition on law enforcement discrimination, but the scope of the prohibition was confined to the emergency federal assistance grant program and to government seizure of crime-related profits. And while the U.S. Sentencing Commission was required to develop race-neutral guidelines and gather information on the race of convicted offenders, these additions were arguably inconsiderable too. They applied only to federal courts, which handle roughly 2.5 percent of the more than 50 million criminal and civil cases litigated in American courts.[5]

An opportunity for legislators to meaningfully address racial disproportionalness in capital sentencing emerged in 1987, but they passed on the opportunity. The U.S. Supreme Court's *McCleskey v. Kemp* ruling placed the statistical disparity in the national political spotlight in a way unmatched in any other period. Pursuant to *Furman v. Georgia* (1972),

thirty-five states revised their death penalty laws with the aim of eliminating bias and arbitrariness in capital sentencing. A study presented in
the 1987 *McCleskey* case revealed stark racial differences in the use of
the death penalty remained. The question before the Court in *McCleskey*
was whether the Court was going to do anything about the decades-old
disparities. The Court answered in the negative and punted the problem
to its coordinate branches and to state governments. Congress's reaction
to *McCleskey* was essentially inaction. All that members in the House
and Senate opted to do in regard to the death penalty disparity was tell
judges to tell jurors not to discriminate. This, plus make jurors promise
not to do so. While more than a verbal affirmation was required by the
1988 Anti-Drug Abuse Act, in that jurors were required to personally
sign a statement certifying their decision was not influenced by racial
considerations, racial justice advocates had hoped for much more.

For example, a measure intended to reduce racial inequality in death
sentencing was introduced by Senator Edward Kennedy during debate
on the 1988 act.[6] Kennedy's amendment provided that, if a defendant
presented statistically significant evidence of racial influences in sentencing decisions, a judge could infer that they were caused by discrimination. The burden would then shift to government prosecutors to prove
the disparities resulted from nonracial factors and rebut the inference by
proving more than just the absence of discriminatory intent or presence
of an aggravating factor.[7] Kennedy's amendment failed on October 13,
1988, with fifty-two senators voting against it and thirty-five in favor.

The rest of the House and Senate's reaction to the *McCleskey* revelations consisted of directing other agencies to study the issue – to study it
and then get back to Congress. Specifically, the crime 1988 bill directed
the General Accounting Office (GAO) to examine state death penalty
statutes and whether they created "a significant risk that the race of a
defendant, or the race of a victim against whom a crime was committed,
influence the likelihood that defendants in those States will be sentenced
to death." It bears mentioning the GAO's charge applied only to death
sentences handed down after 1976. Thus, Congress essentially placed
then-current death row inmates beyond the reach of its research agenda.

Meanwhile, as Congress passed on to other bodies responsibility to act
on (i.e., research) the racial dynamics of criminal justice, members took
it upon themselves to immediately broaden the federal death penalty to a
longer list of drug and violent offenses. They did so without waiting for
evidence of its impact on crime and public safety and with little regard
for its racial effects. The latter step was taken despite the *McCleskey*

ruling, which acknowledged racial influences; the Baldus Study featured in the case, as well as dozens of other studies that indicated capital punishment was used more often in cases involving white victims and, to a lesser extent, black offenders. Also ignored by Congress in 1988 was that the criminal conviction rate for blacks was higher than that for whites. It was immediately clear, then, its decision to expand the death penalty stood to negatively impact blacks more than whites. Still, this fact did not dissuade lawmakers from their strategy. In fact, a handful of legislators outright dismissed it. Rejecting racial justice advocates' proposal to use statistical disparities as a basis for challenging death sentences, Senator Orrin G. Hatch stated "Statistical justice is no justice at all."[8] Later in 1990, Senator Bob Graham would claim more generally that the criminal justice process did not lend itself to statistical analysis.[9]

The GAO death penalty report that Congress commissioned in 1988 was completed and published as of February 1990, yet in October 1990 Congress commissioned another study of racial influences on the death penalty. The report commissioned only two years earlier already detailed how nonracial factors alone did not account for the racial makeup of death row. But in this instance too, while opting to patiently await more research in regard to the racial justice agenda, Congress acted with a sense of urgency in regard to its "get tough" agenda. As such, the general rule of thumb was extreme caution in connection with racial justice, but "full speed ahead" where punitive justice was concerned. What distinguished the 1990 crime policymaking mode from that of earlier proceedings where race was concerned was that the now-standard request for more race-related research was actually in furtherance of punishment more so than reform. The 1990 Crime Control Act's mandate for evaluation of "racial conflict" in Title 34 was folded into the title's establishment of a National Commission to Support Law Enforcement.

As in the 1988 crime policy proceeding, again in 1990 racial advocates fell far short of their goal of instituting legal safeguards against death penalty bias. A racial justice clause was put forth in both chambers as an amendment to the 1990 omnibus crime legislation. If adopted, this clause too would have permitted defendants to appeal death sentences on the basis of statistical disparities and thereby establish a prima facie case that either their or the victims' race was why a death sentence was imposed. This time, reformers won enough votes to move both measures to the floor. However, the clause was struck from the 1990 Senate version of the crime bill in a 58–38 floor vote on May 24, 1990. Reformers moved the proposal farther along in the process on the House side, once a 218–186 floor vote on October 5, 1990, permitted a slightly weaker version of the committee-reported proposal to survive an initial effort to quash the reform initiative altogether. The provision remained in the House version of the overall crime package adopted the same day in a 368–55. It did not, however, survive conference negotiations. A majority of the ninety-four House conferees and twenty-four Senate conferees dropped the racial justice provision altogether from the final bill that was enacted into law.

In 1994, acting this time with what one might have presumed the advantage of a Democrat-controlled Congress and White House, the Congressional Black and Hispanic Caucuses pressed harder than ever for inclusion of race-related safety precautions in a major crime bill. They again met tremendous push-back, this time from members of their own party. Chair of the House Subcommittee on Civil and Constitutional Rights Don Edwards sponsored a racial justice measure addressing capital sentencing. The full committee approved it in a 20–15 vote on March 17, 1994. House Speaker Democrat Thomas Foley beat back an effort to strike it from the bill once it reached the floor, an effort that failed in a close 212–217 vote on April 20, 1994. Like earlier versions, this measure would have prohibited use of the death penalty in cases where statistics indicated its use was racially discriminatory. The measure was adopted in the House as part of the larger crime bill. However, in the end, backers of the measure failed to win the endorsement of Democratic President Bill Clinton. They also failed to win the backing of a majority of the mostly Democratic House and Senate conferees in the first round of negotiations. The reform that managed to survive the second round of conference negotiations was a drastically weaker compromise; it replicated almost verbatim the death penalty provision enacted in 1988. Again in 1994 Congress enacted a crime bill that simply required jurors to certify – in writing – that they did not discriminate when imposing the death penalty.

More studies of race and criminal justice were commissioned by the Democrat-controlled Congress in 1994. This time the request was for an examination of the impact of crime on minority communities as well as "the ability of Federal, State, and local criminal justice systems to administer criminal law and criminal sanctions impartially without discrimination on the basis of race." And, the Sentencing Commission was directed to study the 100-to-1 crack cocaine versus powder cocaine penalty structure implemented earlier by Congress in 1986. Lawmakers also incorporated a handful of provisions in the 1994 Violent Crime

Control and Law Enforcement Act that, for the first time, constituted action-oriented, race-conscious provisions. Still, these provisions are best understood as tiny, incremental departures from the norm – significant in token terms more so than practical terms due to their minuscule reach and negligible impact.

The incremental racial reforms of 1994 consisted of a small grant program used to encourage, though not require enforcement agencies to diversify their workforce. The flat ban on law enforcement discrimination proposed by racial justice advocates was rejected and substituted with a more limited ban made applicable to a handful of small-scale federal law enforcement grant programs. Even this narrowly construed ban was directed not at law enforcement per se but rather state and local governments and private organizations involved with prevention and treatment programs. As to the nondiscrimination mandate in the measure that was squarely aimed at law enforcement officials, it affected only specified seizure operations and traffic stops conducted as part of a pilot motor vehicle theft prevention program.

The 103rd Congress not only dashed racial justice advocates' best hope of incorporating meaningful safety mechanisms into modern crime policy, but the assembly also crippled the racial justice agenda for years to come. Both substantively and politically, the 1994 crime bill represented the final phase of the 1968–1994 march toward the incarceration-centered anti-crime policy that prevails still today. President Bill Clinton described the bill, which he signed into law, as "the toughest, largest and smartest federal attack on crime in the history of the United States of America."[10] From a political standpoint, it marked the point at which Democrats and Republicans lawmakers in Congress and the White House essentially championed the "law and order" agenda together, hand-in-hand.

At a time when at least a 56–44 and 258–176 Democratic majority controlled the Senate and House, the racial justice measures proposed by reformers in the context of the 1994 crime policy proceedings were diluted. The Clinton administration and Democratic leaders split with racial liberals and also the black and Hispanic caucuses in 1994. Clinton and other Democrats opted to drop the death penalty-related racial justice measures from the 1994 crime bill.[11] Then-Senator Joseph Biden urged colleagues to reject the provisions in order to preserve the overall crime bill. In connection with conference negotiations to resolve chamber differences over the House provision banning racially discriminatory use of the death penalty, Biden stated: "The question is whether to accept the House provision, racial justice, which will kill the bill."[12]

While sacrificing racial justice in order to fight crime, the Democrat-controlled Congress demonstrated rather starkly its policy priorities in this sphere. The incarceration-centered enforcement provisions were enormously strengthened. Thanks to the 103rd Congress, the incarceration-mode of crime-fighting would become the American way – at both the federal and state level. In some instances, these policy frameworks were diffused at the state level not by chance or solely state legislators' choice but by way of financial incentives supplied by Congress, including the 32 billion dollar treasure chest set aside in 1994. For all practical purposes and for decades to come, therefore, the 103rd Congress set the threshold for racial reform of criminal justice at a point virtually insurmountable by racial justice advocates.

In what follows, I endeavor to unpack the basic thrust and substantive elements of the existing crime-fighting framework that was developed and implemented during 1968–1994. The discussion highlights the specific components of the "law and order" agenda that made matters worse both for minority groups overrepresented in the criminal process and for the reformist lawmakers advocating on their behalf.

Incarceration Now, Incarceration Tomorrow, Incarceration Forever

The anti-crime strategy settled upon by Congress from 1968 to 1994 made racial justice reform all the more necessary. Critically, moreover, the fact that the strategy was established and continually reinforced over the course of multiple decades, hundreds of votes, and several shifts in party control in Congress and the White House proves that no single political entity is properly blamed. There was a broad bipartisan consensus behind the law and order agenda throughout. It is worth highlighting at the outset that, of the five central features of the agenda, the federalization of criminal law wrought especially harmful consequences for blacks and other disadvantaged groups. The latter entailed expansion of the number and types of criminal offenses subject to federal prosecution. The federalization of criminal law all but guaranteed the massive scope of the agenda's racial impact.

Because of minority groups' overrepresentation among those arrested and prosecuted for street crime, lawmakers effectively bolstered racial tracking each time they increased the number and types of criminalized "street" behaviors, and did so without incorporating racial safety valves. National government powers are ordinarily limited to policy spheres that pertain to "national," inter-state interests – a criterion that day-to-day law enforcement does not easily satisfy, which is why policing matters are traditionally governed chiefly by state law. To legitimately and substantially enlarge the federal government's role in a policy area normally superintended by states, then, national lawmakers needed to proffer a politically compelling rationale. Illegal drugs fit the bill rather neatly. By criminalizing a laundry list of drugs, the federal government fashioned a justification for expanding its role in law enforcement. This process began in earnest with a bill backed by the Nixon administration.[13] The 1970 Comprehensive Drug Abuse Prevention and Control Act put in place a permanent, uniform system for the classification of drugs as legal or illegal based on their potential for abuse, harmfulness, and acceptance in the medical community. This schedule, in turn, became the official basis for criminalizing the distribution and use of select drugs. By empowering the U.S. attorney general to classify drugs within the schedule, instead of the secretary of health, education and welfare, future drug policy strategies would inevitably be heavily centered on enforcement as opposed to prevention and treatment.

The continued federalization of criminal law throughout the 1980s brought numerous other nonviolent and violent criminal offenses under federal crime control policies and practices.[14] As an example, the 1984 Criminal Justice Act Revision classified as federal crimes a wider range of offenses, such as murder and kidnapping, by linking them to racketeering activities. The 1984 law went so far as to make it a federal crime to possess contraband in prison, where before, bringing the contraband into a prison was the crime. The 1986 Anti-Drug Abuse Act made it a federal crime to sell drug paraphernalia, such as water pipes, bongs, roach clips, and even spoons with level capacities of one-tenth cubic centimeter or less. If a person "neglects or refuses to assist" a federal law enforcement officer, namely a U.S. Customs officer upon "proper demand," according to Section 3152 of the 1986 Act, that person was guilty of having committed a federal crime.

Federalization of criminal law ballooned to such an extent that, by 2012, demands for a rollback of federal criminal laws would come from the Republican side of the aisle – where the push toward federalization began in 1968 with the Nixon "law and order" campaign. The 2012 Republican National Party Platform criticized what it called "the overcriminalization of behavior and the over-federalization of offenses." It asserted "federal criminal law should focus on acts by federal employees or acts committed on federal property – and leave the rest to the States."

Republicans also called on Congress to "reconsider the extent to which it has federalized offenses traditionally handled on the State or local level."[15] According to the platform, the number of criminal offenses in the U.S. Code increased from 3,000 in the early 1980s to more than 4,450 by 2008. A 2010 Heritage Foundation publication reported that, when asked by Republican Congressman James Sensenbrenner, the Congressional Research Service was unable to determine how many federal criminal offenses were on the law books because there were more than the agency could count. Not only the Republican Party but others as well made note of Congress's excess. A bipartisan Congressional task force was launched in May 2013. On the basis of a joint study of the Heritage Foundation and the National Association of Criminal Defense Lawyers, the foundation criticized Congress for its "overcriminalization rampage" and added: "Despite this rampant over-criminalization Congress continues to criminalize at an average rate of one new crime for every week of every year including when its Members are not in session)."[16]

The "overcriminalization rampage" was but one of several trends facilitating the expanded criminalization of blacks. An associated contributing factor was the lack of a balanced anti-crime strategy, one that devoted as much attention to prevention, treatment, and rehabilitation as to enforcement. Congressman Charles B. Rangel complained in 1988 it was "hypocritical to go after drug users when there are no real government resources to help with drug treatment or rehabilitation."[17] He was right. Although dozens of rather creative prevention programs were pitched by members of Congress, the financial resources committed to crime prevention across the seven crime bills paled in comparison to that set aside for punitive enforcement.[18] As a case in point, the majority of funds authorized in each of the main three drug-fighting laws were allocated to enforcement rather than rehabilitation.[19] In the 1970 bill, 54 percent of authorized funds were for enforcement; in the 1986 law, 58 percent; and in the 1988 law, 51 percent. Much of the remaining funding was allocated in block grants that left states and agencies considerable leeway in deciding how to appropriate the funds. As to the remaining omnibus bills examined here, the picture is even more lopsided. In the 1968, 1990, and 1994 laws the percentage of funds authorized for domestic law enforcement were nearly 100 percent, 98.6 percent, and 84 percent respectively.

There was a considerable degree of cynicism on Capitol Hill at the time toward programs aimed at leveling the root causes of crime, an atmosphere that further disposed Congress toward lip service in connection with prevention. A history-making Republican policy statement helps to illustrate the environment; it decries the 1994 crime bill because of the amount of social programming included in it. Among the top ten pledges made in the 1994 Republican Contract with America were enactment of "an anti-crime package including stronger truth-in-sentencing, 'good faith' exclusionary rule exemptions, effective death penalty provisions, and cuts in social spending from this summer's 'crime' bill [sic.] to fund prison construction and additional law enforcement."[20]

The second central component of the crime-fighting playbook formulated during 1968–1994 was use of incarceration as the prime means of combating nonviolent as well as violent felony crimes, a choice that entailed especially dire consequences for blacks. Again, because blacks were imprisoned at higher rates than nonblacks, greater reliance on incarceration as the solution to all crime would inevitably multiply still further the number of blacks destined for prison. This effect was all but assured also by the lack of provisions to counteract it. Congressman Robert W. Kastenmeier of Wisconsin remarked that the 1990 crime bill was an appeal "to a vengefulness that society seeks to satisfy."[21] The reality is that the 1990 bill was but one part of a much larger policy pattern. Virtually every major federal crime bill enacted from 1968 to 1994 expanded the use of incarceration, either by way of mandatory incarceration or by way of legislatively mandated sentence lengths.

Continual reinforcements to the country's prison policy by both Congress and state legislatures eventually yielded a nearly 950 percent increase in the number of new prison admissions from courts. Between 1926 and 2011, the number rose from roughly 48,000 to more than 455,000.[22] This increase in new admissions is separate and apart from the overall increase in the sentenced prisoner population from 97,991 to 1,537,415 over the same time period, which includes also readmissions (due to parole violations, and the like).[23] This decades-long trend of incarceration-centered crime policies started in 1970 on a relatively small scale. The 1970 Comprehensive Drug Abuse Prevention and Control Act set a mandatory minimum sentence of ten years for select drug trafficking offences and a sentence of up to twenty-five years for dangerous drug offenders. Next, the 1984 crime law, also known as the Sentencing Reform Act, increased prison terms for trafficking and distribution of drugs such as heroin and cocaine. Significantly, Section 3624 of the 1984 law required that federal offenders serve at least 85 percent of their sentence before release.

The critical watershed in incarceration policy came in 1986. That year lawmakers defined "serious drug offenses" in a way that covered users as well as traffickers, then mandated for those offenses prison terms rising up to life. Much has been made of the 100-to-1 disparity between crack cocaine and powder cocaine offenses put in place by the 1986 Anti-Drug Abuse Act, and for good reason. However, beside this provision were several other seriously problematic provisions also folded into the 1986 law. In addition to establishing a five-year mandatory minimum for 5 grams of crack cocaine and 500 grams of powder cocaine, it also mandated a five-year term for 100 grams of heroin as well as other substances that minorities and the poor were believed to have used more often than their counterparts. Anywhere from a ten-year to life term was required for a second conviction involving a "serious drug offense," inclusive of possession. Owners of buildings in which crack-related offenses occurred on a regular basis were singled out and subject to up to twenty years in prison. Judges were barred from ordering probation for anyone convicted of a narcotics offense. Just two years later, members of Congress voted in favor of a mandatory sentence of five to ten years for simple possession of crack cocaine. And, for the first time ever, the death penalty was authorized for drug-related offenses that resulted in death, thereby reviving the federal death penalty.

The final phase of the "race to incarcerate"[24] came in 1994, when policymakers lengthened the list of violent and nonviolent federal crimes and increased prison terms for dozens more. In addition to lengthening prison terms for assault, manslaughter, murder-for-hire, and gang-related offenses, the prison sentence for mere affiliation with a gang whose members commit a crime was lengthened by ten years as well. Increased penalties were tacked onto drug trafficking in rural areas, near truck stops, within so many feet of schools, playgrounds, public swimming pools, and public housing, and more. Capital punishment was authorized for dozens more federal crimes when a death resulted, though for certain "drug kingpin" crimes a killing was not a necessary precondition for imposing a death sentence. The most oft-noted provision of the 1994 Violent Crime Control and Enforcement Act is the "three-strikes-you're out" provision, that imposes life imprisonment following conviction for a third felony. Seldom noted is that one of the three "violent" offenses could actually be a serious drug offense, according to Title VII, Section 70001 of the law; furthermore, exceptions were made for robbery and arson.

Moreover, much like the increase in their share of the arrestee and prison population in the United States, blacks' above-average share of the lifelong debilitating economic and noneconomic effects of criminal processing was also magnified by modern anti-crime laws. The latter was brought on, specifically, by lawmakers' enactment of a host of new post-prison punishments to go with the new prison-worthy offenses. Officially contrived collateral punishments began as early as 1968, with enactment of anti-riot provisions that disqualified riot participants from federal employment, as noted earlier. The 1980s added to the collection of post-incarceration punishments. A lifetime driver's license suspension was mandated for commercial drivers convicted of a second drug-related DUI (either alcohol or drug-related DUIs) in 1986. Within the space of two years, the list of post-incarceration consequences for a drug conviction multiplied sevenfold under the heading "user accountability," starting with Title V in the 1988 Anti-Drug Abuse Act. Under this act, federal contractors and grantees were required under the 1988 Anti-Drug Abuse Act to discipline or terminate drug users or risk losing their contract or grant. The passport of anyone convicted of a felony drug offense is denied or revoked; the tenancy of any public-housing tenant who engaged in on-site criminal activity or whose guest did so terminated; federal benefits denied for five to ten years or permanently for distribution and for one to five years for possession.

Because "federal benefit" was defined by the law to include only noncontributory benefits that were not "earned" (such as, welfare, student loans, grants), members ensured marginalized minorities and the poor would be chiefly deprived as a result of these post-conviction provisions. The implications of those choices were hardly lost on critics at the time. The decision to deny federal student aid specifically to former drug convicts led House Education and Labor Committee Chair August F. Hawkins to remark in 1988: "So, you can rape and murder and still get student aid," with the distinction being "we currently have a war on drugs and not one on rape and murder."[25] Critiquing the policy from a slightly different angle, then-Congressman Charles Schumer asked "Why do we want to deprive an inner-city kid, who may have been convicted twice of using a small amount of drugs, from getting into a job-training program?"[26]

A fourth major element of the modern anti-crime policy adopted across 1968 to 1994 was diminution of the rights of the accused, the result of which was to further erode the already fragile constitution-legal protections for blacks against the kind of police excess most common in their neighborhoods. The first major legislative enactment of the "law and order" era included provisions that overturned three U.S. Supreme

Court decisions that had strengthened criminal rights. The 1968 crime law took aim at the landmark *Miranda v. Arizona* 1966 ruling, which required police advise detainees of certain fundamental constitutional rights. Although the legislative reversal was later voided in 2000 by the Supreme Court,[27] the fact that it was enacted in the first place serves as a strong indication of lawmakers' stance toward the rights of the criminally accused as early as 1968.

It was a stance that would maintain for decades to come. The erosion of criminal rights continued when lawmakers decided in 1984 to bar parole for federal prisoners and to authorize judges to order government supervision of an individual, even after his prison and/or parole terms ended. The same year, federal prosecutors were authorized to charge as adult juveniles involved in either drug or violent offenses. The legislative roll-back was in full swing by 1994, as Congress endorsed federal prosecution of juveniles for an even broader range of drug-related and violent crimes. As well, re-imprisonment was mandated for probationers and parolees who tested positive under the new mandatory, post-conviction drug testing. This, while Congress made it harder for prisoners to sue for civil rights violations and for federal judges to order relief of prison overcrowding.

Juxtaposed to the dilution of criminal rights was augmentation of law enforcement powers, a means by which modern crime policymaking further extended the justice system's already abnormal reach into black neighborhoods. The provision in the 1968 crime bill that was aimed squarely at predominantly black neighborhoods broadened the scope of police wiretapping beyond the national security sphere to include the race riots of the 1960s. Later, the 1970 federal anti-drug law empowered police officers to forcibly enter homes or other premises with "no knock" warrants. The Criminal Justice Act Revision of 1984 drastically enlarged the plea bargaining power of prosecutors (who act with minimal oversight) and, in the same stroke, shrank the adjudicatory power of judges (whose decisions are subject to appeal). Under the new sentencing law the U.S. Sentencing Commission was created and empowered to set guidelines for federal judges to follow when imposing sentence. As well, prosecutors could now appeal court bail orders, where before only defendants could. Finally, the 1994 omnibus bill led to designation of drug and violent crime "emergency areas" in which federal agencies could pool their manpower together with state and local law enforcement agencies and target specific neighborhoods. These were eventually made up of mostly black and poor neighborhoods, such as the Robert Taylor Homes Projects in Chicago.

The fifth and final trademark of the modern strategy formulated during 1968–1994 was development of a more elaborate institutional infrastructure to help ensure the incarceration strategy would be self-sustaining for years to come and, thus, debilitating to blacks for years to come. This was accomplished by way of repeated enhancements to enforcement structures, over and above prevention and treatment programs. Several policies bolstered state and local law enforcement agency staffing and activities. The primary route to doing so was through federal funding. Congress picked up a significant portion of the cost to replicate its penal policy throughout the states. It also laid the foundation for ongoing enforcement-centered research, starting with the 1968 crime bill's establishment of the National Institute of Law Enforcement and Criminal Justice within the Justice Department. This was coupled with training for local and state police at the Federal Bureau of Investigation National Academy at Quantico, Virginia. To strengthen coordination of federal and state law enforcement, the 1984 law created a liaison in the form of the Office of Justice Programs and also the Bureau of Justice Assistance. The latter was charged with helping to better target state and local resources to reduce drug abuse and award law enforcement block grants to help improve state and local criminal processing.[28] With the 1994 bill came funding to support the salaries of 100,000 new police officers.

Lawmakers enshrined the law and order agenda on the federal front as well. The 1984 law created the Drug Enforcement Policy Board, chaired by no less than the U.S. attorney general and entrusted it with coordination of all federal drug enforcement activities. Further refinements came when the 1988 bill transferred the bulk of these responsibilities to the newly created Office of National Drug Control Policy, headed by a cabinet-level director. More rank-and-file federal law enforcement personnel were added – 300 agents in 1970 to the Bureau of Narcotics and Dangerous Drugs. In addition, as many as 1,000 new federal prosecutors, FBI agents, DEA agents, Secret Service agents, and more were authorized in 1990. The real boon for federal crime fighters came in 1994 in the form of sizeable enhancements to virtually every federal law enforcement agency and, crucially, a dedicated Crime Trust Fund. Nearly half of the fund was allocated for prison construction and hiring new police officers. A total of 30.2 billion federal dollars was committed to the fund and designated for crime-fighting (solely and exclusively) until the millennium. In effect, Congress set aside a segregated fund to help ensure that its exacting penal policy would be financially sustainable for the foreseeable future – no matter the ebb and flow of actual crime rates.

States' interest in increased imprisonment was quite literally incentivized by the 1994 crime bill passed by Congress. The law created dozens of new enforcement grant programs, many of which came with strings attached – strings that called for more criminalization and imprisonment. For example, the 1994 bill required each state to ensure offenders serve no less than 85 percent of their prison sentence in order for the state to be eligible for "Truth in Sentencing Incentive Grants" under Section 20102 of the bill. This section all but guaranteed states would have a need for the crime trust funds. According to the Bureau of Justice, within the space of only four years, fully forty states and the District of Columbia implemented so-called truth-in-sentencing measures,[29] a move that helped to balloon the prison population.

It is important to understand that the amped up incarceration policy and its uniquely disadvantaging impact on blacks could not be sustained in the coming years unless there was an ongoing, active commitment of resources from lawmakers, both financial and nonfinancial. New prison cells and facilities were needed to house, feed, cloth, and confine the new population of prisoners created by the new categories of felony offenses and new classes of felony offenders. This, in turn, required a regular cash flow from public coffers, which required an annual budgetary allocation from lawmakers. Seemingly, as a way to prepare for what was to come, the 1984 Sentencing Reform Act approved a pilot program to help states and localities build new prisons. It also authorized the conversion of federal facilities into state prison or jail facilities. An even more creative initiative was authorization in 1990 for the Federal Bureau of Prisons to set up shock incarceration programs known as "boot camp," and funds in 1994 for states to do the same. This inventive idea was complemented by yet another in 1994 with a call for a study of the suitability of creating federal prison facilities at military bases slated to be closed. All this was in addition to a provision for construction of more old-fashioned prison cells. The duly named "Prisons" section of the bill (Title II) empowered the U.S. attorney general to make grants to states so that they could "construct, develop, expand, modify, operate, or improve correctional facilities," as needed.

On the whole, the main point of the foregoing discussion is that the basic thrust of American crime policy during the formative years of

1968 through 1994 consisted of continual reinforcements to a punitive, incarceration-centered approach to crime reduction. More significantly, the anti-crime policy process was driven by such a strong and widespread zeal for retribution that any effort to moderate its direct negative racial effects or, for that matter, any of its collateral effects encountered virtually insurmountable obstacles. The preceding discussion also shows the racial impact of the "law and order" framework of national crime policymaking was not the making of a handful of legislative enactments and that it was not constructed overnight or in one fell swoop. Rather, it is the byproduct of literally hundreds of deliberate choices made by hundreds of individual lawmakers and successive majorities, across several decades, several presidential administrations, and several shifts in party control of Congress, not to mention in nearly every state in the nation. Some of these provisions accrued through incremental decision making, some by way of bold leaps. Virtually all lean in the direction of what one senator referred to as the rack 'em, stack 'em, and pack 'em approach.

An Inside Job: Pressure Politics, Electoral Politics and Job Security in Crime-Fighting

In what follows, we examine the reasons national policymakers embarked on a crime-fighting strategy sure to deepen the racial divide in criminal justice, while simultaneously rebuffing efforts to ameliorate the strategy's negative racial effects. The fact that so many traditional liberals and conservatives alike were on board makes it difficult to assign purely sinister motives to Congress's race and crime policy choices. We learn, instead, the 1968–1994 crime policy trend was reflective of much broader social and political phenomena. Further, it was not chiefly tied to crime trends, nor to a Republican anti-minority agenda, nor to pressure politics. Rather, the "law and order" approach to crime suited Congressional lawmakers' reelectoral interests. Thus, the exacerbation of racial differences within criminal justice was an inside job.

The politics principle advises that we should not presume that policymakers' reasons for preferring an incarceration-policy were tied solely to the crime problem. In other words, we should not be surprised to find upon close inspection that the "law and order" agenda was not driven chiefly by a need for law and order. If crime and public safety were the primary explanation, then we would observe correspondence between crime rates, on the one hand, and crime policy trends on the other. More precisely, when crime rose, we would expect to see that lawmakers responded in

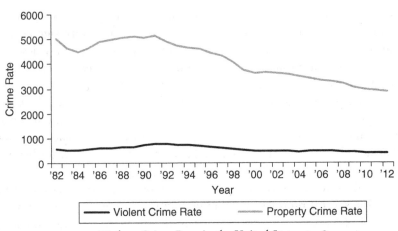

FIGURE 5.1. Violent Crime Rate in the United States, 1982–2012
(Rates Per 100,000 Residents).

kind; conversely, when crime declined, an expected response is that law-makers adjusted their policy approach accordingly. For the earlier part of the 1968–1994 period, this is the case. We observe Congress ratcheting up its crime-fighting efforts and arsenal in line with rising crime rates.[30]

However and critically, the correspondence between crime policymaking and the crime problem dissipated from the 1990s onward, in that crime rates declined yet lawmakers continued to invest more and more of their energies and taxpayer dollars into crime-fighting. Recall that in 1994, Congressional crime fighters made several unprecedented moves, including adoption of the "three strikes you're out" policy, expansion of the death penalty, permanent enhancements to the enforcement infrastructure and the prison industry in particular, as well as a dedicated Crime Trust Fund to help guarantee the future of the get-tough strategy, among other things. These historic, aggressive policy enactments came *after* property and violent criminal offenses were already on the decline throughout the years immediately preceding 1994. Congress nonetheless proceeded to enact what President Bill Clinton bragged was "the toughest, largest and smartest federal attack on crime in the history of the United States of America."[31]

The Federal Bureau of Investigation's crime data in Figure 5.1[32] demonstrate that from 1991 to 1992, the violent crime rate ticked downward from 758 crimes per 100,000 residents to 757; then from 758 to 742 during 1992–1993; and from 747 to 714 during 1993–1994, on the eve of the 1994 enactment. Crime rates continued to decline in the years

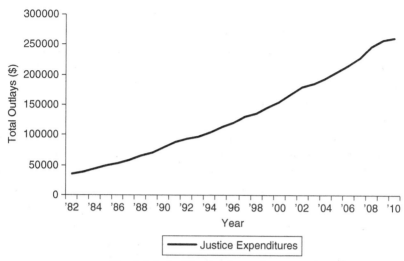

FIGURE 5.2. Total Criminal Justice Expenditures in the United States, 1982–2010.

to follow to the point where, by 2012, the violent crime per capita rate actually flattened to 387, lower than in 1971, when it was 396. Despite this steady decline in violent crime rates, crime expenditures continued to rise steadily as depicted in Figure 5.2.[33] Federal, state, and local outlays to reduce crime continually rose, even as (and despite the fact that) crime continually declined. Thus, the crime policy efforts of 1968 through 1994 were tenuously tied to national crime rates. Viewed against this backdrop, the Violent Crime Control Act of 1994 constituted an historic effort to control a crime problem that was already under control and at the same time help raise the number of blacks in prison to historic levels.

The argument advanced here regarding the attenuated connection between modern crime policymaking and crime trends is warranted, even if it is assumed policymakers had hoped to obliterate every trace of crime from every corner of American society and that this utopian ideal is what led them to commit more and more monies to their crime-fighting machine. However, Figure 5.2 illustrates the incarceration-centered, enforcement-heavy approach pursued by Congress was generally ineffective in reducing the much-talked about violent crime rate. Throughout the thirty years shown, violent crime levels remained generally unresponsive to lawmakers' prison strategy; even during the 1980s and the heyday of mandatory sentencing, violent crime rates remained relatively stable. In essence, the costly incarceration-centered strategy was ineffective, and apparently so.

It is common to assign a significant share of responsibility for the gruelingly punitive thrust of modern crime policy and its disproportionate racial effects on Republican presidents and leaders – perhaps none more than President Ronald Reagan; however, two facts point in a different direction. For all of his much-talked about power to persuade, Reagan cannot be said to have seduced unwitting policymakers into going along with the program, so to speak. Consider the highly criticized 100-to-1 crack-cocaine versus powder-cocaine penalty structure and the racist motives commonly attributed to its enactment. The official record of Congressional debate and proceedings establish that Reagan initially asked Congress to institute a 20-to-1 penalty structure – a ratio very near the 18-to-1 structure eventually signed into law in 2010 by the nation's first black president, Barack Obama. It was actually members of Congress who decided in 1986 to widen the disparity beyond what Reagan initially proposed and to settle instead on the 100-to-1 ratio.[34] The final roll call vote on passage of the widely criticized 1986 bill setting the penalty disparity was 346 representatives in favor and 11 against, together with 87 senators voting in favor and 3 against.[35] Furthermore, the same kind of punishment-heavy "law and order" policies enacted during Reagan's terms in office were enacted also before and after his administration. Finally, it was a Democratic president and Democrat-controlled Congress that in 1994 permanently enshrined the incarceration-centered, anti-crime strategy with little to no regard for its past or future racial effects, as demonstrated in the preceding discussion and analysis.

The scholarly literature on policy subsystems discussed in Chapter 2 suggests a pressure politics-centered lens offers a more compelling account, but it too is unsupported by empirical data. Lawmakers did not cave under the pressure of lobby groups demanding incarceration-centered crime laws from 1968–1994. True, lobby groups exerted a great deal of influence on the legislative process that led to Congress's colorblind "get tough" strategy as well as other relevant policy decisions. Three interest groups in particular met great success in protecting and advancing their policy interests, including advocates for the elderly, gun owners, and also law enforcement agencies and officials. To start with, senior citizen lobbies held the line against the push in 1988 to deny federal benefits to any and everyone convicted of trafficking or possessing illegal drugs. Lawmakers instead exempted beneficiaries of contributory programs by narrowly defining what constituted a "federal benefit" under the bill. The definition expressly excluded "any retirement, welfare, Social Security, health, disability, veterans benefit, public housing, or other similar benefit ... for which payments or services are required for eligibility."[36] In addition to the success of senior lobbies is that of the gun rights advocates, which likewise held the line against gun control proposals from 1968 onward. This, even though members of Congress declared in the 1968 crime bill that "the ease with which any person can acquire firearms other than a rifle or shot gun ... is a significant factor in the prevalence of lawlessness and violent crime in the United States."[37] The 1968 declaration further stated that only through adequate federal control could the "grave problem" of "widespread traffic in firearms" be properly dealt with in states and localities. Yet, lawmakers repeatedly failed from 1968 onward to act resolutely on their own estimation that guns were implicated in the nation's crime problem.

Large and high-powered national law enforcement lobbies sought an enforcement-heavy crime policy approach, and realized greater success than those pressing for a more holistic approach that sufficiently enveloped prevention and rehabilitation-oriented policies. As examples, during the *Narcotics Assistance to State and Local Law Enforcement* hearings before the House Subcommittee on Crime in 1986, representatives of the National Sheriffs' Association, the Fraternal Order of Police, and the International Association of Chiefs of Police presented arguments in favor of increased criminal penalties for drug crimes, along with grants to assist local drug law enforcement efforts.[38] Also, the director of the Bureau of Prisons, J. Michael Quinlan, testified against alternative prisons for federal offenders in 1990.[39] However, earlier in 1988, Quinlan testified in support of a 1988 proposal to allow Federal Prison Industries (UNICOR) to borrow funds from the U.S. Treasury to expand operations in light of projected prison population increases.[40] So did the executive director of the American Correctional Association and the president of the Council of Prison Locals. In the end, law enforcement lobbies such as these and others got much of what they wanted.

In fact, the strategy embraced by Congress proved to be a veritable windfall from which law enforcement agencies and also state and local governments directly benefitted. The federal government's stepped up role in crime-fighting created new revenue streams by way of billions of dollars in new federal grant programs. Indeed, the first major move toward permanent federalization of criminal law was facilitated largely through a block grant program designed to assist law enforcement agencies with the offenses targeted in the 1968 bill, especially the race riots. The bulk of federal funding in the years to follow was channeled through block grants instead of categorical grants, which meant states had more latitude within which to decide how to spend the monies. States typically did not have to match more than 25 cents for every 75 cents on the federal dollar.

Each state was guaranteed a set amount of funding from the grant programs established by the crime laws of 1968–1994, regardless of the size of the state's population or the size of its crime problem. As an example, the minimum amount ranged from $500,000 in the 1986 bill to as much as 50 percent of the $8.8 billion set aside for a myriad of grants programs in the 1994 bill and another 25 percent of the $7.9 billion set aside for prison building and renovations. The start-up monies authorized for the dedicated "crime trust fund" in 1994 equaled $30.2 billion. The drug war proved to be especially rewarding for states. As early as 1972, Nixon bagged: "In 3 years we have provided States and localities with law enforcement assistance grants totaling $1.5 billion. That compares with only $22 million in grants during the final 3 years of the previous Administration."[41] Reagan bragged about a tripling of the anti-drug budget during his administration, on top of more than $500 million in drug-related asset seizures during 1987 alone.[42]

The financial rewards Congress set aside for police officers in particular were considerable. As an example, the 1994 bill supplemented each of the newly authorized 100,000 police officers' salaries with as much as $75,000. This was in addition to the creation of scholarships for police officers, child care, housing subsidies, stress-reduction programs and other services for the families of police officers. This was also in addition to the long-term job security assured by a crime strategy that centered on enforcement drastically more than prevention and rehabilitation. For their part, state and law enforcement agencies reaped the benefit of proceeds generated by asset seizures, which assets crime laws authorized the agencies to convert and/or sell for their own benefit. All totaled, the combined federal, state, and local outlays appropriated to law enforcement agencies – as against prevention, rehabilitation, and educational programs – equaled nearly $260 billion as of 2010, a figure that continually rose throughout the preceding years, as shown in Figure 5.1.

The idea that financial and economic interests on the part of criminal justice officials help undergird the incarceration policy of not only Congress but also states was implied when Governor Andrew Cuomo of New York made a case for prison closures. Cuomo complained in his first State of the State Address in 2011 that the cost to confine one child in the juvenile justice facility was more than $200,000 per year.[43] He continued, explaining "the reason we continue to keep these children in these programs that aren't serving them but are bilking the taxpayers is that we don't want to lose the state jobs that we would lose if we closed the facilities." Cuomo vowed change, declaring "an incarceration program is not an employment program.... Don't put other people in prison to give some people jobs." Within a matter of weeks of vowing to close or consolidate several state prisons despite the objections of criminal justice officials, the *New York Times* reported Governor Andrew Cuomo was forced to scale back his plans as a result of lawmakers vying to fend off the loss of hundreds of state jobs in their districts.[44] According to the article, state Senator Betty Little was among the many state lawmakers who resisted the prison closures. Little stressed that she represented a "very rural" area and added: "we built an economy around these facilities."[45]

Notwithstanding the job security and economic benefits accrued to law enforcement officials and agencies by incarceration policies, three factors strongly suggest the law and order policies enacted from 1968–1994 are not a story of how Congress was unduly pressured by these groups. Besides the fact that the scope of regulatory politics is seldom confined to small group politics, analysis of Congressional hearings on crime policy proposals from 1968–1994 reveals a much wider and more complex set of political forces in play. In every Congress during which the selected anti-crime laws were enacted, dozens of witnesses at committee hearings encouraged lawmakers to pursue a crime-fighting strategy that tilted toward prevention and rehabilitation more than incarceration. They urged a strategy that tackled the socioeconomic causes, and they also expressed concerns about racial justice and civil liberties. For purposes of this discussion, I will term these witnesses "crime-preventers." Recommending an alternative legislative approach were those I will term here "crime fighters." The latter emphasized the importance of tough criminal sanctions, mandatory sentencing, imprisonment, relaxed criminal rights, and the like. Last, Congressional committee members also regularly heard from racial justice and civil liberties advocates.

An estimate of the representational balance across these three camps at Congressional hearings is depicted in Table 5.1.[46] It shows crime preventers and justice advocates consistently outnumbered crime fighters, in some instances by nearly five to one. For example, in the case of the 1970 bill, crime preventers and justice advocates together offered an estimated ninety-three testimonies, while crime fighters provided only twenty. In 1988, Congressional members heard testimony from an estimated sixteen crime fighters, compared to forty-three crime preventers and justice advocates. What information and insights did they present to committee

TABLE 5.1. *Congressional Hearings Witness Testimony: Estimated Number of Testimonies of Crime Preventers, Justice Advocates, and Crime Fighters, 1968–1994*

	Members of Congress	Federal Gov. Officials	State & Local Officials	Nongov. Orgs.	Individuals	Total
CRIME PREVENTERS						
1968	11	2	8	1	1	23
1970	2	15	0	2	1	20
1984	2	13	9	9	10	43
1986	6	5	0	5	0	16
1988	0	7	4	5	0	16
1990	0	8	7	6	3	24
1994	5	4	3	1	0	13
JUSTICE ADVOCATES						
1968	0	0	0	1	1	2
1970	21	11	2	23	32	89
1984	0	0	0	1	0	1
1986	9	5	5	12	2	33
1988	1	3	8	16	6	34
1990	3	6	34	18	20	81
1994	1	1	3	12	17	34
CRIME FIGHTERS						
1968	12	1	3	13	2	31
1970	0	0	0	4	0	4
1984	0	7	3	26	14	50
1986	0	0	0	0	1	1
1988	4	1	0	4	0	9
1990	0	2	0	2	0	4
1994	0	1	1	0	0	2

Note: "Individuals" includes academics, corporate spokespersons, practitioners, and lay citizens.

members? All that one would expect in order for Congress to have realized both the limited utility and also the racial effects of the proposals it adopted. Much of the hearing testimony offered in 1968 concerned several gun control provisions, which were subsequently whittled down to a declaration. But, in 1970, medical experts representing national health organizations dutifully informed members of the House Subcommittee on Public Health and Welfare that drug abuse was a mental health and medical problem. In particular, spokespersons for the American Medical Association, the American Psychiatric Association, the American Public

Health Association, the Committee on Alcoholism, the Council on Mental Health, the American College of Neuro-Psycho Pharmacology, and dozens more stressed the importance of lodging authority to control drug classification and research in the secretary of health, education, and welfare, as opposed to the U.S. attorney general.

If Congress were to do so, these experts carefully explained, it would help ensure the nation's drug policy was effective in controlling illicit drug use.[47] The same messaging came from industry representatives, such as spokespersons for the American Pharmaceutical Association and the National Association of Retail Druggists. The American Civil Liberties Union director, Lawrence Speiser, warned of the likely fallout of the "no-knock" authority and warrant inspection requirements in the 1970 proposal.

Judiciary subcommittees in both chambers of the 98th Congress heard testimony from federal judges, academics, and legal organizations about the likely racial fallout of the mandatory sentencing proposals that were subsequently adopted in 1984.[48] For example, the National Association of Criminal Defense Lawyers, the National Legal Aid and Defender Association, and the National Association of Blacks in Criminal Justice warned of the inequities in rigid sentencing guidelines. Federal judges remarked on the distinction between appropriate and undue disparities in sentencing. A representative of the Vera Institute of Justice underlined the need for additional research on the extent, nature and causes of disparities in judicial sentencing. A representative of the National Conference of Black Lawyers detailed the implications of mandatory sentencing for racial disparity in the criminal justice system. Similarly, an executive officer of the Minnesota Department of Corrections, Leslie R. Green, expressed concern about the long-term effect of mandatory sentencing on blacks and other minorities in Minnesota. The Dean of the School of Criminal Justice at Rutgers University, Don M. Gottfredson, highlighted the need for sentencing guidelines to address prison overcrowding and laid out for committee members various other alternatives to incarceration as a means of reducing repeat offending.

Before Congress enacted the Anti-Drug Abuse Act of 1986, the House Committee on Narcotics Abuse and Control was educated on the importance of drug education programs in schools by Secretary of Education William J. Bennett.[49] Executive directors of the National Association of State Alcohol and Drug Abuse Directors and also the Therapeutic Communities of America advocated drug policies that emphasized drug abuse prevention and treatment.[50] Industry experts, such as the lab director of Toxichem Laboratories, even expressed reservations about the forensic accuracy of the contracted drug testing program, the very kind of testing requirements eventually imposed on parolees by the 1986 law. Contractors and employers represented by the Chamber of Commerce of the United States, Associated General Contractors, Associated Builders and Contractors, the Computer and Communications Industry Association, and other lobby organizations expressed worry that the drug-free workplace mandates in the 1988 bill would push them to err on the side of firing employees, in order to maintain their federal contract.[51]

Again during proceedings on the 1988 and 1990 crime laws, expert testimony drew attention to the importance of drug abuse prevention and treatment, the critical role of education, alternatives to incarceration, and, above all else, the racial implications of these issues.[52] By 1990, a survey of thirty cities and of local policymakers had begun to draw attention to the fact that "only a small portion of the funds" Congress set aside for prevention and treatment in the 1986 bill actually made it to local agencies and organizations, where such needs were typically addressed.[53] The mayor of Alexandria, Virginia, actually complained:

Our new jail cost $15 million. We opened it in 1987. We thought we were going to make money off of it, because normally our prison load was about 200 inmates and we figured we would lease out 100 jail cells to the Federal Government. Their per diem is higher than the actual cost. This morning in that jail with 333 cells we have 510 inmates, and the vast majority of them are there as a result of drugs.[54]

Mayor James P. Moran added: "treatment costs less than incarceration, and incarceration is providing virtually no rehabilitation." Meanwhile, the spokesperson for the National Governors' Association stressed that prevention and education were cheaper, easier, and more effective drug policy strategies.[55]

Chairman of the U.S. Sentencing Commission William W. Wilkins expressed concerns about the disparate impact of the 1994 mandatory life imprisonment proposals. Meanwhile organizations such as the Sentencing Project, the National Association of Criminal Defense Lawyers, and the Black Expo Chicago questioned the premise of mandatory life sentence proposals, underscoring its effect on black citizens.[56] By 1994 criticism of mandatory-minimum sentencing laws and their racial effects came from both ends of the spectrum, from academics such as Alfred Blumstein and also Kathleen M. Hawk, the director of the Bureau of Prisons, to federal public defenders and organizations such as "Families Against Mandatory Minimums."[57]

In sum and substance, Congressional hearings on the 1968–1994 crime laws entailed a far greater proportion of testimony from crime-preventers and justice advocates. Their numbers and the message they carried to Washington lawmakers easily outflanked that of law enforcement lobbies.

Coupled together with the extraordinarily long line of expert witnesses that prodded lawmakers to pursue a more racially sensitive, diversified crime-fighting strategy is the fact that Congress actually took the lead in the nation's march toward an incarceration-centered policy. This further challenges the idea that Congress caved to high-pressured tactics from law enforcement lobbies. Just the opposite is true; it was federal lawmakers who actually incentivized get tough policies at the state and local level. A significant proportion of federal monies appropriated as "law enforcement assistance" to states and localities required implementation of similarly punitive, incarceration-centered policies as a precondition for being awarded federal funds. In the case of the 1994 bill, only those states that required convicts to serve at least 85 percent of their prison sentence could access the $7.9 billion set aside for prison expansion, as explained earlier. Later, when Congress elevated the weight of crime rates in its funding formula, it thereby also increased the incentives for law enforcement to produce large crime counts and, with it, larger numbers of criminalized individuals. From the vantage point of states and localities, the racial justice agenda promised a much smaller return on investment; it was not nearly as financially or politically profitable to them as the "law and order" agenda. Perhaps the most obvious case in point is the $30.2 billion trust fund set up by the 1994 crime law; it easily trumped the $7.5 million set aside in 2005 for the Grant Program to Prohibit Racial Profiling.[58]

The third and more significant factor that exposes the limits of a pressure politics lens for explaining Congress's colorblind crime-fighting agenda is the virtual unanimity with which lawmakers pursued it. In stark contrast to the gridlock and conflict that so often typifies contemporary Congressional decision making,[59] being tough on crime is one of the few policy stances for which political harmony and unity are the rule of the day. Whereas a majority of national lawmakers were regularly silent or otherwise uninvolved in the press for racial justice, the overwhelming majority exhibited a religious-like zeal when asked to give their blessing to policies that centered on incarceration more than rehabilitation for drug addicts, juvenile delinquents, as well as nonviolent and violent offenders alike. Put simply, fervent pursuit of the "law and order"

TABLE 5.2. *Congressional Support for Modern Crime Legislation,*
1968–1994

Crime Law	Final Roll Call Vote on Law (Date of Roll Call Vote)		Percentage Breakdown of Final Roll Vote (% "Yea" Votes)	
	House	Senate	House	Senate
1968 Omnibus Crime Control Act (HR 5037)	369–17 (06/06/68)	72–4 (05/23/68)	96%	95%
1970 Comprehensive Drug Abuse Act (HR 18583)	341–6 (09/24/70)	54–0 (10/07/70)	98%	100%
1984 Criminal Justice Act Revision (H J Res 648)	316–91 (09/25/84)	91–1 (02/02/84)	78%	99%
1986 Anti-Drug Abuse Act (HR 5484)	378–16 (10/17/86)	97–2 (09/30/86)	96%	98%
1988 Anti-Drug Abuse Act (HR 5210)	346–11 (10/22/88)	87–3 (10/14/88)	97%	97%
1990 Crime Control Act (S 3266)	313–1 (10/27/90)	94–6 (07/11/90)	99%	94%
1994 Violent Crime Control Act (HR 3355)	235–195 (08/21/94)	61–38 (08/25/94)	55%	62%

agenda with little to no regard for its racialized effects struck a chord with members of all stripes.

Lawmakers in both the House and the Senate, across both major parties and across the ideological spectrum, lined up in support of passage of the laws. Nearly all sought to avoid the very appearance of casting a vote that could so much as suggest being soft on crime. Even some Congressional Black Caucus members, who initially waged a vigorous fight for racial safety valves, dutifully lined up in support of passage of the bills – after the safeguards they sought were abandoned. Some boycotted the final votes on passage altogether, as a way to avoid being part of the problem but at the same time avoid essentially going on record as soft on crime. For its part, the Democratic Policy Caucuses in the House and Senate fully backed the "law and order" anti-crime strategy over and above that of racial justice aims. They did so with the full support of the leadership and the White House.

Virtually every bill formulating the heart of modern crime policy was enacted by hugely lopsided margins in both the House and Senate.

Table 5.2[60] contains a breakdown of the final roll call vote in each chamber.[61] In a number of instances in which the final vote on passage was accomplished by way of voice vote, there were no objections at all registered. The Anti-Drug Abuse Acts of 1986 and 1988 – the very laws severely criticized by many scholars, journalists, and politicians – were officially endorsed by 96 percent and 97 percent of House members and by 98 percent and 97 percent of senators, respectively. Such unanimity among members of Congress stretching across multiple decades is not ordinarily indicative of a policy process coopted by a special interest group. This is especially so when the lobby group itself or the segments of society for which they speak do not claim a sizeable share of the electorate. It is the kind of unanimity that signals much bigger stakes.

Ultimately, Congress's choice of an incarceration-centered approach to crime-fighting is best understood as having been fundamentally borne of members' electoral interests. It was lawmakers' job security concerns that drove their actions, more so than that of law enforcement spokespersons. All but one of the bills examined here originated in the House, where members are in perpetual reelection mode, more than the Senate.[62] The timing of passage is especially telling too on the question of motives. Every one of the major laws examined here was adopted during an election year. More, the bills were often debated during the heat of the election season and then voted for on the eve of elections. In some instances, they were passed during the early morning hours, just in time for representatives to adjourn and head for the campaign trail with new bragging rights in hand. As an example, the final voice vote on passage of the 1988 crime law came at 1:20 a.m. in the House and at 3:15 a.m. in the Senate, after which both chambers immediately adjourned.[63] Senate passage of the 1994 bill occurred at 11:00 p.m., just before a three-week adjournment.

We learn in the next chapter that the reason lawmakers presumed their crime policy choices were electorally profitable is that those choices were consistent with the tide of anti-crime politics outside of Congress. They followed what was and still is today the playbook where race and criminal justice politics and policy are concerned. This norm was forged by four key national political developments on this policy front, which we turn to in the next chapter.

6

The Politics Principle and the Party Playbook

In the broader political arena beyond of Congress, the disparate treatment and overrepresentation of blacks in criminal justice were downgraded to nonissues during the late sixties. In other words, racial justice concerns were relegated to the sidelines of national crime politics. From the late 1960s onward, the two major national political parties re-fashioned "the problem" in law enforcement to be exclusively a matter of safety, not justice. Crime politics thus metamorphosed from a sphere in which the distinctiveness of the black law enforcement experience mattered briefly into one in which it did not matter for decades to come. This de-racialization of crime politics was facilitated by four major developments.

First, violent crime was effectively nationalized, that is to say re-branded as a serious problem facing all American neighborhoods in equal measure, not chiefly minority or inner city communities. Second, the rights of criminal defendants were pitted against the rights of crime victims in a zero-sum game. The result was the virtual disappearance of concern for the criminally accused, a disproportionate share of whom were black. Third, a new set of primary stakeholders in the crime policy process was designated; it was composed primarily of children, women, and the elderly. These groups were envisaged as the new "special" victims of crime, in place of blacks and other racial minorities. Finally, drugs were declared the most dangerous evil facing American society at large, dangerous enough to render historic levels of black imprisonment tolerable collateral damage.

In sum and substance, the party playbook for modern crime politics instructed politicians to ignore blacks' unique stake in criminal justice policy matters. Critically, moreover, it was a playbook patterned more so after political interests than problem-solving interests, just as the politics principle leads us to believe. It did not matter that the race neutral brand of crime-fighting was disconnected from the reality of crime. Meaning, politicians essentially turned a page regarding crime and law enforcement, even though the acutely racial dimensions of crime and enforcement maintained. The whos, wheres, hows, and whats of crime in the United States remained substantially racial in nature. As such, it was politics, rather than real-life crime trends, that best accounted for lawmakers' stance toward racial justice concerns.

This chapter details the four major shifts in American crime politics from 1968 to 2012 that negatively impacted the fate of racial justice concerns. The discussion focuses specifically on the re-branding of the relation between race and street crime.[1] These transformational changes in the politics of crime are depicted primarily by way of a content analysis of national party platforms and presidential statements.[2] Before we begin, a word about the choice of this analytical focus is in order. A methodological foundation for studies that center on the language and rhetoric of political texts was constructed by Laver, Benoit, and Garry.[3] They detailed the importance of political text for estimating political and policy positions. Subsequent political science studies demonstrate also that party platforms are informative, despite the attenuated link between platform pledges and specific legislative outputs debated in earlier studies.[4] For policymakers, "party platforms provide written guidelines for campaigning and governance" insofar as "the issues covered in these documents are presented to the electorate in the way that the party feels best delineates its philosophy within the context of current issues."[5] For voters, platforms provide a means of assessing candidates for elected office.[6]

For analysts, party platforms approximate the ideological boundaries of U.S. domestic policy, as they are the "one document that spells out the entire program of the party"[7] and also reflects the strategic choices of party activists and elites.[8] Having observed platforms as a participant and scholar, Ronald S. Walters asserted the "final platform document represents the vested interest of the groups within the party."[9] They satisfy a "systemic need for coalition formation" at the national party conventions and, thus, function as a kind of "institutional rhetoric through which these quadrennial syntheses may be built."[10] The heuristic value of party platforms and presidential statements for understanding racial politics in particular is well displayed by the research analysis in Edward G. Carmines and James A. Stimson's groundbreaking book, *Issue Evolution:*

Race and the Transformation of American Politics. Their examination of party platforms and presidential rhetoric and behavior establishes both as expressions of policy positions on a wide range of racial matters dating back to 1932.[11] This study likewise utilizes these indicators to trace the demise of racial justice concerns, in this instance, within the context of national crime politics.

We begin with a look at how parties initially conceptualized the link between race, crime, and justice. Next we trace how they subsequently decoupled the politics of race and criminal justice, notwithstanding the real-life interconnectedness of the two.

All Together Now: Race, Crime, and Criminal Justice

The mid to late 1960s was a time when both parties publicly acknowledged the link between race and crime policymaking. It was apparent for at least a short while that the inner city and ghettos in particular were hot spots for crime, that blacks were concentrated in those areas, and that, as a consequence, black interests necessarily figured prominently in crime politics and policymaking. Foremost among the phenomena that supplied the stage for parties to openly confront the intersection of race, crime, and justice were: the 1960s black civil rights movement, the late 1960s race riots, and the 1968 Richard Nixon presidential campaign.

Much was made of the fact that the marches and demonstrations of the black civil rights movement in the segregated South were marred with violence. Both sides of the aisle publicly acknowledged the otherwise obvious role that racial influences played in the brutal reaction of southern law enforcement officers and assailants. As much is clear in the 1964 Republican and Democratic national party platforms. Upon lauding Congressional passage of the landmark Civil Rights Act of 1964, Democrats' "Democracy of Opportunity" plank stressed: "We reaffirm our belief that lawless disregard for the rights of others is wrong – whether used to deny equal rights or to obtain equal rights. We cannot and will not tolerate lawlessness." The "One Nation, One People" section discussed crime almost entirely in connection with the "march towards the goals of equal opportunity and equal treatment." Later in 1968, Democrats asserted: "We knew that racial discrimination was present in every section of the country.... In this conviction, Democrats took the initiative to guarantee the right to safety and security of the person. "

Republicans also made note of the fact that violence, criminal law administration, and the press for racial equality were inextricably linked during the 1960s. But, the party held a slightly different view of matters. The "Discord and Discontent" section of the 1964 Republican platform complained the Johnson administration had "exploited interracial tensions by extravagant campaign promises, without fulfillment, playing on the just aspirations of the minority groups, encouraging disorderly and lawless elements, and ineffectually administering the laws." The platform pledged "to open avenues of peaceful progress in solving racial controversies while discouraging lawlessness and violence."

The race riots supplied yet another backdrop for candid debate about the racial dynamics of crime and justice during the 1960s. In the wake of some 164 racial disorders during the first nine months of 1967, President Lyndon B. Johnson established the Kerner Commission (officially called the National Advisory Commission on Civil Disorders) to carry out a study of the riots. One of the questions President Johnson charged the Commission to consider was how "police-community relationships affect the likelihood of a riot – or the ability to keep one from spreading once it has started?"[12] The final report of the Commission, released in February 1968, was the boldest national policy statement to date about the linkage between race and policing. The report discussed various aspects of the race problem in criminal justice at length, going so far as to identify it as one of the main factors that caused the disorders. While surveying residents and officials in cities where the disorders occurred, the Commission discovered a precipitating incident almost always occurred just before onset of the riots. In almost half of the disorders, police action was the trigger. The report was careful to note a single incident could not be held responsible and that there were deeply held grievances that spurred rioters, twelve grievances to be exact.

Crucially, the very first grievance on the list of twelve was police practices, with discriminatory administration of justice coming in eighth. The Commission explained:

The police are not merely a "spark" factor. To some Negroes police have come to symbolize white power, white racism and white repression. And the fact is that many police do not reflect and express these white attitudes. The atmosphere of hostility and cynicism is reinforced by widespread belief among Negroes in the existence of police brutality and in a "double standard" of justice and protection – one for Negroes and one for whites.[13]

Foremost among the Kerner Commission recommendations was that city government and police authorities "review police operations in the ghetto to ensure proper conduct by police officers, and eliminate abrasive practices."[14] Significantly, the report did not end at spotlighting the relationship between the police and minority communities. It went on to say emphatically: "The blame must be shared by the total society."[15]

Prior to the Kerner Commission report, President Johnson himself publicly noted the fact that it was blacks who were primarily hurt by the riots. In a live national address in which he announced the establishment of the Kerner Commission, Johnson said: "Let us condemn the violent few. But let us remember that it is law-abiding Negro families who have really suffered most at the hands of the rioters."[16] The Kerner report likewise referenced the special connection between race and crime, claiming crime and drug addiction were the result of segregation and poverty.[17] Whereas Johnson was silent about the final Kerner Commission report, members of his party were not. Democrats agreed with the report's conclusion that racial discrimination was a driving force behind the racial disorders. Their 1968 platform stated: "We acknowledge with concern the findings of the report of the bi-partisan National Advisory Commission on Civil Disorders and we commit ourselves to implement its recommendations and to wipe out, once and for all, the stain of racial and other discrimination from our national life." While they went on to lump the race riots in together with other forms of "lawlessness," such as organized crime and white collar crime, Democrats also pledged to attack the root causes of crime and disorder.

Republicans were equally concerned with the racial roots of the riots and their damaging effects, but they broached the behavior of the rioters from a less empathetic angle. It was the damage caused in black communities that concerned Republicans most. In addressing what it termed the "crisis of the cities," the party expressed in 1968 "concern for the unique problems of citizens long disadvantaged in our total society by race, color, national origin, creed, or sex." Republicans added, however: "Fire and looting, causing millions of dollars of property damage, have brought great suffering to home owners and small businessmen, particularly in black communities least able to absorb catastrophic losses." They promised to alleviate the frustrations that contribute to riots, but added: "We simultaneously support decisive action to quell civil disorder." It was not long before Democrats followed the Republican Party's lead and recast the link between race and crime in terms of its deleterious effects more so than its causes. The 1972 Democratic Party' Platform asserted: "Fear of crime, and firm action against it, is not racism. Indeed the greatest victims of crime today – whether of business fraud or of the narcotics plague – are the people of the ghetto, black and brown."

President Richard M. Nixon too confronted the connection between race and crime, but did so subtly and in ways that disfavored the criminal justice policy interests of minorities. Nixon's 1968 presidential bid provided an outlet for those who were more agitated by than concerned about the linkage.[18] More precisely, it was an outlet for those increasingly frustrated with the press for black equality and the fact that black crime was being whitewashed, in their view.[19] Whereas racial progressives were especially bothered by the nature of the black law enforcement experience and the poor quality of enforcement in black neighborhoods in 1968, Nixon vigorously and unapologetically advocated "law and order." He was significantly less bothered by the racial fallout from uneven criminal justice. In his 1968 speech at the Republican National Convention, Nixon repeatedly underscored the importance of a vigilant fight against crime and was virtually silent on the fight for racial equality. He declared emphatically the "wave of crime" in the country was "not going to be the wave of the future in the United States of America" and he would work to "re-establish freedom from fear in America."[20] When running for his second term in 1972 Nixon made mention of the "frightening trend of crime and anarchy" and pledged to "make the next 4 years a period of new respect for law, order, and justice in America."[21]

Critics assailed the Nixon "law and order" agenda as racist, and Nixon was well aware at the time that his agenda was regarded as such. Still, he defended the stern approach saying: "to those who say that law and order is the code word for racism, there and here is a reply: Our goal is justice for every American. If we are to have respect for law in America, we must have laws that deserve respect." Importantly, moreover, at a time when racial liberals tended to conceptualize racial disturbances and other forms of violence as the result of too little government programing, Nixon reconceived crime and violence as the result of too much government programing. He stated: "For the past five years we have been deluged by government programs for the unemployed; programs for the cities; programs for the poor. And we have reaped from these programs an ugly harvest of frustration, violence and failure across the land." Translated, this meant Nixon had no plans to hamstring his crime policy agenda with additional social programming for crime-ridden neighborhoods, black or otherwise.

Nixon's "law and order" agenda bore a striking resemblance to that of southern segregationists, which is partly why some labeled it racist. Decades later, Republican National Committee chairman Ken Mehlman would apologize for what he termed "some Republicans'" attempts to "benefit politically from racial polarization."[22] The so-called southern strategy employed by Nixon and his followers was designed to win over the Dixiecrat vote.[23] The stiffest competition for that vote was southern segregationist George Wallace, head of the American Independent Party presidential ticket in 1968. Wallace's party platform was a resounding condemnation of the recent civil rights gains made by blacks and other disenfranchised groups. It condemned the landmark Civil Rights Act of 1964 and other federal desegregation initiatives. It condemned the criminal rights revolution spearheaded by the Warren Court. It condemned federal funding for urban development, and more. Critically, Wallace's party declared: "We will not accept violence as the answer to any problem be it social, economic, or self developed. Anarchists and law violators will be treated as such and subjected to prompt arrest and prosecution." Just as Wallace's party merged a vigorous fight against crime together with a repudiation of civil rights advances, so too Nixon's anti-crime rhetoric was coupled with his opposition to racial bussing, federal interference in southern states affairs, and other anti-discrimination measures.[24]

For a period of time during the 1960s, in summary, the two major parties did not shy away from the fact that race, crime, and criminal justice policy were inextricably linked together. It was a time when the linkage took center stage. The criticism of southern law enforcement's brutal reaction to civil rights demonstrations was expressly grounded in an understanding that the reaction was unmistakably racially motivated. Political reaction to the race riots was also informed by a grasp of their discriminatory roots – even as liberals, Nixon, and Wallace calculated the political weight of their causes and effects differently. In the years to follow and for years to come, however, racial concerns and problems were excised from the center point of the national political discourse on crime and criminal justice.

All-American Crime

The first major step parties took toward de-racializing crime policymaking was to nationalize its imagery and, in doing so, decouple the nation's race problem from its crime problem. As long as minority communities were considered to have a unique stake in the fight against crime, their concerns about effective and balanced law enforcement would be at or near the center stage of criminal justice policymaking. This equation changed during the late 1960s. The geopolitical scope of the crime problem was expanded, the result of which was the crime policy process took in a larger number and variety of citizen interests. The nationalization of crime made it extremely difficult, if not impossible, for lawmakers to justifiably focus more intently on the plight of racial minority communities when crafting criminal justice policy. Every Americans' interest was at stake. There were no unique ramifications for minorities. The shift toward a racially neutral approach to crime-fighting is evident, at first glance, from politicians having abandoned rhetoric that honed in on the plight of minorities in crime politics, for terminology and imagery capturing a nonspecific, generalized conception of the impact of crime. The new imagery and language of crime was embraced in equal measure on both sides of the aisle. Both signaled the expanded conception of the geopolitical scope of crime. Both invoked political messaging that highlighted the dangers of crime on a "nationwide," "society," "country," "coast-to-coast," and "American" scale. Crime was no longer a chiefly black American problem it was an "All-American" problem.

The year 1968 marks the key turning point in this evolution. Following that year, the instances in which the racial dynamics of crime and justice were ignored far outweighed and outnumbered those in which they were noted in national crime policy discussions. The overriding post-1968 pattern was one marked by a shift away from segmentation of crime along racial dimensions. Republicans took the lead in nationalizing crime politics. Their 1968 platform reveals that, as far as Republicans were concerned, violent crime and crime-fighting did not have any distinctive effects in minority nor urban communities. Lawlessness was an issue of national proportions, one that was "crumbling the foundations of American society." Republicans pledged a national campaign to undo the consequences of the Johnson administration having purportedly "ignored the danger signals of our rising crime rates." The campaign would amount to an "all-out, federal-state-local crusade against crime" and include a "vigorous nation-wide drive against trafficking in narcotics and dangerous drugs."

The idea that crime was spreading rapidly throughout the country was asserted again in the defining section of the party's 1972 plan for governance, the preamble. It stated: "When our Administration took office, a mood of lawlessness was spreading rapidly, undermining the legal and moral foundations of society. We moved at once to stop violence in America." Republicans' increased emphasis on the federal government obligation is also telling. At a time when the party pressed for a return to traditional federalism in other policy areas,[25] it nonetheless promised "greatly increased Federal aid to State and local law enforcement agencies across the country." It further pledged to continue "vigorous support of local police and law enforcement agencies, as well as Federal law enforcement agencies." Later, the 1976 Republican platform likewise emphasized, the "*American* people have been subjected to an intolerable wave of violent crime" (emphasis added). In neither the 1972 nor the 1976 Republican platform was there any emphasis on race in connection with crime. Rather, the 1972 platform highlighted "the impact of crime in America cuts across racial, geographic and economic lines."

Democrats upped the ante following the 1960s by promising a nation-wide campaign against what they came to label an "urgent national priority." It was a departure from the party's norm. In his 1964 State of the Union Address, President Lyndon B. Johnson linked his remarks about the establishment of the Department of Housing and Urban Development to his recognition of crime as a unique concern of urban areas. Although the speech included an isolated reference to crime as national, Johnson underscored his primary concerns about crime were tied specifically to the city. He averred: "In our urban areas the central problem today is to protect and restore man's satisfaction in belonging to a community where he can find security." He then proceeded to lay out specific crime-control programs as he elaborated his plans for urban renewal.

However, by the 1970s, Democrats became just as unequivocally nationalist in their orientation toward crime policy as their counterparts. Although the "States, Counties and Cities" plank of 1976 noted "the dis-orders of the 1960s were caused by the deteriorating conditions of life in our urban centers," it declared in the very next sentence "many of these same problems plagued rural America as well." The "Law Enforcement and Law Observance" section addressed the "raging and unchecked growth of crime" and claimed that "outside the big cities the crime rate is growing even faster, so that suburbs, small towns and rural areas are no longer secure havens." Finally and bluntly: "we declare the control of crime is an urgent national priority and pledge the efforts of the Democratic party to insure that the federal government act effectively to reverse these trends and to be an effective partner to the cities and states in a well-coordinated war on crime."

Both parties pressed forward with their race neutral approach to crime policy during the 1980s. However, added to their respective strategies during this period were ever bolder position statements regarding the detrimental effects of crime across the country. Republicans promised in 1980 to address the "real problems that face Americans in their neigh-borhoods day by day – deterioration and urban blight, dangerous streets and violent crime that make millions of Americans ... fearful in their own neighborhoods and prisoners in their own homes." They criticized Washington in 1984 for playing "fast and loose" with law enforcement, producing an "epidemic of crime," among other things. Democrats put a similarly alarmist spin on crime by the 1980s. Their 1984 "Crime" subsection asserted, "no problem has worried Americans more persistently over the past 20 years than the problem of crime." Even the six-and-a-half page 1988 platform made clear, "illegal drugs pose a direct threat to the security of our nation from coast to coast, invading our neighborhoods, classrooms, homes and communities large and small."

The march toward nationalization reached a steady enough pace by the 1990s that racial concerns had all but disappeared from the mainstream debate on crime and crime policy. Such concerns effectively took a back seat to crime. Republicans said as much in 1992 by contending, "violent crime is the gravest threat to our way of life." As to just how important crime was on the overall Republican agenda, the 1996 platform pointedly labeled violent crime and drugs as two of the "four deadly threats facing" the country in the early years of the twenty-first century, alongside terrorism and international organized crime." Democrats were no less emphatic. They declared in 1992: "Crime is a relentless danger to our communities. Over the last decade, crime has swept through our country at an alarming rate." In his 1994 State of the Union Address, Clinton said that "every day the national peace is shattered by crime" and asserted, "the problem of violence is an American problem."[26] And while Democrats' assessment of crime levels changed as of 1996, their perception of the national dimensions did not. The "Fighting Crime" plank bragged, "four years ago, crime in America seemed intractable," but "in city after city and town after town, crime rates are finally coming down."

In 2000, even as Democrats praised the Clinton administration's success in lowering the crime rate, they continued to espouse the notion that crime was all of America's problem in equal measure. The "Progress" plank said that eight years ago, "many citizens had come to accept the idea that America's best days were behind her: that crime, welfare, teen births, divisiveness and responsibility would continue to rise," but because of the Democratic Party "America is not just better off, it is better." The tragedy of 9/11 did little to challenge the race-neutral conception of crime on the Democratic side of the aisle. They said in 2004 that "while terrorism poses an especially menacing threat to our nation, a strong America must remain vigilant against the source of homegrown crime as well." In 2008 Democrats' "Metropolitan and Urban Policy" plank made mention of the importance of "public safety" concerns confronting cities, suggesting a return to recognition of the special implications of crime for urban communities where minorities are disproportionally concentrated. However, even this reference was explicitly tied to national security. The only other city-specific, explicit mention of "fighting crime" was in connection with New Orleans and the Gulf Coast.

Democrats clung to the notion that crime was fundamentally indiscriminate even in 2008. The amount of political capital they expended on crime decreased significantly by this point. Still, it was of such national importance to the party in 2008 as to be included among the concerns raised in the platform's defining section, the preamble. Underscored there was the need to "support our communities as they work to save their residents from the violence that plagues our streets" and that "every American ... should have the chance to ... live in safe surroundings." The balance of the platform followed suit with repeated reference to "communities," "our neighborhoods," and commentary on violence as it related to "real human needs" – not especially communities of color. Although there were signs of change at the margins in 2012 as well, still a nationalist bent grounded Democrats' core perspective on crime. For the first time in decades they explicitly acknowledged communities of color were uniquely impacted by crime. They remarked: "We understand the disproportionate effects of crime, violence, and incarceration on communities of color and are committed to working with those communities to find solutions."

That this statement was offered at the very tail end of a much lengthier treatise on the importance of universal crime policies, that it was offered without any elaboration and without any specific policy commitments makes it difficult to claim that Democrats switched to a color-conscious crime-fighting strategy in 2012. Nor was the party's plan to revitalize cities and metropolitan areas expressly tied to its plan for public safety, justice, and crime prevention. As in the past, when laying out their plans for public safety and crime prevention in 2012, Democrats continued to invoke nationalist catchphrases, such as "our neighborhoods," "our communities," "making citizens safer," and the like. Still, their express recognition of the racial dimensions of crime – however isolated and underdeveloped – constituted a noteworthy departure from a nearly forty-five-year trend of colorblind crime-fighting by Democrats.

Republicans, on the other hand, remained steadfast and unmoved in their belief that crime was an omnipresent threat well into the new millennium. In 2000, the party remarked that "most Americans over the age of fifty remember a time when streets and schoolyards were safe, doors unlocked, windows unbarred." The "Justice and Safety" plank concluded, "That world is gone, swept away in the social upheaval provoked by the welfare, drug, and crime policies of the 1960s and later." Their argument in 2004 was that "prosecution of people who violate the peace of communities" was necessary to ensure "all Americans have an opportunity to build better lives." Their "Protecting Our Rights, Fighting Criminals, and Supporting Victims" plank in 2004 endorsed the right of "law-abiding citizens throughout the country to own firearms in their homes for self defense."

The war on terrorism did not generate fundamental adjustments to politicians' assertions about the grave national risks posed by domestic crime. Instead, international terrorism was merged together with domestic crime, particularly in regard to drugs. Republicans said in 2008: "an age of terrorism, drug cartels, and criminal gangs" allowed millions to remain in the country and pose "grave risks to the sovereignty of the United States and the security of its people," and they repeated essentially the same in 2012. The "Ridding the Nation of Criminal Street Gangs" section declared, "Gang violence is a growing problem, not only in urban areas but in many suburbs and rural communities." The "Continuing the Fight against Illegal Drugs" section asserted, "drug addiction and abuse hits all segments of American society." The only distinction it drew concerned the concentration of crime in the District of Columbia, noting "some of the most crime-ridden neighborhoods in the country are blocks from the Department of Justice." As if safety were a pivotal concern for all Americans, the 2012 Republican platform defined the "American Dream" as "a decent place to live, a safe place to raise kids, a welcoming place to retire."

It is critical to understand, moreover, that as the two major parties re-branded crime as an All-American problem from the late 1960s onward, the reality was that crime itself never went "national." It never ceased to be a distinctively urban and black-American problem, something illustrated by statistical data on the actual geographic and racial distribution of violent crime. Violent crime rates in urban areas easily surpassed those anywhere else in the country throughout much of the 1960–2012 period. While crime rose throughout the country following the 1960s, it did not spread. The rising crime rates were chiefly problematic for inner city communities, insofar as it was there that crime was already experienced at above national rates. It was already more of a worry for people living in these neighborhoods than it was for those

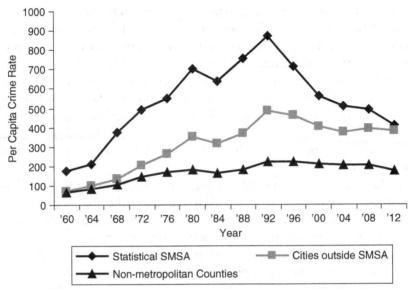

FIGURE 6.1. Geographic Distribution of Violent Crime: Rate,
1960–2012 (Rates Per 100,000 Persons Age 12+).

living beyond city lines. So it was there that crime became even more worrisome. Furthermore, the steepest increase in crime during the late 1960s occurred in urban areas. To the extent there was a newly emerging crime crisis tangential to the absolute increase in crime during that time, then, it was a crisis that mainly impacted urban communities. So, as political leaders embraced a nationalist perspective on crime, crime not only remained segmented along geographic lines but became even more so.

The statistical data from the FBI's *Uniform Crime Reports* (UCR) depicted in Figure 6.1[27] provide an approximate gauge of the geography of crime from 1960 to 2012. It shows the distributional tendency of violent crime remained relatively constant up until the 1990s, with urban communities consistently experiencing higher levels of violent crime than nonurban communities. Viewed from a national angle, moreover, large cities also accounted for the bulk of violent crime in the United States. As such, they were burdened with a greater concentration of crime than that confronting nonurban communities, and they were also burdened with the bulk of all American crime. As much is revealed by the data in Figure 6.2,[28] showing the vast majority of all violent crime offenses in the United States took place in urban areas. According to annual publications of the UCR, the preponderant share of property crimes too were

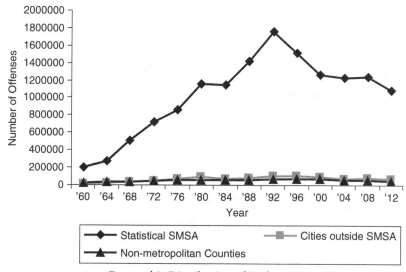

FIGURE 6.2. Geographic Distribution of Violent Crime: Number, 1960–2012.

consistently committed in urban areas. Not shown in the figure are UCR data that pinpoint the inner city in particular, especially the nation's largest cities, as the main locus of America's violent crime problem.

The fact that violent and property crime wearied urban and especially inner city communities more than other areas compounded its dire implications for racial minorities. This is because one of the central demographic shifts of the late 1960s was increased concentration of minorities in the inner city.[29] The re-segregation of minorities in the inner city following the 1960s effectively buttressed minorities' stake in the problems confronting the inner city – most notably, crime.

Supplementary to the data on the geographic containment of crime to communities where minorities mostly resided is more direct evidence of its persistent racial dimensions, as shown in Figure 6.3.[30] The figure establishes it was the racial and ethnic minority segments in the country that consistently suffered more from violent crime than their nonminority counterparts. To borrow the language of the 1980 Republican party platform as applied to Americans at large, it was actually minorities who were comparatively more "fearful in their own neighborhoods and prisoners in their own homes." Thus, their communities had more of an interest in the fight against crime than any other, whether in the context of urban crime policymaking or national crime policymaking. What is

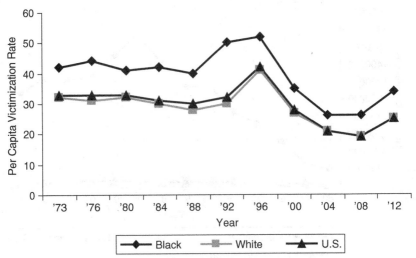

FIGURE 6.3. Violent Crime Victimization Rates, by Race, United States, 1973–2012 (Rates Per 100,000 Persons Age 12+).
Note: Data in figure exclude homicides.

more, blacks bore the brunt of the very worst of violent crime in the United States and did so throughout the period in focus. One could argue that the racialized nature of life-threatening crime was glaringly obvious for any who cared to notice. Homicide rates make unequivocally clear it was black lives that were put in greatest jeopardy by the increased crime rates. Figure 6.4[31] demonstrates that at no point during the more than thirty-year time period shown did the murder of whites approximate the murder of blacks. The rate at which blacks were killed was always between five and seven times greater than the rate at which whites were killed. The rate of black homicides likewise superseded the national homicide rate, by far.

All in all, the hard facts about the geographic and racial distribution of crime debunk the political imagery of crime as an increasingly "national" problem. Contrary to the 1972 Republican party platform claim that "a mood of lawlessness was spreading rapidly," the primary stronghold of crime remained anchored in minority communities. At the time, it actually was not "spreading" beyond the boundaries of inner-city and minority neighborhoods. The same factual data defy also the 1972 Democratic party platform's description of crime as an emerging "urgent national priority" that cut "across racial, geographic and economic lines." Finally and relatedly, Republican attacks on street gangs as one of the primary

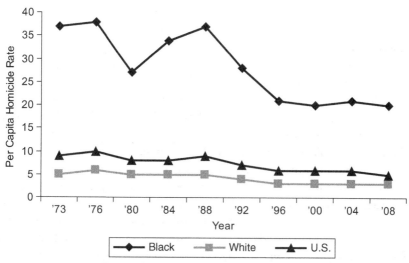

FIGURE 6.4. Homicide Victimization Rates, by Race, United States,
1976–2008 (Rates Per 100,000 Persons).

mediums through which violent crime spread was equally unfounded, not only because crime was actually contained geographically, but also because it was never as randomized as political leaders portended.

The worst of violent crime was largely a function of individualized circumstances, more precisely, a function of one's inner circle. Recall that Republican's 2008 platform referred to an "age of criminal gangs." And their 2012 platform contained a subsection titled "Ridding the Nation of Criminal Street Gangs," which asserted, "gang violence is a growing problem, not only in urban areas but in many suburbs and rural communities." The reality is, neither gangs nor any other organizational mechanism comprised the nonexistent national crime epidemic. As much is suggested by data from the FBI'S Supplementary Homicide Reports. They show lethal gang violence was substantially more circumscribed than politicians proclaimed.[32] Gangs accounted for a mere 1 percent of homicides in 1980 and less than 6 percent as late as 2008. According to data for 1980–2008, the overwhelming majority, fully 80 percent, of homicides during the period were committed by those familiar to the victim, namely nonstrangers, such as acquaintances, spouses, intimate partners, and family members.[33]

Because alarmist assertions about crime "spreading" beyond urban and minority community borders lacked a strong factual base, so too the decoupling of race and crime in the political process also lacked a rational basis, as the politics principle suggests is often the case in regard to policy making. Had crime-fighting Republicans and Democrats acknowledged the continued significance of race in the fight against crime during the late 1960s, 1970s, and 1980s, racial justice advocates might well have had a meaningful say in the development of "law and order" strategies at the ground level, so to speak. Had the crime fighters stayed attuned to the glaring realities of race and crime, they might have fashioned appropriately tailored anti-crime policies that were, on balance, more helpful than damaging to black communities. The manner in which criminal laws were enforced might well have been sufficiently fine-tuned as to actually reduce crime and not further exacerbate longstanding tensions between police and black communities. Instead, crime was re-branded a "national" problem indiscriminately ravaging neighborhoods throughout the country – white neighborhoods no less than black ones. The result was that federal crime policies were crafted to address the alleged national dimensions of crime in a colorblind fashion and with little regard for the racial ramifications of their policy choices.

Victims' Rights, Criminal Rights, Not Black Rights

Notwithstanding politicians' hype about the nationwide destructive impact of crime, at least in theory, there was still room to take into account the likely racial fallout of a heavy-handed approach to tackling crime. The two considerations were not mutually exclusive of one another. Both parties could have aimed to strike a balance between a commitment to tougher criminal justice and a commitment to racially balanced justice. Instead, both chose to embark on a course of action that pitted the two aims against one another. The victims' rights counterrevolution took the wind out of demands for fair and balanced treatment of the criminally accused, a good portion of whom were blacks. It made both the racial justice and the criminal rights agendas appear to suggest that progressives cared more about hardened, murderous predators than the victims upon whom they ostensibly preyed.

It bears mentioning the devaluation of black defendants' rights in crime policymaking was not for lack of persistent effort on the part of justice advocates. They pressed for change decades before and after the ascendance of victims' rights. In fact, organized demands for protection of the constitutional-legal rights of black defendants stretch over nearly a century. They began with efforts to hold law enforcement officers accountable for their part in mob lynchings of blacks, efforts which extended from the late thirties through the first half of the twentieth century. Seven presidents petitioned Congress to pass anti-lynching laws, and nearly 200 anti-lynching bills were introduced in Congress.[34] Two of the earliest, the 1918 and 1922 Dyer anti-lynching proposals, sought to criminalize law enforcement officers' failure to protect blacks from lynching and make it a felony subject to imprisonment, a $5000 fine, or both.[35] Although none of these reform efforts were successful, the cause gained enough momentum to garner a foothold in both major parties. The first time race ever appeared on both the Democratic and Republican national party platforms, in 1940, was directly tied to a call for anti-lynching legislation.[36]

The call for unbiased policing adjusted to changing times and circumstances during the fifties and early 1960s and without dodging the basic fact that much of the systemic bias was fundamentally racial in nature. This, even as the criminal rights revolution spearheaded by the Warren Court during the 1960s called attention to a host of other improprieties plaguing the criminal justice system (e.g., poor prison conditions). The push for racial fairness in criminal justice became much more direct and more explicit over time as well. Democrats' 1980 party platform acknowledged "ethnic, racial and other minorities continue to be victims of police abuse, persistent harassment and excessive use of force." It further noted the Community Relations Service of the U.S. Department of Justice had concluded the use of deadly force by police was a major force of racial unrest in the nation at the time. Notably, the platform called for uniform federal guidelines regarding the use of force and the establishment of civil rights units at U.S. attorneys' offices. In fact, the 1980 Democratic platform highlighted, at length, the problems with racialized policing. It concluded: "Minorities in some areas have been discriminated against by such police actions, and we must take action at the federal, state, and local level to prevent that from happening in the future, including ... swift investigation and prosecution of suspected civil rights violations."

By 2000 reform advocates managed to secure a plank within the Democratic party platform wholly dedicated to the problem of racialized policing, titled "Ending Racial Profiling." It asserted "we need to end the unjust practice of racial profiling in America – because it's not only unfair ... it views Americans as members of groups instead of as individuals, and it is just plain shoddy policing." Again in 2004 and 2008, the party's platform outright condemned racial profiling and committed the party to ending the practice at the federal, state, and local levels. In 2012 it pledged: "We will continue to fight inequalities in our criminal justice system" and bragged about the Democrat-controlled Congress's enactment of the 2010 Fair Sentencing Act.[37] Democrats remarked this bill reduced "racial disparities in sentencing for drug crimes." Moreover, racial profiling of blacks by police officers actually proved to be the only major issue in modern crime politics on which segments within the Democratic Party actually took the lead, and on which Republicans followed.

Fourteen years after Democrats condemned racialized policing, Republicans touted the same message in 2004. That year they praised "President Bush for his strong record on civil rights enforcement, and for becoming the first President ever to ban racial profiling by the federal government." In 2008 and 2012, Republicans went further and warned of the need to not allow correctional facilities to "become ethnic or racial battlegrounds" and calling for public authorities to regain control of the nation's correctional institutions, to protect both the guards and the inmates.

That these political endorsements of justice for black defendants were overshadowed – decisively – by the ground swell of support behind the colorblind approach to victims' rights is succinctly conveyed in the remarks of a president who described himself as an occasional target of racial profiling. In 2012, President Barack Obama stopped short of delineating a substantial federal role in the protection of the rights of black suspects. When addressing the Trayvon Martin tragedy in Florida, Obama took the bold step of validating claims of widespread racial profiling by detailing his own experiences with being profiled as a black man. In the same speech, however, President Obama offered only what he described as "a couple of specifics." In actuality, they were a "couple of specifics" that Obama said he was still "bouncing around" with his staff at the time. Before offering them, Obama cautioned: "I know that [Attorney General] Eric Holder is reviewing what happened down there, but I think it's important for people to have some clear expectations here. Traditionally, these are issues of State and local government, the criminal code. And law enforcement is traditionally done at the State and local levels, not at the Federal levels."[38] Translated, this meant no one should expect the federal government to take the lead in officially sensitizing law enforcement to the concerns of black suspects and defendants, even under Obama's watch.

Well before Obama, racial progressives' calls for concrete policy reform were consistently rebuffed by an abundance of caution. Within the party system, they were most often sidestepped or patently ignored throughout the years leading up to 2012. Starting in the late 1960s, racial reformers' voice in national crime politics was effectively muted by the chorus line of politicians who lined up to sing the praise of victims' rights, over and above civil rights and black rights. A racially charged television ad endorsing Republican presidential candidate George H. W. Bush in 1988 symbolized the peak of the victims' rights counter revolution. The ad was an instance in which victims' rights were pitted directly and unabashedly against racial progressivism. The ad featured a menacing mug shot of a black murder convict (Willie Horton) who was sentenced to life without parole and who later committed rape, assault, and burglary while AWOL from a weekend prison furlough program in Massachusetts. Democratic presidential nominee Michael Dukakis was governor of Massachusetts at the time of Horton's release. Jamieson asserts the ad was effective in helping to defeat Dukakis because, "exposed to Horton's face for weeks by the saturation-level PAC campaign, viewers now saw the convicts through the story of Horton."[39]

Known as the "Willie Horton" ad, launch of the commercial was the tail end of a political trend begun in 1968. That was the year Congress enacted the Omnibus Crime Control and Safe Streets Act in response to an expansion of criminal rights facilitated by a series of U.S. Supreme Court rulings under the leadership of Chief Justice Earl Warren. Title II of the Act purposed to overturn the Court's groundbreaking *Miranda v. Arizona* (1966) ruling that prescribed legal protections for those arrested and interrogated by law enforcement officers.[40] Critics denounced *Miranda* as not only an example of courts overstepping their boundaries; they criticized it also as yet another indication that law enforcement concerns had taken a backseat to concerns for the rights of those targeted by law enforcement. The attempted legislative reversal of *Miranda* in June 1968 marked the start of a vigorous campaign against the rights of the criminally accused. It was a campaign necessarily poised to disproportionally disadvantage blacks and the poor, inasmuch as blacks were continually overrepresented among the criminally accused.

As in most other areas of crime politics, here too the Republican Party led the way by pushing for a contraction of criminal rights and expansion of victims' rights. The party stressed the importance of expediting criminal prosecutions and convictions as early as 1968. The same year it also pledged modernization of the federal judicial system to "promote swift, sure justice." In 1972, Republicans bragged about the appointment of Attorneys General with a "keen sense of the rights of both defendants and victims" and called for mandatory sentences for crimes committed with a lethal weapon. Their 1976 policy plan sharpened the party's focus on the rights of victims in the "Right to Privacy," proclaiming,

"The victim of a crime should be treated with compassion and justice. The attacker must be kept from harming others. Emphasis must be on protecting the innocent and punishing the guilty." And as for discrimination concerns, Republicans were unequivocal in asserting discrimination against crime victims was the priority, as opposed to discrimination against minorities: "The criminal justice system must be more vigilant in preventing rape, eliminating discrimination against the victim and dealing with the offenders."

The Republican Party distinguished itself from the Democratic Party during the 1980s, in part, by contending there was an imbalance of power between crime victims, on the one hand, and criminal defendants and convicts, on the other. With some success, they used the victims' rights mantra as a political weapon against Democratic opponents. It was folded into a larger strategy that enabled Republicans to control the White House in 1980, 1984, and 1988, the Senate from 1980 to 1986, and soon both houses of Congress in 1995.[41] Stressing the need to harshly punish criminals, Republicans' 1980 "Crime" plank stated: "Just as vital to efforts to stem crime is the fair but firm and speedy application of criminal penalties." One of its strongest attacks came in its 1984 "Crime" plank, where the party asserted the "Carter-Mondale legal policy had more concern for abstract criminal rights than for the victims of crime.... Republican leadership has redressed that imbalance." The platform went on to detail specific legislative reforms enacted on behalf of crime victims.

On the flip side, Republicans lauded Senate passage of a bill that toughened bail procedures to enable the detention of "dangerous criminals" and narrowed "the overly broad insanity defense." They were just as proud of administration-backed legislation designed to modify the exclusionary rule and curtail what the party described as "abuses by prisoners of federal habeas corpus procedures." In 1988, the Willie Horton phenomenon was used to take yet another swipe at Democrats in the national platform, which noted: "Republicans oppose furloughs for those criminals convicted of a first degree murder and others who are serving a life sentence without possibility of parole."

The consolidation of Republican power in the Senate and House following the 1994 midterm elections added to the momentum behind the press for more victims' rights and fewer defendant rights. Weeks before the election, the party laid out a ten-point plan for governance in what was titled the "Republican Contract with America." Among the ten initiatives pledged were: "an anti-crime package including stronger truth-in- sentencing, 'good faith' exclusionary rule exemptions, effective death penalty provisions."[42] The party's legislative initiatives on this front were already wide-ranging. Republicans claimed in 1992 to have repeatedly proposed legislation to "end the legal loopholes that let criminals go free." This, they asserted, while "Democrats actually voted to create more loopholes for vicious thugs and fewer protections for victims of crime and have opposed mandatory restitution for victims." The drum beat continued unabated through 1996 as the platform reminded voters "the new Republican majorities in the House and Senate fought back with legislation that ends frivolous, costly, and unnecessarily lengthy death-row appeals." Last, a constitutional amendment to protect the rights of victims became the flag post of a stealthy pro–victims' rights agenda. In 1996, 2000, and 2004, Republicans proposed such an amendment.

The new millennium ushered in a brand of victims' rights politics that was barely distinguishable from what came before. Although in 2008 and 2012 Republicans articulated for the first time in years a deliberate plan for helping juvenile delinquents and prisoners, the very same plat-forms were nonetheless anchored in the party's core belief regarding the one-to-one competition between the rights of victims and the rights of the criminally accused. The balance of their approach in the first decade of the millennium was on par with that of previous decades. The 2000 platform reminded voters that the Republican Congress had "stopped federal judges from releasing criminals because of overcrowding, made it harder to file lawsuits about prison conditions, and, with a truth-in-sentencing law, pushed states to make sure violent felons actually do time." Their reductionist stance toward criminal rights persisted through 2008, when they expressed the belief that "national experience over the past twenty years has shown that vigilance, tough yet fair prosecutors, meaningful sentences, protection of victims' rights, and limits on judicial discretion protect the innocent by keeping criminals off the streets." In 2008 and 2012, Republicans continued to express several telling posi-tions, including opposition to parole for what they termed "dangerous *or* [emphasis added] repeat felons," support for mandatory sentencing and mandatory life imprisonment in various types of cases and support for barring "criminals … from seeking monetary damages for injuries they incur while committing a crime."

That Republicans considered juveniles no less deserving of criminal punishment than adults was also reaffirmed. The 2008 platform declared: "Individuals, including juveniles, who are repeat offenders *or* [emphasis added] who commit serious crimes need to be prosecuted and punished." Both the 2008 and 2012 platforms harkened back to a call from President

Reagan's Task Force on Victims of Crime for a constitutional amendment to secure the rights of crime victims. The notion that criminal rights and victims' rights were directly pitted against one another is conveyed in the following from the 2008 platform: "Innocent victims ... have far fewer rights than the accused. We call on Congress to correct this imbalance by sending to the states for ratification a constitutional amendment to protect the rights of crime victims."

The single most racially charged aspect of the criminal justice system – capital punishment – received more vigorous support from Republicans in 2008 and 2012 than in earlier years. Their 2008 platform outright condemned the U.S. Supreme Court decisions prohibiting capital sentencing of juveniles and mentally retarded, and in emphatic terms: "We object to the Court's unwarranted interference in the administration of the death penalty in this country for the benefit of savage criminals whose guilt is not at issue." It went on to propose restrictions on federal review of death sentences so as to prevent "delaying tactics by defense attorneys"; called for expedited review of death sentences imposed for murdering a police officer; and for permitting retrial of the penalty phase of a defendant's trial in the absence of a unanimous verdict.

By 1992, it was apparent Democrats too had whole-heartedly joined the anti-criminal defendant rights/pro-victims' rights bandwagon and, in doing so, simultaneously abandoned their own prior position on the rights of the criminally accused. Before they turned this corner, Democrats had for years bragged about their efforts to protect the rights of poor defendants to bail and legal counsel, specifically in their 1964 party platform. Then in 1968, Democrats pledged to "rehabilitate and supervise convicted offenders, to return offenders to useful, decent lives, and to protect the public against habitual criminals." Significantly, in 1972, they warned about the dangers of short-term remedies to rising crime rates, noting: "We can protect all people without undermining fundamental liberties." The 1972 platform also warned about the "ever-present danger that alarm will turn to panic, triggering short-cut remedies that jeopardize hard-won liberties." And while Democrats announced support for "major reform of the criminal justice system," in 1976, they opposed "any legislative efforts to introduce repressive and anti-civil libertarian measures in the guide of reform of the criminal code." As late as 1980, Democrats called for a "criminal code which meets the very real concerns about protecting civil liberties." They attended also to victims' rights during the balance of the 1980s, by way of support for federal assistance to victims of crime and "restitution by the perpetrators of crime." However, they did so openly mindful of both sides of the equation, stating in their 1984 platform: "We support fundamental reform of the sentencing process so that offenders who commit similar crimes receive similar penalties."

For Democrats, the take-away lesson from the racially charged "Willie Horton" style attacks of 1988 and later was "to never again be outdone" in this sphere. As chair of the U.S. Senate Judiciary Committee in 1990, then-Senator Joseph Biden reportedly said "one of my objectives, quite frankly, is to lock Willie Horton up in jail."[43] His party's messaging was eventually brought into closer alignment with Republicans'. In 1992, Democrats called for a variety of sentencing and punishment options, including boot camps for first time offenders, and they championed victim-impact statements and restitution, they said, to ensure crime victims were not lost in the complexities of the criminal justice system.

The Clinton years in the White House mark, in many ways, the point at which scaling back on criminal rights, due process, and federal crime prevention became a bipartisan effort. At the start of the new Republican-controlled Congress in 1994, Clinton called on Congress to "find ways as quickly as possible to set aside partisan differences and pass a strong, smart, tough crime bill."[44] Although his 1994 State of the Union Address spoke of the importance of prevention and programming, what his administration actually pursued (with vigor) was an enforcement-centered crime bill. Many of the preventative programs were stripped in bargaining sessions. Clinton would later brag primarily about the "get tough" elements of the 1994 crime bill. In his own words: "we passed a very tough crime bill: longer sentences, "three strikes and you're out," almost 60 new capital punishment offenses, more prisons, more prevention, 100,000 more police."[45] The bipartisan support that enabled passage of the bill was garnered largely because of the Clinton administration's intimate involvement in the proceedings. According to a *Congressional Quarterly Almanac* article, House Democratic whips "set up a command post in a room off the chamber with an open telephone line for Clinton to speak to wavering lawmakers."[46]

The efforts of the Clinton administration added a bipartisan stamp of approval to the conception of criminal rights as a virtual affront to victims' rights, further solidifying the triumph of victims' rights over criminal rights. With Clinton at the helm, Democrats offered the strongest language to date in their 1996 "Fighting Crime" plank; it bore a striking resemblance to Republicans' earlier platforms. Just as Clinton had in 1994, the Democratic Party as a whole two years later likewise touted its version of a "law and order" strategy. Like Clinton, the rest of the party, in lockstep fashion, bragged about having "established the death penalty for nearly 60 violent crimes" and for enacting "a law to limit appeals." It likewise gloated "President Clinton made three-strikes-you're-out the law of the land, to ensure that most dangerous criminals go to jail for life, with no chance of parole." Democrats also called on states to meet President Bill Clinton's challenge to guarantee serious violent criminals serve at least 85 percent of their sentence. And, as if to erase any doubt about its equally impassioned support for victims, Democrats officially announced the party's support for "the President's call for a constitutional amendment to protect the rights of victims."

By the start of the millennium, the difference between Democrats and Republicans in regard to reducing criminal rights protections was, for all practical purposes, a difference without a real distinction. The 2000s platforms called for DNA testing, effective assistance of counsel, and post-conviction reviews in death penalty cases. However, the very same platforms carefully underscored what was Democrats' overriding commitment to victims' rights, as well as the belief they shared with Republicans regarding the one-to-one competition between the rights of victims and the rights of the criminally accused. In 2000 they asserted: "We will put the rights of victims and families first again," intimating yet again there was a zero-sum game between the rights of victims and those of the criminally accused. Democrats also appeared to harken back to the subliminal message of Republicans' infamous Willie Horton television ad of 1988. That ad denigrated early prison release programs, while a 1988 companion to the Willie Horton television commercial ad depicted a line of convicted felons walking through a revolving door. In a strikingly similar fashion, Democrats' 2000 platform included a plank titled "Ending the Revolving Door." It stated: "We should impose strict supervision on those who have just been released on parole." Again in the 2004 platform's Crime and Violence subsection: "We support the rights of victims to be respected, to be heard, and to be compensated."

Election year 2012 witnessed both parties embrace a slightly more complex stance toward prisoner rights, while yet clinging to their core conception of an inherent tension between victims' rights and criminal rights. New in 2012 was the idea that crime reduction was linked to prisoner rehabilitation, that is, a rehabilitative approach was as much a matter of public safety as prisoner rights. Democrats' 2008 criminal justice plank explained the party's conception of "being smart on crime" entailed not only "being tough on violent crime." It encompassed also "getting tough on the root causes of crime" by preventing crime and reducing recidivism through various prisoner reentry initiatives, such as prison-to-work programs. These programs, they argued in 2012, were "making citizens safer and saving the taxpayers money." Democrats also touted the creation of the Federal Interagency Reentry Council in 2011. Republicans followed suit but were even more explicit. Their 2012 platform demanded prisons do more to help those incarcerated, noting prisons "should attempt to rehabilitate and institute proven prisoner reentry systems to reduce recidivism and future victimization."

Notwithstanding these marginal revisions to the playbook, where black interests are concerned, such adjustments arguably constituted a case of "too much, too little too late" when weighed against the aggressive bipartisan assault on criminal rights that was waged throughout the years leading up to 2012. It was an offensive to which black citizens and defendants were more susceptible than any other group. Blacks were left inordinately exposed to not only heavy-handed law enforcement but to criminal justice impropriety as well. Serving as proof, in the first instance, was the fact that racial minorities were primarily the defendants in landmark cases in which the U.S. Supreme Court found evidence of constitutionally suspect behavior on the part of law enforcement.[47] Additionally, minority civilians, arrestees, and convicts more frequently reported the use of excessive verbal and physical force on the part of police officers during various types of police-citizen encounters.[48]

Blacks' greater vulnerability to the rollback of rights of those deemed suspects by the police is evidenced, secondly, by the racial gap in arrest trends across the same time period. These data establish they were consistently overrepresented among the criminally accused. As a result, they were disproportionally in need of robust defendant rights and, thus, inordinately disadvantaged by the curtailment of criminal rights. The *Uniform Crime Reports* data in Figure 6.5[49] help illuminate politicians' lack of sensitivity toward the racial dimensions of criminal defendant rights and, more to the point, blacks' unique vulnerability to their indifference. Throughout the period shown, blacks were arrested at rates substantially greater than those of whites. Their arrest rate actually peaked during the 1990s, when Democrats became a full partner with Republicans in rolling back the rights of the criminally accused.

In effect, when Democrats and Republicans began reading from the same page regarding defendant rights versus victims' rights during the 1990s, the preceding three decades of arrest trend data establish that they did so mostly at the expense of blacks. In legal and political terms, both parties helped to plant firmly in the landscape of American crime

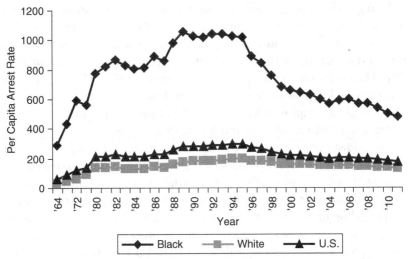

FIGURE 6.5. Arrest Rate for Violent Crime Offenses, by Race, United States, 1964–2011 (Rates Per 100,000 Residential Population).

politics the idea that fighting for the rights of black defendants was synonymous with turning one's back on the victims of crime. The problem that concerned both parties was not blacks' rights within criminal justice but victims' rights instead.

Special Victims in Criminal Justice Policymaking

A third major development in the reconceptualization of criminal justice goals and concerns was the construction of a new set of stakeholders in the crime policy process. Women, children, and the elderly came to be identified as the most vulnerable victims of crime. The guiding principle was, if any demographic needed special attention as crime victims, it was these groups. They were the new faces of victimology. Consequently, politicians were chiefly committed to making the justice system more attuned to the circumstances of these demographic groups and ensuring they received justice – not so much racial minorities. The plight of black victims of crime did not figure prominently, even though they made up a disproportionate share of criminal victims. As such, the newly emergent politics of special victims represented another critical area in which blacks took a back seat to others, in a manner of speaking. There were differences in the degree to which each party singled out the new "special" victims for special attention. Republicans rallied more readily, more frequently, and more vigorously on their behalf than Democrats. However, neither party carried the mantel on behalf of excessive black victimization. Neither envisaged blacks nor other racial and ethnic minorities "special" victims of crime. Neither cared much about the fact that any criminal justice policy strategies and enactments would (or would not) impact disproportionately victimized minority populations more than nonminorities.

Once again, Republicans led the way in re-branding crime and reconceiving which segments in society were chiefly in harm's way. The move in this direction began in earnest during the 1980s. Then, Republicans proclaimed, "dangerous streets and violent crime ... make millions of Americans, especially senior citizens, fearful in their own neighborhoods and prisoners in their own homes." The party asserted in 1984: "We are combating insidious crime against the elderly, many of whom are virtual prisoners in their own homes for fear of violence" and "we support local initiatives to fight crime against the elderly." By 2000, the elderly were such a well-established protected category that the Republican platform reflected back to a time when "the elderly did not live in fear." It was also clear by the 1990s that women and children filled out the remainder of the class of special crime victims. The 1992 Republican platform declared violence "threatens everyone, but especially the very young, the elderly, the weak."

The 1996 platform singled out women. It observed: "Women in America know better than anyone about the randomness and ruthlessness of crime. It is a shameful, national disgrace that nightfall has become synonymous with fear for so many of America's women." The same messaging helped define the party line in 2000, when, once again, as far as Republicans were concerned, "crimes against women and children demand an emphatic response." By 2012, Republicans devoted less space to highlighting the victimization of women, children, and the elderly, but it was a difference in degree more so than in kind. Meaning, at no point did they shift away from their protectionism of these designated special victims, nor did they shift toward recognition of minorities as most vulnerable to criminal victimization.

The political capital devoted to the country's youth was unmatched by that expended on any other group. Little to none of that capital was devoted to black youth specifically. Instead, all the children of America were the poster child for crime politics. The 1980 Republican platform pledged in its "Youth" plank, "a society which is safe and free." In 1988, it was stated further, "schools must be models of order and decorum, not jungles of drugs and violence." Years later the "Principles of the 1996

Republican Platform" section again declared, "Violent crime has turned our homes into prisons, our streets and schoolyards into battlegrounds"; it warned of "danger in schoolyards," and it noted "American children should be able to expect to "attend a safe school." The Republican message about child victims changed after the 1990s to underscore child pornography and missing children more than in previous years, but continued as late as 2004 to stress the need for "rescuing the youngest victims of crime." Following 2004, Republicans would choose the most heinous of crimes as the focal point of their concern for child safety. The party endorsed mandatory prison sentencing for offenses against children in 2008 and 2012 and a mandatory life sentence specifically for child rape – as opposed to all rapes. Election year 2012 also brought a Republican call for a national registry specifically for child murderers – as opposed to all murderers. The 2012 Republican platform declared: "We commit to do whatever it takes, using all the tools of innovative technology, to thwart those who would prey upon our children."

To the extent that any particular subgroup within the youth population commanded special attention from Republicans, it was not minority children. They asserted instead in 1988 that, in connection with their commitment to safer neighborhoods and to full prosecution for child abuse and exploitation, "children in poverty deserve our strongest support." In a similar vein, Republicans complained four years later in 1992 it was "a travesty that some American children have to sleep in bathtubs for protection from stray bullets." The 2000 platform reiterated, "children in poor communities have paid the highest price in the threat of addiction and the daily reality of violence." A slightly different chord was struck by Republicans in 2008, when they expressed concern for the children of prisoners, by noting that "breaking the cycle of crime begins with the children of those who are incarcerated." Important for this discussion is that the party never reached a point of special concern about the disproportional impact of crime specifically on children of color.

In time, Democrats joined Republican politicians in channeling their attentiveness primarily toward children, women, and the elderly in the crime policy process, instead of minorities. This conception of "special victims" was not embraced by Democrats until the 1990s. Up to that point, they were mostly focused on domestic violence. Although late to take up the special victims banner, Democrats more than made up for their delay by pushing the envelope even further than Republicans. Democrats' 1996 "Opportunity" section reasoned, "If young people do not have the freedom to learn in safety, they do not have the freedom to learn at all." Accordingly, the party pledged to "do everything [it] can to help families protect their children, especially from dangerous criminals who have made a dark habit of preying on young people." Democrats soon demanded even tougher sanctions than those advocated by Republicans. Their 2000 plank duly titled "Protecting Our Most Vulnerable Citizens" declared in unequivocal terms, "Our most vulnerable deserve special protections." It went on to highlight crimes against the elderly and women, then endorsed enhanced penalties for those who commit crimes against the elderly and women. Notably, Democrats endorsed enhanced sentences for not only those who committed crimes against children but for those who committed crimes simply in the *presence* of children too.

The party toned down its special victims rhetoric in 2008 and 2012, but did not abandon it. Much of Democrats' retooling consisted of appending the concerns of children, women, and minorities to other bigger ticket items on the party's agenda, such as health care, gun control, and the so-called Republican war on women's rights and health.[50] Their 2008 stance on children and crime was appended partly to gun control, specifically in the "Firearms" subsection. The balance of their 2008 concern for child safety was linked to signature Democratic social programs. The 2008 urban policy plank pledged to protect "our most vulnerable children ... from violence and neglect" and "keep children off the streets by supporting expanded after-school and summer opportunities." Juvenile crime prevention would be accomplished by "providing transitional training to get jobs, removing tax penalties on married families, and expanding maternity and paternity leave" for their absent fathers. Moreover, the fact that women's safety was merged with health care and women's rights is conveyed, first, in the following pledge in the 2008 platform: "We will expand the Family and Medical Leave Act to reach millions more workers than are currently covered, and we will enable workers to take leave to care for an elderly parent, address domestic violence and sexual assault, or attend a parent-teacher conference." Later, the 2012 subsection titled "Women" proclaimed: "We understand that women's rights are civil rights.... That's why we are committed to violence against women."

For Democrats, racial and ethnic minorities were considered special victims of special crimes only. As opposed to violent and property crime generally, hate crimes were noted as especially relevant to minorities and hence justifiable grounds for focused attention from policymakers and law enforcement. From a practical standpoint, this meant identifiable racial bias and discrimination had to be a precipitating cause of violence against minorities in order for law enforcement to act specifically on their behalf. Conversely, it was unnecessary for children, women, and the elderly to be targets of bias in order for law enforcement to take special steps for their protection; it was enough that they were viewed as uniquely vulnerable to victimization. By 2008 and 2012, moreover, racial and ethnic minorities would come to share their recognition as special victims of special crimes with the lesbian, gay, bisexual, and transgender (LGBT) community. In 2008, the Democratic platform called for passage of the Local Law Enforcement Hate Crimes Prevention Act. In 2012, the act was renamed the "Matthew Shepard and James Byrd Jr. Hate Crimes Prevention Act," a move that made explicit its basic goal of targeting hate crimes against LGBTs as well as racial minorities.

Where the 2012 Democratic platform made mention of the "disproportionate effects of crime, violence, and incarceration on communities of color," as noted earlier, it offered little more. That platform only "committed to working with those communities to find solutions." Whereas concrete promises, such as tougher sanctions, narrowly tailored prevention programing, and targeted law enforcement strategies were articulated on behalf of the new stakeholders in the crime policy process, blacks were still not "special" enough in 2012 as to evoke similarly concrete pledges from Democrats.

On the whole, from the 1980s through 2012, children, women, and the elderly were the face of criminal victimization in America, while the disproportional criminal victimization of minorities went largely unnoticed. The former were so heavily favored that, within a decade of the start of this trend, Congress and state legislatures began labeling crime laws with the names of individual children and women who were victims of crime. It was a way to dramatize the brutality of child murders especially as well as call attention to the need for a more proactive policy approach. Nearly all such laws memorialized the death or abduction of select white children. It was the death of white children that most often moved politicians to funnel their energies in this focused, inventive fashion. Among the laws adopted were the 1994 Jacob Wetterling Act, the AMBER Alert system initiated in 1996 in memory of Amber Hagerman, the 2006 Adam Walsh Child Protection and Safety Act, Megan's laws adopted across the states, and others. Rarely were federal or state special victim laws named after minority children.

Minority children did not evoke a similar regard and sympathy from politicians, at least not enough to become a name brand for anti-crime policies. Yet the reality throughout the period in focus is that, as compared

TABLE 6.1. *Child Victimization Rates: Homicide, by Race, United States, 1976–2008 (Rates Per 100,000 Persons Under Age 5 in Each Group)*

Year	Black	White	B-W Ratio	United States
1976	10.2	2.4	4.3	1.6
1980	9.4	2.4	3.9	2.2
1984	8.1	2.3	3.5	2.0
1988	10.2	2.4	4.4	1.3
1992	9.8	2.4	4.1	1.6
1996	8.9	2.7	3.3	2.2
2000	7.9	2.2	3.6	0.9
2004	6.4	2.3	2.8	1.0
2008	7.2	2.3	3.1	2.3

Note: Data for murder and nonnegligent manslaughter.

to their counterparts, it was black children who were the more likely victims of violent crime in the United States. Black children were always most likely to be murdered. According to the Bureau of Justice Statistics data in Table 6.1,[51] black children's risk of being killed was anywhere from three to over four times greater than that of white children, and almost always above the national average, as well. Whether the focus is on the deaths of small children under the age of five or that of teenagers, the picture that emerges is basically the same. Table 6.2 reveals the streets of America were drastically more unsafe for black teenagers than for white teenagers. Although this is true for both black male and female teenagers, the streets were exponentially more dangerous for black male teenagers. The average of their homicide rates from 1976 to 2008 was nearly seven times greater than that of their white male counterparts.

So, when Republicans declared in 1988 it was "children in poverty that deserved their strongest support," it was actually black children most in need of that support. When Democrats in 2000 declared it was "the most vulnerable that deserved special protection," then as well, it was black children and teenagers who were actually the most vulnerable.

Also in relation to women, moreover, there was a disconnect between the rhetoric of special victimization and the reality of special victimization. Data from the National Crime Victimization Survey show black women were consistently the most preyed upon by violent criminals from the late 1960s onward. As politicians embarked on a generalized message about American women overall needing special attention in the crime policy process, it was actually black women whose safety was chiefly

TABLE 6.2. *Teenage Victimization Rates: Homicide, by Race, Gender, 1976–2008 (Rates Per 100,000 Persons Age 14–17 in Each Group)*

Year	Male		Female	
	Black	White	Black	White
1976	24.2	3.7	6.3	2.1
1980	26.3	5.1	6.8	2.6
1984	18.4	3.5	6.4	2.1
1988	43.4	3.9	7.2	2.2
1992	67.3	9.0	12.8	2.4
1996	52.5	7.9	8.9	2.0
2000	25.8	4.1	4.5	1.4
2004	25.6	4.0	3.7	1.1
2008	31.4	4.5	4.6	1.4[*]

Note:
[*] Estimated from data in *Homicide Trends.*

TABLE 6.3. *Female Victimization Rates: Rape, by Race, United States, 1973–2008 (Rates Per 1,000 Persons Age 12+ in Each Group)*

Year	White	Black	B-W RATIO	United States
1973	1.7	2.6	1.53	1.8
1976	1.2	3.2	2.67	1.4
1980	1.5	1.8	1.20	1.6
1984	1.4	3.3	2.36	1.6
1988	0.9	2.6	2.89	1.2
1992	0.8	1	1.25	0.8
1996	2.3	3.3	1.43	2.3
2000	2.1	2.2	1.05	2.1
2004	1.5	2.7	1.80	1.6
2008	0.6	1.9	3.17	1.3

in harm's way. In addition to data in Table 6.2[52] showing black female teenagers' risk of violent victimization was anywhere from three to six times greater than their counterparts', consider also evidence on rape victimization. Rape statistics are a useful indicator of the level of female versus male criminal victimization in the United States in that women are raped at a rate up to six times that of men.[53] Examining the rape statistics shown in Table 6.3[54] helps us grasp more fully the extent to which black women and women of color generally were in need of special attention from crime policymakers. The data tell us that, for every year shown from 1973 to 2008, black women were victimized at higher rates than white women. In fact, in 1988, the year Republicans used Willie Horton in ways that served to emasculate racial justice advocacy with the example of a white female victim, the racial disparity in female victimization had reached its highest level since 1973, with black female victimization nearly three times greater than that of white women.

The Race-Neutral Drug War

The 1980s War on Drugs arguably dealt a fatal blow to the political significance of racial justice during the period in focus, from 1968 to 2012. The perceived menace of illegal drug use and trafficking forcefully justified not only an all-out war on crime; the so-called drug problem also supplied a powerful rationale for ignoring the distinctive law enforcement experience of minorities. The fight against illicit drugs functioned as an anchor for the modern crime politics trifecta detailed in the foregoing discussion, as follows: they posed a grave threat of national proportion, made unflinching criminal punishment all the more necessary, and put the lives of innocent children in greatest jeopardy. So, it was okay to pursue a course of action that made matters worse for racial minorities. Desperate times called for desperate measures. This reasoning was aided by the fact that crime had already been caricatured years earlier as the gravest threat to the American way of life. Because illegal drugs were successfully portrayed as a root cause of crime, it did not take a huge leap of faith to believe drugs were a threat to the American way of life and to everyone's life, literally. In fact, politicians said as much.

Up against an issue of this magnitude – one that stood to destroy the very essence of all that was America – racial justice concerns stood little chance of slowing, let alone halting the march toward blisteringly punitive anti-drug policies. Like so many American wars and conflicts abroad, declaration of the War on Drugs at home in 1983 was simply official recognition of an offensive already underway. Policymakers' claim that drug crimes threatened to topple the American way of life rested on a political foundation laid well before the 1980s. As such, the 1980s drug war did not emerge out of a vacuum. It was the tail end, not the starting point of the de-racialization of national crime politics that began during the late 1960s. It traversed quite a bit of political terrain before making its way to the top of parties' list of criminal justice concerns demanding attention.

The seeds for President Ronald Reagan's War on Drugs were sown well before he entered the White House. As early as 1971, President Richard M. Nixon forcefully argued the tradeoff between saving America from drugs versus saving vulnerable populations, such as the poor and racial minorities, from undue harm. He declared in a June 17, 1971, press conference: "America's public enemy number one in the United States is drug abuse" and that "in order to fight and defeat this enemy, it is necessary to wage a new, all-out offensive," an offensive he likened then to a war.[55] The same day, President Nixon dismissed the assertion that narcotic addiction was a socioeconomic problem, calling the claim "irrelevant" in light of what he characterized as the "universal" nature of the drug problem.[56] When running for reelection later in 1972, Nixon said the 1960s "brought America's narcotics problem to the epidemic stage."[57] This meant drugs posed an untenable risk for everyone. He made as much explicit in 1973 when he asserted: "Drug abuse is one of the most vicious and corrosive forces attacking the foundations of American society today. It is a major cause of crime and a merciless destroyer of human lives."[58] On October 15, 1972, Nixon claimed his administration had "declared total war against heroin and other illicit drugs."[59]

Nixon's "total war" against drugs led to enactment of the Comprehensive Drug Abuse Prevention and Control Act of 1970, which replaced more than 50 pieces of drug legislation already in place. The new law established a single system of control for the first time in U.S. history.[60] At the heart of the newly established single system was a five-part schedule classifying controlled substances based on dangerousness, potential for abuse and addiction, and medical value. Later, the Office of Drug Abuse Law Enforcement was created to focus on street peddlers. Then in 1973, the main arsenal in the drug war was established, the Drug Enforcement Administration (DEA). The DEA was to serve as the single unified command in the war.

It was during Reagan's two terms in the oval office that the drug war escalated into an offensive conducted on both the domestic and the international front, with enemy targets at home and abroad, drug users no less than drug dealers. Nixon had asserted in a 1973 message to Congress his administration "declared all-out, *global* [emphasis added] war on the drug menace," and then proceeded to emphasize the singular importance of foreign interdiction.[61] Reagan, on the other hand, officially declared the War on Drugs here at home in a January 25, 1983 State of the Union address before a joint session of Congress. He remarked "this administration hereby declares an all-out war on big-time organized crime and the drug racketeers who are poisoning our young people."[62] Again, later in a September 14, 1986, national address, President Reagan declared America as a whole was embroiled in a "war for our freedom," and he called on Americans to mobilize for what he termed a "national crusade."[63] The visual imagery Reagan invoked regarding the domestic front of the war was very powerful. The following is a sampling of how Reagan averred drugs a threat to all things held sacred in America:

The revolution out of which our liberty was conceived signaled an historical call to an entire world seeking hope. Each new arrival of immigrants rode the crest of that hope. They came, millions seeking a safe harbor from the oppression of cruel regimes. They came, to escape starvation and disease. They came, those surviving the Holocaust and the Soviet gulags. They came, the boat people, chancing death for even a glimmer of hope that they could have a new life. They all came to taste the air redolent and rich with the freedom that is ours. What an insult it will be to what we are and whence we came if we do not rise up together in defiance against this cancer of drugs.[64]

The following day, Reagan sent to Congress the "Drug-Free America Act of 1986." It supplied the basic framework for what later became the legislative centerpiece of the 1980s War on Drugs, the Anti-Drug Abuse Act of 1986. Reagan's war would prove to be a massive war. He bragged during the last year of his presidency that the antidrug law enforcement budget had tripled under his watch. Drug convictions more than doubled. Prison sentences were 40 percent longer. Tougher sentencing guidelines were issued. The Sentencing Reform Act was passed in 1984, authorizing asset seizure. The Anti-Drug Abuse Act of 1986 imposed mandatory prison sentences for drug dealers as well as drug users. A host of other anti-drug initiatives were undertaken as well, including the 1988 amendments to the Anti-Drug Abuse Act mandating a minimum five-year sentence for simple possession of crack cocaine.

A key distinction between Reagan's War on Drugs and Nixon's global war is that Reagan was not as apt to distinguish the perils of drug use from those of drug trafficking. Nixon repeatedly highlighted important distinctions between the supply side and the demand side of illegal drug activity, and he constantly advocated a treatment approach for drug users while advancing an enforcement strategy for drug traffickers. In his first major message to Congress on drugs in June 1971 Nixon called for compassion as opposed to condemnation for drug users, characterizing them as victims:

The threat of narcotics among our people ... is a problem which demands compassion, and not simply condemnation, for those who become the victims of narcotics and dangerous drugs. We must try to better understand the confusion and disillusion and despair that bring people, particularly young people, to the use of narcotics and dangerous drugs.[65]

The establishment of the Office for Drug Abuse Prevention in 1971 was the administration's way "to begin dealing decisively with the 'demand' side of the drug abuse problem – treatment and rehabilitation for those who have been drug victims, and preventative programs for drug abusers."[66] He reasoned: "We must rehabilitate the drug user if we are to eliminate drug abuse and all the antisocial activities that flow from drug abuse."[67] In essence, Nixon launched his war in 1971 by committing enormous federal funding to drug abuse prevention and rehabilitation programs. It was under Nixon in 1974 that the Drug Abuse Warning Network (DAWN) was created to monitor the extent of drug abuse in the United States.[68] Nixon signed into law the Narcotic Addict Treatment Act in 1974, when he explained the "need for … education in terms of how our younger people can avoid the problems with either drug abuse or alcoholism in the years ahead."[69]

Nixon's war plan was guided by a particular view of the real enemy in the war on drugs. It was informed, more precisely, by a specific conception of the flow of drug activity. According to this conception, drug trafficking preceded drug use, which necessarily meant enforcement was more appropriately targeted primarily toward drug trafficking. Nixon asked for "additional funds to increase our enforcement efforts to further tighten the noose around the necks of drug peddlers, and thereby loosen the noose around the necks of drug users."[70] This was the original intent behind the Drug Enforcement Administration, according to the 1973 message to Congress explaining the rationale for its establishment. There, Nixon stated directly: "I therefore propose creation of a single, comprehensive Federal agency within the Department of Justice to lead the war against illicit drug *traffic* [emphasis added]."[71] As to the focal point of enforcement activity, here too, Nixon had a certain view that called for targeting foreign sources of illicit drugs. He spoke of "the cold-blooded underworld networks that funnel narcotics from suppliers all over the world into the veins of American drug *victims* [emphasis added]" and likened them to "modern-day slave traders."[72] Accordingly, his administration sought improvement on port-of-entry inspections, consolidation of "worldwide drug law enforcement responsibilities," and "high priority emphasis … on the prosecution and sentencing of drug traffickers."[73] Under the Nixon administration, the number of foreign offices opened within the DEA tripled, from eight in 1970 to twenty-nine by 1974.[74]

By comparison, a far fewer seven foreign offices were opened during the first five years of the Reagan drug war, even as the foreign sources of illicit drugs had changed dramatically.[75] As well, the focus shifted under Reagan from interdiction at the border to interruption of domestic flows. This occurred, most notably, by way of concentrated enforcement efforts, such as one the DEA dubbed the "drug corridor" – Interstate-95, running from Florida to the Northeast.

Reagan drew little distinction between the problems posed by drug traffickers and those of drug users and did not consider drug users "victims," as had Nixon. In the 1983 address in which Reagan officially unveiled the War on Drugs, he singled out drug trafficking and organized crime as the prime targets of the War. Prior to this he said: "one of the most critical duties that we faced upon taking office was controlling the influence of illegal drugs into this country."[76] But by 1986, Reagan pledged a commitment to "not tolerate drugs by anyone, anytime, anyplace."[77] By the close of the Reagan administration, he was unequivocal in expressing the view that drug abusers were as much the targets in the drug war as were drug traffickers. In a March 1988 White House briefing on drug abuse, Reagan remarked: "we must be concerned with the personal consequences for the individual, we must demonstrate our great concern for the millions of innocent citizens who pay the high price for the illegal drug use of some."[78] Later, in a July 1988 radio address, he was even more direct in his attack on drug users and said his new set of drug abuse policies sent "a strong message to drug traffickers and illegal drug users that we have a zero tolerance for those who sell or use illegal drugs."[79]

Under Reagan's command, the anti-drug strategy centered on incarceration and punishment for users, more so than drug treatment and rehabilitation. To the extent that governmental funds were committed to drug rehabilitation and treatment, those funds were counterbalanced by the preponderant share of funds having been committed to enforcement and incarceration. (See Chapter 5 on this point.) For Reagan, the bulk of the task of rehabilitating drug offenders was to be entrusted, in the first instance, to volunteerism on the part of private corporations and organizations and only secondarily to government. Upon lamenting the growth and inefficiency of government programs in his 1982 State of the Union Address, Reagan lauded the "three hundred and eight-five thousand corporations and private organizations ... already working on social programs ranging from drug rehabilitation to job training."[80] He later praised his wife, Nancy Reagan, and other parent groups for the work they were doing relative to education and prevention.[81] Nancy Reagan launched in February 1985 the "Just Say No" public awareness program. Among other things, the initiative advised kids in crime-infested, drug-prone, and violent areas to just say "no" to pressure to use or sell drugs. Mackey-Kallis and Hahn argue it was part of a larger strategy that "shifted the responsibility for (drug) problems from the arenas of politics and medicine to that of morality" and it "essentially advocated private solutions to public problems."[82]

As to where and how the federal government would concentrate its enormous resources and power, Reagan made that clear as well. In a signing statement for Executive Order 12368 in June 1982, Reagan named Carlton Turner director of the Drug Abuse Policy Office and made him responsible for the "new campaign against drug abuse." There, Reagan remarked, "we can put drug abuse on the run through stronger law enforcement, through cooperation with other nations to stop the trafficking, and by calling on the tremendous volunteer resources of parents, teachers, civic and religious leaders, and State and local officials."[83]

Among the drugs targeted by politicians such as Nixon and Reagan were cocaine, heroin, and crack. Nixon claimed there was a "raging heroin epidemic" during the late 1960s.[84] The 1972 Republican platform touted the establishment of a "Heroin Hot Line" to report heroin pushers, and the Democratic platform of the same year underscored the importance of focusing on heroin addiction among America's youth. Later, in 1988, Republicans said: "we salute the heroic residents of poor neighborhoods who have boldly shut down crack houses and run traffickers out of their communities." In fact, on the day he transmitted to Congress a draft of the bill that would eventually become the drug war's signature piece of legislation, the 1986 Anti-Drug Abuse Act, Reagan also made clear the main targets of the war. This he did in the following:

> Despite our best efforts, illegal cocaine is coming into our country at alarming levels, and 4 to 5 million people regularly use it. Five hundred thousand Americans are hooked on heroin. One in twelve persons smokes marijuana regularly. Regular drug use is even higher among the age group 18 to 25 – most likely just entering the workforce. Today there's a new epidemic: smokable cocaine, otherwise known as crack. It is an explosively destructive and often lethal substance which is crushing its users. It is an uncontrolled fire.[85]

A key point of this analysis is that Reagan was hardly alone in dramatizing the widespread damage ostensibly caused by drugs. He was actually challenged by Democratic presidential candidate and longtime civil rights spokesperson Reverend Jesse Jackson to wage an even more vigorous drug war than the one already underway in 1988. Jackson propagated much of the same war-like rhetoric articulated by conservative politicians like Reagan and his Republican counterparts. In a hearing before the Senate Labor and Human Resources Committee in June 1988, Jackson said drugs were "the greatest single threat to our Nation's families," "the biggest source of crime," and a "corrupting influence on the entire fabric of our society," that "drug pushers are terrorists" and the nation's security depended on successfully fighting drugs.[86] While the phrase he coined, "up with hope, down with dope," was intended to underscore the importance of compassionately addressing the underlying socioeconomic causes of drug dependency, Jackson fully embraced the combative war concept much like Nixon and Reagan.

Jackson stated: "we must approach the problem as we would a war plan." Further: "The struggle to fight a war on drugs begins with leaders taking very seriously a commitment to end the drugs."[87] "We must address and we must increase assistance to local law enforcement officials to fight drugs."[88] Jackson's hearing testimony was powerful enough that Secretary of Health and Human Services Otis R. Bowen warned President Reagan that Jackson was getting a great deal of political mileage out of his anti-drug message. Specifically, he said: "One of the two remaining Democratic candidates for president is getting some of his highest marks for his passionate and creative oratory on the drug epidemic and is poised to steal from our party what has been a traditional Republican issue – law enforcement."[89]

Toeing the line behind Nixon, Reagan, and Jackson was a host of still more policymakers. Perhaps the most compelling single piece of evidence on the widespread political support behind the drug war strategy is Congress's decision to make the punishment for crack cocaine use five times greater than the Reagan administration initially proposed. The Drug Free America Act introduced on September 23, 1986, in the Senate by Bob Dole on behalf of the Reagan administration (S 2849) called for a 20-to-1 crack versus powder cocaine ratio, a substantially smaller differential than the 100-to-1 ratio eventually enacted by Congress.[90]

The War on Drugs was a broad-based, bipartisan offensive. Absent the virtually unqualified cooperation of politicians across the country, the War on Drugs and the havoc it wreaked in the black community could not have happened. Yet, at no point did the Republican or Democratic party vigorously decry the foreseeable damage a heavy-handed law enforcement approach to drugs would likely yield in racial terms. Republicans actually complained that Democrats had shut them out of the off-floor discussions that culminated in passage of the 1986 Anti-Drug Abuse Act. In a letter to then-Democratic House Majority Leader Tom Foley, Republican House Minority Leader Robert H. Michel complained that Republicans' amendments to the bill were often defeated on party-line votes.[91] As such, when the much-criticized legislative centerpiece of the drug war was enacted by Congress, Democrats were in control literally and figuratively.

Both national parties labeled drugs a contagious and deadly cancer, the devastating effects of which anyone, anywhere, and at anytime could suffer, absent a vigorous government enforcement offensive. The 1972 Republican party platform explicitly labeled drugs a "cancerous social ill" and in 1980 claimed there was a "drug plague." Members of the Republican Party were sympathetic toward drug users in 1968, as alluded to earlier. Their platform pledged "increased research into the causes and prevention of crime … and drug addiction," alongside its "vigorous nation-wide drive against trafficking." But by 1980, the party was definitively more extremist in their view of drug use, referring to "a murderous epidemic of drug abuse" sweeping the country and labeling "drug abuse an intolerable threat" to society. Eight years later and with the drug war in full swing, Republicans again proclaimed, "Drug abuse directly threatens the fabric of our society." In 1996, they blamed President Clinton for surrendering in the war against drugs and called for a crackdown on users. The platform argued, "throughout the 1980s, the Republican approach – no legalization, no tolerance, no excuses – turned the tide against drug abuse" and the party could "do it again by emphasizing prevention, interdiction, a tough international approach, and a crack-down on users." Finally, in 2004, Republicans chose to underscore not so much that drug trafficking was the ultimate culprit, but rather, "drug abuse and addiction ruin lives."

During the years leading up to the 1980s, Democrats consistently employed their own brand of drug scare tactics as well. They asserted in 1972, "Drugs prey on children, destroy lives and communities, force crimes to satisfy addicts, corrupt police and government and finance the expansion of organized crime." Their 1984 platform concluded drug trafficking and abuse had "risen to crisis proportions in the United States," and by 1988, illegal drugs posed a "direct threat to the security of (the) nation from coast to coast." On the question of how best to combat the drug problem, moreover, Democrats were slower to embrace a heavily punitive approach. Initially, they emphasized the importance of intensified enforcement in concert with research and education, as of 1968. Again in 1972, the "importance of treatment and rehabilitation programs for all drug-and-alcohol-addicted veterans" was underscored, as well as "drug abuse treatment and education" for the health of all Americans. Critically, the 1972 platform expressed the idea that "crime and drug abuse cannot be isolated from the social and economic conditions that give rise to them." The party even went so far as to state: "We recognize drug addiction as a health problem and pledge that emphasis will be put on rehabilitation of addicts."

Over time, Democrats abandoned their empathetic perspective on drug addiction and adopted a considerably more condemnatory approach. As of 1992, the party's mantra was scarcely distinguishable from Republicans'. The Democratic platform asserted that year:

We must keep drugs off our streets and out of our schools. President Clinton and the Democratic Party have waged an aggressive war on drugs. The Crime Bill established the death penalty for drug kingpins. The President signed a directive requiring drug testing of anyone arrested for a federal crime.... We established innovative drug courts which force drugs users to get treatment or go to jail.

Then, like Republicans, Democrats linked drug users and criminals together. In 2000, they asserted, pointedly: "Drug and alcohol abuse are implicated in the crimes of 80 percent of the criminals behind bars."

Illegal drugs preoccupied the two major parties less in 2008 than in earlier years due in no small part to the onset of the historic economic crisis that began to take shape that year. Conservatives and liberals alike scaled back on the amount of energy they expended sounding the alarm about drug use. Also, their zeal for imprisoning users, building more prisons, and hiring more police officers waned in the midst of the economic crisis. It bears mentioning that in addition to the economic crisis, a number of high-profile revelations regarding various forms of drug abuse on the part of several notables also coincided with the onset of at least a measure of bipartisan empathy. News media reported eight-time Olympic gold medal winner Michael Phelps, conservative commentator Rush Limbaugh, the late U.S. Supreme Court Chief Justice William Rehnquist, and future president Barack Obama either experimented with illicit drugs, were treated for prescription drug abuse, or were criminally charged for drug abuse.[92] The revelation of substance abuse and addiction by such powerful and productive members of American society added a twist to the long-running storyline in crime politics about drug abuse. They helped make clear that abuse and dependency were, in fact, not as inevitably and indiscriminately destructive to the fabric of American society and to American lives as originally proclaimed.

At least on the surface, it appeared a softer, gentler approach to drug abuse was reintroduced into the parties' drug policy strategy as of 2008. Republicans pledged that year to continue to fight against producers, traffickers, and distributors of illegal substances. They added, however:

We support the work of those who help individuals struggling with addiction, and we support strengthening drug education and prevention programs to avoid addiction. We endorse state and local initiatives, such as Drug Courts, that are trying new approaches to curbing drug abuse and diverting first-time offenders to rehabilitation.

They continued in 2012 to endorse "the right of parents to consent to medical treatment for their children, including mental health treatment, drug treatment, and treatment involving pregnancy." Also lauded were "state and local initiatives that are trying new approaches to curbing drug abuse and diverting firsttime offenders to rehabilitation." Meanwhile, Democrats presented a plan in 2012 for fighting HIV/AIDS that sought to "direct resources to the communities at greatest risk, including gay men, black and Latino Americans, substance users, and others at high risk of infection." Coupled with Democrats' new emphasis on support for substance users was also a pledge in 2008 to "expand the use of drug courts and rehabilitation programs for first-time, non-violent drug offenders."

At a deeper level, nonetheless, the additions to the party drug war playbook that came in 2008 and 2012 were largely editorial in nature and left intact the core themes of the playbook. The society-wide endangerment theme about illegal drugs per se was kept front-and-center in both parties' messaging. The criminal justice subsection of the 2008 Democratic party platform placed equal emphasis on drug crimes as on drug abuse in the following: "We must help, state, local, and tribal law enforcement work together to combat and prevent drug crimes and drug and alcohol abuse." In 2012 Democrats warned "narco-traffickers and criminal gangs" in vulnerable nations "threaten their citizens and ours." For Republicans, election years 2008 and 2012 were an opportunity to actually turn up the volume on their dangerousness rhetoric. In 2008, they equated the war on drugs with the war on terror, blaming "narco-terrorism" for distorting hemispheric progress. Accordingly, they made clear: "Our government must address the increasing role of vicious drug cartels and other gangs in controlling human smuggling across our southern border."

Juxtaposed to parties' persistent claim that illegal drugs posed a threat to American society – even the hemisphere – the reality is that illegal

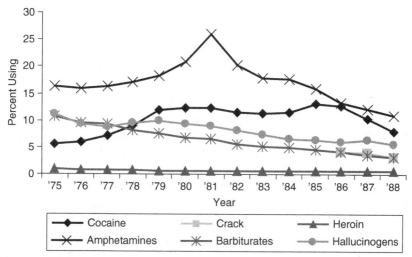

FIGURE 6.6. Illicit Drug Use in the United States: "Hard-Core" Drugs, 1975–1988 (Percent Using).

drugs never posed such a large-scale threat. At no point from the early 1970s onward was the threat of illegal drug use and trafficking in the United States anywhere near the alarming levels claimed by politicians. Not only were Democrats and Republicans unmoved by the absence of an American drug epidemic, they were also undeterred by the fact that the casualties on the law enforcement front of the drug war were disproportionately black.

The available statistical data on substance abuse trends illustrate the first of these points, and are shown in Figure 6.6.[93] The data are drawn from the University of Michigan's *Monitoring the Future* (MTF) annual survey. They are quite useful for our purposes, given that a published report by the federal government's principal source of drug data, the Substance Abuse and Mental Health Services Administration (SAMHSA), states that more is known about cross-racial differences in licit and illicit drug use thanks to the MTF. As well, the MTF is one of only a handful of time-series drug use surveys administered since the early 1970s.[94] Because it is a school-based survey, the MTF series permits us to probe the validity of politicians' heavy emphasis on the special dangers drugs posed for children, which emphasis led to enactment of narrowly focused laws, such as the 1989 Safe and Drug-Free Schools and Communities Act. Additionally, the SAMHSA deems adolescent drug abuse a reliable predictor of adult drug use. It notes a focus on adolescent use is "an appropriate emphasis given that most individuals begin using drugs during adolescence and that adolescent drug use predicts drug use in later life."[95]

The MTF data help to prove that when the War on Drugs was officially launched in 1983, abuse of the drugs mainly targeted by the war was actually on the decline nationally. They demonstrate also that the drugs mainly targeted by drug war strategists were, in fact, not the centrifugal forces of the "murderous epidemic of drug abuse" referenced in Republicans' 1980 platform. The percentage of respondents reporting use of cocaine during a twelve-month period averaged under 10 percent during the years leading up to the war (1975–1982), and it averaged 11 percent from the launch of the war in 1983 through the balance of Reagan's watch. The percentage dipped below 5 percent for much of the period to follow. In fact, during the two years just prior to Reagan's official declaration of war in January 1983, cocaine use was on the decline. It did not tick upward again until 1985, two years after the War on Drugs was declared. Moreover, in addition to the noteworthy elements of drug use trends over time is the scale of drug use. At most, only a tiny percentage of Americans actually faced the dangers of crack cocaine use as of 1986,[96] and an even fewer 1 percent or less were in danger from heroin use. More problematic during the years leading up to the drug war was use of other "hard-core" drugs that were not as vigorously targeted as cocaine, crack, and heroine, namely amphetamines, hallucinogens, and barbiturates. According to these data, neither a murderous epidemic nor any other type of cocaine or crack epidemic ever materialized, certainly not one with large numbers of youth in its cross-hairs.

What we learn from the substance abuse data in Figure 6.7[97] is that the national party system relentlessly sounded the alarm regarding the society-wide impact of drug abuse well after use of the targeted drugs – cocaine, crack, and heroin – had begun to subside. For all but a few years following 1990, neither cocaine, crack, nor heroin reached a 5 percent usage level. Yet, we observe scarcely an adjustment in politicians' rhetoric regarding the national dimensions of the dangers brought on by drug use. In 1988, when cocaine use first dropped to single digit numbers, Democrats were as emphatically committed to the war as ever. They proclaimed in their 1988 platform: "illegal drugs pose a direct threat to the security of our nation from coast to coast, invading our neighborhoods, classrooms, homes and communities large and small." This assertion came after seven consecutive years of declining cocaine use nationally. Undeterred, in 2000, Democrats were still bragging Clinton and Gore had "fought for and won the biggest anti-drug budgets in history, every

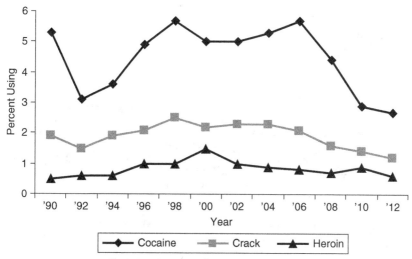

FIGURE 6.7. Illicit Drug Use in the United States: Crack, Cocaine, Heroin, 1990–2012 (Percent Using).

single year" during 1992–2000. These were the very same years during which cocaine use had dipped to single digits (starting in 1989), and it remained there through 2012. Meanwhile, Republicans ratcheted up their dire warnings about the perils of drugs in 2008 and 2012 by explicitly linking drugs to the War on Terror in the ways detailed earlier.

Closer to the heart of this study than the overall disconnect between the rhetoric of the drug war and the reality of drug use in the United States, is the disconnect between those whom politicians said were the intended targets and those actually targeted by law enforcement. In a nutshell, the War on Drugs did not necessarily target drug offenders, it targeted *black* drug offenders. Because politicians uniformly condemned drug users as well as drug traffickers and decried all the evil that drug users wrought throughout the country, one means of gauging racial differences in the execution of the drug war is to compare a racial breakdown of data on drug use to that on drug possession arrests. This is especially true in regard to the most widely vilified drug, crack cocaine. The MTF statistics depicted in Figure 6.8[98] suggest it was whites who used both powder cocaine and smokable cocaine more than blacks. It shows, more precisely, white youth were far more likely than black youth to use the villainous drug crack cocaine, and in every year for which data are available. In most years, white twelfth graders were well more than twice as likely as black twelfth graders to use crack. Not shown in the figure is that other

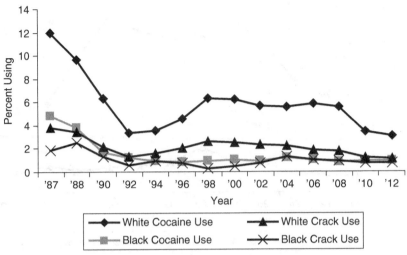

FIGURE 6.8. Cocaine and Crack Use, by Race, 1987–2012
(Percent Using).

hard-core drugs, especially hallucinogens, were likewise used by whites at a rate four times greater than blacks. For example, as of 1983, 22 percent of white twelfth graders reported using amphetamines compared to a much smaller 5.7 percent of black twelfth graders.[99]

Thus, if the level of crack use in the United States was the driving force behind the efforts of federal lawmakers and if the drug war was chiefly about saving America's youth, then crack use on the part of the white majority was the appropriate target – that is, if crack cocaine use were truly the target. While more direct measures of adult crack use have been offered elsewhere, and they intimate crack cocaine as the drug of choice for blacks,[100] the MTF data permit us to speak to the issue of scale from a national perspective. As well, because the MTF is the only data source covering the time period before and after launch of the drug war and for more than a dozen drugs, MTF data allow us to gauge the actual and projected drug trends to which politicians were ostensibly reacting. Moreover, even if we were to concede that crack cocaine use was more prevalent in the black community than in the white community, the MTF data indicate the primary users of crack in the United States as a whole were white. Finally, there is no question that the MTF data establish that among youth – that is, those about whom drug war strategists were purportedly most concerned – crack cocaine

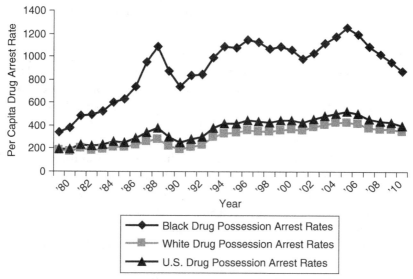

FIGURE 6.9. Drug Possession Arrest Rate, by Race, United States, 1980–2011 (Rates Per 100,000 Residential Population).

use on the part of white high school-age students surpassed that of black high school-age students.

We learn from Figure 6.9[101] that whereas whites literally tipped the scale in regard to use of illicit drugs, it was blacks who were disproportionally targeted for arrest by law enforcement. The Bureau of Justice Statistics data shown demonstrate blacks were more likely to be arrested for drugs before the official start of the drug war, and became even more so once the war was in full swing. Not until halfway into the first decade of the millennium was there noticeable abatement in this trend. Even so, as late as 2011, blacks were still four times more likely than whites to be arrested for drug possession. In sum and substance, politicians claimed during the 1980s and 1990s that the focal point of their drug strategy was incarceration of drug offenders, including drug users. Yet, the actual execution of their strategy did virtually the opposite. It disproportionally ensnared black users, even though whites were disproportionally engaged in hard-core drug use.

There was a marked disconnect between the enforcement solution to drug use and the drug use problem. Perhaps even more problematic for blacks is that hardly anyone cared about the racial dynamics of drug use and drug enforcement.

In the Aftermath: Race, Punishment and Politics

As the two parties went about purging racial concerns and problems from the national politics of crime, the racial divide in criminal justice deepened. Blacks became even more likely than whites to be arrested than before and even more likely than whites to be imprisoned while consistently more likely than whites to be criminally victimized. In short, the problem of racial tracking proceeded on its usual path; it was politicians who changed course.

It is crucial to understand, moreover, the sociopolitical roots of racial tracking ran deep. Well before the de-racialization of crime began during the late 1960s and well before the War on Drugs of the 1980s, American justice had long been a matter of justice to blacks, as opposed to justice for or on behalf of blacks. Together with Figures 6.5 and 6.9, Figure 6.10[102] helps to illustrate this. It depicts the decades-long stretch of time across which justice in the United States evolved into justice against blacks. As of 1964, before the onset of the de-racialization of crime, the number of blacks admitted each year to state and federal prisons had already grown nearly 300 percent since 1926 (from 9,274 to 27,191 annually), whereas the number of whites sent to prison each year had grown only half as much (from 33,559 to 52,458).[103] As of 1986, when the War on Drugs was launched in earnest with passage of its legislative centerpiece (the Anti-Drug Abuse Act of 1986), the number of black prison admissions

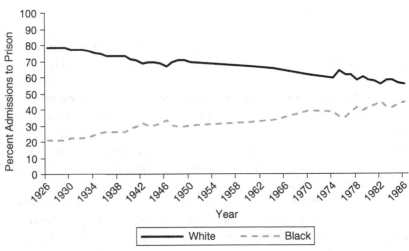

FIGURE 6.10. Admissions to State and Federal Prisons, by Race, 1926–1986.

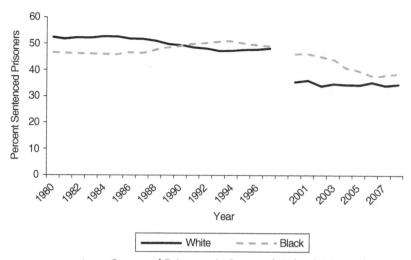

FIGURE 6.11. Sentenced Prisoners in State and Federal Prisons, by Race, 1980–2008.

Note: For 1980–1997 data, "white" and "black" include persons of Hispanic origin as reported by states; data for 2000–2008 "white" and "black" categories exclude persons of Hispanic origin.

had increased 800 percent since 1926 (up to 73,934), juxtaposed to a 275 percent increase in the number of white prisoners admitted over the same time period (up to 92,274). In short, the racial gap in prison admissions due to court commitments or parole violations had been widening for decades, indeed as far back as data are available. The flip side of imprisonment having figured ever more prominently in black America is that American prisons grew darker and darker each year, so that from the 1980s onward, blacks claimed a larger share of the sentenced prisoner population than whites, as depicted by the 1980–2008 data in Figure 6.11.[104] The color of prison justice was disproportionally black.

Hardly new; racial tracking in the United States was old news by the time the War on Drugs was formally declared by President Ronald Reagan in 1983 and officially launched by Congress in 1986. It did not begin with the drug war, nor did it wane in tandem with the drug war.

Though the color of justice in the United States had been manifest partly by skin color for decades, what chiefly set the 1960s apart from the extended history of racial tracking in the United States was politicians' abandonment of the opportunity to do something about it. It was a missed opportunity to reverse or slow the pace of racial tracking. At a time when the country embraced more fully the principle of racial equality and eradicated legal barriers to equal employment, education, and housing for blacks, a very different course of action was followed on the criminal justice front. Rather than embrace more fully the racially conscientious approach to crime-fighting urged by the events of the civil rights movement, the Kerner Commission report and racial justice advocates, mainstream politicians did just the opposite. The practical relevancy of skin color was not only left intact; it was relegated to the sidelines of crime politics. The question is: why?

Why did mainstream policymakers opt to reformulate "the issue" in criminal justice and de-racialize the politics of crime and justice – even as the nature and impact of crime and punishment remained racialized? Whether each politician took part in the de-racialization of crime politics because of, in spite of, or with little knowledge of the racially disadvantaging effects of their choices is the subject of an extended scholarly debate. That they may have had little choice due to blacks' disproportionally high rates of criminal offending is also the focal point of a longstanding academic debate. The various sides of the debate concerning racial animus and other considerations are detailed at length in Chapter 8.

Of special interest at the moment is the extent to which politicians' neglect of racial tracking as of 1968 onward was partly symptomatic of much broader political forces. Given the public origins principle of American policymaking, it makes sense to inquire into the role of the voter. Voters giveth power and voters taketh away power, according to the principle. Were politicians acting in accord with the aggregate preferences of voters – those on whose behalf they were purportedly acting and whose support they needed to win and maintain positions of power?

We know the Democratic Party did not have compelling political reasons to pursue a different course of action. We know based on the data offered in Table 6.4[105] that black voters did not give them sufficient reason to do so. Blacks did not condition their endorsement of the Democratic Party in the voting booth on a tangible commitment from party leaders to follow a more racially sensitive crime-fighting playbook. A vibrant current of scholarly literature carefully dissects the causal dynamics of black voting and sheds light on the wide and complex range of factors that explain black voter preferences.[106] Ultimately, these factors culminated in making the black vote in the United States synonymous with a Democratic Party vote. Starting in 1968 – precisely when the shift toward colorblind crime politics got underway – black voters became overwhelmingly and steadfastly committed to the Democratic Party, and they remained so in every election to follow. At remarkable

TABLE 6.4. *Black Vote in Presidential Elections, by Candidate Party, 1936–2008 (Percent)*

Year	Vote for Democratic Candidate	Vote for Republican Candidate
1936	71	28
1940	67	32
1944	68	32
1948	77	23
1952	76	24
1956	61	39
1960	68	32
1964	94	6
1968	85	15
1972	87	13
1976	85	15
1980	86	12
1984	89	9
1988	88	10
1992	82	11
1996	84	12
2000	90	8
2004	88	11
2008	95	4

levels of between 82 and 95 percent, blacks voted for the Democratic Party ticket in every presidential election during the period in focus. Although black voters' embrace of moderate presidential candidate Bill Clinton in the voting booth in 1992 and 1996 was lower than that of any other Democratic candidate since Lyndon B. Johnson, it too registered at 82 percent and 84 percent respectively.

We also know that black voters were not necessarily unaware of the Democratic Party's compromise of black interests. Black leaders and even right-wing conservatives were at times blunt in their public criticism of the Democratic Party's systematic neglect of black concerns. Longtime Congressional insider and racial justice advocate Democratic Congressman Charles Rangel said during Clinton's run for president:

I don't have any problem when he's talking to black groups. My problem is the campaign and strategy as it relates to bus trips and speeches given on prime time television where he is addressing crowds other than African Americans. We've got to be courted publicly and we've got to be treated as first class voters and cannot be taken for granted.[107]

In a similar vein, national civil rights spokesperson Reverend Al Sharpton's inaugural speech for his 2004 presidential campaign said of the Democratic Party: "They want to have fun with us on Election Day but they can't bring us home to introduce us to their mommies and daddies. We are not going to be the concubines of the national Democratic Party."[108] From the conservative end of the spectrum also, perception of the Democratic Party's complicity was publicly noted. In a radio show titled "Why the Democrats Get the Black Vote" aired during the heat of the 2012 presidential campaign, conservative talk show host Rush Limbaugh asked, "How can they still vote for Democrats after what the Democrat Party has done?" And, "Why do they stick with people and policies that are harming them"?[109]

It would seem, then, the apparent disconnect between Democrats' crime-fighting rhetoric and the racial realities of crime-fighting was not a deal breaker for black voters. At the very least, it did not matter enough to precipitate mass defection or large-scale rallying on the part of the black electorate around a problem that has yielded devastatingly negative racial effects. The discussion and analysis in the next chapter reveals that black voters were not alone in this regard. As with black voters, so too with American voters at large, racial tracking in American criminal justice did not register high enough on the politics radar as to generate mass discontent with national political leadership. The detailed examination of the public mindset regarding race, crime, and criminal justice in Chapter 7 sheds light on a major part of the reason politicians were free to disregard the racial dimensions of crime policymaking.

It tells the story of why the public did not demand from their spokespersons and elected leaders a more racially conscientious stance on crime-fighting. It tells us, more precisely, that politicians did not care essentially because they were not given sufficient reason to care. This, according to the public origins principle, is the primary root of racial tracking.

7

Public Origins

What Americans Believe about Race, Crime, and Criminal Justice Policy

At the root of racial tracking is a public consensus that abides and enables it. A majority of Americans do not consider racial tracking sufficiently problematic as to do something about it. The lack of concern is not due to a lack of awareness, nor to indifference. Most Americans are aware of racial differences in the system and disapprove. But, despite the public's belief that law enforcement officers' treatment of blacks is partly motivated by racial stereotyping, such racial improprieties are not weighty enough to bring the entire system into disrepute. Further, many are convinced that blacks are violence-prone and, therefore, mostly to blame for their overrepresentation in jails and prisons. There is also a sense the country has done all it can and perhaps more than it should to right the wrongs of historically rooted racial inequities.

Transcending all these considerations is the fact that, instead of racial tracking, another criminal justice policy concern is more pressing on the public mind. Americans believe that what the criminal justice system needs most now is a greater commitment to holding criminals accountable and passage of effective crime reduction measures. If lawmakers are to marshal their energies toward any particular criminal justice policy end, that end should be making the system stronger, over and above that of making it racially fair. The same ordering of preferences is evident specifically in black public opinion as well. Because such social, political, and policy preferences cut across racial lines, they are best understood as reflective of a deeply rooted, cross-racial public mind-set.

As expected from the public origins principle of policy process, the analysis to follow establishes that racial differences in criminal law enforcement are ultimately traceable to the American public. More precisely, it illustrates how the public's mind-set is concordant to racial tracking and in full accord also with a much broader set of attitudes toward race and crime in the United States. The analysis draws on nationally representative surveys that authors Howard Schuman, Charlotte Steeh, Lawrence Bobo, and Maria Krysan described as "valuable source[s] of long-term evidence."[1] In their award-winning, book-length treatment of racial attitudes across several decades, Schuman and colleagues utilized data from the General Social Survey (GSS), the National Election Study (NES), the Gallup Organization, and other sources. The discussion to follow utilizes these sources to illuminate, in particular, the three main ways in which national public attitudes toward race, crime, and punishment are conducive to racial tracking. Additionally, a series of national surveys developed specifically for this study are also incorporated.

The discussion begins with a layout of attitudes toward the role of race and racism in law enforcement. Next is a look at the relative weights accorded to racial influences and public safety concerns. The third and final section of the chapter details the substance of the public's legislative preferences regarding race, crime, and criminal justice.

Yeah, We Know, but Those People

A critical point of note regarding public attitudes in this issue domain is that the preponderant share of Americans actually concede there is a race problem in the criminal justice system. To a notable extent, they grasp racial tracking as well. They know blacks are disproportionally ensnared in the criminal process and also subject to differential treatment while entangled in that process. Proof of the public's awareness is depicted in Table 7.1.[2] Whether the focus is on the initial stage of the criminal process, at which black citizens first encounter police officers, the point at which suspects are tried and convicted or imprisoned, we find hard evidence proving a sizeable share of the public knows modern American law enforcement is racially tainted.

When asked whether they think police officers or security guards stop people of certain racial or ethnic groups because these officers stereotype these groups as more criminally oriented, a slim majority consistently responds in the affirmative. In 1999 and in 2003 Gallup polling revealed nearly three out of five Americans believed racial profiling of motorists was widespread.[3] A similar picture emerges also from a 2004 Gallup national survey. The belief in racial profiling is embraced by the bulk of whites (50 percent), blacks (67 percent), and Hispanics

TABLE 7.1. *Beliefs About Racialism in Law Enforcement, United States, Blacks, 2004–2008*

	United States	Blacks
Percent respondents believing ...		
Racial profiling on roads and highways is widespread (2004)	53	67
Discrimination is a *major* factor in imprisonment (2008)	51	80
Percent respondents believing blacks in local community are ... (2007)		
Treated less fairly in dealing with the police	37	73
Treated less fairly on the job	18	53
Treated less fairly in neighborhood shops	15	42
Treated less fairly in stores or shopping malls	19	47
Treated less fairly in entertainment places	16	40

(63 percent). Unnever's statistical analysis explains that it is blacks' personal experiences with police that help to predict their beliefs about criminal justice bias.[4] As would be expected, then, among young black men who report being personally treated unfairly by the police, the perception of police bias is particularly acute. Nearly one in four black males under the age of thirty-five stated in a 2013 Gallup poll that in the past month alone, they were treated unfairly in dealings with the police because they were black.[5]

The average citizen recognizes also that race is a factor in the disproportional imprisonment of blacks. In fact, an overwhelming majority of up to 80 percent of adults in the United States explicitly claim racial discrimination plays at least some role in driving the higher percentage of blacks in prison. Of those, 51 percent consider it a major factor and roughly 28 percent say it is a minor factor. Only 18 percent are under the impression that race has no bearing at all on imprisonment trends. To further ground the point about public awareness of racialism in law enforcement, we place public perception of the role of race in the criminal justice system side by side with the perception of racial influences in other issue areas. Upon doing so, we learn only two out of five consider race a major factor in the lower average education levels of blacks and in the lower average income levels of blacks, and even fewer see it as determinative in the lower average life expectancies for blacks.[6] In essence, the public is far more inclined to attribute racist tendencies to the criminal justice system than to other American institutions and policy spheres.

But there is a caveat to this claim about the public's racial awareness. Most are reluctant to go so far as to pin the "racist" label on local law enforcement. Slightly more favorable views prevail with respect to the treatment blacks receive at the hands of local police. Whereas 53 percent say racial profiling is "widespread" in the country, only 37 percent are willing to say blacks are treated less fairly in respondents' own community. Nonetheless, even when it comes to police officers with whom they are in closer contact, Americans are more prepared to acknowledge officers' susceptibility to racist tendencies as compared to other community actors and institutions. Put differently, if any local institution is most apt to evoke public suspicion of racial unfairness, it is law enforcement. This we can glean from the data in Table 7.1. Those data reveal Americans are about two times more likely to say blacks are treated less fairly in dealings with the police as compared to other contexts, such as on the job, in neighborhood shops, in stores or shopping malls, or in places of entertainment.

Black opinion parallels the general public's on the question of whether racism plays a role in law enforcement. Indeed, blacks are keenly aware that racial minorities are neither treated with the same level of respect and consideration by police officers nor by other actors in the criminal justice system. A number of cross-regional and experimental studies contend there is a statistical relationship between an individual's race and his/her attitudes toward the criminal justice system. Although various factors, such as context, contact, and police force, have been shown to moderate the relationship,[7] most still conclude racial and ethnic minority attitudes diverge from that of the white majority and have been so divided for quite some time. For example, Bobo and Thompson's Race, Crime and Public Opinion Study found that blacks are twice as likely as whites to believe the criminal justice system is racially biased.[8] Also, a 2004 survey of metropolitan areas by Weitzer and Tuch indicates blacks are most likely to harbor negative views of police misconduct in particular.[9]

Later survey data, depicted in Table 7.1, mirror a similar racial divide. They reveal a sizeable majority (67 percent) of blacks say racial stereotyping is often the trigger for black citizen interactions with police officers. A strikingly larger majority (80 percent) see discrimination as a *major* factor influencing the incarceration of blacks. Likewise, the level of distrust toward the criminal justice system surpasses their suspicion toward other institutions. Blacks' lack of faith in law enforcement's propensity to treat racial minorities and whites the same runs both deep and wide, in that they consider the behavior just as concerning at the local level as on

TABLE 7.2. *Attitudes toward Police and Criminal Justice System, United States, Blacks, 2005–2011*

	United States	Blacks
Percent respondents who ...		
Rate honesty and ethical standards of police as very high or high (2011)	54	39
Have much confidence in police (2011)>*	56	43
Have much confidence in police to protect from violent crime (2005)*	53	32
Have much confidence in local police to do a good job enforcing the law (2009)**	71	54
Have much confidence in local police to not use excessive force on suspects (2009)**	63	41
Believe there is no police brutality in their area (2005)	65	29
Have confidence in community police to treat blacks and whites equally (Pew 2009)	63	41
Have confidence in local police to treat blacks and whites equally (Gallup 2007)	73	45
Rate honesty and ethical standards of judges as "very high" and "high" (2010)	47	35
Have confidence in the criminal justice system (2011)***	28	27
Believe the death penalty is applied fairly in the country today (2011)	52	32
Believe the American justice system is not biased against blacks (2008)	59	27

Notes:
 * Includes "a great deal" and "quite a lot" responses.
 ** Includes "a great deal" and "fair amount" responses.
 *** Includes "very fair" and "somewhat fair" responses.

a national scale and just as problematic at the front end of the criminal process as at the back end.

In light of their much greater suspicion toward the criminal justice system's treatment of racial minorities, there should be little wonder why blacks have much lower levels of respect for how criminal law enforcement in the United States is conducted. It bears emphasizing here that blacks' attitudes toward law enforcement personnel and their treatment of blacks are the issue of note, not blacks attitudes toward criminal law enforcement per se. The survey data presented in Table 7.2[10] make clear that even though a not insignificant share of blacks give high marks to police officers in several areas, a pro-police black majority does not exist.

Certainly not in connection with treatment issues and definitely not in comparison to whites. As much is obvious for a wide spectrum of issues – from the run-of-the-mill concern about protection from violent crime to the more controversial issue of police brutality.

In contrast, the general public's recognition of a race problem in law enforcement does not diminish its favorable disposition toward police officers nor the system as a whole. From Table 7.2, we can see that the perceived racist tendencies of criminal justice are neither debilitating nor damning enough to spur public condemnation of the system in its entirety. The vast majority of Americans hold police officers in the highest regard, despite their knowledge of racial bias in officers' decision-making. Indeed, to much of the adult population in the United States, police officers are virtual heroes and are classified among the country's most ethical, effective, and fair professionals. Even clergy, accountants, and bankers fall in line behind police officers, so to speak. A 2011 national survey ranked the honesty and ethical standards of police officers in fifth place and that of clergy in sixth, out of a total of twenty-one ranked professions.[11] Other institutions that are generally well-regarded stand in the shadows of the police force as well.

A separate 2011 survey measuring public confidence in a list of fifteen institutions placed police officers in second place – well ahead of churches, the presidency, and even the U.S. Supreme Court, which tends to enjoy relatively high public approval.[12] Public esteem of police officers' honesty and integrity is more emblematic of recent years than of past decades, which suggests public favor toward police officers is on the rise. In 1977, 37 percent rated police officer ethics high, fifteen years later, 42 percent did so, and by 2011, 54 percent.[13] Last, Table 7.2 also shows solid majorities express either "a great deal" or "quite a lot" of confidence in police offers to protect them from violent crime, to do a good job of enforcing the law, and to use physical force in appropriate ways. To the latter point, nearly two-thirds expressly reject the notion of police brutality in their area.

Other actors within the criminal justice system do not command quite the same high level of respect as police officers; still, the other actors' standing in the public eye is nowhere near paltry. Judges, for example, evoke less enthusiasm than police officers. The same 2011 survey in which 54 percent rated police ethics as very high or high yielded a smaller 47 percent that rated judges' ethics the same. While trend data show police officer ratings growing more positive over time, the opposite is true of judges. An earlier 1999 survey revealed a larger percentage (53 percent) once rated judges' standards as very high or higher than they do now.[14] Today, nonetheless, almost half describe the honesty and ethical standards of judges as "very high" and "high." When sizing up the criminal justice system as a whole, moreover, the public shows less confidence. But here too, despite having comparatively less confidence in it, the public considers the system as fair with respect to its use of the system's greatest power – the death penalty.

What are we to make of the fact that the American public embraces what are seemingly contradictory stances toward law enforcement, namely recognition of racist law enforcement on the one hand and a high regard for the overall system on the other? To start with, we must bear in mind the disconnect between attitudes toward policing on a national scale and attitudes toward local policing, which is the policing most encounter in their own community. The race problem in the criminal process may indeed be a real phenomenon to the larger share of Americans, but it is not *as* real in their own backyard as it is elsewhere. To this point, according to Table 7.2, up to three out of four respondents specifically state that the police in their local community treat blacks and whites equally (albeit less equally than do other local institutions). The vast majority do not believe the justice system is racist through and through and are unwilling to paint the entire system with a broad brush on the issue of race. Asked if "the American justice system is – or is not – biased against blacks," nearly three out of five said that it is not. This latter indicator helps to crystallize a second point embedded in the data, which is that public awareness of racial profiling and its high esteem for police officers are not mutually exclusive of one another.

A sizeable portion of Americans reconcile their belief in police officers as heroes with their recognition of officers' propensity toward racialized decision making by viewing blacks as chiefly responsible for what happens to them. They attribute racial differences in criminal justice outcomes to black criminality more so than law enforcement discrimination. Against this backdrop, blacks are regrettably but understandably arrested and incarcerated at higher-than-usual rates.[15] Aggressive policing tactics and unforgiving prosecutorial strategies are altogether sensible, from this particular vantage point. What is especially important for us to grasp, then, is not simply whether the public realizes that race matters in criminal justice processing, but what it considers the preeminent cause of how and why race matters. According to national public opinion, not only do blacks shoulder a considerable share of the blame for their disproportional entanglement in criminal process; they also come up short in other substantive ways too, as far as the public is concerned.

The belief in greater black criminality is itself grounded in a broader attitudinal framework whereby blacks are adjudged negatively along several dimensions.[16] A vibrant current of literature contends contemporary stereotyping of blacks constitutes a new form of racism, one that supplants the old fashioned Jim Crow-style racism of the past. Such stereotyping fits what political scientists Bobo, Kluegel, and Smith define as a form of laissez-fair racism. It consists of "persistent negative stereotyping of African Americans, a tendency to blame blacks themselves for the black–white gap in socioeconomic standing, and resistance to meaningful policy efforts to ameliorate U.S. racist social conditions and institutions."[17] Psychologist J. F. Dovidio and colleagues advance a similar conclusion and document through experimental research studies what he terms "aversive racism."[18] On the other hand, Quillian and Pager and also Sniderman and colleagues challenge the basic claim of symbolic and modern racism theories. They assert the nature and workings of contemporary racial prejudice are more complex than an anti-black paradigm alone admits and that they are linked also to nonracial factors, such as educational status[19] and neighborhood composition.[20] Consistent with the latter view is research indicating mass media help mediate attitudes toward race and crime in ways that produce different racial belief frameworks for differently situated individuals and groups. (More on the role of the mass media in Chapter 8, "Reasons to Believe.")

For present purposes, what is most significant is that, whatever the proximate political, psychological, or sociological determinants of racial stereotyping, a sizeable portion of Americans settle on a decidedly unflattering portrait of what blackness entails. Perhaps surprisingly, there is a notable level of cross-racial endorsement of the black criminal stereotype. We observe this in regard to public attitudes toward black contributions and values, black characteristics, and the root causes of racial disparities.

To start with, blacks are more often seen by the general public as having little to offer society and, at worst, constituting a liability. The likelihood of blacks being considered a positive and valuable force in society is significantly less than is true of other groups. Table 7.3[21] helps to demonstrate this. Given the option to say whether certain racial and religious groups have made either the most important positive contribution to the country versus an "important," "some," or "little" positive contribution, only 9 percent say blacks have made the most important positive contribution. This, while nearly a third say the same of what the GSS poll labeled "the English." Not shown in the table is that a similar racial

TABLE 7.3. *Beliefs about Racial Subgroups, for United States, Blacks, Whites, 2000–2010*

	United States	Blacks (% in Race)	Whites (% in Race)	B-W Ratio
Percent respondents believing …				
English have made the most important contribution	31	22	32	.69
Blacks have made the most important contribution	9	25	6	4.2
Whites are committed to strong families	54	58	53	1.1
Blacks are committed to strong families	34	50	32	1.6
Asians are committed to strong families	63	62	63	.99
Whites are lazy	14	21	12	1.8
Blacks are lazy	31	19	33	.58
Asians are lazy	11	14	11	1.3
Whites are unintelligent	9	15	7	2.1
Blacks are unintelligent	14	10	15	.67
Asians are unintelligent	11	14	10	1.4
Whites are violent	21	36	18	2.0
Blacks are violent	47	41	47	.87
Asians are violent	17	24	16	1.5
Immigrants increase crime rate	27	19	29	.66

Note: Data on contribution, family commitment, and violence are from the 2000 General Social Survey (GSS). Data on laziness and intelligence from 2010. The exceptions are data on laziness and intelligence for Asians, both from the 2000 GSS.

differentiation inheres at the opposite end of this spectrum. More than one out of ten say blacks have made little positive contribution, whereas about 3 percent say the same of the English. In essence, Americans are three times more likely to regard English contributions to the country as noteworthy but three times more likely to adjudge black contributions as *de minimus*. Coupled with this is that blacks are not believed to embrace certain core values to the same degree as whites. Most consider whites family-oriented, but most do not think the same of blacks.

There is also a sense on the part of many that there is something wrong with black people themselves, according to several years of GSS data. A not insignificant portion of the public looks disparagingly upon black character traits, that is to say upon aspects of blackness itself. As compared to whites, blacks are far more likely to be labeled by the general public as lazy, unintelligent, and, most significantly, violent. The data proving each of these points are depicted in Table 7.3. What stands out most is that, in both relative and absolute terms, violence and blackness are synonymous in the minds of the preponderant share of Americans. Survey data reveal almost half of the country – fully 47 percent of adults – lean toward the view that blacks are violent, and 15 percent lean in the opposite direction. This compares to 21 percent who say whites are violent, and 31 percent who say they are not. Perhaps more than any other aspect of public opinion, the public's beliefs about violence are pivotal. The practical implication of this reasoning is that violent people are deservedly and rightly targeted by police officers and taken off the streets, which in this case is blacks. Similarly, violent people deserve to be treated as such.

Conceptions of laziness constitute another dimension of the public's position on blame. "Lazy" is associated with blacks in the minds of nearly one out of every three Americans, and at a rate more than twice that for whites. As to the issue of innate ability, although a small percentage (14 percent) actually consider blacks unintelligent, the chance blacks will be so regarded is one and a half times greater than that for whites. This is all the more revealing, given that respondents had the option of saying blacks are neither more nor less intelligent than whites. Moreover, the inference to be drawn from the fact that the vast majority reject the notion that blacks are intellectually inferior is not necessarily advantageous. It too comports with the idea blacks have the wherewithal to direct their own life pathways. They can do better, if they so choose, but they choose otherwise.

The negative racial stereotypes to which a significant portion of the public ascribes are fundamentally anti-black, meaning they pertain specifically and chiefly to blacks. They do not extend to other racial and ethnic minorities and, thus, are not necessarily anti-minority. Nor are they pro-white for that matter. The "model minority" concept succinctly conveys the basic mode of thinking about racial minorities. It bears mentioning the very idea there is a "model" minority implies there is a less than exemplary minority, that there are good minorities and also bad minorities. Asians are more often held up as "model" minorities and blacks more often caricatured along opposite lines. Table 7.3 shows the public is nearly three times more likely to say blacks are lazy when comparing them to Asians. Also, whereas nearly half of U.S. adults believe blacks are violent, only 17 percent believe the same of Asians, which is actually less than the percentage for whites. The immigrant population too evokes more favorable assessments than blacks.

The typical American's association of blackness with criminality is an association made in almost equal measure by the typical black American. National civil rights spokesperson Reverend Jesse Jackson is quoted in a *U.S. News & World Report* as having once stated: "There is nothing more painful to me ... than to walk down the street and hear footsteps and start thinking about robbery, then look around and see somebody white and feel relieved."[22] This quote, from no less than a world renowned advocate of black equality, is a powerful indication of the fact that otherwise well-meaning blacks engage in the same kind of negative racial stereotypical thinking as the rest of the public. Based on a review of existing studies of public opinion, Anderson explains in *Benign Bigotry: The Psychology of Subtle Prejudice* that white Americans are more likely to make situation attributions about white criminal suspects (e.g., "I wonder what made that man steal?") and disposition attributions about black suspects (e.g., "Some people act like animals").[23] Quite a few public opinion studies single out whites as the group most likely to associate blacks with violence.[24] However, Anderson also makes clear that the fictional equation of blacks with crime is just as likely for blacks as for whites.

The data in Table 7.3 show black opinion regarding the nature of "blackness" closely parallels that of national public opinion and also white opinion on the all-important question of criminality. From the vantage point of black opinion, blacks emerge as the most violent of all racial groups in the United States. In fact, blacks are more inclined to believe blacks are violent than to believe whites or Asians are violent. Similarly, blacks are less likely to connect immigrants to higher crime rates. Black opinion mirrors national public opinion on more than just the issue of violence. Albeit to a lesser degree, black perceptions of laziness are also differentiated along racial lines in ways that do not bode well for blacks, certainly not as compared to Asians.

A more complex portrait of black-on-black opinion emerges once we move beyond the issues of violence and laziness. Many of the remaining features of blackness are adjudged in a more racially neutral fashion by blacks than by the country as a whole. Whereas only 9 percent of the national public acknowledges black contributions to the country as distinctive, a larger 25 percent of blacks do so. Blacks are just as likely to favorably assess "English" contributions as they are black contributions. The issues of family values and laziness are also points of departure, though not marked departures. Blacks are 16 percent more likely than the general public to say blacks are committed to strong families. However, black attitudes about racial differences in family values tilt slightly in favor of whites, as 50 percent of blacks believe blacks are committed to strong families but a slightly higher 58 percent believe the same about whites.

Notwithstanding these exceptions, cross-racial endorsement of the criminal and lazy stereotypes is what matters most for our look at criminal justice politics. It helps us understand the absence of public outrage regarding racial tracking in criminal justice.

The importance of the blacks-are-criminal stereotype is made even more significant by the fact that much of the country does not believe there is a viable excuse. Structural and institutional explanations for black criminality and for relatively limited black success in general have little sway with the lion's share of Americans. This is irrespective of whether the account centers on poverty, social isolation, fatherless homes, lack of positive role models, or the like.[25] We can see this by examining what most settle upon as the "real" reasons. The data in Tables 7.4[26] and 7.5 reflect national views on the root cause of racial inequality within society at large and within the criminal justice system in particular. These data show that much of the public believes it is the choices blacks make that best account for why they lag behind whites. Specifically, Pew survey data, shown in Table 7.4, indicate blacks who cannot get ahead are mostly responsible for their own condition as far as 67 percent of the public is concerned. Also, the reason blacks have "worse jobs, income, and housing than white people" is that they "just don't have the motivation or will power to pull themselves up out of poverty."

According to GSS data, where 45 percent are inclined to believe poor schooling is the cause of racial inequality, a larger 55 percent believe it is not. Even fewer (36 percent) say discrimination lies at the root of racial inequality, despite the belief that racism against blacks is widespread (as reported earlier). In fact, a two-thirds majority expressly rejects discrimination-centered explanations. A 2013 Gallup survey shows that 77 percent of all U.S. adults and 83 percent of non-Hispanic whites in particular believe blacks have worse jobs, income, and housing for reasons unrelated to discrimination (see Table 7.4). On the whole, blacks are not in the predicament they are in because the country has been unfair to them or because of the perpetuated effects of past discrimination, according to public opinion. Crucially, within the black community itself, opinion is divided on the question of blame. Most point to structural forces such as discrimination (59 percent) and unequal educational opportunity (50 percent). However, a sizeable share of blacks are just as persuaded that individual choices and behavior are the main culprit. Likewise, a Pew survey

TABLE 7.4. *Beliefs about the Causes of Racial Inequality, United States, Blacks, 2009–2010*

	United States	Blacks
Percent respondents believing ...		
Blacks have worse jobs, income and housing due to something other than discrimination (2013)	77	60
Blacks are mostly responsible for their own condition (2009)	67	52
Racial inequality due to lack of will (2006)	50	42
Racial inequality due to lack of education (2006)	45	50
Racial inequality not due to discrimination (2006)	64	41
Racial inequality due to inborn disability (2006)	9	12

shows 52 percent of blacks believe blacks are mostly responsible for their own conditions, as shown in Table 7.4. As many as 43 percent specifically denote a lack of will and motivation. A July 2013 Gallup Poll reports that fully 60 percent of blacks say the reason blacks have worse jobs, income, and housing than whites is not "due to discrimination against blacks" but rather "mostly due to something else."[27] Just as "society" is not accountable for the state of black America, so too are cosmic forces absolved of responsibility. Here as well, survey data that directly prod respondents to explain racial inequality provide solid support. Inborn disability is overwhelmingly rejected by the general public as an explanation. This view connects to the belief that blacks have no excuse but are, at bottom, insufficiently motivated to do better for themselves.

What the public thinks of blacks partly dictates their orientation toward the explanatory significance of race in the criminal justice system. According to McGarty and colleagues, "stereotypes form not just so that individuals can represent the social world to themselves but so that they can also act meaningfully and collectively within it."[28] In this case, the black criminal and lazy stereotypes are both a cognitive and a sociopolitical process.

To further anchor our understanding of the extent to which Americans tie the black law enforcement experience primarily to black choices and behavior, as opposed to the "system," a 2009 national survey was designed to probe precisely this issue. Administered to a 1,000-person, nationally representative sample, the two-part questionnaire prompted respondents, first, to choose between two options, as follows:

U.S. statistics show blacks are more likely than whites to be arrested and imprisoned. As you know, there are many possible reasons why this is the case.

TABLE 7.5. *Reason Blacks Have Higher Arrest and Imprisonment Rates,*
United States, Blacks, 2009

	United States	Blacks
Percent respondents believing …		
Blacks commit more crimes	62	21
Blacks receive unfair treatment by the criminal justice system	38	79

Evaluating two commonly discussed explanations, which do you find more con-
vincing to explain the reason why blacks have higher arrest and imprisonment
rates? Blacks commit more crimes or blacks receive unfair treatment by the criminal justice system?

The open-ended second part of the questionnaire asked them to explain
their choices. The results are depicted in Table 7.5.[29] They illustrate that,
although a sizeable number of blacks concede blacks' own behavior is
a driving force behind societywide inequality (as indicated earlier), they
mostly reject the idea that blacks are primarily to blame for racial disparities in criminal justice. Law enforcement is an altogether different beast
in their view, as the overwhelming majority (nearly 80 percent) fault the
system for higher black arrest and imprisonment rates. Furthermore, a
Gallup poll that offered respondents a choice between "discrimination"
and "something else" as mostly the cause of higher black male incarceration showed the preponderant share (50 percent) of blacks pinpointed
discrimination.[30] In essence, blacks are more likely to attribute differential criminal justice outcomes to the system, despite the fact that 41 percent believe blacks are more criminally oriented.

The general public has a very different orientation. It considers racial
disproportionalness in arrests and imprisonment chiefly the result of the
fact that blacks commit more crime, according to Table 7.5. So, while
in the view of most Americans the observed racial improprieties in law
enforcement are real, disproportional black criminality is apparently
more real.

No Contest: The Race Problem versus the
Crime Problem

In addition to the question of what most believe about the role of racism
in criminal justice is a separate, equally important one. Do Americans

care? Is racial justice considered a worthwhile expenditure of finite political resources, with so many other things believed gone awry? The answer
is not really, certainly not up against the broader range of issues confronting the criminal justice system. For the vast majority, the overriding objective of the criminal justice system should be that of fighting
and preventing crime easily. The preeminent importance of crime-fighting
is so obvious to some as to not even require elaboration. A significant
number of the respondents who, according to Table 7.5, denoted crime
instead of race as the issue to which policymakers should devote more
time offered the following kinds of circular explanations: it is the "more
pressing problem," "it should be common sense to most that out of control crime rates are more important," "people need to worry more about
crime instead of race," "crime is a more pressing issue," and "crime is
more important," and the like.[31] Any other goal the system is expected to
also achieve comes in a distant second place. Ensuring criminal laws are
enforced in a racially fair and equitable fashion is among the significantly
lesser important problems in need of tackling.

To argue that the public does not prioritize racial reform of law
enforcement because it is more committed to other criminal justice concerns, to some degree, begs the question of why one is prioritized over
the other. Analysis of survey data reveals that at least part of the reason
crime-fighting eclipses every other criminal justice policy objective is twofold. On the one hand, the public is convinced great strides have already
been made on the racial front and that the country is well on the way to
overcoming a legacy of bigotry and discrimination. In view of a significant number of adults, the country has already spent more than enough
time and money trying to fix what they see as black people's never-ending
problems. The challenge of crime, on the other hand, presents an altogether different scenario. The trajectory for it is decidedly less positive in
the eyes of the public. Little to no progress has been made toward halting
the rising crime rate, and the country is not on track to doing so either,
or so Americans believe. This reasoning further explains why the seriousness of the crime problem easily trumps that of the race problem, both
in criminal justice and beyond. One might reasonably assume that if the
public were persuaded that the system is adequately handling its first priority of crime-fighting and prevention, it might be inclined to re-channel
at least some attention and resources toward racial reform of the system.
Such is not the case. In what follows, we inquire into the public's assessment of the race problem in the United States and in the criminal justice
system in particular, side-by-side with its opinion of the crime problem.

First of all, there is no public alarm regarding the plight of blacks, neither within the criminal justice system nor in American society as a whole. Most Americans are convinced that, on balance, things are not so bad for blacks and definitely not as bad as they once were. At the same time, they are not under the impression the country has metamorphosed into a racial utopia. Most are aware well into the twenty-first century that the country continues to grapple with what W. E. B. DuBois characterized in 1903 as the preeminent problem of the twentieth century.[32] A host of progressive attitudinal changes since the 1950s have been carefully documented by Howard Schuman, Charlotte Steeh, Lawrence Bobo, and Maria Krysan.[33] The authors establish that, by the 1990s, there was near universal support for the principle of equality, super-majority support for implementation of equality, and growing support for interracial marriage and other aspects of social and cultural change. These shifts in public attitudes are in addition to a plethora of federal and state anti-discrimination legislative advancements.

Even so, a majority in the United States concedes racism is alive and well. Express public acknowledgment of widespread racism is depicted in Table 7.6.[34] Fully 69 percent of all adults in the United States believe there is discrimination against African Americans. This is according to Pew data, which, when broken down by race, show 70 percent of whites, 82 percent of blacks, and 54 percent of Hispanics believe there is either "a lot" or "some" discrimination against blacks. A Gallup survey establishes also a smaller majority of the U.S. adult population (51 percent) is cognizant of the prevalence of anti-black racism.

Oddly, moreover, at least in view of the public, racial discrimination and unequal racial opportunity are not one and the same. The existence of anti-black prejudice does not necessarily mean blacks are denied equal access to employment, housing, and education. Nor does discrimination inevitably spell racial disadvantage. Likely because the overwhelming majority think it possible to have a brand of pervasive racism that somehow peacefully coexists with racially equal opportunity, almost three out of five adults in the United States are satisfied with the way blacks are treated. Yet, Schuman and colleagues show public support for federal implementation of desegregation policies is lower than that for the principle of desegregation. And to the extent any contemporary brand of racism is especially concerning, it is not anti-black racism. According to Table 7.6, the general sense is that there is room for improvement in the treatment of other traditionally marginalized minorities, such

TABLE 7.6. *Attitudes toward the Prevalence and Relevance of Anti-Black Racism, United States, Blacks, 2004–2011*

	United States	Blacks
Percent respondents believing …		
There is discrimination against African Americans in society today (2009)	69	82
Racism against blacks is widespread in the United States (2009)	51	72
Blacks have equal chance for jobs in local community (2011)	72	39
Black children have equal chance for good education in local community (2008)	75	49
Blacks have equal chance for housing in local community (2008)	78	52
Percent respondents who are …		
Satisfied with the way blacks in America are treated (2008)	59	35
Satisfied with the way immigrants in America are treated (2008)	46	38
Satisfied with the way Arabs in the America are treated (2008)	47	38
Proud of America's fair and equal treatment of all groups in society (2004)	75	58

as immigrants and Arabs. Blacks are no longer viewed as the primary victims of discrimination.

Blacks could not disagree more. They see not only racial prejudice and bigotry as continuing problems but racially unequal opportunity as well.

Despite the sharp divide over the current pervasiveness of discrimination, both sides of the divide have a very upbeat outlook. Much of the optimism centers on the trajectory for the race problem. A sizeable majority of Americans, including the black population, cling to the idea there has been a great deal of positive racial change and that even more is on the horizon. The public conception of racial progress encompasses a fairly broad range of issues, from legal rights to socioeconomic status to interpersonal relations and more. Table 7.7[35] suggests the past ten years have witnessed improvement in civil rights for blacks and the years to come promise even more improvement in this area. The gap between black and white living standards is expected to further narrow in the

TABLE 7.7. *Public Opinion on Racial Progress, United States, Blacks, 2008–2009*

	United States	Blacks
Percent respondents believing …		
Civil rights for blacks have improved in the past ten years (2008)*	79	72
Civil rights for blacks will improve ten years from now (2008)*	73	65
Compared to 5 years ago the gap between black and white living standards is narrower (2009)	50	49
Compared to 10 years ago the gap between black and white living standards is narrower (2009)	61	56
Life for blacks in this country will be better in the future (2009)	55	53
Race relations between whites and blacks are good (2008)	68	61
A solution to black and white relations will eventually be worked out (2011)	52	42

Note:
* Includes "greatly improved" and "somewhat improved" responses.

years to come, just as most believe it already has. The same applies to the perception of overall life prospects for blacks going forward.

As to the dream Dr. Martin L. King, Jr. had more than fifty years ago in 1963 about little black boys and black girls joining hands together with little white boys and white girls as sisters and brothers, that too is expected to materialize at some point in the future. This particular aspect of King's dream does not resonate quite as forcefully, though. The public does not exhibit the same level of enthusiasm toward the future of race relations as for legal rights and socioeconomic opportunity. Fully 68 percent regard relations between whites and blacks as currently good. But, compared to the 73 percent that expect black civil rights to improve going forward, a slimmer majority of 52 percent believes a solution to relations between blacks and whites will eventually be worked out. Of course, as a logical matter, it would seem a change in relations with blacks is a necessary precondition to a change in behavior toward blacks. But, apparently in the minds of the general American public, the interpersonal aspects of race are disconnected from the racial status quo. There are indications of a similar disconnect in the minds of blacks too. Except, they are comparatively less enthusiastic about race relations, while still quite hopeful about the future of rights and opportunity. Table 7.7 shows sizeable majorities of blacks note improvement in civil rights over the past decade and envision an even brighter future ahead in this area. Nearly half also say the gap in living standards has narrowed in the past five years, and a smaller 36 percent say it has widened.[36] Last, black optimism about what the future holds for their overall life prospects is nearly the same as that of the general public.

Oddly, the survey data in Table 7.8[37] supply grounds to argue that the candidacy and election of Barack Obama significantly dampened the prospects for mobilizing a critical mass of Americans around the race problem in criminal justice, or any other aspect of the race problem in the country. It could be said that his election whittled away at public disquietude on this front. A remarkable 85 percent of blacks stated outright in 2008 that his impending election would be a sign of progress in racial equality in the United States, as did 74 percent of the overall public. Critically, moreover, Obama's 2008 campaign did much to alter also the nation's grasp of the obstacles and problems average black citizens face on a daily basis. Right from the start, Americans expected the election of candidate Obama to the White House in 2008 to singlehandedly work wonders on the racial front. The data in Table 7.8 show fully 80 percent of both the general public and blacks in particular expected his election to open up opportunities for blacks in national politics. A solid majority of the general public and a two-thirds majority of blacks thought it would improve race relations also. His impending election was even expected to somehow swing open doors of opportunity in black careers across the country.

The social, political, and historical significance attached by so many to Obama's election in 2008 overshadowed the continued relevance of race and, in some cases, caused many to question it. The first black presidential candidate ever to be nominated by one of the two major political parties, let alone actually win the general election, Obama's victory was momentous enough to generate discussion about a "post-racial" society. The term connoted America was no longer shackled with the effects of its shameful history of slavery and discrimination, as evidenced by the fact that a black man could now become president. An article in the opinion section of *The Washington Post* noted: "Obama's election isn't just about a black president. It's about a new America. The days of confrontational identity politics have come to an end."[38] "Post-racial" signified also the advancement of blacks from being the group that symbolized the nation's proclivity toward racial subjugation to the group whose experience most poignantly captured the limitless possibilities of the great American dream.

The news media pontificated at length about post-racialism.[39] Two days following the 2008 election conservative scholar Abigail Thernstrom remarked in the *National Review Online*: "An Obama presidency – in addition to the pride it evokes – will allow black parents to tell their children, it really is true: the color of your skin will not matter. You can grow up to be our president, the most powerful person on earth, the leader of the free world."[40] One week after the 2008 presidential election, the Thernstroms together asserted in a *Wall Street Journal* editorial that while the "results do not mean we now live in a color-blind society," "we can say the doors of electoral opportunity in America are open to all."[41] Calling for an end to federal protections in the 1965 Voting Rights Act and amendments, the Thernstroms read Obama's election to mean: "American voters have turned a racial corner."[42]

Not only his election but Obama himself was frequently presented as Exhibit A, proof positive of how far blacks had come. Meaning, for many, Barack Obama personified the racial transformation believed to be underway, making it that much more difficult to grasp the idea the black masses remained handicapped by skin color, let alone targeted by law enforcement because of it. The 2012 Democratic national party platform highlighted he was "the son of a single mother" and others underscored he was the son of an African immigrant father.[43] Much of the country saw him as one who admirably rose from humble beginnings to become a Harvard law graduate and a charismatic, transformative presidential candidate turned president. He was able to work his way up the ranks through old-fashioned hard work, not affirmative action, without any problems with the police. If he could do it, then so could other blacks – despite widespread racism. And if Obama's ascendance out of the ashes were not proof enough, there were plenty of other phenomenal personal stories chronicling the extraordinary triumph of otherwise ordinary blacks in the face of prejudice. Supreme Court Justice Thurgood Marshall, U.N. Ambassador Andrew Young, Oprah Winfrey, the late business entrepreneur John H. Johnson, to name a few. Indeed, the very existence of a black middle class alone constituted solid proof for many that insurmountable racial barriers no longer existed. Alas, a majority voted Obama, a black man, into the highest office in the land. Admonishing the National Association for the Advancement of Colored People (NAACP) for its harsh critique of the Tea Party, former presidential candidate Sarah Palin challenged the organization: "Isn't it time we put aside the divisive politics of the past once and for all and celebrate the fact that neither race nor gender is any longer a barrier

TABLE 7.8. *Public Opinion on 2008 Election of Barack Obama, United States, Blacks, 2008–2011*

	United States	Blacks
Percent respondents believing election of Obama would ...		
Be a sign of progress in racial equality in the United States (2008)	74	85
Be among most important advances for blacks in 100 years (2008)	50	59
Open up opportunities for other blacks in national politics (2008)	80	79
Make black career advancement easier (2008)	54	56
Improve race relations (2008)	56	65
Percent respondents believing that due to Obama election...		
Race relations better (2009)	36	54
Race relations had gotten better (2011)	35	48
Race relations will get better in the years ahead (2011)	52	64

to achieving success in America – even in achieving the highest office in the land?"[44]

A marked decline in the high hopes attached to Obama's candidacy ensued in the wake of his succession to the White House, starting as early as 2009. The more tempered attitude toward the Obama presidency was evident on racial matters as well as many other issues. Whereas in 2008, 56 percent expected his election would improve race relations, in late 2009, only 36 percent reported race relations had actually gotten better as a result of his election, according to Table 7.8. Among blacks, the stock put into Obama's likely effect on race relations did not dip quite as steeply, still it decreased from 65 percent in 2008 to 54 percent in 2009 and then 48 percent two years later.

Blacks were less inclined to abandon their hopes for a brighter future on the racial horizon. Not since the era of Dr. Martin L. King, Jr. had any single individual proven so inspiring to the black community as Barack Obama. According to a 2010 Pew survey report of blacks only,[45] an astounding 95 percent indicated their overall opinion of Barack Obama was favorable. Of those, fully 77 percent specifically said they had a "very" favorable opinion, and the rest "mostly" favorable. More than any other racial or ethnic group, blacks believed Obama shared the values and interests of black people in this country, fully 61 percent, compared to 40 percent of all adults who said the same.[46] We can say, then, blacks felt a special bond with President Obama that went beyond the connection most of the country felt toward him. He gave blacks a renewed faith on the racial front. Pre-Obama election (between 2001 and 2007) the percentage of blacks dissatisfied with the way blacks are treated in U.S. society increased by 8 percent, from 60 percent to 68 percent, but post-Obama election (between 2008 and 2013) that number declined by 12 percent, from 64 percent to 52 percent.[47] In sum, blacks were still more dissatisfied than most with the racial portrait of America but less so since Obama was in the nation's highest office.

Although talk of a post-racial society eventually disappeared or was dismissed by most scholars and journalists, much of the rest of the country opted to "keep hope alive." As late as August 2011 – in the midst of a lagging economy, continued high unemployment, soaring gas prices, increased uncertainty on the international front, among other concerns – a 52 percent majority of all adults continued to expect race relations in the country would get better in the years ahead "as a result of Barack Obama's presidency" (see Table 7.8). This, while 35 percent expected no change, and only 11 percent anticipated things would get worse. For blacks, the future of race relations appeared all the more promising because of Obama. Nearly two out of three stated as much.

Few high-profile demands were put on the Obama administration to do more to actively improve race relations or the racial status quo. No ultimatums. A case in point is the initial reaction to the jury verdict acquitting a white man, George Zimmerman, of fatally shooting an unarmed black teenager, Trayvon Martin, while on Neighborhood Watch Patrol in Florida. This, *after* being advised by the 911 dispatcher to stop following Martin. Further complicating the incident was the local police department's initial failure to fully investigate, arrest, or charge Zimmerman and the state's "stand your ground law," believed by some to tacitly condone Zimmerman's actions. Although President Obama indicated in a news conference Attorney General Eric Holder was "reviewing what happened down there,"[48] all that resulted in the immediate aftermath were massive marches and speeches condemning the verdict. There were no pressing demands for a U.S. Justice Department investigation and prosecution. Television commentator and author Tavis Smiley deemed Obama's reaction to the Zimmerman verdict "weak as pre-sweetened Kool-Aid,"[49] and later chastised Obama for not laying out a definitive pathway to reform. Smiley was met with swift and harsh criticism mainly from liberals for his comments.[50]

While the president did in fact lay out what he described in his own words as a "couple of specifics" as to what could be done in the wake of the tragedy, he concluded the news conference by saying:

As difficult and challenging as this whole episode has been for a lot of people, I don't want us to lose sight that things are getting better. Each successive generation seems to be making progress in changing attitudes when it comes to race. It doesn't mean we're in a postracial society. It doesn't mean that racism is eliminated. But when I talk to Malia and Sasha, and I listen to their friends, and I see them interact, they're better than we are – they're better than we were – on these issues. And that's true in every community that I've visited across the country.[51]

Crucially, Obama added that law enforcement is typically a matter handled by state and local governments, not the federal government.

Strangely, then, it would appear Obama's electoral success and his reign in the White House inadvertently served to undermine efforts to rally broad public support for racial reform in criminal justice. This, even on the rare occasion of large-scale discontent with a jury verdict stunningly dismissive of racial profiling, and even on the watch of a president who actually went to greater lengths than any before him to tell Americans racial profiling was real, as Chapter 4 reveals.[52]

As blacks and whites settled on a revised narrative regarding the nation's treatment of blacks and their future, a new and very different narrative for the white experience in America was taking shape. This narrative told of how whites are discriminated against and denied equal opportunity because of their skin color, of how bad things are for the white man. Before delving into the particulars of this new narrative chronicling anti-whiteness, it should be noted this aspect of the country's racial transformation actually began to manifest in national politics as early as the 1960s.[53] However, the ideological framework for it is a new form of racial conservatism, one that rivals its predecessors. Whereas 1964 presidential candidate Barry Goldwater aligned himself with opponents of the traditional civil rights agenda under the banner of states' rights and limited federal power, his Republican successors from Richard Nixon through George H. W. Bush outright denounced certain parts of the agenda as contrary to the American way. Once championed as a means of rectifying the legacy of slavery, affirmative action was soon decried as nothing more than a form of reverse discrimination against whites. Questions about the proper balance of power between the federal and state government under the Equal Protection Clause were supplanted with questions about the legitimacy of contemporary race reform advocacy itself.

The tables had turned so much, that national civil rights spokespersons, such as Reverends Jesse Jackson and Al Sharpton, were now publicly disparaged in more than a few corners, not as impatient or misguided, as Dr. Martin L. King was often described by his critics during the 1950s and 1960s.[54] Worse, Sharpton and Jackson were divisive race-baiters and opportunists. Adolph Reed, Jr.'s book *The Jesse Jackson Phenomenon: The Crisis of Purpose in Afro-American Politics* asserted Jackson's "message of hope" during his 1988 presidential campaign "was not grounded in politics" but "manipulated its adherents' fear and despair."[55] The *Washington Post* opinion piece lauding the emergence of a "new America" with Obama's election began with the following: "African Americans have just entered the no-excuses zone." The self-described African American writer chastised the National Association for the Advancement of Colored People (NAACP), liberal black author and commentator Tavis Smiley, and noted political scientist Ronald Walters for expecting newly elected President Obama to pursue racial reform. She declared "some African Americans don't get it. Despite measurable advances over the past thirty years, they still perceive themselves as beleaguered, as the once and present victims of discrimination."[56] Somewhat less delicately, conservative radio commentator Rush Limbaugh remarked "for 50 years, the race hustlers, the Jacksons, the Sharptons have been complaining and moaning and whining about the same stuff for 50 years."[57]

For some, then, the gravamen of today's race problem is not that blacks continue to lag behind whites socioeconomically and are subject to a different brand of law enforcement but that they continue to complain about it.

The racial rhetoric that emerged on the far right does not contrast all that sharply with the core sense of the public at large. Americans seem to have reached a point of fatigue in regard to continued advocacy on behalf of blacks in any sphere of American life. Many appear tired of nearly 150 years of bemoaning all the wrong society has perpetrated against black people. Indeed, there is growing frustration over what some see as a misguided and incessantly persistent emphasis on race. Among the responses to a partly open-ended survey asking whether race or crime should be prioritized by policymakers were the following: "Race is not an issue unless you are a politician"; "dwelling on race is not the cure.... Stop trying to incite prejudice"; "race issues are more political than a real problem"; "because the biggest crime is the way that they try to push the

TABLE 7.9. *Attitudes toward the Prevalence of Anti-White Racism, United States, Blacks, 2009–2010*

	United States	Blacks
Percent respondents stating …		
White opportunities hurt by affirmative action (2010)	61	43
There is a lot or some discrimination against white Americans (2010)	45	41
Racism against whites widespread (2009)	44	39

race card and illegal aliens"; "race is only an issue these days because people continue to make it one"; and "race issues are trumped up for political leverage and advantage."[58]

Some even go so far as to question whether there is any such thing as "race." Consequently, demands for redressing the perpetuated effects of slavery, for compensatory justice, for stronger civil rights oversight and regulation gain little to no traction in public opinion. Cries of racially discriminatory actions against individual blacks fall on virtually deaf ears too, as many have come to believe the so-called race card is overplayed to the point that it lacks legitimacy and amounts to little more than a smokescreen for those who fall short in terms of their own individual merit, choices, and behavior. The race card has lost much of its potency. Perhaps nowhere is this truer than in regard to crime and punishment, given that a substantial portion of the public believes blacks are more criminally oriented than most.

Americans are now convinced that whites have been hurt by what they consider an over-the-top preoccupation with making things better for blacks. Table 7.9[59] contains evidence on this point. Nearly two-thirds of adults in the United States say whites have been hurt by affirmative action and other kinds of preferential programs. Whites are believed to be almost as much the victims of discrimination as racial minorities. As many as 44 percent think racism against whites is widespread in the United States, a difference of only seven points from the number believing racism against blacks is widespread, as reported in Table 7.6. Perhaps remarkably, there are only a few percentage points separating blacks and the general public on the issue of anti-white racism. Blacks are almost just as likely as the rest of the public to claim there is widespread racism and discrimination against whites. That as many as 56 percent of blacks in 2008 and 43 percent of blacks in 2010 also embrace the concept of reverse discrimination and its disadvantaging effect on whites is further indication of the extent to which worries about anti-white racism are broadly and firmly rooted in the public mind.

To sum up, there is little concern on the part of the public about racial disproportionalness in criminal justice or in society at large partly because most are convinced its eventual resolution is already in the works. The lion's share of work to be done on the racial front is accomplished and what remains is *de minimis* or beyond the reach of government. And to the extent there is a serious concern on the racial front, it is how whites are treated, not so much blacks. Against this backdrop, efforts to reform the status quo in criminal justice are at odds with the public mind-set.

That Americans are decidedly less optimistic about the trajectory of the crime problem goes a long way toward helping to explain why so few actively worry about reforming the criminal justice system along racial lines, whereas so many are up in arms about improving the system's ability to protect public safety. The general consensus on crime is that it has yet to be sufficiently brought under control, and the pathway forward is not especially promising either. It is important to clarify at the outset that, when Americans say they are concerned about the crime rate, it is not their own personal safety driving the concern. Most generally feel safe in their own homes, safe in their own neighborhoods, and safe as they go about their day-to-day activities. The data in Table 7.10[60] demonstrate crimes that potentially cause bodily harm are not at the top of the list of particularized anxieties. None of the top three most worried-about crimes have to do with the safety of one's own person but rather identify theft followed by home burglary and car theft – in that order.

Being personally victimized by a violent crime is not something that weighs heavily on the mind of most, according to Table 7.10. Roughly a third fret about the possibility of being mugged or their child being hurt while in school; even fewer worry about crimes such as murder, carjacking, and sexual assault. This is not to make light of the fact that one in five have some fear of being murdered. Rather the point is the types of offenses that most directly affect personal safety are the source of anxiety for what amounts to a minority of the overall adult population in the United States. The same can be said of the black population in particular. Coupled with a relatively limited concern for personal safety is the fact that most Americans also believe their neighborhoods are safe. This we can glean from the last line in Table 7.10, which shows only a third of all U.S. adults report being afraid to walk alone at night near where they live. Although a slightly larger share of blacks consider neighborhood safety a problem, for them too personal safety is of lesser importance

TABLE 7.10. *Concern about Crime Victimization, United States, Blacks, 2010–2011*

	United States	Blacks
Percent respondents reporting concern about …		
Being the victim of identity theft	67	71
Home being burglarized while at home	47	43
Car being stolen or broken into	44	43
Getting mugged	34	36
Having a child harmed while in school	32	38
Home being burglarized while away	30	28
Being a victim of terrorism	30	35
Being sexually assaulted	22	16
Getting murdered	20	30
Being attacked while driving a car	19	26
Being the victim of a hate crime	17	29
Being assaulted or killed on the job	6	6
Walking alone at night near where they live (GSS 2010)	33	41

than the safety of their property. The fact that most feel safe in their own neighborhoods also points to crime being increasingly problematic for them as the lens is expanded outward – beyond their safety zone, where they do not live.

Serving as additional evidence that public safety worries are not exactly personal safety concerns is the fact that the vast majority of Americans do not take steps to protect their person. Were they to do so, we could reliably conclude they are indeed "on guard," or at least unsettled enough as to do something. Consistent with their slightly higher concerns about protection of property, a sizeable percentage of blacks take steps to protect their home. Beyond this, however, none of the property-related worries noted earlier are serious enough to goad the average citizen to take action. As much is proven by the data in Table 7.11.[61] At the top of the list of precautionary steps taken is installation of a home burglar alarm. Yet, even this is something fewer than a third bother to do, and the second most common anti-crime measure (gun purchase) is taken by less than a quarter.

The most likely reason so few are worried about personal safety is that only a tiny percentage actually experience violent crime, a very tiny percentage. Fully 99 percent are never even in danger of being a violent crime victim, let alone actually being one. Data from the National Crime Victimization Survey (NCVS) in Table 7.12[62] help to illustrate this.[63]

TABLE 7.11. *Steps Taken to Avoid Criminal Victimization, United States, Blacks, 2007*

	United States	Blacks
Percent respondents reporting they engaged in selected behaviors because of concern over crime		
Had a burglar alarm installed in home	31	43
Bought a gun for protection of self or home	23	16
Carry mace or pepper spray	14	17
Carry a knife for defense	12	20
Carry a gun for defense	12	17
Avoid going to certain places or neighborhoods	48	55

TABLE 7.12. *Criminal Victimization Rates, United States, Blacks, 2008 (Rates per 1,000 Persons Age 12 or Older)*

	United States	Black
Personal Crimes ...		
Crimes of violence	19.3	25.9
Completed violence	5.4	10.1
Attempted/threatened violence	13.9	15.7
Rape/sexual assault	0.8	1.9
Robbery	2.2	5.5
Aggravated assault	3.3	5.2
Simple assault	12.9	13.3
Purse snatching/pocket picking	0.5	0.7
Property Crimes ...		
Household burglary	26.3	42.0
Motor vehicle theft	6.6	12.6
Theft	101.8	103.3

The NCVS data are measures of criminal victimizations and not crime victims. But, even if we were to assume each victimization represents one person, these numbers would indicate actual crime is rarely experienced by the vast majority of the U.S. population, if ever. More precisely, the data would mean that about one half of 1 percent (or 5.4/1000) are actual victims of crime and just over 1 percent (or 13.9/1000) are *almost* crime victims, that is to say the target of threatened or attempted violence. Even the most common criminal offense, simple assault, affects just over 1 percent. Slightly in contrast to this, the black criminal victimization rate for completed crimes of violence is twice the national average;

TABLE 7.13. *Public Worries about Crime Trends, United States, Blacks, 2006–2011*

	United States	Blacks
Percent respondents believing there is ...		
More crime in local community than there was a year ago (2011)	48	50
More crime in the United States than there was a year ago (2011)	68	70
An extremely or very serious drug problem in local community (2009)	30	32
An extremely or very serious drug problem in the United States (2009)	68	73
Percent respondents believing ...		
Government successful in controlling crime (2006)	35	24
Nation has stood still or lost ground in coping with illegal drugs (2011)	66	41

still this comparatively higher rate translates into only a small percentage of the black population in the United States being personally affected by crime. The public's greater concern about identity theft appears grounded in reality, as it corresponds to greater property crime victimization.

What underlies public violent crime worries is, in essence, a fear of potential threats to personal safety, a fear of what *could* happen. This fear is based on a perception of what is occurring beyond the borders of their individual lives and neighborhoods. Many Americans view the crime problem as something that presently affects "other" neighborhoods more so than their own. This is clear from the data in Table 7.11, shown earlier. At the top of the list of precautionary steps taken to ensure personal safety is that of avoiding "going to certain places or neighborhoods." Whereas anywhere from 12 to 31 percent report taking measures geared to protect their person or property, a significantly larger 48 percent of all U.S. adults and 55 percent of black adults say they simply avoid unsafe areas. Yet another indication of the fear of crime somewhere "out there" is that the number characterizing the drug problem as a serious problem facing the United States is more than double that saying the same about the drug problem in their own community. (See Table 7.13.)

Add public perception of crime levels somewhere "out there" together with public opinion on crime trends, and it becomes clear that in the public mind the crime problem is fundamentally a matter of the direction in which things are moving. It is a fear that someday crime might actually arrive at their doorstep. It has not yet, but someone has to stop it before it does. The data in Table 7.13[64] indicate a large majority is convinced current crime rates are higher than they were in the past. General Social Survey (GSS) data reveal the public has held to this perception since as far back as 1972. Besides the fact that the trajectory of crime is unsettling is yet another concern. The government's success in changing the course of crime trends falls short of the desired mark and, thus, further dashes hopes things will get better anytime soon. While blacks are more convinced than most that the War on Drugs made some headway, they are also more apt to believe the drug problem in the United States remains a serious one.

Significantly, moreover, the threat of violent crime and the need to confront it are serious enough as to trump any and all concerns about the problems facing blacks in the criminal justice system. It should be noted that David Cole has persuasively argued that one concern cannot be resolved without addressing the other. Cole lays out this argument in *No Equal Justice*, namely that racially uneven law enforcement effectively diminishes respect for the law and the force of law.[65] To extend Cole's reasoning, how can the youth of any color be fully persuaded to respect and follow the law when they personally observe or experience unlawful or constitutionally suspect behavior on the part of those in whose hands the law is entrusted? Viewed in this light, the racial dynamics of the criminal justice system could be said to undermine what most consider the overriding goal of the system. Yet, most Americans still make what they consider the "obvious" (and what one respondent pertaining to the data in Table 7.16 considered the "duh") choice of self-preservation over racial justice.

Turns out, the so-called crime problem is not so obviously a problem, if we examine actual crime statistics. They show crime has steadily declined in recent decades and virtually everywhere in America.

Yet, no matter the angle from which one examines the question of whether crime or race is most concerning to the public, the unequivocal answer is "crime." Thus, the de-racialization of crime by politicians was firmly anchored in public thinking. Neither crime nor race actually tops the public's list of national policy priorities, something that is most apparent against the economic crisis that began in 2008. The claim made here is not that public safety is considered the most important issue facing the country; rather, crime is considered *more* important than race. There are earlier times in history when race weighed more heavily on the public mind. However, the last time the political importance of race trumped that of crime and occupied the center stage of national politics was during the mid-1960s. From the late 1960s onward, race has taken a back seat to crime, in a manner of speaking.[66]

Among the local concerns cited in a 2009 Pew Research Center open-ended survey, not only do "crime/drugs" issues easily outrank "racism/discrimination" problems[67]; racial issues are the least mentioned of all of the roughly twenty-six categories, with fewer than 0.5 percent of all U.S. adults and only 1 percent of blacks mentioning race as "the most important problem facing [their] local community today." Conversely, crime and drug issues were the most frequently mentioned outside of economic and financial issues. Furthermore, whereas 14 percent of the general population identifies crime concerns as most important locally, an even larger 27 percent of blacks do so.

Blacks are more worried about crime than the rest of the country. A 2012 Gallup poll solicited feedback on a list of fifteen issues.[68] For each, respondents were asked to indicate whether they worried a "great deal," a "fair amount," or "only a "little/not at all." Here too, the economy along with gas prices and the federal deficit topped the list. But crime and violence along with drug use again easily outranked race relations, which came in last with only 17 percent of Americans naming it as something they worried about a great deal. This compared to more than three times that figure saying the same for crime and violence (42 percent) and for drugs (42 percent). The survey did not gauge the views of blacks separately but did report "nonwhites" elevate crime and violence (53 percent) and drug use (52 percent) well above race relations (28 percent). These data tell us as well that, even though racial issues are comparatively more important to minorities than to the general public, minorities also do not consider racial issues as high a priority as crime.

Safety concerns have tremendous significance within the black community. A Pew survey of black respondents shows that not only is the competition between economic issues and crime concerns more intense among blacks than among Americans at large; crime is believed to be one of the top three challenges confronting the black community. Indeed, crime is closely linked by blacks to survival of the most basic institution within the community structure, namely the black family. The survey asked respondents to comment on how problematic certain issues are for black families. While 79 percent cite a lack of decent-paying jobs as foremost important, a comparable 74 percent also assert drugs and alcoholism are a big problem for black families today. Sixty-seven percent specifically note neighborhood crime as a big problem. None of the other issues were as important to blacks, insofar as the percentage naming public schools (56 percent), unwed parents (50 percent), and lack of successful role models for young people (42 percent) trailed by double digits.[69]

Fight Crime, Not Racial Inequity

As for policy preferences, voters want lawmakers to prioritize policies that bolster greater efficiency in the criminal justice system over and above policies that foster greater racial parity within the system. They are not nearly as interested in eliminating racial influences as they are in getting rid of crime. And when forced to choose between the two, anti-crime policy wins. The public's specific criminal justice policy preference is to strengthen the system's crime-fighting capacity and to do so both by increasing the penalties for criminals and by preventing crime. There is an ever-growing sense among Americans that criminals get off too easily and are too often coddled by the system. According to Gaubatz, the get-tough consensus of recent decades satisfies a "need for an outlet for insufficiently actualized negative feelings about the behavior of their fellow citizens."[70]

Against the backdrop, quite literally, the last thing the American public wants to hear about is scaling back heavy-handed criminal law enforcement against blacks, whom many consider the most violent.

The "get tough" stance on the part of average citizens is partly evidenced by Table 7.14.[71] It shows a sizeable majority believes courts do not deal harshly enough with criminals and that violent juvenile delinquents ages fourteen to seventeen should be treated as adults. Gallup time-series data reveal public endorsement of capital punishment stretching back to 1953.[72] Presented with the alternative option of life imprisonment for persons convicted of murder, the proportionate share still opts for the more exacting death penalty as of 2010, specifically 49 percent preferring it versus the 46 percent who prefer "life imprisonment without the possibility of parole." The reasons people offer to explain their support for capital punishment underscore the desire for retribution. A 2011 Pew Research Center survey shows fully 53 percent of supporters say the punishment fits the crime or it is what murderers deserve, and a very small percentage say they support the death penalty because it acts as a deterrent (6 percent), according to Table 7.14. An earlier 2003 Gallup survey reveals pretty much the same. Among the sixteen response categories emerging from the poll asking why respondents support capital punishment, retribution tops the list, having been cited by as many as 40 percent, followed by cost (12 percent) and then deterrence (11 percent).

A number of scholars link the public's get-tough stance to anti-black sentiment on the part of whites. In fact, several studies assert the "racialization" of a range of public-policy attitudes, with attitudes toward crime

TABLE 7.14. *Criminal Justice Policy Preferences, United States, Blacks, 2003–2011*

	United States	Blacks
Percent respondents believing (or support)		
Courts do not deal harshly enough with criminals (2010)	68	54
Juvenile delinquents should be treated the same as adults (2003)	59	54
Death penalty for persons convicted of murder (GSS 2010)	68	47
Death penalty for persons convicted of murder (Gallup 2011)	61	28
Life imprisonment the better penalty for murder (2010)	46	77
Death penalty acts as a deterrent to murder (Pew 2011)	6	NA
Death penalty acts as a deterrent to murder (Gallup 2003)	11	NA
Best crime approach is to attack social and economic causes (2010)	64	85
System should try to rehabilitate, and not just punish (2003)	72	NA

policy being the most frequently noted.[73] Unnever, Cullen, and Jonson note: "Taken together, the extant studies reach remarkably consistent results: negative views toward African Americans – what scholars in this area have called 'racism' or 'racial animus' – predict a range of political attitudes, including greater support for capital punishment."[74] Support for tough criminal justice measures, according to this work, is masked white racism. Zubrinsky and Bobo[75] and also Bobo and Gilliam[76] establish statistical linkages between size of the black population and fears about safety, among other things. Bobo and Johnson observe more directly: "The most consistent predictor of criminal justice policy attitudes is, in fact, a form of racial prejudice."[77]

Episodic renderings of black opinion in the wake of controversial incidents certainly hint at a very liberal orientation on the part of blacks as to how the system should operate. Gallup, Inc. polling showed 48 percent of blacks found the 1993 jury acquittal of officers involved in the Rodney King incident wrong, 89 percent believed the "not guilty" verdict in the O. J. Simpson 1993 criminal trial a right decision, and fully

85 percent considered the 2013 acquittal of George Zimmerman in the shooting death of unarmed teenager Trayvon Martin a wrong decision.[78] This compared to markedly fewer adults in the overall U.S. population who believed the same, 27 percent, 42 percent, and 40 percent, respectively. On the surface, raw data on support for capital punishment also appear to link crime policy attitudes to racial identity. Capital sentencing has a very different political meaning in the black community as compared to elsewhere. Owed in no small measure to the history of racially disproportionate use of death sentencing, blacks are far more critical and distrustful of capital sentencing than most. The data in Table 7.14 show only a minority of blacks support capital punishment, while the overwhelming majority endorse life imprisonment as the better of the two penalties for murder.

Whereas these raw data and the aforementioned research studies evidence a link between racial factors and crime policy attitudes, experimental studies by Hurwitz and Peffley suggest that not all crime policy attitudes are linked to racial animus. They find racial stereotypes are only modestly correlated with attitudes toward generic crime issues, such as the death penalty, and unimportant as determinants of responses toward nonviolent crimes and preventive polices.[79] Aside from this research, one could reasonably theorize that being tough on crime stems from circumstances that vary for blacks and whites. That is, blacks and whites could want the same thing – more stringent criminal justice policies – for very different reasons.[80] Then, there is also the strange possibility that blacks are no less susceptible than whites to the kind of race-based criminal justice policy preferences highlighted in many public opinion studies. (Recall, Table 7.3 shows that 41 percent of blacks believe that blacks are violent.)

Significant for this discussion is that, whatever the precise racial animus shaping attitudes toward criminal justice policies, blacks, much like whites, settle upon a list of policy priorities that elevates crime policies. National survey data show blacks' lower support for the death penalty in no way signifies they are any softer on crime or any less desirous of criminal accountability than most other Americans. In their case, the limited support for the death penalty reflects simply that blacks support *capital punishment* at much lower levels. Otherwise, blacks are just as interested as the next in making criminals pay for their crimes, according to Table 7.14. That blacks share the general public's sense of the system's failure to punish adequately is also revealed by the data, which depict their negative assessments of court sentencing and criminal justice responses to juvenile delinquency.

In addition to a cross-racial public preference for policies that bolster criminal accountability, there is also a cross-racial consensus behind the goal of making the criminal justice system proactive and not merely reactive.[81] Rehabilitative and preventative approaches are preferred by the general public more than a purely punitive approach. As shown in Table 7.14, the overwhelming majority of Americans (72 percent) either completely or mostly agree the system should try to rehabilitate criminals and not just punish them, including fully 85 percent of blacks. On a similar note, measures designed to prevent crime are backed by very wide margins. Such that, given the choice between attacking the social and economic roots of criminal behavior, on the one hand, and bolstering law enforcement to punish such behavior, on the other, two-thirds prefer the former.

In essence the public may indeed desire a system that punishes, but it likewise desires a system that deters and rehabilitates criminal behavior. It is this aspect of public crime policy preferences that politicians seem to miss and, thus, where public preferences diverge slightly from national politicians' policy choices. When it comes to making changes in the criminal justice system, Americans want those changes to not only center upon punishment, but also upon improving the system's capacity to reduce crime.

Just the opposite is true of public policy preferences regarding racial tracking. At the core of the public's racial policy stance is a desire for lawmakers to do less and, in fact, to scale back, most especially in regard to racial influences in criminal justice. We can even go so far as to say there is strong aversion to any kind of government legislation specifically targeting minority interests. In *Reaching Beyond Race* Sniderman and Carmines utilized randomized experiments imbedded in survey interviews in their Race and Politics Study to demonstrate the extent of "resentment and sense of betrayal" generated by race-conscious policies.[82]

More recent national survey data also show that Americans do not want government to do much of anything further on behalf of blacks – whether it is more civil rights laws, affirmative action, socioeconomic support, educational opportunity, employment, or anything else. According to Table 7.15,[83] it is their view that blacks should overcome prejudice without favors, "like Irish, Italian, Jews, and other minorities." A Pew Center survey on American values finds nearly three quarters of U.S. adults do not endorse the proposition that "we should make every possible effort to improve the position of blacks and other minorities, even if it means giving them preferential treatment." A Gallup survey reveals

TABLE 7.15. *Racial Policy Preferences, United States, Blacks, 2003–2013*

	United States	Blacks
Percent respondents believing		
New civil rights laws are not needed to reduce discrimination against blacks (2011)	76	48
Government should play either no or a minor role in improving the social and economic position of blacks and other minorities (2011)	72	40
Government programs to address economic inequality should not give special consideration to blacks (2008)	87	78
Every effort should be made to improve the position of blacks and other minorities, even if it means giving preferential treatment (2003)	25	67
Racial preference in hiring and promotion is wrong (2010)*	80	53
College applicants should be admitted solely on merit, even if the result is fewer minorities (2013)	67	44
Blacks should overcome prejudice without favors, like Irish, Italians, Jews, and other minorities (2006)**	73	55

Notes:
* Includes "strongly oppose" and "oppose" responses.
** Includes "strongly agree" and "agree somewhat" responses.

the same distaste for preferential policies. It indicates fully 87 percent of U.S. adults believe government programs designed to address economic inequality should only take into account a person's economic situation, whereas a mere 9 percent believe special consideration should be given to blacks because of past racial discrimination. A 2010 GSS poll reveals 80 percent believe racial preference in hiring and promotion is wrong, and a 2013 survey indicates fully 67 percent feel students should be admitted to college solely on the basis of merit.

While it is argued by some that the public's negative reaction to special preference programs and policies is also a form of modern racism,[84] the fact is either a majority or the preponderant share of blacks have a similarly negative reaction to such policies. Neither a majority of blacks nor a majority of whites roundly endorse greater investments in traditional racial policy reform.

Neither are they vested in policies geared toward reform of the criminal justice system along racial lines. Upon balancing enactment of policies

TABLE 7.16. *Racial Policy Problems and Crime Policy Problems, United States, Blacks, 2010*

	United States	Blacks
Percent respondents believing policymakers should devote more time and energy to ...		
Crime-related problems	88	76
Racial problems	12	25

to protect public safety against redress of racial tracking, the former carries considerable policy weight among blacks as well as whites. GSS and Pew data illuminate the public's rank ordering of crime and racial issues, along with other major domestic issues. When asked in a GSS survey to say for which policy issues "we're spending too much on ... too little money, or about the right amount," more than three out of five U.S. adults expressed the belief that too little is spent "halting the rising crime rate" and just as many believe the country is spending too little on "dealing with drug addiction.[85] Increased crime expenditures are even more of a top priority for blacks specifically, with as many as 75 percent describing current funding levels inadequate. Perhaps surprisingly, black public opinion ranks anti-crime policy about as high as "improving the conditions of blacks" (79 percent). In addition to GSS data, broad public support behind crime-fighting is illustrated also by a Pew survey.[86] Racial policies were not included on the preselected list of twenty-two problems. Crime was, however, and nearly half of respondents (48 percent) named it a "top priority" for the president and Congress to consider in 2012 and 62 percent did so five years earlier before the onset of the 2008 economic crisis. With financial and economic policy concerns grouped together, crime places in the top third of the Pew list.

To gauge more directly how the two policy priorities stack up against one another, a nationally representative, 1,000 person survey developed for this study asked respondents to choose between the two. It posed the following: "Which of the following problems do you think policymakers should devote more of their time and energy to?" Only two options ("Crime" or "Race") were listed in randomized order. The results, shown in Table 7.16,[87] are unequivocal. Nearly 90 percent of respondents said policymakers should concentrate on crime-related policies, and only about 10 percent consider race-related measures more deserving of policymakers' attention. While blacks cite racial policies as a top priority at a rate twice the national average, they otherwise endorse the exact same

TABLE 7.17. *No. 1 Criminal Justice Policy Priority of Public, United States, Blacks, 2011*

	United States	Blacks
Percent respondents believing No. 1 priority should be to ...		
Reform prison system to create productive members of society	27	29
Provide police more crime-fighting resources	20	15
Provide police with more power to prevent and solve crimes	19	15
Provide judges the power to give stiffer penalties	16	6
Ensure minorities are treated fairly in justice system	12	29
Reduce overrepresentation of poor and minorities in prison	6	7

ordering of policy preferences as the rest of the country. They too line up behind a policy agenda that centers more upon anti-crime measures (76 percent) *instead of* racial reform measures (25 percent).

The fact is, racial reform of criminal justice does not compete well with anti-crime policy goals under any circumstances. A 2011 follow-up survey gave respondents wiggle room in which to include racial reform along with other top criminal justice policy goals. They were not forced to choose between the "obvious" policy option (secure public safety) and the not-so-obvious option (ensure racial justice), but could actually lend top support to both.[88] The survey asked respondents to choose from among six criminal justice policy reforms, to select two of the six, and to designate which constituted the number one policy goal and which the number two. It asked: "Of the following criminal justice policy goals, which two goals do you think lawmakers should focus more of their time and energies on?"[89] Among the six policy options delineated in the survey questionnaire were two pertaining specifically to racial unevenness in the system, while the remaining four concerned the system's crime-fighting capacity.

Still, under these circumstances too, respondents passed on the opportunity to lend meaningful support to the goal of redressing the racial dynamics of criminal justice. As to the Number 1 criminal justice policy goal depicted in Table 7.17,[90] the largest share (26.9 percent) cited reforming the prison system to create productive members of society. Competing closely with this goal as a number one priority is that of providing police with more crime-fighting resources. Significantly, moreover,

TABLE 7.18. *No. 2 Criminal Justice Policy Priority of Public, United States, Blacks, 2011*

	United States	Blacks
Percent respondents believing No. 2 priority should be to ...		
Reform prison system to create productive members of society	22	25
Provide police more crime-fighting resources	18	15
Provide police with more power to prevent and solve crimes	20	19
Provide judges the power to give stiffer penalties	15	5
Ensure minorities are treated fairly in justice system	16	26
Reduce overrepresentation of poor and minorities in prison	9	10

both policy options pertaining to race were least likely to be selected as a top criminal justice policy goal. Even as a possible Number 2 goal for policymakers, racial reform garnered the least public support, as shown in Table 7.18.[91] In short, race-related criminal justice policy options failed to make either the first or the second cut. And although race-related criminal justice policies enjoy more support from blacks than the general public, blacks too place a high premium on anti-crime goals. Rehabilitation and racial fairness were selected as the Number 1 goal by the preponderant share of blacks surveyed (29 percent). Still, the aim of reducing racial disproportionalness in imprisonment was ranked next to last by blacks, whether as a primary or secondary criminal justice policy goal. Crucially, in neither instance did blacks put racial reform squarely at the top of the list of things they want from the criminal justice policymaking process.

Conclusion

To conclude, the public origins principle tells us that any effort to fully understand the persistence of a public policy problem in the United States must weigh the extent to which public interest, opinion, and policy preferences are more or less contributory. In the foregoing discussion and analysis, we learned that indeed the American public's disposition toward race, crime, and criminal justice policy effectively undergirds racial tracking. The public mind-set as it pertains to racial tracking may be summed up in four points. One, the country has a serious and growing violent crime problem, and the race problem in the criminal justice system must take a backseat to fixing the supposed growing crime problem. Otherwise, violent crime will be coming soon to neighborhoods where things like murder, rape, robbery, and the like do not normally happen. Two, most do not believe the admitted racial improprieties in law enforcement are weighty enough to counterbalance the fine job police officers do in protecting their local communities, especially not once blacks and their propensity to violence are figured into the equation. Besides which, the country has elected a black man to the highest office in the land and is well on its way to a brighter racial future. As to those blacks left behind, their plight is no longer owed to having been locked out of jobs and educational opportunity, or in this case, locked in prison due to widespread racism. On the contrary, the fate of black citizens, black defendants, and black convicts alike is ultimately the making of their own individual choices and failings. Finally and critically, those choices and failings are not the concern of anti-crime policymakers. Nor do Americans believe they should be – certainly not when there are more important criminal justice policy matters at hand to tackle, such as the crime problem that could soon arrive at their doorsteps.

8

Streams of Thought

Belief Options Concerning Race, Crime, and Justice

Scholars have provided ample evidence to counter the thrust of the public and lawmakers' policy position where race, crime, and justice are concerned. There are, more precisely, compelling reasons for the public and policymakers to believe the problem of racial tracking in criminal justice is amenable to public policy reform, and not just a matter of individual choice. Decades of carefully constructed analyses by reputable academicians, working from a mix of disciplinary angles and armed with a variety of hard data and rigorous methodologies prove the significant role that macro-context factors play in generating racially uneven criminal justice outcomes. This body of research tells us, in essence, the plight of blacks within the criminal justice system does not stem from a special affinity blacks have for crime and punishment. It is not solely the making of black choices; rather, societal forces are at play.

True, there are differing perspectives on the question of which of these forces is most immediately responsible. There are the racial theorists, who argue the primacy of traditional racism; the legal-processual theorists, who emphasize the role of institutional-policy bias; structural theorists, who contend disadvantage is chiefly responsible; and cultural theorists, who tell us the problem is directly tied to subcultures of violence and that these subcultures are, in turn, a byproduct of bias and disadvantage. Despite the existence of multiple academic perspectives, they generally point toward the same basic idea. They suggest systemic factors are at the root of racial tracking – that racial disproportionalness and racial disparate treatment are not simply a matter of individual choice. Therefore, the lack of attentiveness in the political arena is not because of a lack of knowledge among experts as to whether something can be done, or what can be done, or where to begin doing something. The considerable scholarly insight brought to bear on the dynamics of racial tracking, however, is effectively lost in transmission.

What gets transmitted to the public instead is a grossly oversimplified message about blacks as criminals – neatly compressed and packaged in a scary black face. Mainstream television news in particular thwarts a grounded public understanding of the core reasons for blacks' distinctive criminal justice experience. The entertainment industry transmits the same blacks-are-criminal narrative as TV news – including segments that purportedly endeavor to do more. It is also a case in which pecuniary interest trumps public interest. Add to this equation the public's already ingrained predisposition to "buy into" individualist explanations over and above structural determinism, and the absence of public alarm regarding the causal dynamics of the black law enforcement experience is more easily calculable.

The discussion to follow pursues three objectives. The first is to provide an in-depth look at the understanding of race, crime, and justice that is supplied by academic researchers. In order to prove a primary claim made here – that we know a great deal about the subject – the review details at length the data and findings of studies that support the four main schools of thought on the subject. These include racial theory, legal-processual theory, structural theory, and cultural theory. A cross-disciplinary perspective is provided on each of these schools of thought; it synthesizes insights from public policy, political science, legal studies, criminology, sociology, psychology, economics, and media communications. Following this review of extant research, the chapter considers the extent to which these grounded insights make their way into public discourse. In this regard, the role of mass media outlets, especially television news, is examined. Finally and critically, we learn more of how the public origin principle comes into play. We learn, more specifically, the public is predisposed toward individualist ideals, and, thus, TV news and mass media essentially sell the public what the public chooses to buy. In the final analysis, here as well the American voter is the original source of control regarding the politics of race, crime, and justice. We begin with a look at the empirical evidence that supports one of the oldest themes in the study of race, crime, and criminal justice, namely the race-discrimination thesis.

Social Science Research

Racial Theory

Racial theories point to traditional bias and discrimination as the driving force behind racial tracking and disproportionalness. Racial analyses of criminal justice trends are most often (though not always) put forth by political scientists, legal analysts, and psychologists who, as a matter of course, typically emphasize power and attitudinal frameworks. One of the two main strands of racial theory argues individual actors in the criminal justice system are consciously or subconsciously prejudiced against racial minorities and carry out their responsibilities partly on the basis of such built-in prejudice. In doing so, law enforcement officials help to generate the observed disparities. The race discrimination thesis has, over the years, shed important light on each of the individual stages of the criminal process. Perhaps no stage of the criminal process has received greater scholarly and political scrutiny than the police investigation stage.

The results of five separate studies revealed to Eberhardt and colleagues that racial stereotypes affect visual processing, which, in turn, influences law enforcement decision making and behavior. In one of the studies, a survey of 182 police officers indicated police officers tend to associate black faces with criminality. The officers were presented with black and white male faces and asked, "Who looks criminal?" The more black an individual appeared, the more criminal that individual was seen to be by police officers.[1] Moreover, work by social psychologists Plant, Peruche, and Butz suggests racial considerations help to explain the use of deadly police force. In an experimental study in which fictional black and white criminal suspects were and were not carrying guns in simulated situations, whites were less likely than blacks to be "shot" by participants.[2] A study of drug arrests in Seattle, Washington, led Beckett and colleagues to conclude that the racialization of imagery surrounding illegal drugs in general and crack cocaine in particular generated long-lasting institutional and cultural effects that shape police perceptions and practices. In their view, these effects explain much of the disparity that characterizes drug possession arrests in Seattle.[3]

Racial effects at the trial and sentencing phase of the criminal process have been documented as well. Evidence indicates court officers are influenced by race. Guervara, Spohn, and Herz used data from a sample of juvenile court referrals to examine the interaction of race and type of counsel on court outcomes. Non-white youth represented by a private attorney were found significantly more likely than similar white youth to receive a secure confinement disposition.[4] Bridges and Steen combined information from probation officers' reports on juvenile offenders with court records about offenders in order to assess the relation between court officials' perceptions of offenders and the officials' classification, assessment, and sentence recommendations. The authors uncovered pronounced differences in officers' attributions about the causes of crime by white youth versus the crimes of minority youth.[5] Offering us a wider lens, Engen, Steen, and Bridges' undertook a review of the extant literature on race and punishment. Their examination of the major theories of disparity in juvenile justice, the methodological components of the studies, and the studies' findings as to the effects of race led to the following conclusion:

> Race effects are more prevalent among studies that examine earlier stages in the juvenile justice process or that examine cumulative measures of dispositional severity, and among studies that compare outcomes for white youth to those for black youth.... Race effects are not contingent upon whether or not studies control for differences in the seriousness of offending. These findings offer support for a structural-processual perspective on the role of race in juvenile justice, and suggest that disproportionately punitive treatment is more clearly associated with being black than with being "non-white."[6]

Studies show that judges and jurors are also subject to racial bias. An experimental study conducted by Law Professors Rachlinski, Johnson, and Guthrie and a federal judge, the Honorable Andrew J. Wistrich, set out to ascertain whether judges hold implicit racial biases and whether those biases affect their judgments in courts. The sample for the study included 133 judges drawn from different jurisdictions. It exposed hidden biases against blacks among white judges and also a link between judges' biases and the sentences they indicated they would impose on those convicted.[7] Additionally, experimental studies by Bodenhausen and Wyer (involving undergraduate students) revealed participant decisions regarding punishment and parole were influenced by racial and ethnic stereotyping.[8] To gauge the relative significance of jury bias and judges' instructions to jurors, Rector, Bagby, and Nicholson carried out simulations involving more than 200 university students.[9] Their study found that when judge's instructions to jurors are absent, then jurors' decisions are influenced by the race of the defendant, as well as the attractiveness of the defendant. As such, the work of Rector and his colleagues point up the importance of considering situational conditions when assessing the presence or absence of racial bias. On the other hand, Sunnafrank and

Fontes's experimental study settled upon more pervasive effects where prospective jurors are concerned, namely that crime-related racial stereotypes exist for nine of ten index offenses examined.[10] From this vantage point, different situations do not result in different outcomes. Race matters – all of the time, most of the time, and sometimes.

Besides being black, looking black too has been found to generate criminological consequences at the court stage. In fact, Pizzi, Blair, and Judd assert that racial stereotyping in sentencing is actually not a function of the racial category of the individual. "Instead, there seems to be an equally pernicious and less controllable process at work. Racial stereotyping in sentencing still occurs based on the facial appearance of the offender.... Those offenders who possess stronger Afrocentric features receive harsher sentences for the same crimes."[11] This conclusion was informed by examination of photographs of 216 randomly selected Florida prison inmates incarcerated during 1998–2002. A separate analysis by Blair, Judd, and Chapleau poured over a random sample of Florida state inmate records; it likewise showed inmates with more Afrocentric features received harsher sentences than those with less Afrocentric features.[12] Afrocentric physical features matter even after controlling for factors that are often the centerpiece of nonracial theories of criminal justice (e.g., offense type, socioeconomic status, and various demographic factors). Turns out, across a spectrum of social and economic indicators, influences such as complexion, skin tone, colorism, the skin color paradox, and the like all appear to matter. Hochschild and Weaver report that, in a study of more than 67,000 male felons incarcerated between 1995 and 2002 in Georgia, first-time black offenders with medium and dark skin received lengthier sentences. Conversely, light-skinned black defendants received sentences more commensurate with their white counterparts. The authors ultimately deemed color preference "a cousin of racial prejudice."[13]

No facet of American criminal justice has received more scholarly attention over the years than capital sentencing. The death penalty has been the focal point of numerous publications stretching back to the early 1900s, many of which identify race as a causal factor operating through one or more mechanisms. Contemporary work in psychology indicates the decisional processes leading to death sentences are tainted by racial biases on the part of jurors and judges. Using an experimental study involving Stanford undergraduates, Eberhardt and colleagues analyzed cases in which a death sentence was a possibility. The study's focus was specifically on the effect of perceived stereotypicality of black defendants on jurors' death-sentencing decisions in cases with both white and black victims. It showed black defendants who were more "stereotypically black" were also more likely to be "sentenced" to death.[14] Most of the research on capital sentencing focuses on use of the death penalty in actual cases. More than a few of these works document the lengthy history of state-sponsored and illegal lynchings of blacks.[15]

Of interest here are accounts that proffer statistical data and analysis. Earlier quantitative studies tended to center on the race of defendants, and claim black convicts are more likely than their white counterparts to be sentenced to death. In 1919 the National Association for the Advancement of Colored People (NAACP) began publishing reports that detailed systematic racial disparities in capital sentencing. Its first, *Thirty Years of Lynching in the U.S. 1889–1918*, showed that of the 3,224 persons lynched during that period, fully 2,522 or 78 percent, were black and only 702 white.[16] In addition to advocacy organizations, defense attorneys too have employed statistical data and analyses to bolster legal challenges to individual death sentences. The first case in which such evidence was used is known as the "Martinsville Seven" case, in which seven black men were sentenced to death in Martinsville, Virginia, for raping a white woman.[17] Defense attorneys argued on appeal that the policy, practice, and custom in the state of Virginia between 1908 and 1949 was to impose the death penalty on blacks convicted of raping a white woman but never on whites convicted of raping a black woman. Also, in *State v. Culver*, a 1958 federal appeal on behalf of a black male defendant sentenced to death in a Florida state court for rape, statistics were submitted to show that during a period of roughly twenty years, twenty-four blacks were executed for rape while no white persons were.[18]

Among the more common criticisms lodged against earlier analyses of race and death sentencing is that these analyses often rested their case on the mere existence of statistical disparity. Racial unevenness in and of itself was considered proof of racial discrimination. They failed to take into account nonracial factors also relevant in the decisional processes lead to death sentences, such as criminal record, seriousness of crime, aggravating circumstances, among other things. It bears mentioning, however, this criticism does not apply to one of the more sophisticated early studies that did control for nonracial factors. Garfinkel examined more than 800 homicide cases in North Carolina from 1930 through 1940 and found defendants who killed whites were more likely to be sentenced to death than those who killed blacks.[19] After controlling for race-of victim, Garfinkel still found that in both white-victim and black-victim cases, black defendants were more likely to be sentenced to death than their white counterparts. Like Garfinkel, Bowers and Pierce too found capital sentencing in Florida, Georgia, Texas, and Ohio during the late 1970s produced racial differences, both in connection with race-of-victim as well as race-of-defendant. Blacks who killed whites were more likely to receive death sentences than whites who killed whites.[20]

The pivotal turning point in race and death penalty research came in 1987 in the context of the landmark U.S. Supreme Court case, *McCleskey v. Kemp.*[21] There, the Court addressed the constitutional significance of statistical disparities in death sentencing. To support the claim that legally impermissible racial influences help to produce the observed disparities, the defense presented a study done by university Professors David C. Baldus, Charles Pulaski, and George Woodworth. Known as "the Baldus Study," it addressed head-on the question of whether the death sentence rate for blacks was higher because they were black or for nonracial reasons that also matter for capital sentencing decisions. Following an extensive probe of over 2,000 murder cases in Georgia during the 1970s, Baldus and colleagues concluded disparities in the imposition of the death penalty are based partly on the race of the victim and, to a lesser extent, the race of the defendant. A total of 230 variables that could have explained the disparities on nonracial grounds were taken into account in the study's regression analysis. Even after weighing thirty-nine of the more pertinent nonracial variables, Baldus, Pulaski, and Woodworth found defendants charged with killing white victims were 4.3 times more likely to receive a death sentence than those killing black victims.

Although a later multivariate analysis of capital sentencing trends revealed a decrease in the racial gap associated with race-of-victim in the years following *Furman*, the analysis still led Baldus and colleagues to conclude: "Defendants whose victims were white were nearly as disadvantaged after *Furman* as they were before."[22] Whereas Baldus, Pulaski, and Woodworth's studies relating to *McCleskey* and *Furman* examined murder cases in the state of Georgia during the 1970s, Gross and Mauro examined death sentencing patterns in as many as eight different states.[23] Upon taking into account a number of nonracial variables, such as race-of-victim, felony circumstance, offender-victim relationship, number of victims, female versus male victim, and use of a gun, they too found capital sentencing disparities by race-of-victim.

This claim – that differences pertaining to race-of-the-victim are determinative – became the consensus in the race and capital sentencing, from the 1980s onward.[24] This is true even of studies that focused on use of prosecutorial discretion as to whether to pursue the death penalty. Radelet and Pierce's analysis of 1,400 homicides in Florida demonstrated prosecutors' handling of police report descriptions of killings varied by race-of-defendant but chiefly because homicides with white victims were disproportionately categorized by prosecutors as "aggravated," an evidentiary requirement that grew out of the U.S. Supreme Court's *Furman v. Georgia* decision.[25] Similarly, Jacoby and Paternoster report prosecutors seek the death penalty more often in white-victim cases than in black-victim cases.[26] Casting a much wider net, the U.S. General Accounting Office (GAO) reviewed all death penalty studies done at the national, state, and local level in both published and unpublished sources; surveyed twenty-one criminal justice researchers and directors of relevant organizations; and screened more than twenty-eight studies, twenty-three data sets, and 200 annotated citations and references. The 1990 report concluded its synthesis of studies "shows a pattern of evidence indicating racial disparities in the charging, sentencing, and imposition of the death penalty after the *Furman* decision."[27] Last, in a 2010 publication probing data on male offenders sentenced to death in Texas between 1974 and 2009, Petri and Voerdill used regression analysis to show that cases involving minority victims and black or Latino offenders have lower hazards of execution than cases in which both victims and offenders are white. Besides the imposition of death sentences, race effects are evident also in actual execution rates.[28]

While the theories explored thus far pertain to individual facets of the criminal process, the concept of racial threat is used in conflict theory to offer an overarching account of racial influences in the process. In simplified form, conflict theory holds that too many black people is too many black people; and, when there are too many black people, other people (usually white people) turn to drastic measures. Fear of blacks and other racial minorities more so than racial animosity is why race figures prominently throughout law enforcement – from the formulation of criminal policy to its implementation. Often tied to the concept of "racial context" and "racial composition," the primary assertion of conflict theory is that the larger the size of the black or minority population, the greater the perceived threat of crime and, hence, the more punitive the political, policy, and law enforcement response desired by non-minorities. Like many, Taub, Taylor, and Dunham qualified the racial threat thesis by essentially noting some neighborhoods are more adept at surviving an influx of black people than others. Middle-class neighborhoods, for example, adapt more successfully to racial change than working-class areas due to the buffering effect of things like appreciating housing values and quality of life amenities (e.g., parks).[29] Still, the main take-away from racial threat studies – even considering the mitigating effects of secondary forces – is that white fear of blacks is relevant and sometimes decisive.

Racial threat is argued important at multiple levels. In a book-length treatment of the minority group threat thesis, Jackson used quantitative analysis of the determinants of municipal police force spending in U.S. cities to illustrate cities with sizeable black populations tend to devote more to police spending.[30] Stults and Baumer establish that racial context and police force size are positively correlated, and that whites' fear and perceived economic threat account for more than one-third of the effect of percentage black population on police size.[31] According to Myers and Talarico, racial composition of county partly explains also disparate sentencing outcomes.[32] Larger minority populations also help dictate the legality and use of capital punishment across jurisdictions. An assessment of the statistical relationship between lynchings and size of African American population led Jacobs, Carmichael, and Kent to claim racial threat and lynchings combine to produce increased death sentences.[33] Finally, Liska and Tausig observed that, even after taking into consideration various legal variables (e.g., prior arrests, first offender status, legal experience, seriousness of crime, etc.), a racial differential is still found to operate at each decision level within the criminal justice system.[34]

In addition to voters and law enforcement officials, policymakers responsible for appropriating the power and resources of the criminal justice system have also been shown to fulfill their responsibility partly in reaction to white fear of racial minorities. Historical analyses detail the racial origins of national drug policy from the early 1900s onward. Musto's classic study *The American Disease: Origins of Narcotic Control* details how fear of Chinese immigrants, Mexican migrants, and blacks influenced many of the country's first narcotics control policies.[35] Likewise, Whitebread and Bonnie's government-commissioned study shows marijuana drug policy from the 1930s to the 1970s was driven from the outset by anti-immigration sentiment. It was aimed, more precisely, at Mexican laborers whose migration to western states was met by hostile, working-class whites.[36] Last, as in macro-contexts, so too in micro-contexts an increase in the number of minorities generates coarse policy reactions. Employing a national sample of 294 public schools to test the racial threat hypothesis, Welch and Payne established school disciplinary policies are often shaped in part by racial threat. The authors observe: "Results of multivariate analyses support the racial threat perspective, finding that schools with a larger percentage of black students are not only more likely to use punitive disciplinary responses, but also more likely to use extremely punitive discipline and to implement zero tolerance policies."[37]

Legal-Process Theory

The legal-process thesis, a variant of race discrimination theory, tackles the overall operational mode of the criminal justice system. It argues that blacks' current plight in the system stems from institutional and policy biases. These biases are quite different from the blatant forms of past racism in that they are imbedded in laws, enforcement regulations, and court rulings that systematically ensnare racial minorities and the poor. Although race-neutral on their face, these legal mechanisms are very much racialized in operation and effect. They stack the odds against society's least advantaged, especially blacks. It is important to note that implicit in the legal-processual thesis is the idea that blacks are punished at higher rates because they do indeed break the law more often than others. However and importantly, it is argued black criminality is in many ways artificially contrived in that anti-crime laws typically criminalize the kinds of behaviors in which blacks and the poor disproportionately engage. By extension, then, the higher-than-usual black arrest and imprisonment rate is engendered by the basic *modus operandi* of the American anti-crime strategy.

Glenn C. Loury avers: "Race helps to explain why the United States is exceptional among the democratic industrial societies in the severity and extent of its punitive policy."[38] A wide range of criminal policies and rules are deemed culpable.[39] Quite a few research studies probe in great detail the policy choices of the 1980s and later. Among these policies, the most frequently noted are: overcriminalization, determinate sentencing; the War on Drugs, the crack-cocaine differential; and court decision making. For Miller, the reformulation of criminal law during the 1980s and the resultant devastating impact on minority communities was hardly happenstance. Policymakers needed bad guys for the "newly energized" system to work. Utilizing a mix of qualitative and quantitative data sources, Miller explains that because few violent offenders could be found among the millions of underclass citizens of color, the definitions of dangerousness were twisted and stretched to include as many among them as possible, as often as possible.[40] Other studies indicate mandatory state and federal sentencing laws in particular hamstring blacks and other minority defendants, more so than their white counterparts.[41] While the stated intent of many of these laws was to ensure the "punishment fit the crime" and to engender consistency in the use of judicial discretion, the guidelines they instituted are intertwined with socioeconomic status. By extension, these guidelines interact also with race. As an example, in order to merit a lesser penalty under many sentencing laws, an individual must show s/he has maintained consistent employment. Stable residency is another common requirement for leniency. Finally, a clean juvenile record is often stipulated as well. Due to the high correlation between race and socioeconomic status and the younger age structure of the black population, such requirements inordinately work to the detriment of blacks.

A host of studies highlight a direct correlation is between the War on Drugs launched during the 1980s and the burgeoning racial gap in imprisonment that followed in its wake. Where researchers differ on this subject is mostly in regard to whether the racial effects of the war were intentional. The first of three starting points for almost all of these works is that the number of inmates in custody of state or federal correctional facilities (excluding private facilities) increased by almost 450 percent between 1980 and 2010; specifically, from nearly 320,000 to nearly 1.4 million.[42] A second point of note is that state incarceration rates for drug offenses grew fourteen-fold between 1980 and 2008, from 19,000 to 265,000 respectively. The third starting point is that blacks constitute a disproportional share of the newly imprisoned drug offenders, as many as 80 percent of persons incarcerated in federal prisons for crack offenses.[43] Michael H. Tonry and Joan Petersilia report that, of the many explanations put forth to explain the incarceration policy of the 1980s, racism is one.[44] They point to Beckett's work that indicates fears about crime and demands for punishment were mobilized by conservative politicians regrouping after the disaster of supporting segregation. Also highlighted is Tonry's *Malign Neglect*,[45] published in 1995, which suggests penal policies that drive up minority imprisonment are a form of "malign neglect" reflecting the foreseeable but unintentional consequences of policy choices. Fifteen years after publication of *Malign Neglect*, Tonry, together with Melewski, revisited his original analysis and found not much had changed with respect to the "litany of ways crime control policies disproportionately affect black Americans."[46] Importantly, 2008 data were used to revisit Blumstein's landmark 1982 study disputing the significance of racial bias. The new data led Tonry and Melewski to a slightly different conclusion. Namely, Blumstein's original analysis left 20.5 percent of imprisonment disparities unexplained. Still, though "such large unexplained variation creates a strong presumption of racial bias," it is not necessarily the kind of traditional bias and stereotyping of the past.[47]

A number of works are less constrained to declare outright that the War on Drugs was fundamentally racist. Indeed, for Nunn, the War on Drugs could just as well be dubbed a "War on Blacks."[48] Porter and Wright wrote in 2011: "Although drug war penalties never explicitly referred to race, the 'tough on crime' rhetoric in response to the crack epidemic demonized crack as a 'black' drug and thereby shaped the drug problem among political leaders and law enforcement."[49] Based on field interviews of law enforcement officials at various levels of law enforcement, Cole revealed those responsible for street level enforcement of drug offenses were well aware of the likely racial effects of the War on Drugs before its launch.[50] They knew blacks and the poor would be hardest hit. In Provine's view, both latent and manifest racism helped shape a punitive U.S. drug policy whose onerous impact on racial minorities is willfully ignored by Congress and the courts.[51]

Compared to other aspects of the drug war, the crack cocaine versus powder cocaine differential has commanded the greatest attention from scholars, journalists, and some national policymakers. Under the Anti-Drug Abuse Act of 1986, a prison sentence was mandated for 500 grams of powder cocaine but only five grams of crack cocaine. In 1988, the act was amended to mandate prison sentences for simple crack cocaine offenses, the only such mandatory sentence for simple possession. Many consider Congress's enactment of this 100-to-1 ratio penalty structure racially motivated.[52] It was believed when the policies were adopted that white cocaine users would be minimally affected and that black users would be drastically impacted. Just before enactment, a 1985 National Institute on Drug Abuse report revealed up to two-thirds of cocaine users at the time were powder cocaine users as opposed to crack cocaine users.[53] It also revealed 90 percent of young cocaine users in particular were sniffing, not smoking. Further the adverse health legal consequences of each method of administration were about the same – crack was no more dangerous to health than was powder cocaine.[54] A 2002 U.S. Sentencing Commission Report later indicated the same.[55] In essence, policymakers did not have amply grounded reasons to institute the differential, although there was evidence pointing out its likely consequences for blacks and the poor.

Several studies in *Crack in America* offer a critique of the main reasons put forth by policymakers as justification for the 100-to-1 ratio.[56] Editors Reinarman and Levine assert that, much like drug scares of the past, the drug scare of the 1980s essentially linked a scapegoated substance to working-class immigrants, racial or ethnic minorities, or rebellious youth.[57] Notably, the book's lengthy list of analysts (representing a variety of fields) all "agree about the central role played by poverty and racism in shaping the sets and settings that created the crack crisis."[58] Two conclusions are argued on the basis of the time-series and cross-sectional statistical data presented throughout. One, although crack was never widely used beyond minority neighborhoods, politicians and the mass media portrayed crack as the most contagiously addicting and destructive substance known. Secondly, as did the U.S. Sentencing Commission in 2002, these authors too found that widespread claims about crack's dangerous pharmacological effects were not corroborated by data from the Drug Abuse Warning Network (DAWN), nor several other surveys of medical professionals and drug users. As opposed to its allegedly destructive impact, in view of these authors, "crack attracted the attention of politicians and the media because of its downward mobility to and increased visibility in ghettos and barrios."[59]

The constitutional-legal foundation for the War on Drugs was laid by American courts, most notably the U.S. Supreme Court. Court approval of the intrusive enforcement tactics characteristic of the drug war allowed it to proceed virtually unfettered. Consequently, legal analysts consider modern criminal law procedure a pivotal institutional mechanism linking race and punishment. Cole presents numerous examples of federal and state court decisions upholding police officers' disparate treatment of minorities via unconstitutional seizures, consent searches, pretext stops, "stop-and-frisk" tactics, and drug courier profiles. Also problematic is courts' handling of racial disparities in death sentencing, three strikes laws, and the different penalties for crack versus powder cocaine offenses. The impact of all of these decisional trends is worsened by the problem of overburdened and underfunded public defenders offices. Of special note is the Supreme Court's diminution of constitutional protections established by the Warren Court, which diminution led Cole to conclude: "The Court has imposed nearly insurmountable barriers to persons challenging race discrimination at all stages of the criminal justice system, from policing to judging to sentencing."[60]

Over the years, many have compared the criminal justice system to the "Jim Crow" system of the Old South. Quoting the U.S. Commission on Civil Rights in 1970, Bell wrote that the justice system manifests the essence of "institutional subordination," which entails "placing or keeping persons in a position of status of inferiority by means of attitudes, actions, or institutional structures which do not use color itself as the subordinating mechanism, but instead use other mechanisms indirectly related to color."[61] The Jim Crow thesis was advanced in Glasser's 2000 analysis of racial disparities in the prosecution of drug laws in "American Drug Laws: The New Jim Crow"[62] and also Tonry and Melewski's 2008 "The Malign Effects of Drug and Crime Control Policies on Black Americans"[63]

In the first book-length treatment of the Jim Crow thesis, Alexander situates the relation between race and legal process in a much broader context. She contends that, much like the Jim Crow system of old, the modern criminal justice system and especially its dependence on mass incarceration operate as a "tightly networked system of laws, policies, customs, and institutions that operate collectively to ensure the subordinate status of a group defined largely by race."[64] Alexander's analysis demonstrates that not only did the U.S. Supreme Court construct barriers to lawsuits against law enforcement; civil rights organizations have been relatively quiet on the issue too, and their inaction owes to the fact that they are overly affected by the prevailing public consensus and racial stereotyping[65] and are thus uncomfortable championing the cause of criminals.[66] As evidence, Alexander provides an in-depth historical analysis of racial progressivism covering the Founding to the present, along with a detailed review of Fourth Amendment Supreme Court decisions governing police investigations and the use of prosecutorial discretion.

To sum up, there is a mass of well-researched academic studies that pinpoint macro-level forces, such as systemic racial discrimination and institutional bias, as key among the underlying drivers behind uneven criminal justice outcomes.

Structural Theories

As do racial and legal-processual theories, structural theories likewise note the impact of macro-context forces. The primary claim of structural studies, however, is that disadvantage lies at the root of blacks' overrepresentation in jails and prisons. Implicit in virtually all of these studies too is the idea that blacks do indeed engage in criminal behavior more frequently than whites. So instead of the motivations of law enforcement and crime policymakers, the chief analytical goal of such works is to dissect the reason black crime outpaces white crime. Sociologists and criminologists ask: what are the avenues through which structural deprivation gives rise to black criminality? While a range of avenues have been mapped, the prevalence of criminogenic factors within black communities is considered key. That is, the things that normally cause crime in any community are considered more widespread in black communities than in non-black communities. Primarily for this reason, higher crime rates are to be expected within the black population, according to structural theorists.

Leading research within this school of thought pinpoints socioeconomic status as the primary reason blacks commit crime at a higher rate than whites. Specifically, blacks' higher joblessness rate, higher poverty rate, lower income, lower educational achievement, and the like make them more prone to criminal activity. One of the hotly debated issues in this vein of scholarship is whether the connection between class status and criminality is negotiated through absolute economic deprivation or through relative deprivation. Is it tied to racial inequality or to poverty? Relevant to our discussion here is simply that there is a shared emphasis on the impact of economic strain, setting aside for now the precise pathways through which it is mediated.

In a groundbreaking work by Blau and Blau, the nexus between interracial socioeconomic inequality and black crime rates was probed. Their 1982 study examined data for the 125 largest standard metropolitan statistical areas (SMSAs) in the United States. The database comprised 1.2 million persons and *Uniform Crime Reports* (UCR) violent crime data for four offense categories (murder, forcible rape, robbery, and aggravated assault). Regression analysis was employed to assess the relation between crime and the SMSAs population size, percent black, percent poor, geographical region, income inequality, percent divorced, and racial socioeconomic inequality. The authors concluded much of the racial difference in crime commission "is attributable to the socioeconomic inequality between blacks and whites and the great income inequality in SMSAs with many blacks and, consequently, cannot be attributed to distinctive racial attributes – such as genetic traits or family composition (single-parent families) – that predispose blacks toward violence."[67]

A host of studies published in the wake of Blau and Blau's analysis advance a similar thesis regarding race, crime and resource deprivation. Blau and Golden later reconfirmed Blau and Blau's original thesis that racial inequality in socioeconomic status raises rates of violent crime.[68] Williams found that racial disparities in median family income have a significant positive effect on official homicide rates, although he found poverty more impactful than racial inequality.[69] Also, Corzine and Huff-Corzine concluded racial income inequality has a positive, significant influence on homicides.[70] Land, McCall, and Cohen expanded the usual analytic scope of research on structural covariates of homicide rates.

Their work included *all* cities and SMSAs identified by the Census Bureau in 1960, 1970, and 1980, as many as eleven explanatory variables, and also UCR homicide rates.[71] Their results too indicated race is consistently significant statistically in explaining homicide rates, but like others, Land and colleagues found also that race is substantially tied to resource deprivation. Especially numerous are works that underscore linkages between black crime and poverty, including those by Hawkins, Parker and Pruitt, and Parker.[72]

Racial invariance theses tell us that black crime is no more tied to blackness than white crime is tied to whiteness. The cross-racial criminological consequences of structural disadvantage render it colorblind, as it increases crime among whites in much the same way that it increases crime among blacks – at least in theory anyway. Drawing on U.S. Census Bureau data, the Community Survey of the Project on Human Development in Chicago Neighborhoods, and Chicago Police Department homicide reports, Morenoff, Sampson, and Raudenbush examined structural characteristics of nearly 9,000 Chicago residents to predict homicide variations across more than 300 neighborhoods. Morenoff and colleagues concluded: "evidence is more favorable than not to the idea that the fundamental causes of neighborhood violence are similar across race."[73] Also, Wooldrige and Thistelethwaite's study of census tracts in Hamilton County, Ohio revealed "comparable effects of neighborhood disadvantage ... on assault rates for African-American males and white males."[74] As part of an attempt to tease out variation across levels of disadvantage, Krivo and Peterson compared predominantly white high-poverty neighborhoods to predominantly black high-poverty neighborhoods. They concluded "extremely disadvantaged communities have qualitatively higher levels of crime than less disadvantaged areas, and that this pattern holds for both black and white communities."[75] Finally, based on analysis of vital records for seventy-five Chicago community areas, Almgren and colleagues found that joblessness and family disruption are tied to not only homicide rates but all violent deaths, including accidental and suicidal deaths. Further, these relationships have strengthened in both black and non-black communities alike over time.[76]

Lending still more fuel to the claim "racially different effects (in homicide offending rates) occur because the crime-generating process itself is conditioned by the social situations of blacks and whites" is a 2000 study by Krivo and Peterson.[77] The authors partly respond to studies[78] that dispute the claim that similar social conditions are at the root of violent crime for all racial groups. Krivo and Peterson highlight the fact that variation in levels of structural disadvantage may cease to provide meaningful distinctions among cities once disadvantages reach very high levels. Some analysts overlook the fact that there is an upper threshold or tipping point beyond which they should not expect to find meaningful differences in the relation between structural variables and violent crime outcomes (or, more aptly, be surprised by the lack thereof). Crucially, blacks more often live in areas that lie beyond that tipping point than do whites.

Disadvantaged whites may well be more susceptible to criminal behavior than their well-to-do white counterparts, but the reality is that disadvantage itself is more prevalent among blacks. In reality, then, blacks' greater disadvantage makes them more susceptible to criminogenic forces than their white counterparts at any class stratum. In Shihadeh and Shrum's view, it is not enough to highlight that factors such as poverty, joblessness, transient populations, or criminal opportunities are important causal factors.[79] It is necessary to clarify also these factors are spatially concentrated in certain neighborhoods, often black neighborhoods. Even critics of the racial invariance thesis admit as much. Among those that allege certain weaknesses in racial invariance analyses is McNulty, who highlighted what he termed the problem of "restricted distributions."[80] It means there are not enough high disadvantage white cities to compare to high disadvantage black cities to reliably assess variations across levels of disadvantage and criminal activity, at least not at the macro-level. McNulty asserted: "race and class are so geographically conflated – consolidated in social structure in Blau's (1977) terms – that it may be impossible to empirically differentiate race from class effects with macro-level data."[81]

Partly for this reason, researchers have devoted more nuanced attention to ecological considerations, that is the particular forces at play in the communities in which blacks live. Specific structural characteristics of neighborhoods are strongly correlated with crime, which means some have all the ripe ingredients for a high crime rate. As to the signposts of crime-prone neighborhoods, three are frequently pinpointed. Racial segregation is cited as one of the more important ecological conditions driving black crime. It is not the case that large black populations are a formula for violence. Rather, racial segregation per se is problematic because it functions as an invisible wall separating inner-city blacks from mainstream society. Massey's work suggests black crime is tied to high levels of racial segregation.[82] Peterson and Krivo examined the impact of racial residential segregation on rates of black homicide victimization.

Their analysis of FBI Supplementary Homicide Reports data for more than 125 large U.S. central cities demonstrates racial segregation leads to higher rates of black killing. Their probe also made clear social isolation is the primary mechanism by which segregation leads to higher levels of homicide among blacks.[83] The association between racial segregation and structural disadvantage was highlighted again in a later study by Peterson and Krivo where they observed: "Segregation has an important effect on black but not white killings, with the impact of segregation on African-American homicides explained by concentrated disadvantage."[84] Shihadeh and Flynn too concluded: "Black isolation [is] a strong predictor of the rates of black violence in the U.S."[85]

The term "concentrated poverty" connotes the idea that not all forms of poverty and deprivation are equal; some are more unequal than others. And it is the spatial configuration of poverty that helps to distinguish one form from another. The consolidation of poverty along geographic lines intensifies a range of behavioral pathologies typically associated with deprivation, including delinquency and violence. It follows that, because poverty is more often concentrated in black neighborhoods, "concentrated poverty" is part of the reason black crime is typically higher than white crime. Based on a probe of homicide data from case files of the St. Louis Metropolitan Police Department stretching over a decade, Kubrin and Wadsworth proved concentrated disadvantage is associated with many types of black killings.[86] Lee's examination of FBI arrest statistics for 121 U.S. central cities led him to assert the concentration of poverty increases the homicide rate for both blacks and whites.[87] Further underscoring the importance of ecological conditions, Pattillo–McCoy's study revealed that even the black middle class is not immune to violence if they live close to areas of concentrated poverty. Her study of a predominately black middle class area in Chicago (Groveland) showed that it too was susceptible to the spillover of violence from nearby areas of high deprivation.[88]

In addition to racial segregation and concentrated poverty, the labor market context is yet another structural correlate of black criminality. The anemic job market in a sizeable number of black communities matters. According to Smith, Devine, and Sheley, "unemployment affects the crime rates of most age groups and both races, even when controlling for a number of other influences that have been linked theoretically and empirically to criminal offending."[89] As to precisely how labor market context translates into violent crime, Shihadeh and Ousey examined the relationship between the industrial structure of central cities and the rates of homicide and found a "decline in the access to low-skill jobs increases violence indirectly by first increasing economic deprivation."[90] Crutchfield, Glusker, and Bridges' study of homicide rates and labor market conditions in three cities found that work operates primarily through education. So that, "children who grow up in an inner-city neighborhood where few adults are legally employed may be less likely to believe that getting good grades will really make a difference for their futures."[91]

Social disorganization theory, an especially influential body of literature on delinquency and context, claims it is the organizational capacity of a community that is most directly associated with its level of crime. The higher the community's level of organization, the lower its crime rate, and vice versa. The theory centers broadly on the ability (or, more aptly, inability) of a community structure to facilitate realization of the common values of its residents and to maintain effective social controls.[92] More concretely, it has to do with a community's means to supervise and control teenage groups (e.g., gangs), the viability of local friendship networks, and the level of local participation in formal and voluntary organizations. The extent of social disorganization in a community is itself a function of several factors, so that the lower a community's socioeconomic status, the higher its residential mobility, the greater its racial and ethnic heterogeneity, family disruption, and urbanization, the greater its level of social disorganization will be. First articulated in a classic 1942 work by Shaw and McKay,[93] social disorganization theory was refined later in 1960 by Cloward and Ohlin, who devoted special attention to how the milieu in which individuals find themselves shapes the types of adaptations that develop in response to the kind of pressures that ordinarily lead to deviance.[94] Not until decades later was social disorganization theory subjected to rigorous empirical testing, when researchers Sampson and Groves analyzed data for 238 localities in Great Britain.[95]

Other empirical investigations validate the explanatory power of social disorganization theory in regard to black criminality in the United States. Phillips found that weak forms of social control factors (measured in terms of female-headed households, divorce, teen pregnancy, labor force participation, gun control, and migration) are consistently associated with high black homicide rates.[96] Focusing on the role of family in facilitating social control, Sampson's work indicates certain labor market conditions hurt, at the outset, the black male and, ultimately, the black family. In fact, as early as 1939, Frazier asserted "disorganization of the Negro family life in the urban environment, together with the absence of communal controls, [resulted] in a high delinquency rate among Negro boys and girls."[97] Sampson's empirical probe decades later unpacked the process at work. His study of rates of robbery and homicide by juveniles and adults in over 150 U.S. cities revealed the effect of black adult male joblessness on black crime is mediated through its effects on family disruption. The "scarcity of employed black men increases the prevalence of families headed by females in black communities. Such black family disruption, in turn, substantially increases the rates of black murder and robbery, especially by juveniles."[98] Parker and Johns offer a review of the scholarly literature, which they say largely confirms "the family is a mechanism of social control and is essential for reducing crime."[99] Their own study clarifies family diversification (i.e., single-parent structure) does not always and in every instance yield a statistically positive effect on homicide, but rather there is something going on within the home itself.[100] Finally, from 1995 to 2002 Sampson, Morenoff, and Raudenbush collected and analyzed data from about 3,000 study participants aged 18–25 and also a separate community survey of some 9,000 Chicago residents.[101] Like others, their study found the majority of the racial gap in violence is explained by family structure and neighborhood social context.

The definitive work on the link between ecological conditions and delinquent behavior is Wilson's *The Truly Disadvantaged: The Inner City, the Underclass, and Public Policy*.[102] Informed partly by his look at the behavioral patterns of residents of the Robert Taylor Homes projects of Chicago, Wilson set out to explain the emergence of the black urban underclass, defined as individuals who experience severe economic distress and engage in street crime and other aberrant behaviors (e.g., teenage pregnancy, high school dropout, illegal drug use, and welfare dependency). Especially informative is Wilson's answer to the question of why black poverty yields behavioral pathologies distinguishable from those of white poverty. He makes clear, first, black poverty is more geographically concentrated. As a result and second, persons living in black high-poverty census tracts are less likely to interact with working class and middle-class individuals. They are effectively cut off from those who are employed and embrace mainstream values. Wilson's work goes a step further to detail precisely how and when black poverty came to be so concentrated and isolated and when the associated evils emerged thereby – when, in essence, the bottom fell out.

Wilson avers a social transformation thesis. Social isolation of the black underclass was largely brought on by the shift from a mostly goods-producing to a mostly service-producing labor economy and associated changes during the early sixties. The newly emergent labor economy presented serious problems for laborers in urban black communities. Due to limited educational opportunities, this labor market shift produced a skill mismatch between inner-city blacks and the higher-skill jobs available in more plentiful supply within the inner city. It also produced a spatial mismatch between inner-city blacks and the preponderant share of lower-skill jobs that moved out of the inner city to the suburbs, to the western and southwestern parts of the country, and abroad. By happenstance, the sixties black civil rights movement solidified further the social isolation of the urban black underclass. The movement opened doors of opportunity for skilled and educated black workers and, in the process, facilitated a black middle-class exodus from inner-city areas.[103] As a result, Wilson writes, "the residents of these areas, whether women and children of welfare families or aggressive street criminals, have become increasingly socially isolated from mainstream patterns of behavior."[104] Crucially, "poor whites rarely live in such neighborhoods."[105]

On the whole, scholars have put forth a mix of empirically grounded, methodologically sophisticated structural analyses that highlight the role of absolute and relative economic deprivation and its cross-racial effects, as well as the significance of ecological context and social disorganization in particular.

Cultural Theories: Sub-Culture of Violence, Code of the Street, and Cultural Adaptation

One of the more provocative and controversial explanations for racial differentials in criminal justice is cultural theory. Provocative because it partly reifies the role of individuated decision making in the production of racially uneven criminal justice outcomes. Controversial because it shifts attention away from the role of aggregate phenomena, although not entirely. Within the assortment of culture-centered explanations of race and criminal justice are two main variations. These include those that center on the violence-prone values, attitudes, and beliefs of inner-city black individuals and communities as determinative, on the one hand, and those that explicate how violent subcultures are themselves a response to structural forces, on the other. Between the two variations, the latter commands the endorsement of leading cultural theorists and is more widely accepted in sociology, largely because it is grounded in more conceptually sound methodology. Despite this, Darnell F. Hawkins reports conceptualizations that chiefly stress the importance of cultural differences are the "preeminent choice of nonscholarly commentators and observers, including the media and many public officials."[106] Crucial to this discussion is that, much like racial, legal-processual, and structural theorists, cultural theorists too, in the main also link black criminality to broad forces.

A key tenet of cultural theses is that certain cultural predispositions are more conducive to the use of violence than others. These predispositions comprise a "subculture of violence" or "code of the street" that leads to violence. As to the conceptual elements of street codes, the following are among the most oft noted: "never back down from a fight," "violence gains respect," "got your back," "retaliate when one's crew is disrespected," and "project a tough image to avoid being punked."[107] Street codes carry more weight than mainstream societal codes in certain neighborhoods, according to cultural theorists. Consequently, violent crime can result from anything as simple as an individual wearing the wrong color of clothing to merely staring too long at another. Contemporary studies of the cultural determinants of black crime actually evolved from early classic cultural works that were little concerned with black behavior. Merton offered the first extended version of the subculture of violence thesis in 1938. Drawing on Emile Durkheim's analysis of cultural conditions and crime, Merton analyzed how cultural structures explained white organized crime in Chicago (e.g. the Al Capone syndicate) and also crime in southeastern Europe.[108] Early studies of the cultural roots of violence in the United States originated in a focus on regionally (as opposed to racially) based subcultures, with the South consistently identified as the most violent region in the United States.[109] Coupled with more direct evidence below, these foundational studies help debunk the claim that violence-prone values in poor black neighborhoods are internalized, at least no more so than is true of southern or European whites.

The definitive work on subculture of violence theory as applied to race in the United States is Wolfgang and Ferracuti's *The Subculture of Violence: Towards an Integrated Theory of Criminology*. It offers the following exposition of its main tenets:

A subculture implies that there are value judgments or a social value system which is apart from and a part of a larger central value system.... There are shared values that are learned, adopted, and even exhibited by participants in the subculture, and that differ in quantity and quality from those of the dominant culture. Just as he is born into a culture, so he may be born into a subculture."[110]

The authors further theorized:

whatever may be the learned responses and social conditions contributing to criminality, persons visibly identified and socially labeled as Negroes in the United

States appear to possess them in considerably higher proportions than do persons labeled white. Our subculture-of-violence thesis would, therefore, expect to find a large spread to the learning of, resort to, and criminal display of the violence value among minority groups such as Negroes."[111]

The subculture of violence thesis has been advanced in some empirical investigations that aim to cast doubt on the idea that structural disadvantage undergirds higher black crime rates. Bailey's work tackled the race versus economic deprivation puzzle and led him to conclude: "minority status has an independent effect on killings that is not simply a function of economic disadvantage."[112] Huff-Corzine, Corzine, and Moore found poverty positively impacted official white homicide rates but did not have a similar effect on non-white homicide rates.[113] Curtis, in a major work on subcultural influences (*Violence, Race, and Culture*), argues that while racial-economic constraints are important, culture is an important intervening variable. A point of emphasis in Curtis's work is the extent of departure from the dominant culture, namely a "contraculture."[114] In an attempt to demonstrate the significance of cultural factors over and above socioeconomic factors, Messner regressed UCR homicide rates for 1959–1961 onto several variables, including percent black.[115] He concluded: "both southern region and the relative size of the black population exhibit significant partial effects on the homicide rate even with controls for theoretically important socioeconomic and demographic variables." More directly, "high levels of homicide for southern SMSAs and for SMSAs with large populations of blacks cannot, in short, be accounted for simply by the high levels of poverty characteristic of these areas."[116] A later work by Messner also argued that the impact of economic deprivation on rates of violent crime is likely to vary appreciably depending on the general cultural context.[117] In short, the problem is culture, not economic stress, according to these analysts.

It is important to point out, however, that for Curtis, Messner, and certain other analysts who use the subculture of violence thesis to debunk structural theory, "percent black" is the statistical measurement used to operationalize "culture." That is, "racial category" and "culture" are treated methodologically as if they are one and the same. This measurement approach has been criticized as problematic, not the least of which because of the conceptual conundrums it runs up against. Reliance on "percent black" necessarily assumes not only that blackness is the issue and that it is a reliable indicator of "culture"; it perhaps assumes as well that all black people have black ways of thinking and living, irrespective of socioeconomic status and background. The methodology quite literally lumps all under "percent black." It thus obscures cultural and value-related variation within the black community. Covington's extended critique of such "aerial" analyses underscores their failure to distinguish between lots of black people and lots of violent black people.[118]

Obviously, being black does not explain why some blacks engage in violence and other blacks do not. From a purely common sense perspective, skin color is probably not the best way to gauge one's cultural values and mores. The "percent black" methodology is problematic also because other researchers have cast doubt on its empirical validity. Sampson set out to determine whether in fact "percent black" continued to have a statistical correlation with black offending rates, once other structural characteristics (like poverty and inequality) were taken into account. It did not. An examination of demographically disaggregated homicide rates for the fifty-five largest cities in the United States led Sampson to conclude: "overall, 70 percent of the variance in aggregate homicide is explained by the constellation of structural characteristics."[119]

Like Sampson, most subculture of violence theorists show cultural factors are ultimately traceable to structural disadvantage. Very early on, Hannerz's field work in a black Washington, DC, neighborhood over a two-year period highlighted the existence of a "ghetto culture" but demonstrated also its macrostructural determinants.[120] A number of works have since formed a subset of cultural theory; they highlight the convergence of cultural and structural factors. The cultural underpinnings of black crime, according to this research, is best understood as a response to or adaptation to deprivation. In other words, violent subcultures or street codes of violence constitute the means by which individuals mediate, negotiate and come to terms with their disadvantage. Poverty pushes people to live by a set of rules and mores that others with more resources are not forced to contemplate. These street codes help them to cope and survive in the underworld in which they live.

The analytical goal of much of the cultural-response research is to detail how factors such as racism and disadvantage generate "oppositional culture" and "street codes of violence." Anderson offers the most cogent statement on the intersection of racism, disadvantage and street codes of violence. His ethnographic research makes clear: "The inclination to violence springs from the circumstances of life among the ghetto poor–the lack of jobs that pay a living wage, the stigma of race, the fallout from rampant drug use and drug trafficking, and the resulting alienation and lack of hope for the future."[121] Further, although there are often forces in the community which can counteract the negative influences, by far the most powerful being a strong, loving, "decent" ... family committed to middle-class values, the despair is pervasive enough to have spawned an oppositional culture, that of "the streets," whose norms are often consciously opposed to those of mainstream society.[122]

The code of the street is, thus, a defensive mechanism that acts as a shield from the physical violence of the inner-city ghetto and the psychological detriment of racist rejection from mainstream society.[123] Alongside Anderson's study of street codes and oppositional culture is Massey and Denton's extended look at the cultural impact of racial segregation. Their book claims "segregation created the structural conditions for the emergence of an opposition culture that devalues work, schooling, and marriage and that stresses attitudes and behaviors that are antithetical and often hostile to success in the larger economy."[124]

Statistical studies further bolster the cultural adaptation thesis. Kubrin and Weitzer's examination of quantitative data and narrative accounts of homicides in St. Louis over a two-year period found a twofold reason as to why retaliatory homicides are more common in disadvantaged minority neighborhoods.[125] The first is that problematic policing causes residents to turn to alternative forms of problem resolution. The second reason is that cultural codes legitimate the use of violent forms of problem resolution. Sampson and Bartusch's study of 343 Chicago neighborhoods similarly notes "an ecological structuring to normative orientations."[126] They stress orientations toward law and deviance are rooted more in experiential differences associated with neighborhood context than in a racially induced subcultural system. "Because race and neighborhood are confounded, the tendency in the literature has been, incorrectly in our view, to attribute to African Americans a distinct culture of violence."[127] Guided by specific measures of codes of violence (as opposed to simply "percent black"), Matsueda, Drakulich, and Kubrin examined data from a multi-level survey of nearly 5,000 households within 123 census tracts in Seattle.[128] Like others, they similarly concluded neighborhood codes and violence are highly correlated and that neighborhood codes are disproportionately found in extremely impoverished black and Hispanic neighborhoods. McCord and Ensminger followed a novel approach and tracked a group of black individuals from childhood to the age of thirty-two to evaluate the association of a variety of life experiences with criminal records (collected through courts and the FBI).[129] The researchers found the perception of racial discrimination on the part of the individuals they tracked helped to explain why some became violent and others did not.

Crucially, the cultural adaptation thesis envisages the code of the street to exist separate and apart from the internal makeup of an individual and, thus, changeable by external forces. Sampson and Wilson's "Toward a Theory of Race, Crime, and Urban Inequality" underscores the significance of the very different ecological contexts in which blacks and whites live, they note: "macro-social patterns of residential inequality give rise to the social isolation and ecological concentration of the truly disadvantaged, which in turn leads to structural barriers and cultural adaptations that undermine social organization and hence the control of crime."[130] Thus, "if cultural influences exist, they vary systematically with structural features of the urban environment."[131] It follows, then, that the culture of poverty thesis – which intimates ghetto culture and values are internalized and transformative at the individual level – misses the mark, according to Wilson. He clarifies elsewhere: "the concept of *social isolation* does not mean that cultural traits are irrelevant in understanding behavior in highly concentrated poverty areas; rather, it highlights the fact that culture is a response to social structural constraints and opportunities."[132] Together, Sampson and Wilson make the point even more plainly: "social isolation does not mean that ghetto-specific practices become internalized, taking on a life of their own, and therefore continue to influence behavior no matter what the contextual environment. Rather, it suggests that reducing structural inequality would not only decrease the frequency of these practices; it would also make their transmission by precept less efficient."[133]

In the main, then, structural and cultural theorists explicitly or implicitly endorse the notion that a decline in structural inequality or disadvantage will spur a decline in criminal activity and, eventually, change in the racial status quo in the justice system.

Agreement in Theory

At first glance, structural and cultural theories may appear to be at odds with racial theories, insofar as the former posit black behavior as the direct impetus for disparate criminal justice outcomes, whereas the latter are chiefly concerned with the behavior and policies of law enforcement. A closer look, however, reveals a degree of commonality across these seemingly opposite perspectives. To start with, racial theories do not necessarily contradict nor refute the black criminality premise. To acknowledge that discrimination and bias affect the criminal justice process does not require wholesale dismissal of the idea that crime is more prevalent among minorities. Besides, raw crime data would make the latter position difficult to maintain, analytically. Before illustrating this difficulty, it is worth noting that more than a few racial theorists highlight *bona fide* weaknesses in the government crime data typically proffered as proof in studies that dispute racial theories. Widely cited works by Blumstein and Graddy in 1982[134] and by Blumstein in 1982[135] and 1993[136]; a 1983 work by Blumstein, Cohen, Martin, and Tonry[137]; a 1987 book publication by Wilbanks[138]; a 1988 study by Klein, Turner and Petersilia[139]; a 2000 publication of Steffensmeier and Demuth[140]; as well as 2003 analyses by Pope and Snyder[141] and D'Alessio and Lisa Stolzenberg[142] all ground their refutation of the race-discrimination thesis chiefly and, in most instances, solely upon arrest and imprisonment data supplied by law enforcement, namely the *Uniform Crime Reports* (UCR).

The UCR was conceived in 1929 by a law enforcement body (the International Association of Chiefs of Police), is administered by a law enforcement agency (the FBI), consists of data on crimes either discovered by or reported to state and local law enforcement agencies, and then compiled and submitted as reports by these agencies to the FBI.[143] Given that UCR data are effectively law enforcement data, it is logical to question their suitability as grounds for dismissing the race-discrimination thesis, especially since the thesis points the finger of blame mainly at law enforcement. This is doubly so in light of the fact that relations between blacks and police agencies have almost always been fraught with tension,[144] thus making blacks potentially less likely to report crimes to law enforcement while making law enforcement potentially more likely to record crimes committed by blacks but less likely to record crimes against blacks. Moreover, the UCR data program excludes roughly half of violent crimes and up to 40 percent of property crimes never reported to the police.[145] Because of this, we can theorize with good cause that blacks are overrepresented in the roughly 50 percent of violent crimes reported by law enforcement agencies to the UCR data clearinghouse but underrepresented in the crimes that are not reported by those agencies. In short, UCR data are legitimately suspected of possible bias.

The foregoing critique of UCR data is not as readily applicable to data from the National Crime Victimization Survey (NCVS), however. NCVS data are supplied not by law enforcement but by crime victims. As a result, racial theorists are not as well-positioned to challenge the picture that emerges from this alternate data source, certainly not when they are corroborated by other nongovernmental sources such as ethno-graphic studies and proprietary surveys. These nongovernmental sources of crime data make a compelling case for the claim of criminal inequality along racial lines. As do UCR data, NCVS data also indicate blacks claim a disproportional share of violent crime. Specifically, NCVS data indicate blacks constitute roughly 12 percent of the U.S. population as of 2008 but are responsible for nearly 23 percent of violent crime; whites, for comparison, constitute about 65 percent of the population but only about 58 percent of violent criminal offenses.[146]

Besides the empirical data confirming criminal inequality along racial lines are the political blows rendered to the overall race-discrimination thesis. Wilson chronicles the decline of racial theory in academe in the wake of the 1960s, a decline that was engineered at the outset first by racial conservatives.[147] But a number of popular critiques of the perspective have since been added to the fray, and at the hands of otherwise sympathetic black celebrities and spokespersons. This includes some who identify with extremist "pro-black" sects. Speeches made during the 1995 Million Man March on Washington, headed by black Muslim leader Minister Louis Farrakhan, centered as much on self-help and community responsibility themes as societal discrimination and exclusion.[148] A number of less extreme prominent blacks postulate more straightforwardly how blacks contribute to their own demise. Bill Cosby is one such figure. Star and producer of a 1980s television sitcom that featured an upper-middle-class black family and marked a departure from the black exploitation entertainment, Cosby sparked a firestorm in the wake of remarks at a celebration of the 50th anniversary of the *Brown* decision in 2004. He criticized the high rates of teenage pregnancy, single-parent homes, and imprisonment among blacks, and said: "We can't blame white people.... *Brown v. Board* is no longer the white person's problem."[149]

Endorsing Cosby's critique of black failings from the political right, Juan Williams's New York Times bestseller *Enough: The Phony Leaders, Dead-End Movements, and Culture of Failure That are Undermining Black America – and What We can Do About It* presented a stinging critique of black leaders too. Reflecting on the civil rights demonstrators brutally attacked in the South during the Sixties Movement, Williams wrote "major national black politicians invoke these icons and perform shallow reenactments of the powerful marches of the movement as hypnotic devices to control their audiences. And if people try to break the spell by suggesting we move beyond those ancient heroes and tired tactics, they are put down with language that implicates them as tools of the white establishment."[150] Finally, President Barack Obama himself remarked during an interview on the *Tonight Show with Jay Leno*: "We all know that young African American men disproportionately have involvement in criminal activities and violence – for a lot of reasons, a lot of it having to do with poverty, a lot of it having to do with disruptions in their neighborhoods and their communities, and failing schools and all those things."[151] In sum, the race-discrimination thesis has lost ground over the years.

It is crucial to understand, nonetheless, the primary claim of most racial theorists is not that blacks and whites engage in criminal activity in equal measure or that there should be racially proportional representation in jails and prisons. The claim of criminal inequality along racial lines and the claim of racially discriminatory law enforcement are not mutually exclusive of one another. Rather, the central point of the discrimination thesis is that racist law enforcement is very real – just as real as the other proven correlates of racial unevenness. A distinctive strength of racial theories is that they offer something structural and cultural theories do not, namely, an account of why individual black citizens encounter a less considerate and lenient brand of law enforcement than whites. The fact that this is the experience even for those blacks who are never arrested, let alone imprisoned, suggests the uniqueness of the black law enforcement experience stems from more than criminality alone. This is especially so if being arrested and imprisoned constitute evidence of wrongdoing, as many structural and cultural theorists apparently believe, given their heavy reliance on arrest and prison statistics as measures of criminal offending. Legal theorists, for their part, deepen both the race-discrimination thesis as well as structural and cultural theories. By detailing the institutional bias and policy mechanisms that help drive up the black crime rate above what it would be in the absence of certain criminal policy decisions, legal-processual theories help synthesize the research findings across the four main schools of thought.

Taken as a whole, racial theories supply an important piece of the puzzle of race and punishment and, as such, are best understood as a complement (as opposed to an alternative) to the remaining theories.

Just as racial theorists do not (and cannot) cast aside evidence of greater black criminality, most structural and cultural theorists also do not summarily dismiss the relevance of racial discrimination. The most prominent expressly concede that the proximate structural and cultural causes of black criminality are themselves borne of past or present racial discrimination. This acknowledgment is, in many ways, a matter of necessity. Without it, the enormously important theoretical and empirical insights proffered by sociological and criminological studies of race and crime would do little more than beg the ever-recurring question of whether and how race matters. They would, in other words, tell us a great deal about how disadvantage is tied to criminal inequality but little about why it is blacks who make up the most structurally disadvantaged subgroup. Unless one recognizes there are racialized historical and sociopolitical processes that precede and initially dictate blacks' overrepresentation among the structurally disadvantaged, one cannot fully account for the existence of criminal inequality along racial lines nor the greater impact of criminal laws on black communities.

Put differently, if blacks are disproportionally represented among the arrested and imprisoned, because they are plagued by higher crime rates, because they are disproportionally disadvantaged, the all-important question that still remains is: why are blacks disproportionally disadvantaged in the first place? What initially led to their segregation in inner-city ghettos and social isolation from mainstream society – which led to their higher crime rates, which led to their overrepresentation in America's jails and prisons? In essence, what are the contemporary and historical sociopolitical mechanisms that fused these now interlocked racial and macro-structural forces together in the first place? Of course, besides these questions remain still others, most notably that of why there was a widening of the racial gap through the 1980s, 1990s, and 2000s, then some retraction later.[152] Unless one postulates a corresponding spike and decline in "street codes" or sharp dip and rise in blacks' class status during the same relatively short time period, then structural and cultural theories still leave much unexplained. Alas, how is it that innocent (i.e., "not arrested," "not charged," "not guilty") black citizens are nonetheless more likely to encounter intrusive and heavy-handed law enforcement, as demonstrated earlier in the book in Chapter 1?

That racial forces are indispensable to a comprehensive account of racial disproportionalness in criminal process is a point acknowledged repeatedly over the years and, critically, by leading analysts of black crime and deviance. The point was made in the groundbreaking 1942 work in which the race and subculture of violence thesis was applied in the United States. There, quoting one of their earlier works, Marvin E. Wolfgang and Franco Ferracuti wrote:

"If a careful, detached scholar knew nothing about crime rates but was aware of the social, economic and political disparities between whites and Negroes in the United States, and if this diligent researcher had prior knowledge of the historical status of the American Negro, what would be the most plausible hypothesis our scholar could make about the crime rate of Negroes? Even this small amount of relevant knowledge would justify the expectation that Negroes would be found to have a higher crime rate than whites."[153]

Having worked during the height of the civil rights movement with the director-counsel of the National Association for the Advancement of Colored People, Jack Greenberg, and others in the NAACP, Wolfgang's own personal politics mirrored his belief that race remained relevant, even if not determinative.[154]

William Julius Wilson – by far the most influential contemporary scholar of the black urban underclass and author of the infamous *Declining Significance of Race* (1980)[155] – likewise noted the lasting effects of historic racism. In a separate 1987 book, he wrote:

My own view is that historic discrimination is far more important than contemporary discrimination in explaining the plight of the ghetto underclass, but that a full appreciation of the effects of historic discrimination is impossible without taking into account other historical and contemporary forces that have also shaped the experiences and behavior of impoverished urban minorities.[156]

Together with Sampson, Wilson wrote again in 1995 that, among the macrostructural factors that have combined to concentrate urban black poverty in the inner city are racial segregation and housing discrimination, as well as economic transformation and class-linked out-migration from the inner city.[157] A decade later, in one of the more thorough reviews of the sociological and criminological literature on race and crime, Ruth D. Peterson and Lauren J. Krivo intimated broader scholarly recognition of preexisting privilege. The reviewers noted:

Significant structural, political, and social factors have created extraordinary freedom from criminogenic conditions for some groups but deep embeddedness in such conditions for others. By articulating and exploring these forces, we will begin to focus attention on how privileged conditions perpetuate the mechanisms by which some communities are able continually to avoid high levels of crime and violence, and why it is so difficult for others to alter the social forces that produce and perpetuate these problems.[158]

In summary, there is a common thread across the various disciplinary angles on race and crime that runs along one important dimension: societal influences matter. Macro-forces ultimately explain racial disproportionalness in arrests and imprisonment – notwithstanding the fact that the avenues through which these forces come into play vary from traditional discrimination and bias to institutional and policy bias, to structural disadvantage, to cultural adaptation. It follows, then, that as these macro-forces shift, so will black crime and, thereby, the problem of racial inequity in criminal justice. In sum, academe has supplied ample reason to believe it is a problem that is fixable. There is no lack of understanding about the prospects for *public* policy reform, at least not on the part of experts in the field.

Lost in Transmission: Academic Theory in the Public Arena

What has been the fate of scholarly reasoning and analysis in the larger political arena, beyond the Ivory Tower, and especially during the 1980s, when the push for stringently punitive crime laws was amped up tenfold? In light of the public's relative disinterest in prioritizing racial tracking in criminal justice and its doubt concerning the significance of societal forces (as laid out in the preceding chapter), the real question of note at this juncture is: why has the consensus in academe failed to translate into a public consensus? The answer is that these explanations have been all but roundly cast aside, decades ago. A declaration by the most popular president in modern times helps to illustrate the point. President Ronald Reagan claimed his administration spoke on behalf of a new consensus among the American people on the crime problem, one that pointedly rejected the vast body of scholarly research on crime and punishment. Speaking directly to the issue of causation, Reagan disparaged what he called "misguided social philosophy" in 1982. He noted:

At the root of this philosophy lies utopian presumptions about human nature that see man as primarily a creature of his material environment. By changing this environment through expensive social programs, this philosophy holds that government can permanently change man and usher in an era of prosperity and virtue. In much the same way, individual wrongdoing is seen as the result of poor socioeconomic conditions or an underprivileged background. This philosophy suggests in short that there is crime or wrongdoing, and that society, not the individual, is to blame.[159]

Reagan further declared:

A new political consensus among the American people utterly rejects this point of view.... The American people are reasserting certain enduring truths – the belief that right and wrong do matter, that individuals are responsible for their actions, that evil is frequently a conscious choice.[160]

A remark made later in 1994 by Republican Congressman Henry J. Hyde again conveyed the standard retort to social science in certain political quarters. Criticizing an initial House of Representatives version of the 1994 crime bill, Hyde said: "This bill satisfies the academics and the sociologists, but God help you if you work the midnight shift and have to walk home."[161] Lauding the proposal's eventual failure in the House, then-Senate Minority Leader Bob Dole said the bill failed because it was "an over-hyped, multibillion-dollar boondoggle that emphasized social theory over law enforcement."[162]

To what or whom, then, do we attribute solidification of a political and public consensus centered on an individualist perspective around the same time a substantial body of empirical evidence had amassed in support of an opposite perspective? Obviously, a critical mass of lay citizens do not pour through sometimes hard-to-decipher scholarly books and journal articles, as evidenced by the latter's usually small circulation and sales numbers. It is arguably unreasonable to expect that the public would, especially in connection with an issue of minor personal importance to a majority of Americans.

Daily Doses of a Scary Black Face: Mass Media and the Blacks-are-Criminal Script

Instead of scholarly publications, a majority of Americans rely on their television sets for news and information about public policy issues and problems, most notably where racial matters are concerned. Consequently, television news is enormously influential in shaping what the public thinks about policy issues pertaining to blacks. According to a 2013 Gallup Poll, 55 percent of Americans say television is their main source of news.[163] Reliance on the internet (as one among several sources of news) has dramatically increased from 13 percent in 2001 to 41 percent by 2010, and a decline has occurred in the percentage citing television as a source of news.[164] Despite these shifts, a 2011 Pew Center study reports a combined majority still get most of their news from cable news networks (36 percent), broadcast network news (22 percent), and local news programing (16 percent).[165] A 2012 study further indicates that 48 percent regularly watch local news.[166] Although digital platforms figure more largely in news consumption, they are not displacing traditional news platforms, according to the Pew Center's biennial news consumption survey. "Instead of replacing traditional news platforms, Americans are increasingly integrating new technologies into their news consumption habits."[167] The overall "net impact of digital platforms supplementing traditional sources is Americans are spending more time with the news than was the case a decade ago."[168] Dutta-Bergman further observes that, instead of competition-based displacement, there is complementarity in consumption of news types across traditional and new media.[169]

Where whites' grasp of the black experience in the United States is concerned, the impact of the news media is especially great because it often functions as *the* source of information on the subject. Due to segregation and the resultant limited interracial contact on the part of whites, many lack the means to independently develop perspectives on racial issues. Whites are far less likely to have regular contact with blacks in their personal lives, as compared to the reverse. As a result, what a sizeable number of whites see and hear about blacks in the news enormously shapes what they come to "know" and believe about blacks. That residential segregation remains prevalent throughout the United States is well documented by Orfield, Massey, and Denton and others.[170] It is well established too that residential segregation minimizes interracial personal relationships and contact, most notably for whites.[171] High levels of segregation in conjunction with low interracial contact are evident also in schools, churches, and other social contexts.[172] Segregated contexts yield segregated lives, which in turn yield narrow perspectives. Precisely because of the lack of firsthand information about blacks, Sigelman and Welch assert whites must base their attitudes toward blacks on whatever information they may have at their disposal.[173] This source is television news.

It is important to understand that television news does far more than just pass along facts to the informationally challenged. It also engages in what communication scholars refer to as "framing." Meaning, it selects "some aspects of a perceived reality and make them more salient in a communicating context, and in such a way as to promote a particular problem definition, causal interpretation, moral evaluation, and/or treatment recommendation."[174] In choosing which stories to report, news organizations are effectively allocating meaningfulness in a given society, as well as mediating the social construction of humanity and how a society defines "us" and "them."[175] Framing also entails interjection of reporters' and editors' prejudgments into the reporting and editing process. The media affect both what people think about as well as what they think.[176] Sometimes the public understanding engendered by news reporting on particular issues and problems is flawed. Entman explains: "*Reality* [sic] is problematic not only because news stories inevitably select only some aspects of reality and leave out others. More important, over time, the specific realities depicted in single stories may accumulate to form a summary message that distorts social reality. Each in a series of news stories may be accurate, yet the combination may yield false cognitions within audiences."[177]

What is the racial reality constructed by mainstream American news and daily consumed by up to 55 percent of Americans? More precisely, what is the message mass media convey to Americans about blacks?[178] It is, on balance, a substantially negative message. The history of racial stereotypes in everything from newspapers, magazines, and television to school textbooks and children's music books from the Civil War era through the 1970s has been studied at length.[179] But, numerous works illustrate a varied range of anti-black imagery and themes in television news persist still today, decades after standard industry use of "Sambos," "Mammies," "Toms," and "Coons."[180] The predominant contemporary message about blacks comprises a mix of negative concepts that are imbedded in the subtext of news stories, movie scripts, commercial ads, music lyrics, and more. Among these are: blacks are lazy, dependent, reckless, untrustworthy, overly demanding, over-sexed, overly materialistic, untrustworthy, unreliable, and lacking in family and mainstream values. As if these character stereotypes are not enough, Gilens details how television news exaggerates also the extent of poverty among blacks, making its unflattering image of the poor even more unflattering for poor blacks in particular.[181]

Television news often evinces the kind of anti-black attitudes and beliefs collectively known as "modern racism" or "aversive racism."[182] As compared to yesteryear's racism, today's is far more subtle and is reinforced at subconscious levels.[183] It is exhibited by whites who outwardly endorse egalitarian values, profess themselves colorblind, and showcase their black friend as proof. Yet, they unconsciously discriminate in subtle ways rationalized on the basis of otherwise plausible concerns (such as, concern for safety, cost of welfare, etc.).[184] As part of their probe of what they term the "post-Willie Horton Era," Hurwitz and Peffley expose the use of racialized code words that carry racial connotations equally as strong and impactful as those of the past.[185] And, while there is a recent new wave of mass media images of blacks as rich, accomplished, and smart (think Oprah Winfrey, Tyler Perry, and Bill Cosby), it has not washed away the tidal wave of images of black deviance.[186] Black success stories do not counterbalance black failures partly because black success is given a unique interpretation, explains Russell-Brown.[187] Successful blacks are often caricatured as the select few "articulate" and "well-spoken" stand-outs in a mass of inarticulate, ungrammatical, wayward blacks.

At the core of negative media messaging regarding blacks is that they are criminal and/or regularly associated with crime. Blackness and criminality are treated as if the two concepts are one and the same, particularly in television news reporting. Study after study carefully unpacks the many ways in which television news interlocks crime news stories with news coverage of blacks.[188] As one set of analysts put it: "TV news, especially local news, paints a picture of Blacks as violent and threatening toward whites."[189] Gilliam and Iyengar further assert that the media's overemphasis on the racial dimensions of crime gives rise to a narrative "script." We will refer to it in this book as the blacks-are-criminal script. Entman's research sheds crucial empirical light on how the script merges blackness together with violence.[190] Although a bit dated, his study of local television news programing in Chicago remains the most comprehensive, carefully done statistical probe of television coverage of race and crime. It reveals crime is one of the most common subjects of stories featuring blacks. To be exact, one of the top two subjects in local news. In Entman's study, approximately 41 percent of local TV stories about blacks in the Chicago TV news market were crimes of violence explicitly reported as committed by blacks. Entman's work also delineates some of the main features of the script.

First and foremost, the blacks-are-criminal script consists of more favorable treatment of white suspects, as compared to black suspects. Entman found the names of accused blacks (49 percent) were reported less frequently than whites (65 percent), which at a symbolic level means the black suspect's name and individuality are not as important. Black suspects (52 percent) were more likely than whites (66 percent) to be shown in motion video, which motion tends to symbolize a person as a human being and to disclose something about his size, facial expressions, and other elements of individuality. Blacks (38 percent) were much more likely to be shown in the grip of a restraining officer than whites (18 percent), led around in handcuffs, their arms held by uniformed white police officers or otherwise surrounded with symbols of menace, such as glowering mug shots. Meanwhile, none of the accused violent white criminals during the period studied were shown in mug shots or in physical custody. Also, 11 percent of stories about blacks and 29 percent of stories about whites included quotes from pro-defense actors, which further suggests a less humanized treatment of the black accused. A second central feature of the blacks-are-criminal script is the idea that black suspects and criminals are far more violent and dangerous than white suspects and convicts. Partial proof of this is that white victimization by blacks appeared to have especially high priority across the television stations studied.

Network news reporting follows much the same racialized pattern as local television news. Because crime is one of the major topics for local news, it enjoys less prominence in the network news. Thus, images of threatening, violent blacks occupy a smaller proportion of the network news reports. Still, stories about blacks for the three-network sample in Entman's analysis fall into three categories. The most frequent classification is crime, with blacks either committing crime and/or victims of violent, drug, and nonviolent crime. The second most common is politics, namely the activities of black politicians and community leaders. The third most common topic is blacks as victims of social misfortunes other than crime, such as poverty, bad schools, and racial discrimination. All total, "the crime plus the victim categories account for 46.4 percent of the stories; thus nearly half the coverage depicted blacks as threats to or non-contributing victims of American society."[191] And, among the crime stories in which blacks are portrayed as perpetrators, 77 percent consist of violence or drug-related crimes, while only 42 percent of crimes involving white perpetrators were for violent or drug-related offenses.

Crime reporting in dozens of other major news markets likewise portrays blacks and Hispanics as criminal suspects. In Orlando, Florida, blacks were nearly two and a half times more likely than whites to be so portrayed and Hispanics over five and a half times, according to Chiricos and Eschholz.[192] Poindexter, Smith, and Heider examined portrayals of racial minorities in 596 local television news stories from forty-eight newscasts for twenty-six stations in twelve cities over a twelve-year period. They found blacks more likely to be newsworthy because they had committed a crime, roughly twice as likely when compared to stories about whites.[193] Likewise, blacks are depicted as criminals at a much higher rate than whites. At the same time, whites are more often shown as victims than as perpetrators.[194]

The issue here is not simply that television news reporting on black crime compares unfavorably to that on white crime. Rather, as noted earlier, the news media engage in a much bigger enterprise, namely reality construction. Tierney, Bevc and Kugligowski provide concrete support for "constructionist" accounts of race and crime. Their study of news coverage of the 2005 Hurricane Katrina disaster revealed the mass media promulgated erroneous beliefs about disaster behavior.[195] Of special note for purposes of this discussion is Beckett's assertion that "it is the definitional activities of the state and the media, rather than the reported incidence of crime or drug use and abuse, that has shaped public concern regarding those issues."[196] In the case of blacks and crime, the news media help construct and define the "reality" of black offending and victimization. This is done partly by way of over-reporting (i.e., exaggerating) the incidence of black crime.[197] Similarly, black victimization is underreported, a fact that conveys the news media's vulnerability to what is euphemistically known as "missing white woman syndrome."[198]

It is the pervasive lack of contextual information in news reporting that chiefly empowers the blacks-are-criminal script. The script is seldom accompanied by substantive explanation. As such, the heart of the problem with mass media's construction of black imagery is as much a matter of omission as commission. For the vast majority of crime stories, it is the criminal offense itself that is the headliner, more so than the reasons behind the offense or crime patterns in "those" neighborhoods. The absence of explanatory depth leaves audiences with scarcely a superficial grasp of the dynamics of the relationship between race and crime. It is a grasp that captures the connection to skin color, but little else beyond that. The fact that local newscasters often consider it important to explicitly identify the race of blacks in suspect descriptions on a consistent basis but not to do the same for white suspects speaks volumes about the extent to which black crime is implicitly linked to skin color while white crime is not. Often, when the race of suspects is not made explicit, it is implicit by way of mug shots or reference to an area known to be predominately black (e.g., the "south side" of Chicago). The shallow nature of crime reporting is acutely characteristic of daily local crime reporting. It often relays almost verbatim what "police say." What "police say" often extends no further than the word-on-the-street about localized gang- and drug-related activity.

Lost in transmission are the all-important nuances carefully articulated and explored in scores of academic studies. Discussions in mass media about racialized law enforcement, about imbedded biases in crime policy, about structural disadvantage, about cultural adaptation and the like are abysmally rare. As Wilson explains in *Truly Disadvantaged*: "When figures on black crime, teenage pregnancy, female-headed families, and welfare dependency are released to the public without sufficient explanation, racial stereotypes are reinforced."[199] It is not unreasonable to expect more in-depth insight from mass media, especially news media. "Ideally, a media system suitable for a democracy ought to provide its readers with some coherent sense of the broader social forces that affect the conditions of their everyday lives."[200] This is all the more so in an era of information overload, and one in which media outlets are empowered to flourish with a bare minimum of external controls – governmental or otherwise.

Yet, the dominant informational mediums in the United States generally fail to proffer an integrative account of the individual *and* structural forces that bear on the intersection of race and crime. The recurring racial themes in film and television reinforce the existing racial status quo by ignoring social structures, by focusing on individuals, and by denying inequality.[201] Admittedly, the lack of in-depth coverage on the subject is characteristic of TV news reporting on most other subjects. Scholars have long documented and lamented the superficiality of news reporting.[202] Iyengar describes contemporary news reporting as fitted to one of two frames. The first kind, episodic framing, focuses on specific events, causes, or individuals. The second kind, thematic framing, locates issues in a larger context.[203] Episodic framing is most often the rule of the day. Even lay audiences consider television news an unlikely place to look for deep reporting, as most use television news for the latest headlines and consider newspapers a more reliable source of in-depth reporting.[204] Oddly, though, fewer and fewer actually read newspapers.[205] It bears emphasizing also that a sizeable percentage of Americans only dabble in television news. As of 2010, 57 percent of Americans say they get their news from TV only "from time to time" versus "regular times," up from 48 percent in 2006.[206]

Inasmuch as the public eschews more informative news sources and then skims the surface of its primary news source – which itself skims the surface – all that can reasonably be expected is a severely limited public understanding of a public policy matter with which many have limited personal involvement to begin with – namely, race.

In addition to television news outlets, the racial messaging of other mass media segments is similarly devoid of contextual information and balance. Millions are reached through these outlets, which include everything from prime-time dramas and sitcoms to television commercials, modern music, and Hollywood movies.[207] Storylines, character roles, personality, dress, dialect, and more serve to embellish the script. Of course, any discussion of entertainment industry portrayals of race and crime would be incomplete without consideration of the unique role and impact of rap music. It is the segment within the entertainment industry most often tied to inner-city ghetto life and black deviance. Rap music reaches sizeable audiences well beyond the urban black community,[208] as evidenced by its enormous cross-over appeal that extends even to international audiences.[209] The "script" followed by rap music is well-positioned to influence a not insignificant proportion of public thinking on the relation between race and crime. This is all the more so since rap artists are typically portrayed as having actually lived the "ghetto life" and are sometimes presumed to speak with greater authenticity than Ivory Tower academics who explore inner-city black life from the confines of their campus offices.

It is arguable that rap music messaging straddles the fence where race, crime, and punishment are concerned and, in doing so, inadvertently bolsters the same negative messaging endemic to mainstream media. On one side of the fence, the music is expressive and gives voice to underprivileged black youth and the difficult life choices they are forced to make on a regular basis, according to a number of scholars.[210] As Kubrin puts it, rap music evinces the "code of the street."[211] It tells the story of blacks in the ghetto, of the lives behind the violence and drug use, of how hard things are for "ghetto blacks." More, it does so at a time when so many others could care less. Significantly, rap lyrics are said to also artistically convey the racial, structural, and cultural forces that lie behind racially disproportional offending and imprisonment. The very same forces scholars point to by way of sophisticated empirical studies that reach primarily academic audiences. On this side of the fence and in this light, rap music contextualizes and, thus, improves upon the blacks-are-criminal script.

On the other side of the fence, however, the framing of rap music messaging effectively changes the tune of the music, so to speak. Graphic rap lyrics and videos frame otherwise valid messaging in images and themes that seemingly condone hyper-materialism, hyper-sexualization, misogyny, illegal drugs, gangs, and violence.[212] Certainly, gangsta rap artists seldom condemn the behavioral pathologies about which they rap. The resultant takeaway varies in accordance with audience predilections. For those familiar with the reality of racial inequality and injustice in the United States, rap music exposes the deeper institutional and structural roots of behavior that deviates from societal norms. For these, rap music tells a familiar story.[213] For those not connected to or cognizant of the reality of racial disadvantage – such as white audiences living in homogenous residential and social contexts – rap music constitutes irrefutable proof of poor inner-city blacks' low regard for mainstream values and law-abiding behavior. For these, rap music repeats the same refrain found in the standard messaging of mainstream media.[214] Only this time, it comes from those who are "in-the-know." Therefore, even where it endeavors to deepen the blacks-are-criminal script, much like the rest of the entertainment industry and television news, rap music often falls short of adequately showcasing the important causal forces linking race, crime, and punishment.

But, alas, gangsta rap music is not the source to which most Americans turn for news and information about blacks in the United States. To recap, this role is played by television news.

Real-Life Impact of the Script

There are real-life consequences that flow from the blacks-are-criminal script followed by mass media, and by television news in particular. Existing studies indicate it does more than simply mirror racial stereotypes; it actually reinforces them and in doing so effectively diminishes public support for racial reform of the criminal justice system. The impact on younger viewers is especially potent in that their exposure to the script occurs during formative years, ensuring perpetuation of the narrative and its impact for years and generations to come. Russell-Brown's study suggests the onslaught of criminal images of black men leads the public to conclude that most black men are criminals. Hence is borne what she terms the myth of the *criminalblackman*.[215] The script is potent enough, Russell-Brown argues, that dozens of white individuals have perpetrated racial hoaxes whereby they blame unnamed and nonspecific (and, in reality, nonexistent) minority suspects for crimes that they themselves committed.[216] Other empirical analyses and experimental studies also supply proof the blacks-are-criminal narrative activates and reinforces negative racial stereotypes.[217] They illustrate white viewers who are exposed to a violent black perpetrator in the news tend to embrace negative stereotypes about blacks.[218] In addition to Domke's[219] experimental study, Bjornstrom and colleagues' multiple regression analysis establishes real-life effects not only with respect to public perception but possibly in regard to public policy preferences too, as follows:

If viewers repeatedly see white victims, their world view will be altered to reflect this such that whites come to believe they have more reason to be fearful of crime than other groups or than is realistic. Moreover, the consequences may reach beyond an unrealistic assessment of the likelihood of victimization for whites. The minimization of attention to groups that, in fact, bear the brunt of victimization may lead to a lack of support for policies oriented to addressing their vulnerability to violence.[220]

Patton and Snyder-Yuly offer a close-up look at how racial stereotyping in the media prompts local community law enforcement to embark on witch hunts for black males to the point that "any four black men will do."[221]

Juxtaposed to the news media's persistent racialization of public opinion on crime is the media's potential to meaningfully inform the public about the linkage between race, crime, and justice. The media can do better. A series of experimental studies by Mutz suggests the media have the capacity to encourage greater awareness.[222] So do numerous other analyses that demonstrate shifts in public attitudes and attentiveness are proximally related to shifts in news reporting.[223] Even in the face of widespread residential segregation, news media can move the needle toward a more sophisticated public discourse on race and crime. Gilliam, Valentino, and Beckmann prove television is in a position to reinforce negative racial stereotypes in the absence of racial residential integration. Whites from heterogeneous neighborhoods are either unaffected or moved in the opposite direction, endorse less punitive crime policies, less negative stereotypes, and feel closer to blacks as a group as a result of exposure to stereotypic coverage. On the other hand, when exposed to racial stereotypes in the news, white respondents living in homogenous white neighborhoods endorse more punitive policies to address crime, express more negative stereotypic evaluations of blacks, and feel more distant from blacks as a group.[224] When whites in segregated contexts read the script, they tend to believe it. It follows then that less stereotyping in news coverage stands to yield less stereotyping on the part of whites who do not know any better. More than just a change in public opinion, the available evidence suggests informative and comprehensive media reports on race can also deter politicians from race-baiting[225] as well as discourage racial profiling on the part of law enforcement.[226]

There is reason to believe that, were mass media to engage the public in an informed and empirically grounded conversation about crime and race, the public would rise to the occasion. It possesses the intellectual capacity to be so engaged. The average American may not be able to digest the methodological nuance of academic research, but s/he can make sound judgments about the credibility of academic studies over and above that of drive-thru reporting. The American public was dubbed by Page and Shapiro a "rational public" in their classic work on public opinion because the public is responsive to external stimuli, such as new information and changing times, among other things.[227] Iyengar's work illustrates that TV viewers who are exposed to episodic news framing tend to focus on specifics and make fewer connections to larger societal forces, whereas viewers exposed to thematic framing tend to confront larger questions about cause and effect.[228]

Perhaps most striking of all is that news stories about experts or research studies produce the greatest amount of change in public opinion. Page, Shapiro, and Dempsey probed the statistical relation between variations in opinion change and media content change and found news stories about experts or research studies produce a "very substantial amount" of public opinion change.[229] In fact, "news commentary and experts remain the most powerful sources of opinion change."[230] And, where the effect of commentaries is lagged (meaning, it takes time to operate), the same is not true of expert information. They explain:

According to our estimates ... those we have categorized as "experts" have quite a substantial impact on public opinion. Their credibility may be high because of their actual or portrayed experience and expertise and nonpartisan status. It is not unreasonable for members of the public to give great weight to experts' statements and positions, particularly when complex technical questions affect the merits of policy alternatives.[231]

Further, they add, "experts are less likely than presidents or other elected officials to bend quickly with the winds of opinion."[232] Interestingly, Jerit's 2009 examination of fifty-three cross-sectional surveys administered by Princeton Survey Research Associates from 1992 to 2004 proved that not only expert commentary in news stories but also contextual coverage helps to improve public knowledge about political issues.[233]

Supply and Demand: Pecuniary Interest, Public Interest, and the American Ethos

Given these three things – that more informed accounts of race, crime, and justice are available, that TV news reporting could go deeper, and that the public is bright enough to keep up – it is worth asking why the news about blacks so often ends up being negative and shallow anyway. The answer lies partly in the organizational structure and makeup of the news reporting process.[234]

Market forces are the driving engine behind the media's reliance on sound bites over and above sound explanations. Competition for audiences and the advertising revenues they bring are the most powerful market forces.[235] Jamieson explains the reason the infamous Willie Horton ad used by the 1988 George H. W. Bush presidential campaign (which featured a menacing-looking furloughed-turned-murderer and rapist black male) garnered widespread news coverage is that it fit the requirements of news.[236] Patterson argues time pressures, what he terms "the mindnumbing confines of the 24-hour news cycle," are a key reason journalists do not dig deeper.[237] The all-important goal is to hurriedly generate a storyline before a competitor does, even if important substance is lost in the process and even if racial stereotypes are reinforced in the process. Few issues are better-suited to the financial motives and time constraints of TV news reporting than crime. Stories about crime dominate local television news programming; it is the most frequent subject of lead stories in television news.[238] The Pew Research Center's 2013 *Annual Report on American Journalism* indicated nearly one in five local news stories was on crime.[239] What is more, TV news conveys the misguided notion that crime is violent.[240] Jamieson explains that "because violent crime is dramatic, conflict ridden, evokes intense emotions, disrupts the social order, threatens the community, and can be verified by such official sources as police, it is 'newsworthy.'"[241] "If it bleeds, it leads" because, for the news industry, crime actually helps to pay the bills.

Instead of changing these dynamics, the impact of the massive increase in digital news platforms over the past two decades has been to strengthen and expand the influence of market influences. Klinenberg's ethnographic studies indicate the convergence of news media in recent decades – that is, the merging of content from different providers, such as television stations, Internet companies, magazines, and newspapers – makes matters worse. Convergence has "undermined the conditions of news production, mainly by reducing the time available to report, research, write, and reflect on stories."[242] Even though the news media was "born as a commercial medium and has always been deeply entangled with corporate, profit-driven interests, insiders fear the logic of the market has penetrated to unprecedented depths of the modern newsroom."[243] Meanwhile, recent shifts within television news reporting, such as the explosion of cable news programing, hardly signal things are changing for this platform either. Rather, they enable us to see more clearly the dominant industrial practices of past television eras, according to Lotz.[244]

Alongside (and in some ways ushered in by) the burgeoning online news media are unprecedented changes in the economics of the news industry, which changes stand to exacerbate still further the tendency toward drive-thru reporting on racial matters. Earlier in the discussion it was noted that the industry *can* do a better job of educating the public about the complex interactions between race, crime, and punishment. The question at hand is whether we have reason to expect the industry *will* do better. The answer is not an unequivocal "yes." The Pew Center's annual report on journalism asserted news organizations' ability to distinguish between "high-quality information of public value and agenda-driven news has become an increasingly complicated task, made no easier in an era of economic churn."[245] The news industry's share of new digital advertising is shrinking considerably, so that advertisers who previously turned to local media now turn to Google, Facebook, and other large networks to buy ads.[246] Major cutbacks have occurred in precisely those parts of the news industry most likely to provide in-depth coverage of issues. For example, CNN, a cable channel that brands itself around deep reporting, cut produced story packages in half from 2007 to 2012.[247] For cable news generally, commentary and opinion (63 percent of airtime) are far more prevalent on the air than straight news reporting (37 percent).[248] Black news media outlets, such as the *Chicago Defender*, which are more likely to offer critiques of law enforcement, are not immune from market retrenchment. According to the Pew report, all of these changes add up to a "news industry that is more undermanned and unprepared to uncover stories, dig deep into emerging ones."[249]

On the basis of television news' prioritization of pecuniary interests over public interests, it would be easy to lay all of the blame for the public's limited understanding of racial matters on the media. However, existing evidence cautions against doing so. According to Entman, the impact of news treatment of blacks in the news markets he examined systematically fostered modern racism but not because journalists intentionally set out to do so. He avers:

Journalists who repeatedly transmit these images may not themselves support modern racism. News personnel shape reports in accordance with professional norms and conventions. When confronted with events or issues that the social structure and political process routinely produce, these journalistic practices yield visuals and sound bites that fit audience stereotypes.... What reinforces stereotypes from the perspective of the communication theorist is simply following news conventions and audience expectations to the journalist.[250]

Entman's probe of network news indicates the patterns observed there as well are "not because of conscious bias, but because of the way conventional journalistic norms and practices interact with political and social reality."[251] Others settle on the same conclusion, that news reporter interviews as well as the editing of news stories are guided by "narrative relevance," meaning a preliminary idea of what the emerging story should look like.[252]

In short, the determination of what news reports "should look like" is based on audience preferences – on what sells and on what audiences will buy as well as buy into. At the same time that mass media engages in reality construction and helps mold public attitudes about specific issues and problems, its approach to doing so is very much informed by audience predilections.

It is for this reason, then, that it would be a mistake to attribute public stereotyping of blacks wholly to the inner workings of mass media, or to expect that a change in news reporting alone would foster massive attitudinal shifts on racial matters. Public opinion is not entirely the making of mass media. Research studies demonstrate there is a measure of autonomy in public opinion formation. Gamson and colleagues note that while media engage in social construction of reality, many "viewers ... are wide awake and draw on their wisdom and experience in making sense of what they see on television."[253] Crucially, the public not only thinks for itself, so to speak, but there is a cyclical relationship between TV news reporting and public thinking, such that public preferences help shape TV news reporting. Erbring, Goldenberg, and Miller developed what they call an "audience-contingent effects model," which illustrates "media coverage interacts with the audience's pre-existing sensitivities."[254] Although much has been made in recent years of the widely noted conservative bias in Fox News reporting and liberal bias in MSNBC News reporting, Gentzkow and Shapiro's 2010 study of daily newspapers' news content establishes media "slant is highly related to consumer ideology" and generally unrelated to owner ideology.[255] They find readers have an economically significant preference for like-minded news.[256] With respect to online news consumption as well, public endorsement of particular content is evident.[257] The Pew Center's 2013 *State of the News Media 2013* report too shows TV audiences select news sources partly based on their ideological and partisan preferences.[258]

Therein lies the second part of the answer to the question of why TV news reporting about blacks heavily emphasizes criminal behavior and de-emphasizes its systemic roots. Where race, crime, and justice are concerned, American mass media tell a familiar story, a story that fits seamlessly with what the public already thinks. As compared to social scientists' emphasis on structural determinism, the blacks-are-criminal script is more closely aligned with fundamental American beliefs about individualism and self-determination. The basic thrust of the blacks-are-criminal script is ultimately traceable to the preexisting audience belief framework that mediates informational inputs on public policy matters. According to the ideology of individualism, it is the individual, not society, that ultimately dictates one's fate. In the widely cited *Race and*

Inequality: A Study in American Values, Paul M. Sniderman with Michael Gray Hagen explains:

Individualism ... is an ethic: It is a bedrock belief in an ethic of self-reliance. Individuals must take care of themselves. They must not pretend to be victims of circumstance, or ask for special favors, in an effort to get others to do for them what they should do for themselves. It is up to them to do what it takes to get ahead. They themselves must shoulder the responsibility for their lives.[259]

More to the point, "individualists believe that blacks have only themselves to blame for not getting ahead."[260] It was during the time period 1977 to 1989 that whites' explanations of racial inequality became more firmly fixed.[261] Perhaps decisively, Sniderman and Hagen find that while individualists tend to fit a certain demographic profile (viz., less educated, older, and southern), their beliefs about personal responsibility are not confined to blacks only but extend to other groups as well, such as women and the poor. The ideology of individualism is applied to everyone and everything on an equal basis – including racial inequality

Americans' propensity to embrace individualism and, thus, reject explanations that blame society extends as far back as the Founding. Individualism is deeply rooted in American sociopolitical thought, manifest and reinforced on a continual basis. Everything from classic fairy tales to religious expositions predictably point in unison to the basic idea that everyone can make it if they only work hard and play by the rules. The myth of Horatio Alger nicely symbolizes this core American ideological and cultural tradition. A self-actualization theme runs throughout the famed Horatio Alger fictional writings of the late nineteenth century, which chronicle the rise of poor boys from poverty to wealth and fame through perseverance and hard work.[262] Max Weber theorized long ago in *The Protestant Ethic* that a belief in individual entrepreneurship is an essential element of the spirit of capitalism. The definitive phrases in the American *Declaration of Independence* too underscores not only that all have the right to life, liberty, and the pursuit of happiness; all men are also created equal. For the average citizen in the United States, the latter has come to mean an equal chance at a good life. Each individual has the power to succeed. Educational and work opportunities are available to all. If one's life turns out poorly, it is primarily because one did not work hard or did not play by the rules. At bottom, life outcomes are a function of individual phenomena, not societal forces. Necessarily, then, structural explanations of any kind conflict with the fundamental ideals embraced by the vast majority of Americans.

TABLE 8.1. *American Beliefs in Self-Actualization, 1994–2010*

Percent Believing	1994	2000	2004	2010
Everyone has it in their own power to succeed	79	80	78	75
Most people who want to get ahead can make it if they're willing to work hard	68	74	68	64

TABLE 8.2. *American Attitudes toward Opportunity and Life Success, 1984 and 1987*

	Year	Percent Agreeing
Everyone in country has educational opportunity	1984	71
Social standing reflects what people made out of their opportunities	1984	74
Life achievement depends on one's ability and education	1984	85
Natural ability is important for getting ahead in life	1987	96
Hard work is important for getting ahead in life	1987	98

When asked whether blacks are responsible for their disproportional share of arrests and imprisonment or their comparatively limited success in society generally, Americans are predisposed to say "yes." Survey data help to illustrate the extent to which they embrace explanations of life outcomes that center on the individual, as opposed to society. Table 8.1[263] shows that four out of five consistently expressed the opinion that "everyone has it in their own power to succeed" and that "most people who want to get ahead can make it if they're willing to work hard." Furthermore, Table 8.2[264] makes clear that systematic measures ground Americans' individualist ideology dating back over decades, to the 1980s, precisely the time when social scientists had begun to produce mountains of evidence to the contrary.

Conclusion

To conclude, what substantially diminishes Americans' receptivity toward macro-level explanations for blacks' overrepresentation and disparate treatment in the criminal justice system is that most believe individual fate is, fundamentally, a function of individual choice. In addition to this basic belief framework is the fact that a majority are daily reminded by mass media of blacks' disproportional involvement in drugs, violence, and other deviant behaviors. What they purportedly see with their very own eyes, then, is blacks habitually running afoul of law and order – by choice. The root causes of criminal activity or, more to the point, racial disproportionalness in arrests and imprisonment are seldom broached in news reporting and, thus, less apparent to most. The rare occasions on which the twin problem of disparate treatment is deemed worthy of head-line news are likewise occasions on which the widespread and systemic nature of such treatment is under-explored, if at all. The scarcity of news reporting on the Rodney King, Amadou Diallo, and Oscar Grant inci-dents creates the impression they are isolated. Out of sight, out of mind. Meanwhile, the richly informative, decades-long conversation among academics regarding the relevance of institutional bias, resource depriva-tion, ecological contexts, cultural adaptation, and the like is an exchange carried on mostly behind the walls of the Ivory Tower. The empirically grounded scholarly explanations for racial differences in criminal process that have been published over the years are not the stuff of headline news. The news coverage they generate hardly competes at all with the seem-ingly daily incidence of black-on-black crime and does not compete at all with black-on-white crime.

These contraindications notwithstanding, a grounded public under-standing of how and why race figures prominently in criminal justice is not out of reach. Studies show that voters can discern the difference between empiricism and sensationalism. When exposed to expert knowl-edge on a subject matter, in the words of James Madison, that knowledge serves to "refine and enlarge" public thinking. Still, where the black law enforcement experience is concerned, more than just the facts are needed to spur a transformative public dialog. Also needed is a change, or at the very least an adjustment in the belief framework within which public atti-tudes toward individual opportunity and outcomes are negotiated. The extant literature on public opinion and media influences supply cause to expect that a shift in the individualist ideology of most Americans would potentially alter television news' reliance on the blacks-are-criminal script. Absent such a shift in their belief framework, most Americans will continue to rationalize and abide racial tracking in the criminal justice system and will do so on the basis of what they think they know about race and crime. Most will continue to believe the burden of responsibility for change rests on the shoulders of black individuals, beyond the reach of public policy reform, and beyond the power of the public.

Appendix

Methodology for Hearings Analysis

The methodology used to gather the data and information for the hearings analysis in Chapter 5 utilizes two sources, namely the "Legislative History" page of the Pro Quest Congressional website (at http://www. congressional.proquest.com) and hearings testimony published in print form by the U.S. Government Printing Office. (*Pro Quest) The Pro Quest listing of hearings under the enacted laws "PL" number and also the hearings summary descriptions provided there was especially useful for determining at the outset which of the hearings to select for analysis. For purposes of manageability and also my interest in probing witness testimony as systematically as possible, the hearings contained in the Pro Quest listing were selected on the basis of several criteria. First, only those hearings held during the Congress in which the crime laws were adopted are examined. Second, hearings listed by Pro Quest as "published" or "related" were included and unpublished hearings excluded.

Next, I selected hearings that involved direct advocacy. This included both those hearings held to address crime bills formally introduced in the House or Senate as well as those that involved testimony in which witnesses expressly recommended or objected to legislative action or in which witnesses offered "lessons" or policy approaches for Congress to follow or implement. This list was then further narrowed by way of eliminating hearings described on the Pro Quest listing as chiefly concerned with agency coordination, creation and oversight of grant programs, and budget authorization and appropriations hearings. To help maintain the study's focus on street crime, also excluded were hearings on subjects such as domestic violence, bank fraud, money laundering, juvenile justice, pornography and obscenity, Indian Lands, anabolic steroid and prescription drug abuse, mail fraud, foreign interdiction, foreign aid, and the like. Of special interest were hearings and testimony that dealt with enforcement and prevention issues in the United States as a whole, as opposed to those pertaining to individual states or cities. The opening statements of committee members were excluded, since committee members are the intended receivers of hearing information and testimony.

Witness panels were then grouped into three categories, as follows. The "crime fighters" category includes witness testimonies that advocated chiefly or exclusively enforcement-centered approach to crime-fighting. "Crime-preventers" include witness testimonies that chiefly or exclusively advised a prevention and treatment-centered approach. In the third category of "justice advocates" are witnesses who urged adoption of a crime policy approach that was informed by racial justice or civil liberties-related concerns. Finally, the data in Table 5.1 depict the number of witness testimonies, not the number of witnesses, though I occasionally use the terms "witness" and "testimony" interchangeably. Doing so does not substantially detract from the accuracy of my conclusions because of three considerations. First, there are but a few instances in which a single witness is counted twice. Second, duplicate witnesses sometimes offer perspectives that are properly classified separately, though the witness' administrative or political role is consistently lodged in one category. For example the head of the Bureau of Prisons on most occasions stressed the importance of traditional prison confinement but on a few also highlighted the importance of more funding for prison programming. Finally and most importantly, the primary concern of the hearings analysis in Chapter 5 is the nature and extent of expert information and issue advocacy to which members of Congress were exposed. It concludes, on the basis of the hearings data gathered, the policy choices eventually adopted by Congress were not congruent with the witnesses and testimony lineup across the hearings. Table A.1 contains a listing of the hearings selected for this analysis

TABLE A.I. *List of Selected Hearings*

Year of crime law enactment	Hearing dates	Subcommittee/full committee
1968	Mar. 15–16, 22–23, Apr. 5, 7, 10, 12, 19–20, 26–27, 1967	Subcommittee No. 5; House Judiciary
1970	Feb. 4, 17–20, 1970	Subcommittee on Public Health; House Interstate and Foreign Commerce
1970	Feb. 25–27, Mar. 2–3, 1970	Subcommittee on Public Health; House interstate and Foreign Commerce
1970	Mar. 16–17, 23–25, 1970	Special Subcommittee on Alcoholism and Narcotics; Senate Labor and Public Welfare
1970	Mar. 26, Apr. 13–15, 1970	Special Subcommittee on Alcoholism and Narcotics; Senate Labor and Public Welfare
1984	Feb. 22, 29, Mar. 21, Apr. 4, 12, 1984	Subcommittee on Criminal Justice; House Judiciary
1984	May 3, 9, 10, Jun. 7, 1984	Subcommittee on Criminal Justice; House Judiciary
1984	May 4, 11, 18, 19, 23, 1983	Subcommittee on Criminal Law, Senate Judiciary
1984	Jun. 30, July 14, 1983	Subcommittee on Courts, Civil Liberties, and the Administration of Justice; House Judiciary
1984	Jun. 29, 1983, Feb. 22, 1984	Subcommittee on Crime; House Judiciary
1986	May 20, 1986	House Committee on Narcotics Abuse and Control
1986	Sep. 18, 1985	Senate Judiciary Committee
1986	Mar. 13, 1986	Subcommittee on Crime; House Judiciary
1986	Jun. 12, 1986	Subcommittee on Crime; House Judiciary
1986	Aug. 7, 1986	Subcommittee on Crime; House Judiciary
1986	Sep. 27, 1985	Select Committee on Narcotics Abuse and Control
1986	Aug. 6, 1986	House Education and Labor Committee
1988	Jun. 15, 1988	Subcommittee on Legislation and National Security; House Government Operations
1988	May 14, 1987	Senate Judiciary Committee
1988	Jun. 14, 1988	Senate Judiciary Committee

(*continued*)

TABLE A.I *(continued)*

Year of crime law enactment	Hearing dates	Subcommittee/full committee
1988	Mar. 23, 1988	Subcommittee on Courts, Civil Liberties, and the Administration of Justice; House Judiciary
1988	June. 16, 1988	Senate Labor and Human Resources Committee
1988	May 12, 1987	Subcommittee on Children, Family, Drugs, and Alcoholism; Senate Committee on Labor and Human Resources
1988	Feb. 26, 1987	House Select Committee on Children, Youth, and Families
1988	Mar. 11, 1987	House Select Committee on Narcotics Abuse and Control
1988	June 9, 1987	House Select Committee on Narcotics Abuse and Control
1990	Jan. 29, Mar. 1, 1990	Subcommittee on Oversight of Government Management; Senate Governmental Affairs Committee
1990	Sep. 21, 1989	Senate Governmental Affairs Committee
1990	Sep. 14, 1989	Subcommittee on Criminal Justice; House Judiciary
1990	Jul. 25, 1989	Senate Judiciary Committee
1990	Apr. 10, 1989	Senate Judiciary Committee
1990	Mar. 27, Apr. 19, Jul. 23, Aug. 15, 1990	Subcommittee on Criminal Justice; House Judiciary
1990	Mar. 21, 29, May 24, 1990	Subcommittee on Crime; House Judiciary
1990	Aug. 2, 1989	Subcommittee on Crime; House Judiciary
1990	Mar. 6, 1990	Subcommittee on Crime; House Judiciary
1994	Feb. 9, 1994	Subcommittee on Juvenile Justice; Senate Judiciary
1994	Mar. 1, 1994	Subcommittee on Crime and Criminal Justice; Senate Judiciary
1994	May 12, Jul. 29, 1993	Subcommittee on Intellectual Property and Judicial Administration; House Judiciary
1994	Feb. 10, 1994	Subcommittee on Intellectual Property and Judicial Administration; House Judiciary

Notes

Preface

1   Steinberg, N. (1994, April 12). "Cisneros: CHA May Be Most Violent // HUD Chief Spends Night at the Robert Taylor Homes." *Chicago Sun-Times.* Retrieved June 20, 2013, from http://www.highbeam.com

2   Wilson, William J. (1987). *The Truly Disadvantaged: The Inner City, the Underclass, and Public Policy.* Chicago: University of Chicago Press.

3   Madden v. O'Leary, 915 F.2d 715 (1990).

1 Racial Tracking: Two Law Enforcement Modes

1   However, for a broad descriptive account of treatment (versus processing) based primarily on local and state data, see Mann, C. R. (1993). *Unequal Justice: A Question of Color.* Bloomington: Indiana University Press.

2   Black motorist Rodney King was subject to a videotaped beating by four Los Angeles police officers in 1991, which included fifty-six baton blows, six kicks, and shots from a taser gun. African immigrant Amadou Diallo was killed in 1999 by four New York City police officers after being wounded by nineteen of forty-one shots fired at him. Two black sisters, Gladys and Jamie Scott, ages nineteen and twenty-one, were sentenced to life in prison in 1994 in Forest, Mississippi, for setting up an armed robbery that netted eleven dollars. Both were pardoned by the state governor after serving sixteen years in prison. Harvard Professor Henry Louis Gates was handcuffed and arrested in 2009 because of comments he made to a police officer while on his own front porch. In 2009, black twenty-two-year-old Oscar Grant was shot and killed by a transit cop while face down on the ground of a subway platform in Oakland, California. All five cases grabbed national news headlines for an extended period of time.

3   See, for example, Leadership Conference on Civil Rights. (April 2000). *Justice on Trial: Racial Disparities in the American Criminal Justice System.* http://www.civilrights.org; Hanley, R. (March 28, 2002). "NAACP Head Criticizes

Study of Turnpike Arrests." *New York Times.* http://www.nytimes.com; American Civil Liberties Union. (June 20, 2009). *The Persistence of Racial and Ethnic Profiling in the United States.* http://www.aclu.ogr; Gibney, S. (2009). "NAACP President Outlines Agenda for Next Century." *Crisis*, 116, 44–45; Rights Working Group. (September 2010). "Faces of Racial Profiling: A Report from Communities Across America." http://www.rightsworkinggroup.org; Winston, B. (2010). "The NAACP's New Smart and Safe Campaign Calls for Law Enforcement Accountability." *Crisis*, 117, 41–47.

4 Arrests by federal agencies make up a tiny percentage of total arrests in the United States. For example, according to the *Sourcebook on Criminal Justice Statistics* website, in 2004 140,755 persons were arrested by a federal agency. This compares to well more than 10 million total arrests in the United States during the same year.

5 For an excellent review of racial trends in various states and localities, see Georges-Abeyie, D. (1984). *The Criminal Justice System and Blacks.* New York: Clark Boardman Company, Ltd.; Mann, C. R. (1993). *Unequal Justice: A Question of Color.* Bloomington: Indiana University Press; Hawkins, D. F. (ed.). (1995). *Ethnicity, Race, and Crime: Perspectives across Time and Place.* Albany, NY: State University of New York Press; Meeks, K. (2000). *Driving While Black.* New York: Broadway Books; Gabbidon, S. L., Greene, H. T. and Young, V. D. (2002). *African American Classics in Criminology and Criminal Justice.* Thousand Oaks, CA: Sage Books; Harris, D. A. (2003). *Profiles in Injustice: Why Racial Profiling Cannot Work.* New York: The New Press; Heumann, M. and Cassak, L. (2003). *Good Cop, Bad Cop: Racial Profiling and Competing Views of Justice in America.* New York: Peter Lang Publishing; Gabbidon, S. L. and Greene, H. T. (2005). *Race and Crime.* Thousand Oaks, CA: Sage Publications, Inc.; Western, B. (2006). *Punishment and Inequality in America.* New York: Russell Sage Foundation; Decker, S. H., Alarid, L. F., and Katz, C. M. (eds.). (2007). *Controversies in Criminal Justice: Contemporary Readings.* New York: Oxford University Press.

6 Amnesty International U.S.A. (1999). *United States of America: Race, Rights and Police Brutality.* New York: Amnesty International U.S.A.

7 Figures in Table 1.1 calculated from data in: Bureau of Justice Statistics. (2008). *Police-Public Contact Survey, 2005* [Computer file]. Conducted by the Bureau of the Census. ICPSR020020-v1. Ann Arbor, MI: Inter-University Consortium for Political and Social Research [distributor]. Population data on U.S. residential population 16 sixteen years and older taken from the *Statistical Abstract of the United States 2007*, table 14.

8 Figures in Table 1.2 calculated from data in: *Police-public contact survey, 2005* [Computer file] and *Statistical Abstract of the United States, 2007*, table 14.

9 By "objective indicia," I mean a radar detector in the case of speed-related stops, a blood alcohol test in the case of driving under the influence offenses (DUISs), vehicle defects, and records checks.

10 Russell-Brown, K. (2009). *The Color of Crime: Racial Hoaxes, White Fear, Black Protectionism, Police Harassment, and Other Macroaggressions* (2nd ed.). New York University Press, 64.

11 In many states, law enforcement officers have the authority to detain a stopped driver or vehicle until drug-sniffing dogs are brought to the scene, should the driver object to a search of the vehicle or his person.

12 Figures in Table 1.3 calculated from data in: *Police-Public Contact Survey, 2005* [Computer file] and *Statistical Abstract of the United States, 2007*, table 14.

13 Bureau of Justice Statistics. (April 2005). *Contacts between Police and the Public: Findings from the 2002 National Survey* (NCJ 207845). http://www.bjs.gov

14 Figures in Table 1.4 calculated from data in: *Police-Public Contact Survey, 2005* [Computer file] and *Statistical Abstract of the United States, 2007*, table 14.

15 For a description of the three main sources of police homicides, see Bureau of Justice Statistics. (October 2007). *Arrest-Related Deaths in the United States, 2003–2005* (NCJ 219534). For a comparative trend analysis, see: Bureau of Justice Statistics. (March 2001). *Policing and Homicide, 1976–1998* (NCJ 180987).

16 Figures in Table 1.5 calculated from data in Bureau of Justice Statistics. (October 2007). *Arrest-Related Deaths in the United States, 2003–2005* (NCJ 219534), Appendix table 4. Population data on 2005 U.S. residential population sixteen years and older taken from the *Statistical Abstract of the United States 2007*, table 14.

17 Figures in Table 1.6 calculated from data in *Arrest-Related Deaths in the United States, 2003–2005*. Population data for residents 16 years and older taken from the *Statistical Abstract of the United States 2007*, table 14.

18 Arrest figures in Table 1.7 calculated from data in Federal Bureau of Investigation. (September 2010). *Crime in the United States, 2009*. Arrest tables 43A, 43B, 49A, 55A, 61A, and 67A. Population figures for one race, non-Hispanic blacks and whites obtained from U.S. Census Bureau. Annual estimates of the resident population by sex, race, and Hispanic origin for the United States: April 1, 2000, to July 1, 2009.

19 Bynam, A. E. (1988). "Eighth and Fourteenth Amendments – The Death Penalty Survives." *Journal of Criminal Law and Criminology.* 78:1080–1118, 1116.

20 Bynam, p. 1116.

21 In plea negotiations, prosecutors can use the threat of a first, second, or third felony conviction as incentive for a defendant to plead guilty and avoid triggering the three-strikes mandate in place at the federal level and in many states.

22 Although these data do not permit us to probe the frequency with which prosecutors decide against pursuit of police arrest charges, they do allow us to examine the thrust of the decisive choices they make from the point of initial court appearance through adjudication.

23 Figures in Table 1.8 calculated from data in Bureau of Justice Statistics. (2007). *State Court Processing Statistics, 1990–2004: Felony Defendants in Large Urban Counties.* ICPSR02038-v3. Ann Arbor, MI: Inter-University Consortium for Political and Social Research [distributor].

24 Figures in Table 1.9 calculated from data in *State Court Processing Statistics, 1990–2004.*

25 Figures in Table 1.10 calculated from data in *State Court Processing Statistics.*

26 Figures in Table 1.11 calculated from data in *State Court Processing Statistics.*

27 Figures in Table 1.12 calculated from data in *State Court Processing Statistics.*

28 Figures in Table 1.13 calculated from data in *State Court Processing Statistics.*

29 Figures in Table 1.14 calculated from data in *State Court Processing Statistics.*

30 Figures in Table 1.15 calculated from data in *State Court Processing Statistics.*

31 Figures in Table 1.16 calculated from data in *State Court Processing Statistics, 1990–2004.*

32 Figures in Table 1.17 calculated from data in *State Court Processing Statistics, 1990–2004.*

33 Figures in Table 1.18 calculated from data in *State Court Processing Statistics, 1990–2004.*

34 Tonry, M. (1995). *Malign Neglect: Race, Crime, and Punishment in America.* New York: Oxford University Press; Mauer, M. (1999). *The Sentencing Project.* New York: The New Press; Tonry, M. and Petersilia, J. (eds.). (1999). *Prisons.* Chicago: University of Chicago Press.

35 Figures in Table 1.19 calculated from data in *State Court Processing Statistics, 1990–2004.*

36 Figures in Table 1.20 from Bureau of Justice Statistics. (December 2009). *Felony Sentences in State Courts, 2006–Statistical Tables* (NCJ 226846). http://www.bjs.gov, tables 1.3 and 3.6.

37 Figures in Table 1.21 from Bureau of Justice Statistics. (December 2010). *Capital Punishment, 2009–Statistical Tables* (NCJ231676). http://www.bjs. gov. Calculations based on data in tables 4, 8, and 13. U.S. residential figures based on 2009 Census Bureau online population estimates.

38 Schudel, M. (December 11, 2005). "With Humor and Anger on Race Issues, Comic Inspired a Generation." *Washington Post.* http://www.washington-post.com

39 Figures in 1.22 derived from data in: Bureau of Justice Statistics (BJS). (December 2011). *Prisoners in 2010* (NCJ 236096), Appendix tables 12–13 and BJS. (December 2012). *Prisoners in 2011* (NCJ 239808), table 9, http://www.bjs.gov. Population data from 2010 and 2011 U.S. census.

40 All data in Table 1.23 (except the sexual assault and mortality data) were derived from Bureau of Justice Statistics. 2004 *Survey of Inmates in State and Federal Correctional Facilities.* ICPSR04572-v1. Ann, Arbor, MI: Inter-university Consortium for Political and Social Research Producer, 2007-02-28. The sexual assault 2008–2009 data were calculated from Bureau of Justice Statistics. (August 2010). *Sexual Victimization in Prisons and Jails Reported by Inmates, 2008–2009* (NCJ 231169), table 6. Mortality data

for state prisoners for 2001–2001 obtained from Bureau of Justice Statistics. (August 2005). *Suicide and Homicide in State Prisons and Local Jails* (NCJ 210036), table 3.

41 See Tonry, M. and Petersilia, J. (eds). (1999). *Prisons.* Chicago: University of Chicago Press.

42 Data in Table 1.24 derived from 2004 *Survey of Inmates in State and Federal Correctional Facilities.*

43 Holzer, H. J., Raphael, S., and Stoll, M. A. (May 19–20, 2003). *Employment Barriers Facing Ex-Offenders.* Urban Institute Reentry Roundtable. New York: New York University Law School. http://www.urban.org

44 All data in Table 1.25 (except HIV infection and AIDS-related death data) obtained from the 2004 *Survey of Inmates in State and Federal Correctional Facilities.* HIV infection data for 2004 obtained from BJS. (September 2007). *HIV in Prisons, 2005* (NCJ 218915). AIDS-related deaths data for 2007 obtained from BJS. (December 2009). *HIV in Prisons, 2007–2008* (NCJ 228307), table 5.

45 Data in Table 1.26 derived from BJS. (November 2010). *Sentence Length of State Prisoners, by Offense, Admission Type, Sex, and Race – Statistical Tables.* ncrp0811.sav, table 11.

46 Arrest data in Figure 1.1 derived from: FBI. *Crime in the United States* serial editions for year of arrest data. Population data for one race, non-Hispanic blacks and whites obtained from the *Statistical Abstract of the United States* editions 1970, 1980, 2004, and 2007 and also the U.S. Census Bureau. Annual estimates of the residential population by sex, race, and Hispanic origin for the United States: April 1, 2000, to July 1, 2009.

47 Data in Table 1.27 derived from: Langan, P. A. (May 1991). *Race of Prisoners Admitted to State and Federal Institutions, 1926–1986* (NCJ-125618); BJS. (December 2011). *Prisoners in 2010* (NCJ 236096); BJS. (June 1996). *Correctional Populations in the United States, 1994* (NCJ-160091), table 1.8; and, data for 2000 obtained from: BJS. (December 2009). *Prisoners in 2008* (NCJ 228417). Population obtained from the U.S. Census Bureau.

2 Policy Process Theory of Racial Tracking: An Overview

1 Among the excellent exceptions are: Provine, D. M. (2007). *Unequal under Law: Race in the War on Drugs.* Chicago: University of Chicago; Weaver, V. M. (2007). "Frontlash: Race and the Development of Punitive Crime Policy." *Studies in American Political Development,* 21, 230–265; Loury, G. C. with Karlan, P. S., Shelby, T., and Wacquant, L. (2008). *Race, Incarceration, and American Values.* Cambridge, MA: MIT Press; Tonry, M. (2010). "The Social, Psychological, and Political Causes of Racial Disparities in the American Criminal Justice System." *Crime and Justice,* 39: 273–312; Tonry, M. (2011). *Punishing Race: A Continuing American Dilemma.* New York: Oxford University Press.

2 More of the evidence concerning the viability of public policy intervention is laid out in Chapter 8.

3 Bonczar, T. P. (August 2003). *Bureau of Justice Statistics Special Report: Prevalence of Imprisonment in the U.S. Population, 1974–2001* (NCJ 197976). Washington, DC: Bureau of Justice Statistics, table 9; Schmitt, J. and Warner, K. (November 2010). *Ex-Offenders and the Labor Market.* Washington, DC: Center for Economic and Policy Research (CEPR). http:// www.cepr.net, table 4.

4 Schmitt and Warner, *Ex-Offenders and the Labor Market,* table 4.

5 Carson, E. A. and Sabol, W. J. (December 2012). *Prisoners in 2011* (NCJ 239808). Washington, DC: Bureau of Justice Statistics.

6 Schmitt and Warner, *Ex-Offenders and the Labor Market*; Pager, D. (2007). *Marked: Race, Crime, and Finding Work in an Era of Mass Incarceration.* Chicago: University of Chicago Press.

7 U.S. Equal Employment Opportunity Commission. (September 7, 1990). Notice No. N-915, *Policy guidance on the consideration of arrest records in employment decisions under Title VII of the Civil Rights Act of 1964.* Notice No. N-915-061.

8 Schmitt and Warner, *Ex-Offenders and the Labor Market,* 2.

9 Holzer, H. J., Raphael, S., and Stoll, M. A. (May 19–20, 2003). *Employment Barriers Facing Ex-Offenders.* Urban Institute Reentry Roundtable. New York: New York University Law School. http://www.urban.org

10 Pager, *Marked: Race, Crime, and Finding Work.* See also Holzer, H. (1996). *What Employers Want: Job Prospects for Less-Educated Workers.* New York: Russell Sage Foundation; Holzer, H. and Lalonde, R. (2000). "Job Stability and Job Change among Young Unskilled Workers." In D. Card and R. Blank (eds.) *Finding Jobs: Work and Welfare Reform.* New York: Russell Sage Foundation.

11 Holzer, Raphael, and Stoll, *Employment Barriers Facing Ex-Offenders.*

12 Holzer, H. J., Raphael, S., and Stoll, M. A. (2006). "Perceived Criminality, Criminal Background Checks and the Racial Hiring Practices of Employers." *Journal of Law and Economics,* **49,** 451–480.

13 Mukamal, D. (June 2001). *From Hard Time to Full Time: Strategies to Help Move Ex-Offenders from Welfare to Work* No. AS-10868-00-40. Washington, DC: U.S. Department of Labor.

14 Schmitt and Warner, *Ex-Offenders and the Labor Market,* 14.

15 Schmitt and Warner, *Ex-Offenders and the Labor Market,* table 6. See also Holzer, H. J., Offner, P., and Sorensen, E. (2005). "Declining employment among young black less-educated men: The role of incarceration and child support." *Journal of Policy analysis and Management,* **24,** 329–350.

16 Grogger, J. (1992). "Arrests, Persistent Youth Joblessness, and Black/ White Employment Differentials." *Review of Economics and Statistics,* **74,** 100–106.

17 For more on this theme, see the discussion in Chapter 8 pertaining to the research identifying the socioeconomic causes of racial disproportionalness in incarceration.

18 See Mirsch, A. E., Dietrich, S. M., Landau, R., Schneider, P. D., Ackelsberg, I., Bernstein-Baker, J., and Hohenstein, J. (2002). *Every Door Closed: Barriers Facing Parents with Criminal Records.* http://www.clasp.org

19 For a review of this literature as it pertains to criminal justice matters, see: Murray, J. (2005). "Effects of Imprisonment on Families and Children of Prisoners." In A. Liebling and S. Maruna (eds.), *The Effects of Imprisonment* (NCJ211241). Portland: Willan Publishing. http://www.ncjrs.gov

20 Wilson, W. J. (1987). *The Truly Disadvantaged: The Inner City, the Underclass, and Public Policy*. Chicago: The University of Chicago Press.

21 Western, B., Pettit, B. and the Pew Charitable Trusts. (2010). *Collateral Costs: Incarceration's Effect on Economic Mobility*. http://www.pewtrusts.org

22 See Western, Pettit, and the Pew Charitable Trusts, *Collateral Costs*, 21 and Murray, "Effects of Imprisonment on Families and Children of Prisoners."

23 Manza, J. and Uggen, C. (2006). *Locked Out: Felon Disenfranchisement and American Democracy*. New York: Oxford University Press.

24 The Brennan Center. (March 23, 2011). *Restoring Voting Rights*. http://www.brennancenter.org

25 The Sentencing Project. (June 2013). *Felony Disenfranchisement Laws in the United States*. http://sentencingproject.org

26 Pew Charitable Trusts. (June 12, 2012). *The High Cost of Corrections*. http://www.pewstates.org; Maguire, K. (ed.) *Sourcebook of Criminal Justice Statistics*. State University of New York at Albany. http://www.albany.edu/sourcebook, table 1.9.2010.

27 Pew Center on the States. (March 2009). *One in 31: The Long Reach of American Corrections*. Washington, DC: The Pew Charitable Trusts. http://www.pewstates.org

28 Carson, E. A. and Sabol, W. J. (December 2012). *Prisoners in 2011* (NCJ 239808). Washington, DC: Bureau of Justice Statistics. http://www.bjs.gov

29 Carson and Sabol, *Prisoners in 2011*.

30 Pew Center on the States. (April 2011). *State of Recidivism: The Revolving Door of America's Prisons*. Washington, DC: The Pew Charitable Trusts. http://www.pewtrusts.org, 2

31 Holzer, Raphael, and Stoll, *Employment Barriers Facing Ex-Offenders*; Mukamal, *From Hard Time to Full Time*.

32 Fagan, J., West, V., and Holland, J. (2002). "Reciprocal Effects of Crime and Incarceration in New York City Neighborhoods." *Fordham Urban Law Journal*, 30, 1551–1602, 1554.

33 Fagan, J., West, V., and Holland, J. (2005). "Neighborhood, Crime, and Incarceration in New York City." *Columbia Human Rights Law Review*, 36, 71–108.

34 Western, B. (2007). *Punishment and Inequality in America*. New York: Russell Sage Foundation.

35 Loury with Karlan, Shelby, and Wacquant, *Race, Incarceration, and American Values*, 34.

36 Amnesty International US. (February 2000). *Police Brutality and International Human Rights in the United States*. New York: Amnesty International US, 39.

37 Rights Working Group, American Civil Liberties Union. (June 30, 2009). *The Persistence of Racial and Ethnic Profiling in the United States: A Follow-Up*

Report to the U.N. Committee on the Elimination of Racial Discrimination.
http://www.aclu.org

38 Lasswell, H. (1956). *The Decision Process*. College Park: University of Maryland Press; Jones, C. (1970). *An Introduction to the Study of Public Policy*. Belmont, CA: Wadsworth; Anderson, J. (1975). *Public Policy-Making*. New York: Praeger; Brewer, G. and deLeon, P. (1983). *The Foundations of Policy Analysis*. Monterey, CA: Brooks/Cole.

39 Nakamura, R. (1987). "The Textbook Process and Implementation Research." *Policy Studies Review*, 1, 142–154.

40 Dahl, R. (1961) *Who Governs: Democracy and Power in an American City*. New Haven, CT: Yale University Press; Dahl, R. (2000). *On Democracy*. New Haven, CT: Yale University Press; Polsby, N. W. (1960). "How to Study Community Power: The Pluralist Alternative. *Journal of Politics*, 22, 474–484.

41 Ferguson, T. (1995). *Golden Rule: The Investment Theory of Party Competition and the Logic of Money-Driven Political Systems*. Chicago: University of Chicago Press.

42 Bachrach, P. and Baratz, M. S. (1962). "Two Faces of Power." *American Political Science Review*, 56, 947–952, 949.

43 Gaventa, J. (1982). *Power and Powerlessness: Quiescence and Rebellion in an Appalachian Valley*. Champaign: University of Illinois Press.

44 Erikson, R. (1976). "The Relationship between Public Opinion and State Policy: A New Look at Some Forgotten Data." *American Journal of Political Science*, 20, 25–36; Monroe, A. D. (1979). "Consistency between Public Preferences and National Policy Decisions." *American Politics Quarterly*, 7, 3–19; Page, B. I. and Shapiro, R. Y. (1983). "Effects of Public Opinion on Policy." *American Political Science Review*, 77, 175–190; Wagner, J. (1983). "Media Do Make a Difference: The Differential Impact of the Mass Media in the 1976 Presidential Race." *American Journal of Political Science*, 27, 407–430; Weissberg, R. (1976). *Public Opinion and Popular Government*. Englewood Cliffs, NJ: Prentice-Hall; Abbe, O. G., Goodliffe, J., Herrnson, P. S., and Patterson, K. D. (2003). "Agenda Setting in Congressional Elections: The Impact of Issues and Campaigns on Voting Behavior." *Political Research Quarterly*, 56, 419–430.

45 Lowi, T. J. (1964). "American Business, Public Policy, Case-Studies, and Political Theory." *World Politics*, 16, 677–715.

46 See, for example: Hayes, M. T. (2001). *The Limits of Policy Change: Incrementalism, Worldview, and the Rule of Law*. Washington, DC: Georgetown University Press; Hayes, M. (2007). "Policy Characteristics, Patterns of Politics, and the Minimum Wage: Toward a Typology of Redistributive Policies." *Policy Studies Journal*, 35, 465–480.

47 Mayhew, D. R. (1974). *Congress: The Electoral Connection*. New Haven, CT: Yale University Press.

48 Fenno, R. (1973). *Congressmen in Committees*. Boston: Little Brown and (2008). *Home Style: House Members in Their Legislative Districts*. New York: Longman Publishing Group. For an excellent discussion of how Fenno's 1973 theory of committees remains applicable, see: Aldrich,

J. H., Perry, B. N., and Rohde, D. W. (2013). "Richard Fenno's Theory of Congressional Committees and the Partisan Polarization of the House." In L. C. Dodd and B. I. Oppenheimer (eds.) *Congress Reconsidered* (10th ed.). Washington, DC: CQ Press.

49 Fiorina, M. P. (1989). *Congress: Keystone of the Washington Establishment* (2nd ed.). New Haven, CT: Yale University Press.

50 For a broad overview of many of these influences and related studies, see: Jacobson, G. C. (2012). *Politics of Congressional Elections* (8th ed.). New York: Pearson; and Davidson, R. G. and Oleszek, W. J. (2013). *Congress and Its Members* (14th ed.). Washington, DC: CQ Press.

51 Lindblom, C. E. (1959). "The Science of Muddling Through." *Public Administration Review*, 14, 79–88, 84.

52 See also: March, J. G. and Simon, H. A. (1958). *Organizations*. New York: Wiley; Heclo, H. (1974). *Modern Social Politics in Britain and Sweden*. New Haven, CT: Yale University Press; Lindblom, C. E. (1979). "Still Muddling, Not Yet Through." *Public Administration Review*. 39, 517–526; and Hayes, M. T. (1992). *Incrementalism and Public Policy*. New York: Longman Publishing Group.

53 Jones, B. D. (2001). *Politics and the Architecture of Choice*. Chicago: University of Chicago Press.

54 Fenno, R. (1966). *Power of the Purse*. Boston: Little Brown, p. 410.

55 Wildavsky, A. (1979). *The Politics of the Budgetary Process* (3rd ed.). Boston: Little Brown.

56 Wildavsky, A. (1992). *The New Politics of the Budgetary Process* (2nd ed.). New York: HarperCollins Publishers.

57 Hayes, M. T. (1992). *Incrementalism and Public Policy*. New York: Longman Publishing Group, 27 and Chapter 3.

58 For additional critiques or modifications of incrementalism, see: Bailey, J. T. and O'Connor, R. J. (1975). "Operationalizing Incrementalism: Measuring the Muddles." *Public Administration Review*, 35, 60–66; Berry, W. D. (1990). "The Confusing Case of Budgetary Incrementalism: Too Many Meanings for a Single Concept." *Journal of Politics*, 52, 167–196; Dezhbakhsh, H., Tohamy, S. M., and Aranson, P. H. (2003). "A New Approach for Testing Budgetary Incrementalism." *Journal of Politics*, 65, 532–558.

59 Baumgartner, F. R. and Jones, B. D. (1993). *Agendas and Instability in American Politics*. Chicago: University of Chicago Press.

60 Among these are: McDonough, J. (1998). *Interests, Ideas, and Deregulation*. Ann Arbor: University of Michigan Press; True, J. L. and Utter, G. (2002). "Saying 'Yes', 'No', and 'Load Me Up' to Guns in America." *American Journal of Public Administration*, 32, 216–241; Ceccoli, S. J. (2003). "Policy Punctuations and Regulatory Drug Review." *Journal of Policy History*, 15, 158–191; Repetto, R. (ed.). (2006). *By Fits and Starts: Punctuated Equilibrium and the Dynamics of US Environmental Policy*. New Haven, CT: Yale University Press; Manna, P. (2006). *School's In: Federalism and the National Education Agenda*. Washington, DC: George University Press.

61 Kingdon, J. W. (2002) *Agendas, Alternatives, and Public Policies*. New York: Longman, 227.

62 Cohen, M. D., March, J. G., and Olson, J. P. (1972). "A Garbage Can Model of Organizational Choice." *Administrative Science Quarterly*, 17, 1–25.

63 Kingdon, *Agendas, Alternatives, and Public Policies*, 88.

64 Kingdon, *Agendas, Alternatives, and Public Policies*, 20.

65 Kingdon, *Agendas, Alternatives, and Public Policies*, 140.

66 Kingdon, *Agendas, Alternatives, and Public Policies*, 20.

67 Flemming, R. B., Bohte, J., and Wood, B. D. (1997). "One Voice among Many: The Supreme Court's Influence on Attentiveness to Issues in the United States, 1947–92." *American Journal of Politics*, 41, 1224–1250; McCloskey, R. G. (2010). *The American Supreme Court* (5th ed). S. Levinson, ed. Chicago: University of Chicago Press. For a variation on this theme, see: Rosenberg, G. N. (2008). *Hollow Hope: Can Courts Bring About Social Change?* (2nd ed.). Chicago: University of Chicago Press.

68 Mayhew, *Electoral Connection*, 138.

69 Marshall, T. R. (2008). *Public Opinion and the Rehnquist Court*. Albany: State University of New York Press; For an excellent summary of the research on the Court and public opinion, see Segal, J. A. and Spaeth, H. J. (2002). *The Supreme Court and the Attitudinal Model Revisited*. New York: Cambridge University Press.

70 Rehnquist, W. H. (1986). Constitutional law and public opinion. *Suffolk University Law Review*, 20, 751–769, 768–769.

71 Kingdon, *Agendas, Alternatives, and Public Policies*, 20.

72 Brady, D. W. (1988). *Elections and Congressional Policy Making*. Stanford, CA: Stanford University Press. See also Burnham, W. D. (1970). *Critical Elections and the Mainspring of American Politics*. New York: W. W. Norton Company.

73 Lindblom, C. E. (1980). *The Policy-Making Process*. 2nd ed. Englewood Cliffs, NJ: Prentice-Hall, 116–121.

74 Page, B. I. and Shapiro, R. Y. (1992). *The Rational Public: Fifty Years of Trends in Americans' Policy Preferences*. Chicago: University of Chicago Press.

75 Pew Research Center. (March 3, 2011). *Fewer Are Angry at Government, but Discontent Remains High*. http://www.people-press.org, Section 3; Loper, B. (May 23, 2012). "After President Obama's announcement, opposition to same-sex marriage hits record low." *Washington Post*. http://www.washingtonpost.com; Jones, R. P., Cox, D., and Navarro-Rivera, J. (2013). *Shifting Landscape: A Decade of Change in American Attitudes about Same-Sex Marriage and LGBT Issues*. Washington, DC: Public Religion Research Institute. http://www.publicreligion.org

76 Lowi, "American Business, Public Policy, Case-Studies, and Political Theory," 697.

3 A Color-Blind Problem: U.S. Supreme Court and Racial Influences in Law Enforcement

1 **Color-blind** Bickel, A. M. (1986). *The Least Dangerous Branch: The Supreme Court at the Bar of Politics* (2nd ed.). Binghamton, NY: Vail-Ballou Press, Inc., xi.

2 Guinier, L. and Torres, G. (2002). *The Miner's Canary: Enlisting Race, Resisting Power, Transforming Democracy*. Cambridge, MA: Harvard University Press.

3 Kennedy, R. (1997). *Race, Crime, and the Law*. New York: Pantheon Books; Cole, D. (1999). *No Equal Justice: Race and Class in the American Criminal Justice System*. New York: The New Press; Alexander, M. (2010). *The New Jim Crow: Mass Incarceration in the Age of Color-blindness*. New York: The New Free Press.

4 See Cole, *No Equal Justice*, and Alexander, *The New Jim Crow*; Cole provides an extended look at *Gideon v. Wainwright* and its progeny.

5 For this particular construction of the chapter's argument, I have Professor Lani Guinier to thank.

6 Cases were selected primarily on the basis of the Court's recognition of a case as controlling or relevant to the issues raised.

7 Prior to this, civil and criminal rights protections were inapplicable to the almost 90 percent of the black population in the United States who resided specifically in the South. Besides which, the Court did not begin superintending criminal cases until 1889. On the latter point, see Witt, D. (1990). *Congressional Quarterly's Guide to the U.S. Supreme Court* (2nd ed.). Washington, DC: Congressional Quarterly, Inc., 258.

8 The following indicators were used to note a "racial factor": (1) racial-ethnic minority defendant(s); (2) explicit references to race-ethnicity in the official opinion of the U.S. Supreme Court or lower courts; (3) racial-ethnic references in the briefs and other materials submitted by counsel; (4) use of racial stereotyping language; (5) the racial climate and events surrounding the crime itself or the investigation and prosecution of the crime; (6) the attendant historical and contemporary racial trends and climate; and (7) media coverage of the racial elements of a case. The presence of two or more of these indicators was the general rule of thumb for determining whether a case contained racial dimensions (or was "racialized").

9 See Dickson, D. (2001). *The Supreme Court in Conference (1940–1985): The Private Discussions Behind Nearly 300 Supreme Court Decisions*. New York: Oxford University Press.

10 Chapter 8 of this book presents an in-depth discussion of race and media patterns.

11 Rehnquist, W. H. (1986). "Constitutional Law and Public Opinion." *Suffolk University Law Review*, 20, 751–769.

12 Barnum, D. G. (1985). "The Supreme Court and Public Opinion: Judicial Decision Making in the Post-New Deal Period." *Journal of Politics*, **47**, 652–666; Stimson, J. A. (1991). *Public Opinion in America: Moods, Cycles, and Swings*. Boulder, CO: Westview Press; George, T. E. and Lee Epstein, L. (1992). "On the Nature of Supreme Court Decision Making." *American Political Science Review*, 86, 323–337; Mishler, W. and Sheehan, R. S. (1994). "Popular Influence on Supreme Court Decisions." *American Political Science Review*, 88, 711–724; Roesch, B. J. (2006). "Crowd Control: The Majoritarian Court and the Reflection of Public Opinion in Doctrine." *Suffolk University Law Review*, 39, 379–423.

13 Washington v. Davis, 426 U.S. 229 (1976).

14 For a similar argument addressing a different area of law, see Rose, M. (1996). "Race Obliviousness and the Invisibility of Whiteness: The Court's Construction of Race – *Miller v. Johnson.*" *Temple Law Review*, 69, 1549–1570 and also Gotanda, N. (1991). "A Critique of 'Our Constitution Is Color-Blind.'" *Stanford Law Review*, 44, 16–21.

15 Maguire, K. and Pastore, A. A. (eds.) (2002). *Sourcebook of Criminal Justice Statistics 2002.* Washington, DC: USGPO, 536.

16 National Association for the Advancement of Colored People (NAACP). (2002). *Death Row U.S.A. Summer 2002.* http://www.naacpldf.org/death-row-usa, 12.

17 Banner, S. (2002). "The Death Penalty's Strange Career." *Wilson Quarterly*, 26, 70–82.

18 NAACP. (April 1919). *Thirty Years of Lynching in the United States 1889–1918.* http://www.naacp.org/pages/naacp-history

19 Leadership Conference on Civil and Human Rights (2000). *Justice on Trial: Racial Disparities in the American Criminal Justice System,* Executive Summary. http://www.civilrights.org, 17–18.

20 Pervear v. Commonwealth, 72 U.S. 475 (1867).

21 Wilkerson v. Utah, 99 U.S. 130 (1878); In re Kemmler, 136 U.S. 436 (1890); O'Neil v. Vermont, 144 U.S. 323 (1892); and, Howard v. Fleming, 191 U.S. 126 (1903). Hints of leftward movement surfaced in *Weems v. United States* (1910), which invalidated a sentence of fifteen years in chains for falsification of a government document. *Louisiana ex rel. Frances v. Resweber* (1947) forbade infliction of unnecessary pain, but permitted the re-electrocution of a black convict after the first electrocution attempt failed.

22 NAACP. (2002). *Death Row U.S.A. Summer 2002.* http://www.naacpldf.org/death-row-usa

23 Trop v. Dulles, 356 U.S. 86 (1958).

24 Witherspoon v. Illinois et al., 391 U.S. 510 (1968).

25 Furman v. Georgia, 408 U.S. 238 (1972).

26 Gregg v. Georgia, 428 U.S. 153 (1976).

27 Brief for Petitioner at 8, *Furman.*

28 Brief for Petitioner at 11–12, *Furman.*

29 Goldman, R. and Gallen, D. (1992). *Thurgood Marshall: Justice for All.* New York: Carroll & Graf Publishers, Inc; Bland, R. W. (1993). *Private Pressure on Public Law: The Legal Career of Justice Thurgood Marshall 1934–1991* (Rev. ed.). Lanham, MD: University Press of America; Tushnets, M. V. (1994). *Making Civil Rights Law: Thurgood Marshall and the Supreme Court 1936–1991.* New York: Oxford University Press; Tushnets, M. V. (1997). *Constitutional Law: Thurgood Marshall and the Supreme Court 1961–1991.* New York: Oxford University Press.

30 See also the companion cases decided with *Gregg* on July 2, 1976: *Proffitt v. Georgia* (428 U.S. 242), *Jurek v. Texas* (428 U.S. 262), *Woodson v. North Carolina* (428 U.S. 280), and *Roberts v. Louisiana* (428 U.S. 325).

31 Later cases granted states even greater latitude. See, for example, *Barclay v. Florida* (1983), which allowed states to control the weight a judge or jury

may assign to aggravating and mitigating evidence; *Blystone v. Pennsylvania* (1990), which permitted capital sentencing upon a finding of only one aggravating circumstance; and *Payne v. Tennessee* (1991), which permitted victim impact statements to be construed as objective evidence in capital sentencing.

32 McCleskey v. Kemp, 481 U.S. 279 (1987).

33 Its prior acceptance of statistics as proof of discrimination was limited to jury selection and statutory violations under Title VII of the Civil Rights Act of 1964.

34 An alternative view is offered by Rudovsky, D. (2007). "Litigating Civil Rights Cases to Reform Racially Biased Criminal Justice Practices." *Columbia Human Rights Law Review*, 39, 97–123, in which he argues that, while some litigation challenges have been precluded by *McCleskey*, litigation that focuses on racialized police practices offer great promise of systemic relief.

35 Thompson v. Oklahoma, 487 U.S. 815 (1998).

36 Stanford v. Connecticut, 492 U.S. 361 (1989).

37 Roper v. Simmons, 543 U.S. 551 (2005).

38 Atkins v. Virginia, 536 U.S. 304 (2002).

39 Penry v. Lynaugh, 492 U.S. 302 (1989).

40 Powell v. Alabama, 287 U.S. 45 (1932).

41 Klarman, M. (2000). "The Racial Origins of Modern Criminal Procedure." *Michigan Law Review*, 99, 48–97. See also Harcourt, B. E. (2006). *Against Prediction: Profiling, Policing, and Punishing in an Actuarial Age.* Chicago: University of Chicago Press.

42 Brief for Petitioner at 7, *Powell.*

43 Brief for Petitioner at 8, *Powell.*

44 Brief for Petitioner at 20, *Powell.*

45 Brief for Petitioner at 20, *Powell.*

46 *Powell,* 51.

47 *Powell,* 45, 50, 51.

48 Johnston v. Zerbst, 304 U.S. 458 (1938).

49 Bute v. Illinois, 333 U.S. 640 (1948).

50 Brief for Petitioner at 10, *Bute.*

51 Brief for Petitioner at 23, *Bute.*

52 Brief for Respondent at 11, *Bute.*

53 Betts v. Brady, 316 U.S. 455 (1942).

54 Gideon v. Wainwright, 372 U.S. 335 (1963).

55 Moore v. Michigan, 355 U.S. 155 (1957).

56 People v. Moore, 344 Mich. 137, 144.

57 Oliver, M. B. (1994). "Portrayals of Crime, Race, and Aggression in 'Reality-Based' Police Shows: A Content Analysis." *Journal of Broadcasting & Electronic Media*, 38, 179–192; Rose, W. (2002). "Crimes of Color: Risk, Profiling, and the Contemporary Racialization of Social Control." *International Journal of Politics, Culture, and Society*, 16, 179–205; Brunson, R. K. and Miller, J. (2006). "Young Black Men and Urban Policing in the United States." *British Journal of Criminology*, 46, 613–640.

58 Brief for Petitioner at 7–8, *Moore.*

59 Brief for Petitioner at 10, *Moore*.

60 Brief for Petitioner at 11, *Moore*.

61 Brief for Petitioner at 12, *Moore*.

62 Carnley v. Cochran, 369 U.S. 506 (1962).

63 Brown v. Education, 347 U.S. 483 (1954).

64 Carnley v. Cochran, 122 So. 2d 249.

65 Hamilton v. Alabama, 368 U.S. 52 (1961).

66 Hamilton (1961), 52.

67 Editorial note. (May 6, 1957). "Texas: Bad Day in Longview 1957." *Time*. http://www.time.com

68 Editorial note. "Texas: Bad Day in Longview 1957."

69 In re Gault, 387 U.S. 1 (1967).

70 The earlier case was Haley v. Ohio, 332 U.S. 596 (1948).

71 Coleman v. Alabama, 399 U.S. 1 (1970).

72 Brief for Petitioner at 7, *Coleman*.

73 Graham, F. P. (June 23, 1970). "High court rules city must widen jury-trial right." *New York Times*.

74 Aronstam, D. and Tyson, G. A. (1980). "Racial Bias in Eye-Witness Perception." *Journal of Social Psychology*, 110, 177–182; Egeth, H. E. (1993). "What Do We Not Know about Eyewitness Identification?" *American Psychologist*, 48, 577–580; Rutledge, J. P. (2001). "They All Look Alike: The Inaccuracy of Cross-Racial Identifications." *American Journal of Criminal Law*, 28, 206–228; Smith, S. M., Pryke, S., and Dysart, J. E. (2001). "Eyewitness Identification: Postdictors of Eyewitness Errors: Can False Identifications Be Diagnosed in the Cross-Race Situation?" *Psychology, Public Policy and Law* 7: 153–169; Olson, G. L. and Olson, E. Z. (2001). "The other-race effect in eyewitness identification: what do we do about it?" *Psychology, Public Policy and Law*, 7, 230–246; Oliver, M. B. (2002). "Race and Crime in the News: Whites' Identification and Misidentification of Violent and Nonviolent Criminal Suspects." *Media Psychology*, 4, 137–156; Sherman, J. W. (2003). "Bearing False Witness under Pressure: Implicit and Explicit Components of Stereotype-Driven Memory Distortions." *Social Cognition*, 21, 213–246; Welch, K. (2007). "Black Criminal Stereotypes and Racial Profiling." *Journal of Contemporary Criminal Justice*, 23, 276–288; Edlund, J. E. and Skowronski, J. J. (2008). "Eyewitness Racial Attitudes and Perpetrator Identification: The Lineup Method Matters." *North American Journal of Psychology*, 10, 15–26.

75 Owens-Patton, T. and Snyder-Yuly, J. (2007). "Any Four Black Men Will Do: Rape, Race, and the Ultimate Scapegoat." *Journal of Black Studies* 37, 859–895.

76 Brief for Petitioner at 7, *Coleman*.

77 Brief for Petitioner at 6, *Coleman*.

78 U.S. v. Wade, 388 U.S. 218 (1967).

79 Kirby v. Illinois, 406 U.S. 682 (1972).

80 National Advisory Commission on Civil Disorders. (1968). *Report of the National Advisory Commission on Civil Disorders: Summary of the Report*. Washington, DC: Government Printing Office.

81 See reports by the U.S. Civil Rights Commission as well as dozens by local and state civil rights commission.
82 Brief for Petitioner at 14, *Kirby*.
83 U.S. v. Ash, 413 U.S. 300 (1973).
84 U.S. v. Ash, 461 F.2d 92, 95.
85 *Ash*, 302.
86 *Ash*, 302.
87 Avery v. Alabama, 308 U.S. 444 (1940).
88 Although the victim in this case was his estranged black wife, her murder was itself a low priory to local law enforcement, as evidenced by several things. Avery's arrest in Pittsburgh on March 21, 1938, came more than six years after her murder and was the result of pure happenstance more so than diligent police investigation. Also, the prosecution was unable to pinpoint the date of her murder with any degree of precision, establishing only that it occurred sometime in February 1932.
89 Brief for Petitioner at 2, *Avery*.
90 Geders v. U.S., 425 U.S. 80 (1976).
91 Perry v. Leeke, 488 U.S. 272 (1989).
92 *Perry*, 273.
93 Brief for Petitioner at 9, *Geders*.
94 Argersinger v. Hamlin, 407 U.S. 25 (1972).
95 Justice Douglas was replaced by Justice Stevens in December 1975, who sided with the defendant Scott.
96 Scott v. Illinois, 440 U.S. 367 (1979).
97 U.S. v. Morrison, 449 U.S. 361 (1981).
98 The research on these issues is detailed at length in the discussion of racial theories in Chapter 8.
99 Her plea was conditioned on the outcome of her appeal.
100 Bram v. U.S., 168 U.S. 532 (1897).
101 Twining v. Jersey, 211 U.S. 78 (1908).
102 Brown v. Mississippi, 297 U.S. 278 (1936).
103 Brief for Petitioners at 34, *Brown*.
104 *Brown*, 282.
105 *Brown*, 281.
106 Malloy v. Hogan, 378 U.S. 1 (1964).
107 Adamson v. California, 332 U.S. 46 (1947).
108 Brief for Petitioner at 3, *Adamson*.
109 Brief for Petitioner at 3, *Adamson*.
110 Brief for Petitioner at 8, *Adamson*.
111 Brief for Petitioner at 8, *Adamson*.
112 See 4 N.Y. 2d 256.
113 Escobedo v. Illinois, 378 U.S. 478 (1964); The defendant in the companion case to *Escobedo* was also a minority, a twenty-eight-year old black male, Nathan Jackson, who reportedly told a detective, when asked for his name: "Nathan Jackson, I shot the colored cop" (Jackson v. Denno, 378 U.S. 368, 1964).

114 The officer, described as "Officer Montejano," was said to have grown up in Escobedo's neighborhood and as having used "Spanish language in [his] police work."

115 *Escobedo*, 482.

116 28 Ill. 2d 41 (1963).

117 28 Ill. 2d 41 (1963).

118 Special to the *New York Times*. (June 23, 1964). Use of confession in trial is curbed. *New York Times*.

119 Miranda v. Arizona, 384 U.S. 436 (1966).

120 Brief for Petitioner at 2, *Miranda*.

121 Brief for Petitioner at 3, *Miranda*.

122 See also Mathis v. U.S., 391 U.S. 1 (1968, 1968); Beckwith v. U.S., 425 U.S. 241 (1976); Oregon v. Mathiason, 429 U.S. 492 (1977).

123 Orozco v. Texas, 394 U.S. 324 (1969).

124 428 S.W.2d 666.

125 428 S.W.2d 666.

126 428 S.W.2d 666.

127 U.S. v. Mendenhall, 446 U.S. 544 (1980).

128 *Mendenhall*, footnote 1.

129 Brief for Respondent at footnote 24, *Mendenhall*.

130 Brief for Respondent at footnote 26, *Mendenhall*.

131 American Civil Liberties Union Brief at 5, *Mendenhall*.

132 American Civil Liberties Union Brief at 5, *Mendenhall*.

133 American Civil Liberties Union Brief at footnote, *Mendenhall*.

134 Estelle v. Smith, 451 U.S. 454 (1981).

135 See, for example, a *Texas Monthly* article published in July 1978. The caption under Dr. Grigson's picture read: "Affable, believable," while that under Ernest Smith's picture read "Smith: the one who didn't pull trigger."

136 See the extended discussion of research on race and the media in Chapter 8, and also: Jamieson, K. H. (1992). *Dirty Politics: Deception, Distraction and Democracy*. New York: Oxford University Press; Lule, J. (1995). "The Rape of Mike Tyson: Race, the Press, and Symbolic Types." *Critical Studies in Mass Communication*, 12, 176–195; Gilliam, F. D., Iyengar, S., Simon, A., and Wright, O. (1996). "Crime in Black and White: The Violent, Scary World of Local News." *Harvard International Journal of Press/Politics*, 1, 6–23; Mann, C. R. and Zatz, M. S. (eds.). (1998). *Images of Color, Images of Crime*. Los Angeles: Roxbury Publishing Co.

137 Community Involvement. (n.d.). http://www.kinara.com

138 Brief for Respondent at 13, *Estelle*.

139 *Estelle*, 460.

140 See Brunson and Miller, "Young Black Men and Urban Policing," Oliver, "Portrayals of Crime, Race, and Aggression," and Rose "Crimes of Color."

141 Edwards v. Arizona, 451 U.S. 477 (1981).

142 Michigan v. Mosley, 423 U.S. 96 (1975).

143 Brief for Petitioner at 3, *Edwards*.

144 Brief for Respondent at 16, *Edwards*.

145 Brief for Respondent at 16, *Edwards*.

146 Brief for Respondent at Footnote 13, *Edwards*.

147 Brief for Respondent at 51, *Edwards*.

148 Brief for Petitioner at 25, *Edwards*.

149 Fare v. Michael, 442 U.S. 707 (1979).

150 Bridges, G. S. and Steen, S. (1980). "Racial Disparities in Official Assessments of Juvenile Offenders: Attributional Stereotypes as Mediating Mechanisms." *American Sociological Review*, 63, 554–570.

151 While there was also a witness identification, the California Court of Appeals observed: "It appears that absent the confession the evidence was insufficient to sustain the conviction. No argument to the contrary is presented by the People." Michael C. v. Fare, 66 Cal. App. 3d 239 footnote 1.

152 66 Cal. App. 3d 239; 135 Cal. Rptr. 7672 at 767–1977.

153 Hurwitz, J. and Peffley, M. (2005). "Explaining the Great Racial Divide: Perceptions of Fairness in the U.S. Criminal Justice System." *Journal of Politics*, 67, 762–783.

154 Brief for Petitioner at 9, *Fare*.

155 Brief for Petitioner at 15, *Fare*.

156 Brief for Petitioner at 16, *Fare*.

157 Harris v. New York, 401 U.S. 222 (1971).

158 New York v. Quarles, 467 U.S. 649 (1984) set a broad public safety exception to the rule. It too involved a black male along with detailed suspect descriptions in the Court's opinion, the state's brief, and a *New York Times* June 13, 1984, article.

159 Brief for Petitioner at 6, *Harris*.

160 Brief for Petitioner at 2, *Harris*.

161 According to the New York appellate court opinion, Harris stated shortly after his arrest that "everybody in his area was selling narcotics" (31 A.D.2d 828, 829).

162 Brief for Respondent at 8 and Brief for Petitioner at 7, *Harris*.

163 Dershowitz, A. M. and Ely, J. H. (1971). "Harris v. New York: Some Anxious Observations on the Candor and Logic of the Emerging Nixon Majority." *Yale Law Journal*, 80, 1198–1227.

164 Brief for Petitioner at 5, *Harris*.

165 McCloskey, R. G. (1960). *The American Supreme Court*. Chicago: University of Chicago Press, 225.

166 McCloskey, *The American Supreme Court*, 182.

167 Bickel, A. M. (1986). *The Least Dangerous Branch: The Supreme Court at the Bar of Politics* (2nd ed.). Binghamton, NY: Vail-Ballou Press, Inc., 200.

168 Bickel, *The Least Dangerous Branch*, 240.

169 Dickerson v. U.S., 530 U.S. 428 (2000).

170 The discussion in Chapter 6 details this trend at length.

171 McAdam, D. (1999). *Political Process and the Development of Black Insurgency, 1930–1970* (2nd ed.). Chicago: University of Chicago Press.

172 For a more in-depth historical analysis of race in presidential politics, see: Carmines, E. G. and Stimson, J. A. (1989). *Issue Evolution: Race and the Transformation of American Politics*. Princeton, NJ: Princeton University Press; Shull, S. A. (1989). *The President and Civil Rights Policy*. New

York: Greenwood Press; Shull, S. A. (1999). *American Civil Rights Policy from Truman to Clinton: The Role of Presidential Leadership.* New York: M.E. Sharpe; Riley, R. L. (1999). *The Presidency and the Politics of Racial Inequality: Nation-Keeping from 1831–1965.* New York: Columbia University Press.

173 The discussion in Chapter 5 contains a fuller account of the 1968 bill's provisions and its passage in Congress.

174 Stroup, R. H. (2007). "The Political, Legal, and Social Context of the McCleskey Habeas Litigation." *Columbia Human Rights Law Review*, 39, 74–96, 94.

4 Opportunities for Change: The Racial Justice Agenda in Congress

1 The measures are categorized as "racial justice agenda" measures by virtue of their official title, their stated purpose or justification, the issues raised in the "Findings" section of the bill, or the legislative profile and/or introductory remarks of the lead sponsor(s).

2 End Racial Profiling Act of 2011, S. 1670 and H.R. 118, 112th Cong. (2011).

3 A series of articles culminated in reporters offering advice for dealing with racial profiling, such as the following: National Report Section (March 1999). "Rash of Racial Profiling Forces Parents to Prepare Young Drivers for Police Stops." *Jet.* http://www.lexisnexis.com

4 Barovick, H. (June 1998). DWB: "Driving while Black." *Time Magazine.* http://content.time.com; Webb, G. (April 1999). "Driving while Black: Tracking Unspoken Law-Enforcement Racism." *Esquire Magazine.* http://www.esquire.com

5 Brown v. City of Oneonta, 221 F.3d 329 (2d Cir. 2000).

6 Goldberg, J. (June 20, 1999). "The Color of Suspicion." *New York Times.* http://www.nytimes.com

7 Goldberg, "The Color of Suspicion."

8 Joint Application for Entry of Consent Decree, *United States v. State of New Jersey and Division of State Police of the New Jersey Department of Law and Public Safety* (Civil No. 99–597).

9 For a more complete look at the studies lawmakers took into account, see the following Judiciary Committee report: H.R. Rep. No. 106–517 (2000).

10 Representative Conyers (MI). "Traffic Stops Statistics Act." *Congressional Record (Daily Edition)* 143:105 (January 7, 1997) E10. http://www.gpo.gov/fdsys

11 Senator Feingold (WI). "Statements on Introduced Bills and Joint Resolutions ... S. 989. A Bill to Prohibit Racial Profiling" *Congressional Record (Daily Edition)* 147:107 (June 6, 2001) S5891. http://www.gpo.gov/fdsys

12 Expressing the Sense of the House of Representatives that Congress and the States Should Act to End Racial Profiling, H. Res. 515, 108th Cong. (2004).

13 Traffic Stops Statistics Study Act of 1998, H.R. 118, 105th Cong. (1997); Traffic Stops Statistics Study Act of 2000, H.R. 1443, 106th Cong. (1999); Traffic Stops Statistics Study Act of 1999, S. 821, 106th Congress (1999).

14 H.R. Rep. 105–435, at 2 (1998).

15 H.R. Rep. 105–435, at 2 (1998).

16 Racial Profiling Education and Awareness Act of 2001, S. 2114, 107th Cong. (2002).

17 End Racial Profiling Act of 2011, S. 1670 and H.R. 118, 112th Cong. (2011).

18 End Racial Profiling Act of 2011, S. 1670 and H.R. 118, 112th Cong. (2011).

19 End Racial Profiling Act of 2001, H.R. 2074, 107th Cong. (2001).

20 Senator Feingold, "Statements on Introduced Bills and Joint Resolutions ... S. 2132." *Congressional Record (Daily Edition)* 150:108.

21 Senator Feingold, "Statements on Introduced Bills and Joint Resolutions ... S. 2138." *Congressional Record (Daily Edition)* 151:109.

22 See Representative Conyers (MI). "Introduction of End Racial Profiling Act of 2007." *Congressional Record (Daily Edition)* 153:110 (December 13, 2007) E2576. http://www.gpo.gov/fdsys and "Introduction of End Racial Profiling Act of 2010." *Congressional Record (Daily Edition)* 156:111 (July 15, 2010) E1341. http://www.gpo.gov/fdsys

23 Senator Cardin (MD). "Statements on Introduced Bills and Joint Resolutions ... S. 1670. A Bill to Prohibit Racial Profiling" *Congressional Record (Daily Edition)* 157:112 (October 6, 2011) S6340. http://www.gpo.gov/fdsys

24 End Racial Profiling Act of 2011, S. 1670, 112th Cong. (2011).

25 Leung, R. (February 11, 2009). "Targeted in Tulia, Texas?" www.cbsnews.com

26 Representative Lee (TX). "Science, State, Justice, Commerce, and Related Appropriations Act, 2006." *Congressional Record (Daily Edition)* 151:109 (June 16, 2005) H4590. http://www.gpo.gov/fdsys

27 Representative Lee, "Science, State, Justice, Commerce, and Related Appropriations Act, 2006." *Congressional Record (Daily Edition)* 151:109.

28 Justice in Sentencing Act of 2004, H.R. 5103, 108th Cong. (2004).

29 Representative Doggett (TX). "Science, State, Justice, Commerce, and Related Appropriations Act, 2006." *Congressional Record (Daily Edition)* 151:109 (June 16, 2005) H4591. http://www.gpo.gov/fdsys

30 Representative Doggett, "Science, State, Justice, Commerce, and Related Appropriations Act, 2006." *Congressional Record (Daily Edition)* 151:109.

31 No More Tulias: Drug Law Enforcement Evidentiary Standards Improvement Act of 2005, H.R. 2620, 109th Cong. (2005); No More Tulias: Drug Law Enforcement Evidentiary Standards Improvement Act of 2007, H.R. 253, 110th Cong. (2007); No More Tulias: Drug Law Enforcement Evidentiary Standards Improvement Act of 2009, H.R. 68, 111th Cong. (2009).

32 Senator Durbin (IL). "Statements on Introduced Bills and Resolutions ... S. 1789. A Bill to Restore Fairness to Federal Cocaine Sentencing." *Congressional*

Record (Daily Edition) 155:111 (October 15, 2009) S10492. http://www. gpo.gov/fdsys

33   United States Sentencing Commission. (May 2007). *Report to Congress: Cocaine and Federal Sentencing Policy.* http://www.ussc.gov

34   Senator Durbin, "Statements on Introduced Bills and Resolutions ... S. 1789." *Congressional Record (Daily Edition)* 155:111.

35   See the Justice in Sentencing Act of 2004, H.R. 5103, 108th Cong. (2004); Drug Sentencing Reform Act of 2006, S. 3725, 109th Cong. (2006); Powder-Crack Cocaine Penalty Equalization Act of 2007, H.R. 79, 110th Cong. (2007); Crack-Cocaine Equitable Sentencing Act of 2007, H.R. 460, 110th Cong. (2007); Drug Sentencing Reform and Cocaine Kingpin Trafficking Act of 2007, H.R. 4545, 110th Cong. (2007); Drug Sentencing Reform Act of 2007, S. 1383, 110th Cong. (2007); Fairness in Drug Sentencing Act of 2007, S. 1685, 110th Cong. (2007); Drug Sentencing Reform and Cocaine Kingpin Trafficking Act of 2007, S. 1711, 110th Cong. (2007); Fairness in Cocaine Sentencing Act of 2008, H.R. 5035, 110th Cong. (2008); Drug Sentencing Reform and Cocaine Kingpin Trafficking Act of 2009, H.R. 265, 111th Cong. (2009); Fair Sentencing Act of 2010, S. 1789, 111th Cong. (2009).

36   Justice in Sentencing Act of 2004, H.R. 5103, 108th Cong. (2004).

37   Drug Sentencing Reform Act of 2006, S. 3725, 109th Cong. (2006).

38   See the Fair Sentencing Act of 2010, S. 1789, 111th Cong. (2009) and Drug Sentencing Reform and Cocaine Kingpin Trafficking Act of 2009, H.R. 265, 111th Cong. (2009).

39   Senator Durbin (IL). "Fair Sentencing Act of 2009." *Congressional Record (Daily Edition)* 156:111 (March 17, 2010) S1680. http://www.gpo.gov/ fdsys

40   Racial Justice Act of 1988, H.R. 4442, 100th Cong. (1988).

41   See Representative Conyers (MI). "Introduction of Law Enforcement Trust and Integrity Act of 2000." *Congressional Record (Daily Edition)* 146:106 (March 15, 2000) E321. http://www.gpo.gov/fdsys

42   Law Enforcement Trust and Integrity Act of 2000, H.R. 3981, 106th Cong. (2000).

43   Law Enforcement Trust and Integrity Act of 1999, H.R. 2656, 106th Cong. (1999).

44   Law Enforcement Trust and Integrity Act of 2000, H.R. 3927, 106th Cong. (2000).

45   See the Death in Custody Reporting Act of 2000, Pub. L. No. 106–297, 114 Stat. 1045 (2000).

46   Justice Integrity Act of 2008, S. 3245 and H.R. 6518, 110th Cong. (2008); Justice Integrity Act of 2009, S. 495, 111th Cong. (2009).

47   Senator Biden (DE). "Statements on Introduced Bills and Joint Resolutions ... S. 3245. A Bill to Increase Public Confidence in the Justice System and Address Any Unwarranted Racial and Ethnic Disparities." *Congressional Record (Daily Edition)* 154:110 (July 10, 2008) S6565. http://www.gpo.gov/ fdsys

48   Senator Biden, "Statements on Introduced Bills and Joint Resolutions ... S. 3245." *Congressional Record (Daily Edition)* 154:110.

49 Representative Conyers (MI). "Introduction of Law Enforcement Trust and Integrity Act of 1999." *Congressional Record (Daily Edition)* 145:10 (July 30, 1999) E1707. http://www.gpo.gov/fdsys

50 Representative Conyers, "Introduction of Law Enforcement Trust and Integrity Act of 1999." *Congressional Record (Daily Edition)* 145:10.

51 Commission on Accreditation for Law Enforcement Agencies, Inc. About us: The Commission." http://www.calea.org

52 Law Enforcement Trust and Integrity Act of 1999, H.R. 2656, 106th Cong. (1999); Law Enforcement Trust and Integrity Act of 2000, H.R. 3927 and H.R. 2981, 106th Cong. (2000).

53 Moore, N. (2000). *Governing Race: Policy, Process, and the Politics of Race.* Westport, CT: Praeger.

54 Racial Profiling Prohibition Act of 2001, H.R. 965 and H.R. 1907, 107th Cong. (2001); Racial Profiling Prevention Act, H.R. 4398, 112th Cong. (2012).

55 End Racial Profiling Act of 2010, H.R. 5748, 111th Cong. (2010).

56 End Racial Profiling Act of 2001, H.R. 2074, 107th Cong. (2001); End Racial Profiling Act of 2011, S. 1670, 112th Cong. (2011).

57 Racial Profiling Prevention Act, H.R. 4398, 112th Cong. (2012).

58 National Criminal Justice Association. (May 2011). *Cornerstone for Justice: Byrne JAG and Its Impact on the Criminal Justice System.* http://www.ncja. org/cornerstone-for-justice-report

59 Bureau of Justice Assistance, Office of Justice Programs, U.S. Department of Justice. Edward Byrne Justice Assistance Grant (JAG) Program Fact Sheet. http://www.bja.gov/Publications/JAG_Fact_Sheet.pdf

60 Nancy Pelosi, Office of the Democratic Leader. (April 22, 2009). COPS Improvement Act. http://www.democraticleader.org/floor

61 Office of Community Oriented Policing Services, U.S. Department of Justice. (FY 2011). Cops and the Hiring Program – By the Numbers. http://www. cops.usdoj.gov/pdf/2011AwardDocs/.../2011CHPQuickFacts.pdf

62 Safe, Accountable, Flexible, Efficient Transportation Equity Act: A Legacy for Users, Pub. L. No. 109–159, 119 Stat. 1144 (2005).

63 H.R. Rep. No. 109–203 (2005).

64 Gormley, Jr., W. T. (2006). "Money and Mandates: The Politics of Intergovernmental Conflict." *Publius* 36, 523–540; Kettl, D. F. (1987). *The Regulation of American Gederalism.* Baltimore: Johns Hopkins University Press.

65 The classic statement on this theme is offered in: Fenno, Jr., R. F. (1978). *Home Style: House Members in Their Districts.* Boston: Little, Brown.

66 Dilulio, J. J. and Kettl, D. F. (1995). *Fine Print: The Contract with America, Devolution, and the Administrative Realities of American Federalism.* Washington, DC: Brookings Institution; Ray, M. R. and Conlan, T. J. (1996). "At What Price? Costs of Federal Mandates since the 1980s." *State and Local Government Review* 28, 7–16; Super, D. A. (2005). "Rethinking Fiscal Federalism." *Harvard Law Review* 118, 2544–2652.

67 Racial Profiling Education and Awareness Act of 2002, S. 2114, 107th Cong. (2002).

68 Fair Sentencing Act of 2010, Pub. L. 111–220, 124 Stat. 2372 (2010).

69 U.S. Sentencing Commission (n.d.). Most frequently asked questions: The 2011 retroactive crack cocaine guideline amendment. http://www.ussc.gov/ Meetings_and_Rulemaking/Materials_on_Federal_Cocaine_Offenses/FAQ/ index.cfm#faq03

70 Senator Durbin (IL). "Statements on Introduced Bills and Resolutions ... S. 1789." *Congressional Record (Daily Edition)* 155:111. S10491.

71 Senator Abraham. "Statements on Introduced Bills and Resolutions ... S. 1254. A Bill to Disapprove of Amendments to the Federal Sentencing Guidelines Relating to Lowering of Crack Sentences." *Congressional Record (Daily Edition)* 141:104 (September 18, 1995) S13739. http://www.gpo.gov/ fdsys

72 United States Sentencing Commission. (May 2007). *Report to Congress: Cocaine and Federal Sentencing Policy.* http://www.ussc.gov, 9.

73 United States Sentencing Commission. (April 6, 2011). News release: U.S. Sentencing Commission promulgates permanent amendment to the federal sentencing guidelines covering crack cocaine, other drug trafficking offenses. http://www.ussc.gov/Legislative_and_Public_Affairs/Newsroom/ Press_Releases/20110406_Press_Release.pdf

74 See remarks of Senator Hatch (UT). "Statements on Introduced Bills and Joint Resolutions ... S. 1685. A Bill to Reduce the Sentencing Disparity Between Power and Crack Cocaine Violations." *Congressional Record (Daily Edition)* 153:110 (June 25, 2007) S8358-59. http://www.gpo.gov/fdsys

75 Safe, Accountable, Flexible, Efficient Transportation Equity Act: A Legacy for Users, Pub. L. No. 109–159, 119 Stat. 1144 (2005).

76 Representative Norton (DC). "Introduction of the Racial Profiling Prevention Act." *Congressional Record (Daily Edition)* 158:112 (April 18, 2012) E573. http://www.gpo.gov/fdsys

77 Moving Ahead for Progress in the 21st Century Act (MAP-21). Pub. L. No. 112–141, 126 Stat. 405 (2012). See also: Federal Highway Administration, U.S. Department of Transportation. (July 17, 2012). Moving Ahead for Progress in the 21st Century Act (MAP 21): A summary of highway provisions. http://www.fhwa.dot.gov/map21/docs/map21_summary_hgwy_pro- visions.pdf

78 Anderson, J. W. (1964). *Eisenhower, Brownell, and the Congress.* Tuscalossa: University of Alabama Press; Bullock, C. and Lamb, C. (1984). *Implementation of Civil Rights Policy.* Monterey, CA: Brooks/Cole Publishing Company; Graham, H. D. (1990). *The Civil Rights Era: Origins and Development of National Policy, 1960–1972.* New York: Oxford University Press; Moore, N. (2000). *Governing Race: Policy, Process, and the Politics of Race.* Westport, CT: Praeger; Schuman, H. (1957). "Senate Rules and the Civil Rights Bill: A Case Study." *American Political Science Review,* 4, 955–975; Sundquist, J. L. (1968). *Politics and Policy: The Eisenhower, Kennedy, and Johnson Years.* Washington, DC: Brookings Institution; Walton, Jr., H. (1988). *When the Marching Stopped: The Politics of Civil Rights Regulatory Agencies.* State University of New York Press.

79 Deering, C. J. and Smith, S. S. (1997). *Committees in Congress* (3rd ed.). Washington, DC: Congressional Quarterly, Inc.

80 See Shapiro, R. (May 26, 2009). "Bills of the 110th Congressional Session" http://sunlightfoundation.com/blog/2009/05/26/bills-110th-congressional-session/. See also Shapiro, R. "The Life and Death of Congressional Bills in the 110th Congress: A Window into What Happens to Bills in Congress." http://assets.sunlightlabs.com/billvisualization/graphs/bill_death_log.html; Deering, C. J. and Smith, S. S. (1997). *Committees in Congress*, 3rd edition. Washington, DC: Congressional Quarterly, Inc.

81 Bessette, J. M. (1997). *The Mild Voice of Reason: Deliberative Democracy and American National Government*. Chicago: University of Chicago Press; Binder, S. A. (1997). *Minority Rights, Majority Rule: Partisanship and the Development of Congress*. New York: Cambridge University Press. See also Sinclair, B. (2011). *Unorthodox Lawmaking: New Legislative Processes in the U.S. Congress*. 4th edition. Washington, DC: Congressional Quarterly, Inc.

82 For an in-depth discussion of formal Congressional process and procedures and how they intersect with external politics, see Davidson, R. H. and Oleszek, W. J. (2013). *Congress and Its Members*. 14th edition. Washington, DC: Congressional Quarterly, Inc.; Deering, C. J. and Smith, S. S. (1997). *Committees in Congress*, 3rd edition. Washington, DC: Congressional Quarterly, Inc.; Dodd, L. C. and Oppenheimr, B. I. (eds.) (2005). *Congress Reconsidered*. Washington, DC: Congressional Quarterly, Inc.; Oleszek, W. J. (2013). *Congressional Procedures and the Policy Process* (9th ed.). Washington, DC: Congressional Quarterly, Inc.; Sinclair, B. (2011). *Unorthodox Lawmaking: New Legislative Processes in the U.S. Congress* (4th ed.). Washington, DC: Congressional Quarterly, Inc.

83 U.S. General Accounting Office. (2000). *U.S. Customs Service: Better Targeting of Airline Passengers for Personal Searches Could Produce Better Results* (GAO/GGD-00-38), 2. http://www.gao.gov/assets/230/228979.pdf

84 U.S. General Accounting Office. (2000). *Racial Profiling: Limited Data Available on Motorist Stops* (GAO/GGD-00-41). http://www.gao.gov/new.items/gg00041.pdf

85 The first time a racial justice measure was reported out of committee and adopted by the floor was when Republicans controlled both houses of the 105th Congress.

86 Senator Voinovich (OH). "Statements on Introduced Bills and Joint Resolutions … S. 2114. A Bill to Authorize the Attorney General to Carry Out a Racial Profiling Educating and Awareness Program." *Congressional Record (Daily Edition)* 148:107 (April 11, 2001) S2584. http://www.gpo.gov/fdsys

87 Senator Durbin, "Statements on Introduced Bills and Resolutions … S. 1789." *Congressional Record (Daily Edition)* 155:111.

88 Senator Hatch (UT). "Statements on Introduced Bills and Joint Resolutions … S. 1685. A Bill to Reduce the Sentencing Disparity Between Power and Crack Cocaine Violations." *Congressional Record (Daily Edition)* 153:110 (June 25, 2007) S8358. http://www.gpo.gov/fdsys

89 Senator Durbin (IL). "Fair Sentencing Act of 2009." *Congressional Record (Daily Edition)* 156:111 (March 17, 2010) S1681. from http://www.gpo.gov/fdsys

90 Representative Conyers (MI). "Introduction of Traffic Stops Statistics Act of 1999." *Congressional Record (Daily Edition)* 145:106 (April 15, 1999) E673. http://www.gpo.gov/fdsys

91 Racial profiling within law enforcement agencies: Hearings before the Senate Committee on the Judiciary, 106th Cong. (2000), S. Hrg. 106–996/Serial No. J-10674 (opening statement of Senator John Ashcroft).

92 S. 989: The End Racial Profiling Act of 2001: Hearings before the Subcommittee on the Constitution of the Senate Committee on the Judiciary, 107th Cong. (2001), S. Hrg. 107–537/Serial No. J-107-36 (opening statement of Senator Russell Feingold).

93 Originally introduced and referred to committee as: Transportation Equity Act: A Legacy for Users, H.R. 3, 109th Cong. (2005).

94 H.R. Rep. No. 109-203 (2005).

95 Representative Lee (TX). "Science, State, Justice, Commerce, and Related Appropriations Act 2006." *Congressional Record (Daily Edition)* 151:109 (June 16, 2005) H4589. http://www.gpo.gov/fdsys

96 Representative Wolf (VA). "Science, State, Justice, Commerce, and Related Appropriations Act 2006." *Congressional Record (Daily Edition)* 151:109 (June 16, 2005) H4590. http://www.gpo.gov/fdsys

97 Representative Wolf (VA). "Science, State, Justice, Commerce, and Related Appropriations Act 2006." *Congressional Record (Daily Edition)* 151:109 (June 16, 2005) H4591. http://www.gpo.gov/fdsys

98 End Racial Profiling Act of 2001, H.R. 2074 and S. 989, 107th Cong. (2001); End Racial Profiling Act of 2004 H.R. 3847 and S. 2132, 108th Cong. (2004).

99 Senator Feingold (WI). "Statements on Introduced Bills and Joint Resolutions … S. 989. A Bill to Prohibit Racial Profiling." *Congressional Record (Daily Edition)* 147:107 (June 6, 2001) S5891. http://www.gpo.gov/fdsys

100 Traffic Stops Statistics Study Act of 1998, H.R. 118, 105th Cong. (1997).

101 End Racial Profiling Act of 2011, S. 1670 and H.R. 118, 112th Cong. (2011).

102 Reasonable Search Standards Act, S. 799, 107th Cong. (2001).

103 S. 989: The End Racial Profiling Act of 2001: Hearings before the Subcommittee on the Constitution of the Senate Committee on the Judiciary, 107th Cong. (2001), S. Hrg. 107–537/Serial No. J-107-36 (testimony of Steve Young, national vice president, Fraternal Order of Police).

104 William J. Clinton. Memorandum on Fairness in Law Enforcement. (June 9, 1999). G. Peters and J. T. Wooley (eds.), *American Presidency Project.* http://www.presidency.ucsb.edu

105 William J. Clinton. Memorandum on Fairness in Law Enforcement.

106 William J. Clinton. Opening Remarks at a Roundtable Discussion on Increasing Trust Between Communities and Law Enforcement Officers. (June 9, 1999). *American Presidency Project.*

107 George W. Bush. Memorandum on Racial Profiling. (February 27, 2001). *American Presidency Project.*

108 George W. Bush. Address Before a Joint Session of the Congress on Administration Goals. (February 27, 2001). *American Presidency Project.*

109 See remarks of Senator Feingold (WI). "Statements on Introduced Bills and Joint Resolutions ... S. 989. A Bill to Prohibit Racial Profiling." *Congressional Record (Daily Edition)* 147:107 (June 6, 2001) S5891-2. http://www.gpo.gov/fdsys

110 See remarks of Senator Feingold, "Statements on Introduced Bills and Joint Resolutions ... S. 989." S5893.

111 U.S. Department of Justice. (June 17, 2003). "Justice Department Issues Policy Guidance to Ban Racial Profiling: Action Fulfills President Bush's Promise." http://www.justice.gov/opa/pr/2003/June/03_crt_355.htm

112 Civil Rights Division, U.S. Department of Justice. (June 2003). *Guidance Regarding the Use of Race by Federal Law Enforcement Agencies.* http://www.justice.gov/crt/about/spl/documents/guidance_on_race.pdf

113 American Civil Liberties Union. (May 7, 2012). *Coalition Letter to Eric Holder on the Department of Justice's June 2003 Guidance Regarding the Use of Race by Federal Law Enforcement Agencies.* https://www.aclu.org/criminal-law-reform-immigrants-rights-national-security/coalition-letter-attorney-general-eric

114 Institute on Race and Justice, Northeastern University. (2008) *Promoting Cooperative Strategies to Reduce Racial Profiling.* (COPS Evaluation Brief No. 1). Washington, DC: Office of Community Oriented Policing Services, U.S. Department of Justice. http://www.cops.usdoj.gov/Publications/e08086157.pdf

115 Senator Durbin (IL). "Statements on Introduced Bills and Joint Resolutions ... S. 799. A Bill to Prohibit the Use of Racial Profiling in connection with Searches and Detentions." *Congressional Record (Daily Edition)* 147:107 (April 30, 2001) S4046. http://www.gpo.gov/fdsys

116 Senator Corzine (NJ). Statements on Introduced Bills and Joint Resolutions ... S 2138. A Bill to Prohibit Racial Profiling." *Congressional Record (Daily Edition)* 151:109 (December 16, 2005) S13808. http://www.gpo.gov/fdsys

117 Senator Corzine, Statements on Introduced Bills and Joint Resolutions ... S 2138." 151:109.

118 Office of the President-Elect Barack Obama. (n.d.). Plan to Strengthen Civil Rights. http://change.gov/agenda/civil_rights_agenda/

119 Barack Obama: The President's News Conference. (July 22, 2009). *American Presidency Project.*

120 Barack Obama: Remarks on the Verdict in *State of Florida v. George Zimmerman.* (July 19, 2013). *American Presidency Project.*

121 For more on the facts and media coverage of the Trayvon Martin incident, see Andrus, A. K. (2012). *A Textual Analysis of Media Frames: The Coverage of the Shooting of Trayvon Martin.* (Master's thesis). http://www.nelson.usf.edu/

122 Barack Obama: Remarks on the Nomination of Jim Yong Kim to be President of the World Bank and an Exchange with Reporters. (March 23, 2012). *American Presidency Project.*

5 Congress as Power Player: Racial Justice versus "Law and Order"

1 Omnibus Crime Control and Safe Streets Act, Pub. L. 90–351, 82 Stat. 197 (1968); Comprehensive Drug Abuse Prevention and Control Act of 1970, Pub. L. 91–513, 84 Stat. 1236 (1970); Comprehensive Crime Control Act of 1984 (a.k.a. Sentencing Reform Act and the Criminal Justice Revision Act of 1984), Pub. L. 98–473, 98 Stat. 2027 (1984); Anti-Drug Abuse Act of 1986, Pub. L. 99–570, 100 Stat. 3207 (1986); Anti-Drug Abuse Act of 1988, Pub. L. 100–690, 102 Stat. 4181 (1988); Crime Control Act of 1990, Pub. L. 101–647, pub. L. 104 Stat. 4789 91990); Violent Crime Control and Law Enforcement Act of 1994, Pub. L. 103–322, 108 Stat. 1796 (1994).

2 The analysis draws on information from the *Congressional Record*, Congressional committee hearings and reports, and the following *Congressional Quarterly Almanac* articles: Staff. (1968). "Congress Passes Extensive Anticrime Legislation." *1968 CQ Almanac*. Washington, DC: Congressional Quarterly, Inc.; Staff. (1970). "Comprehensive Drug Control Bill Cleared by Congress." *1970 CQ Almanac*. Washington, DC: Congressional Quarterly, Inc.; Staff. (1984). "Major Crime Package Cleared by Congress." *1984 CQ Almanac*. Washington, DC: Congressional Quarterly, Inc.; Staff. (1986). "Congress Clear Massive Anti-Drug Measure." *1986 CQ Almanac*. Washington, DC: Congressional Quarterly, Inc.; Staff. (1988). "Election-Year Anti-Drug Bill Enacted." *1988 CQ Almanac*. Washington, DC: Congressional Quarterly, Inc.; Staff. (1990). "Bush Signs Stripped Down Crime Bills." *1990 CQ Almanac*. Washington, DC: Congressional Quarterly, Inc.; Staff. (1994). "Lawmakers Enact $30.2 Billion Anti-Crime Bill." *1994 CQ Almanac*. Washington, DC: Congressional Quarterly, Inc.

3 Excluded from the analysis to follow are bills with a particularized focus, such as the Law Enforcement Assistance Acts, the Juvenile Justice and Delinquency Acts, and the Violence Against Women Acts, among others.

4 See Table 5.1.

5 Federal Judicial Center. (2006). *Federal Courts and What They Do*. http://www.fjc.gov

6 On the House side, Congressman John Conyers introduced the Racial Justice Act of 1988. However, it was referred to the House Judiciary Committee's Subcommittee on Criminal Justice instead of the Subcommittee on Crime, which reported the Judiciary Committee's version of the omnibus crime bill to the floor.

7 For a fuller account of the various views aired in Congress in regard to racial justice proposals and HR 3355, see Doyle, C., Congressional Research Service. (May 4, 1994). *Racial Justice and Capital Punishment: The Racially Discriminatory Capital Sentencing Provisions of the House Passed Crime Bill (H.R. 4092/3355) 94–386 S*. Washington, DC: The Congressional Research Service.

8 Staff, "Election-Year Anti-Drug Bill Enacted," 108.

9 Staff, "Bush Signs Stripped Down Crime Bills," 491.

10 Staff, "Lawmakers Enact $30.2 Billion Anti-Crime Bill," 282.

11 Staff, "Lawmakers Enact $30.2 Billion Anti-Crime Bill," 282.

12 Staff, "Lawmakers Enact $30.2 Billion Anti-Crime Bill," 282.

13 Congress's earlier approach to illicit drug control was conducted in a more ad hoc, piecemeal fashion and lacked the kind of standardized provisions and administrative infrastructure established by the 1970 bill.

14 For a more complete listing of federalized criminal offenses, see Task Force on the Federalization of Criminal Law, American Bar Association, Criminal Justice Section. (1998). *The Federalization of Criminal Law.* Washington, DC: American Bar Association, Criminal Justice Section.

15 Republican National Party Platform. (2012). G. Peters and J. T. Wooley (eds.), *American Presidency Project.* http://www.presidency.ucsb.edu

16 Heritage Foundation. (August 17, 2010). Overcriminalization. *Solutions for America.* http://www.heritage.org/solutions

17 Staff, "Election-Year Anti-Drug Bill Enacted," 93.

18 Bear in mind also, budget authorizations are not the same as appropriations. The latter are actual outlays, i.e. spending.

19 These figures were calculated using the "Major Provisions" summary reports published in *Congressional Quarterly Almanac* for years 1968, 1970, 1984, 1986, 1988, 1990, and 1994. Enforcement figures include funds for various interdiction activities, such as border patrol, military defense expenditures, and foreign assistance. Neither enforcement nor prevention totals include funds authorized exclusively for Indian tribal lands, military veterans, victims funds, or prosecution of telemarketing fraud. Nor does the total account for funds allocated pursuant to "Such Sums as Necessary" legislative authorizations for either enforcement or prevention.

20 Republican Contract with America. September 13, 1994. http://www.gvpt. umd.edu/jgloeckler/documents/contract.pdf

21 Staff, "Bush Signs Stripped Down Crime Bills," 494.

22 Langan, P. A. (May 1991). *Race of Prisoners Admitted to State and Federal Institutions, 1926–1986* (NCJ-125618). https://www.ncjrs.gov, Table 7; Carson, E. A. and Sabol, W. J. (December 2012). *Prisoners in 2011* (NCJ 239808). Washington, DC: Bureau of Justice Statistics. http://www.bjs.gov

23 Langan, P. A., Fundis, J. V., Greenfeld, L.A., and Schneider, V. W. (May 1988). *Historical Statistics on Prisoners in State and Federal Institutions, Yearend 1925–86* (NCJ 111098). https://www.ncjrs.gov; Carson and Sabol, *Prisoners in 2011.*

24 Loury, G. C. with Karlan, P. S., Shelby, T., and Wacquant, L. (2008). *Race, Incarceration, and American Values.* Cambridge, MA: MIT Press.

25 Staff, "Election-Year Anti-Drug Bill Enacted," 96.

26 Staff, "Election-Year Anti-Drug Bill Enacted," 99.

27 *Dickerson v. U.S.* (No. 99–5525, 2000).

28 Staff, "Election-Year Anti-Drug Bill Enacted," 90.

29 Ditton, P. M. and Wilson, D. J., Bureau of Justice Statistics. (January 1999). *Special Report: Truth in Sentencing in State Prisons* (NCJ 179932). http:// www.bjs.gov

30 See Figures 6.1 and 6.2 in Chapter 6 for more details on the crime rates of earlier years.

31 Staff, "Lawmakers Enact $30.2 Billion Anti-Crime Bill," 282.

32 Data in Figure 5.1 obtained from: FBI. *Uniform Crime Reporting Statistics* UCR Data Online. www.ucrdatatool.gov

33 Data in Figure 5.2 for 1982 through 2006 from Maguire, K. (ed.). *Sourcebook of Criminal Justice Statistics*. http://www.albany.edu/sourcebook, table 1.1.2006; Bureau of Justice Statistics. *Justice Expenditure and Employment Extracts* for years 2007, 2008, 2009, and 2010. http://www.bjs.gov

34 Drug-Free America Act of 1986, S. 2849, 99th Cong. (1986); United States Sentencing Commission. (February 1995). *Report to Congress: Cocaine and federal sentencing policy*. http://www.ussc.gov; See also remarks of Senator Hatch (UT). "Statements on Introduced Bills and Joint Resolutions ... S. 1685. A Bill to Reduce the Sentencing Disparity Between Power and Crack Cocaine Violations." *Congressional Record (Daily Edition)* 153:110 (June 25, 2007) S8358-59. http://www.gpo.gov/fdsys

35 See Table 5.1 for further details.

36 Anti-Drug Abuse Act of 1988, Pub. L. 100–690, 102 Stat. 4181 (1988).

37 Omnibus Crime Control and Safe Streets Act, Pub. L. 90–351, 82 Stat. 197 (1968).

38 Narcotics Assistance to State and Local Law Enforcement. Hearing before the Subcommittee on Crime of the Committee on the Judiciary, House of Representatives, 99th Congress, 2nd Session (1986). http://congressional.proquest.com

39 Federal Role in Promoting and Using Special Alternative Incarceration. Hearing before the Subcommittee on Oversight of Government Management of the Committee on Governmental Affairs, U.S. Senate, 101st Congress, 2nd Session (1990). http://www.congressional.proquest.com

40 Federal Prison Industries Reform Act of 1988. Hearing before the Subcommittee on Courts, Civil Liberties, and the Administration of Justice of the Committee on the Judiciary, U.S. House of Representatives, 100th Congress, 2nd Session (1988). http://www.congressional.proquest.com

41 Richard M. Nixon: Radio Address on Crime and Drug Abuse. (October 15, 1972). *American Presidency Project*.

42 Ronald Reagan: Radio Address to the Nation on Drug Abuse and Trafficking. (April 16, 1988). *American Presidency Project*.

43 Governor Andrew M. Cuomo. (January 5, 2011). *State of the State Address*. https://www.governor.ny.gov

44 Hakim, B. (January 28, 2011). "As Republicans Resist Closing Prisons, Cuomo is Said to Scale Back Plan." *New York Times*. http://www.nytimes.com

45 Governor Cuomo, *2011 State of the State Address*.

46 See Appendix for the methodology notes on the data in Table 5.1.

47 Drug Abuse Control Amendments, 1970, Part 1. Hearing before the Subcommittee on Public Health and Welfare of the Committee on Interstate and Foreign Commerce, U.S. House of Representatives, 91st Congress, 2nd Session (1970). http://www.congressional.proquest.com

48 Federal Sentencing Revision, Parts 1 and 2. Hearings before the Subcommittee on Criminal Justice of the Committee on the Judiciary, U.S. House of Representatives, 98th Congress, 2nd Session (1984); Comprehensive Crime Control Act of 1983. Hearing before the Subcommittee on Criminal Law of the Committee on the Judiciary, U.S. Senate, 98th Congress, 1st Session (1983). http://www.congressional.proquest.com

49 Drug Abuse Education. Hearing before the Select Committee on Narcotics Abuse and Control, U.S. House of Representatives, 99th Congress, 2nd Session (1986). http://www.congressiona.proquest.com

50 Narcotics Assistance to State and Local Law Enforcement. Hearing before the Subcommittee on Crime of the Committee on the Judiciary, House of Representatives, 99th Congress, 2nd Session (1986). http://congressional.proquest.com

51 Drug-Free Workplace Act of 1988. Hearing before the Subcommittee on Legislation and National Security, Committee on Government Operations, U.S. House of Representatives, 100th Congress, 2nd Session (1988). http://www.congressional.proquest.com

52 See list of hearings in Appendix Table A1.

53 Oversight of Federal Drug Policy Programs Affecting State and Local Governments. Hearing before the Committee on Governmental Affairs, U.S. Senate, 101st Congress, 1st Session (1989). http://www.congressional.proquest.com

54 James P. Moran. (1989). Prepared Statement in Oversight of Federal Drug Policy Programs Affecting State and Local Governments. Hearing before the Committee on Governmental Affairs, U.S. Senate, 101st Congress, 1st Session (1989). http://www.congressional.proquest.com, 39.

55 Incarceration and Alternative Sanctions for Drug Offenders. Hearing before the Committee on the Judiciary, U.S. Senate, 101st Congress, 1st Session (1989). http://www.congressional.proquest.com

56 Correcting Revolving Door Justice: New Approaches to Recidivism. Hearing before the Subcommittee on Crime and Criminal Justice of the Committee on the Judiciary, U.S. House of Representatives, 103rd Congress, 2nd Session (1994). http://www.congressional.proquest.com

57 Federal Prison Population: Present and Future Trends. Hearing before the Subcommittee on Intellectual Property and Judicial Administration of the Committee on the Judiciary, U.S. House of Representatives, 103rd Congress, 1st Session (1993). http://www.congressional.proqeust.com

58 For more on the grant program, see Chapter 4.

59 Sinclair, B. (2000). *Unorthodox Lawmaking: New Legislative Processes in the U.S. Congress* (2nd ed.). Washington, DC: CQ Press; Binder, S. A. and Smith, S. S. (1997). *Politics or Principle? Filibustering in the U.S. Senate* Washington, DC: Brookings Institution.

60 Data in Table 5.2 obtained from editions of the *Congressional Quarterly Almanac*, as listed in Note 2.

61 The final conference report on the 1970 law was adopted by voice vote in each chamber. The Senate voted 82-0 on January 28, 1970, to pass S3246, which was later incorporated into HR 18583. The 1984 crime law was appended to an appropriations resolution (H J Res 648); it represented a

compromise between HR 5690 passed in the House on September 25, 1984 (243–166), and HR 5963 passed in the House on October 2, 1984 (406–16). The final conference report on the 1990 law was adopted in the Senate without objection in a voice vote on October 27, 1990.

62 For the classic statement on the extent that electoral interests influence Congress members' activities both on and off the floor, see Fiorina, M. P. (1989). *Congress: Keystone of the Washington Establishment* (2nd ed.). New Haven, CT: Yale University Press.

63 Staff, "Election-Year Anti-Drug Bill Enacted," 85.

6 The Politics Principle and the Party Playbook

1 The analysis focuses chiefly on violent street crime, to the exclusion of other crimes such as white collar crime, cyber-crime, domestic and child abuse, elder abuse, and the like.

2 Except where otherwise noted, all of the national party platforms and presidential documents cited in this chapter were obtained from the *American Presidency Project*, an online documents archive established in 1999 as a collaboration between John T. Woolley and Gerhard Peters at the University of California, Santa Barbara. The archive contains 104,406 documents related to the study of the presidency and political parties and can be accessed at http://www.presidency.ucsb.edu.

3 Laver, M., Benoit, K., and Garry, J. (2003). "Extracting Policy Positions from Political Texts Using Words as Data." *American Political Science Review*, 97, 311–331.

4 For more on this debate, see Budge, I. and Hofferbert, R. I. (1990). "Mandates and Policy Outputs: U.S. Party Platforms and Federal Expenditures." *American Political Science Review*, 84, 111–131 and King, G., Laver, M., Hofferbert, R., Budge, I., and McDonald, M. D. (1993). "Party Platforms, Mandates, and Government Spending." *American Political Science Review*, 87, 744–750.

5 Fine, T. S. (1994). "Lobbying from Within: Government Elites and the Framing of the 1988 Democratic and Republican Party Platforms." *Presidential Studies Quarterly*, 24, 855–863, 855.

6 Simas, E. N. and Evans, K. A. (2011). "Linking Party Platforms to Perceptions of Presidential Candidates' Policy Positions, 1972–2000." *Political Research Quarterly*, 64, 831–839.

7 Kidd, Q. (2008). "The Real (Lack of) Difference between Republicans and Democrats: A Computer Word Score Analysis of Party Platforms, 1996–2004." *PS: Political Science and Politics*, 41, 519–525.

8 Poutvaara, P. (2003). "Party Platforms with Endogenous Party Membership." *Public Choice*, 117, 79–98.

9 Walters, R. W. (1990). "Party Platforms as Political Process." *PS: Political Science and Politics*, 23, 436–438, 437.

10 Smith, L. D. (1992). "The Party Platforms as Institutional Discourse: The Democrats and Republicans of 1988." *Presidential Studies Quarterly*, 22, 531–543, 532.

11 Carmines, E. G. and Stimson, J. A. (1989). *Issue Evolution: Race and the Transformation of American Politics*. Princeton, NJ: Princeton University Press, 16–17, 55.

12 Lyndon B. Johnson: Remarks Upon Signing Order Establishing the National Advisory Commission on Civil Disorders. (July 29, 1967). G. Peters and J. T. Wooley (eds.), *American Presidency Project*. http://www.presidency.ucsb. edu.

13 National Advisory Commission on Civil Disorders. (1968). *Report of the National Advisory Commission on Civil Disorders: Summary of the Report*. Washington, DC: Government Printing Office, 10.

14 National Advisory Commission on Civil Disorders, 15.

15 National Advisory Commission on Civil Disorders, 14.

16 Lyndon B. Johnson: The President's Address to the Nation on Civil Disorders. (July 27, 1967). *American Presidency Project*.

17 National Advisory Commission on Civil Disorders, 9.

18 For more on racial conservatism, presidential voting and partisan identification in the white South, see Valentino, N. A. and Sears, D. O. (2005). "Old Times There Are Not Forgotten: Race and Partisan Realignment in the Contemporary South." *American Journal of Political Science*, 49, 672–688.

19 For more on this theme, see Mendelberg, T. (2001). *The Race Card: Campaign Strategy, Implicit Messages, and the Norm of Equality*. Princeton, NJ: Princeton University Press; Weaver, V. M. (2007). "Frontlash: Race and the Development of Punitive Crime Policy." *Studies in American Political Development*, 21, 230–265.

20 Richard Nixon: Address Accepting the Presidential Nomination at the Republican National Convention in Miami Beach, Florida. (August 8, 1968). *American Presidency Project*.

21 Richard M. Nixon. (October 15, 1972,). Radio Address on Crime and Drug Abuse. *American Presidency Project*.

22 Allen, M. (July 14, 2005). "RNC Chief to Say It Was 'Wrong' to Exploit Racial Conflict for Votes." *The Washington Post*. http://www.washington-post.com

23 For more on the southern strategy, see Kalk, B. H. (2001). *The Origins of the Southern Strategy: Two-Party Competition in South Carolina, 1950–1972*. Lanham, MD: Lexington Books; Black, E. and Black, M. (2003). *Rise of Southern Republicans*. Cambridge, MA: Harvard University; Brown, F. (2004). "Nixon's 'Southern Strategy' and Forces against Brown." *Journal of Negro Education*, 73, 191–208; Knuckey, J. (2006). "Explaining Recent Changes in the Partisan Identifications of Southern Whites." *Political Research Quarterly*, 59, 57–70.

24 See Shull, S. A. (1999). *American Civil Rights Policy from Truman to Clinton: The Role of Presidential Leadership*. Armonk, NY: M.E. Sharpe.

25 Ferejohn, J. A. and Weingast, B. R. (eds.). (1997). *The New Federalism: Can the States Be Trusted?* Stanford, CA: Hoover Institution Press; Robertson, D.B. (2011). *Federalism and the Making of America*. New York: Routledge.

26 William J. Clinton: Address Before a Joint Session of the Congress on the State of the Union. (January 25, 1994). *American Presidency Project*.

27 Data for Figure 6.1 from: Federal Bureau of Investigation, *Crime in the United States*, 1960 through 2012 editions.

28 Data for Figure 6.2 from; Federal Bureau of Investigation, *Crime in the United States*, 1960 through 2012 editions.

29 Massey, D. S. and Denton, N. A. (1993). *American Apartheid: Segregation and the Making of the Underclass.* Cambridge, MA: Harvard University Press; Orfield, G., Eaton, S. E., and Harvard Project on School Desegregation. (June1996). *Dismantling Desegregation: The Quiet Reversal of Brown v. Board of Education.* New York: The New Press; Frey, W. H., and Myers, D. (2005). "Racial Segregation in U.S. Metropolitan Areas and Cities 1999–2000: Patterns, Trends, and Explanations." http://www.psc.isr.umich.edu/pubs/pdf/rro5-573.pdf

30 Data for Figure 6.3 from: Bureau of Justice Statistics (BJS). (July 1994). *Criminal Victimization in the United States: 1973–1992 Trends* (NCJ 147006); BJS. *National Criminal Victimization in the United States – Statistical Tables,* various editions 1996 through 2012; BJS. (October 2013). *Criminal Victimization, 2012* (NCJ 243389). http://www.bjs.gov

31 Data for 1976–2005 in Figure 6.4 from: Bureau of Justice Statistics (BJS). (July 1, 2007). *Homicide Trends in the United States.* http://www.bjs.gov; Data for 2008 from BJS. (November 2011). *Homicide Trends in the United States, 1980–2008* (NCJ 236018) and FBI, Department of Justice. (September 2009). *Crime in the United States, 2008.* http://www.fbi.gov

32 Bureau of Justice Statistics. (November 2011). *Homicide Trends in the United States, 1980–2008* (NCJ 236018). http://www.bjs.gov/content/pub/pdf/htus8008.pdf

33 Bureau of Justice Statistics. (November 2011). *Homicide Trends in the United States, 1980–2008.*

34 Lynching Victims Senate Apology Resolution, S. Res. 39, 109th Cong., (2005).

35 National Association for the Advancement of Colored People. *NAACP History: Anti-Lynching Bill.* http://www.naacp.org/pages/naacp-history-anti-lynching-bill

36 Moore, N. M. (2000). *Governing Race: Policy, Process, and the Politics of Race.* Westport, CT: Praeger Publishers.

37 See Chapter 4 for more on the Fair Sentencing Act of 2010.

38 Barack Obama: Remarks on the Verdict in *State of Florida v. George Zimmerman.* (July 19, 2013). *American Presidency Project.*

39 Jamieson, K. H. (1992). *Dirty Politics: Deception, Distraction, and Democracy.* New York: Oxford University Press, 27.

40 Miranda v. Arizona, 384 U.S. 436 (1966).

41 Koopman, D. L. (1996). *Hostile Takeover.* Lanham, MD: Rowman & Littlefield Publishers.

42 Republican Contract with America. (September 13, 1994). http://www.gvpt.umd.edu/jgloekler/documents/contract.pdf

43 Staff. (1990). "Bush Signs Stripped Down Crime Bills." *1990 CQ Almanac.* Washington, DC: Congressional Quarterly, Inc., 487.

44 William J. Clinton: Address Before a Joint Session of the Congress on the State of the Union.

45 William J. Clinton: Address Before a Joint Session of the Congress on the State of the Union.

46 Staff. (1994). "Lawmakers Enact $30.2 Billion Anti-Crime Bill." *1994 CQ Almanac*. Washington, DC: Congressional Quarterly, Inc., 284.

47 For more on this point, see the discussion and analysis in Chapter 3.

48 For more on this point, see the discussion and analysis in Chapter 1; see also reports of the U.S. Commission on Civil Rights.

49 Data for 1980–2011 in Figure 6.5 from Bureau of Justice Statistics. (June 2013). *Arrest in the United States, 1980–2011* (Arrest Data Analysis Tool). http://www.bjs.gov; Data for 1964–1976 calculated using data from FBI, *Crime in the United States*, serial editions and U.S. Census Bureau. *National Estimates by Age, Sex, Race: 1900–1979*. (PE-11). http://www.census.gov.

50 "The Campaign against Women." (May 19, 2012). *New York Times*. http://www.nytimes.com

51 Data for 1976–2005 in Table 6.1 from: Bureau of Justice Statistics (BJS). (July 1, 2007). *Homicide Trends in the United States*; Data for 2008 from BJS. (November 2011). *Homicide Trends in the United States, 1980–2008*.

52 Data in Table 6.2 from: Maguire, K. (ed.) *Sourcebook of Criminal Justice Statistics*. State University of New York at Albany. http://www.albany.edu/sourcebook, table 3.126.2005; Data for 2008 from BJS. (November 2011). *Homicide Trends in the United States, 1980–2008*.

53 For trend data on sexual assault for 1972–1990, see Bureau of Justice Statistics. (July 1994). *Criminal Victimization in the United States: 1973–1992 Trends* (NCJ-147006). https://www.ncjrs.gov/pdffiles1/Digitization/147006NCJRS.pdf

54 Data in Table 6.3 from: Bureau of Justice Statistics (BJS). *Criminal Victimization in the United States: 1973–1992 Trends*; BJS. *National Criminal Victimization in the United States – Statistical Tables*, various editions 1996 through 2012.

55 Richard Nixon: Remarks About an Intensified Program for Drug Abuse Prevention and Control. (June 17, 1972). *American Presidency Project*.

56 Richard Nixon: Special Message to the Congress on Drug Abuse Prevention and Control. (June 17, 1971). *American Presidency Project*.

57 Richard M. Nixon: Radio Address on Crime and Drug Abuse.

58 Richard Nixon: Message to the Congress Transmitting Reorganization Plan 2 of 1973 Establishing the Drug Enforcement Administration. (March 28, 1973). *American Presidency Project*.

59 Richard M. Nixon: Radio Address on Crime and Drug Abuse.

60 Drug Enforcement Administration. (n.d.). *DEA History in Depth, 1970–1975*. http://www.justice.gov/dea/about/history/1970-1975.pdf.

61 Richard Nixon: Message to the Congress Transmitting Reorganization Plan 2 of 1973 Establishing the Drug Enforcement Administration.

62 Ronald Reagan: Address Before a Joint Session of the Congress on the State of the Union. (January 25, 1983). *American Presidency Project*.

63 Ronald Reagan: Address to the Nation on the Campaign Against Drug Abuse. (September 14, 1986). *American Presidency Project.*

64 Ronald Reagan: Address to the Nation on the Campaign Against Drug Abuse.

65 Richard M. Nixon: Special Message to the Congress on Drug Abuse Prevention and Control.

66 Richard Nixon: Message to the Congress Transmitting Reorganization Plan 2 of 1973 Establishing the Drug Enforcement Administration.

67 Richard M. Nixon: Special Message to the Congress on Drug Abuse Prevention and Control.

68 Drug Enforcement Administration. (n.d.). *DEA History in Depth.*

69 Richard M. Nixon: Remarks on Signing Two Bills Providing for Drug and Alcohol Abuse Prevention. (May 14, 1974). *American Presidency Project.*

70 Richard M. Nixon: Special Message to the Congress on Drug Abuse Prevention and Control.

71 Richard Nixon: Message to the Congress Transmitting Reorganization Plan 2 of 1973 Establishing the Drug Enforcement Administration.

72 Richard Nixon: Message to the Congress Transmitting Reorganization Plan 2 of 1973 Establishing the Drug Enforcement Administration.

73 Richard Nixon: Message to the Congress Transmitting Reorganization Plan 2 of 1973 Establishing the Drug Enforcement Administration.

74 Drug Enforcement Administration. (n.d.). *DEA History in Depth.*

75 Drug Enforcement Administration. (n.d.). *DEA History in Depth.*

76 Ronald Reagan: Remarks Announcing Federal Initiatives Against Drug Trafficking and Organized Crime. (October 14, 1982). *American Presidency Project.*

77 Ronald Reagan: Address to the Nation on the Campaign Against Drug Abuse.

78 Ronald Reagan: Remarks to Media Executives at a White House Briefing on Drug Abuse. (March 7, 1988). *American Presidency Project.*

79 Ronald Reagan: Radio Address to the Nation on the Resignation of Attorney General Meese and the War on Drugs. (July 9, 1988). *American Presidency Project.*

80 Ronald Reagan: Address Before a Joint Session of the Congress Reporting on the State of the Union. (January 26, 1982). *American Presidency Project.*

81 Ronald Reagan: Remarks on Signing Executive Order 12368, Concerning Federal Drug Abuse Policy Functions. (June 24, 1982). *American Presidency Project.*

82 Mackey-Kallis, S. and Hahn, D. F. (1991). "Questions of Public Will and Private Action: The Power of the Negative in the Reagans' 'Just Say No' Morality Campaign." *Communication Quarterly,* 39, 1–17, 1. See also: Beck, J. (1998). "100 Years of 'Just Say No' Versus 'Just Say Know': Reevaluating Drug Education Goals for the Coming Century." *Evaluation Review,* 22, 15–45.

83 Ronald Reagan: Remarks on Signing Executive Order 12368, Concerning Federal Drug Abuse Policy Functions.

84 Richard M. Nixon: Radio Address on Crime and Drug Abuse.

85 Ronald Reagan: Address to the Nation on the Campaign Against Drug Abuse.

86　Rev. Jesse Jackson. (1988). Prepared Statement in "Drug Abuse – Prevention, Education and Treatment." Committee on Labor and Human Resources, U.S. Senate, 100th Congress, 2nd Session. S. Hrg. 100–803. Washington, DC: Government Printing Office, 24–27.

87　Jackson, Committee on Labor and Human Resources, 27.

88　Jackson, Committee on Labor and Human Resources, 26.

89　Staff. (1988). "Election-Year Anti-Drug Bill Enacted." *1988 CQ Almanac.* Washington, DC: Congressional Quarterly, Inc., 86.

90　Drug-Free America Act of 1986, S. 2849, 99th Cong. (1986); United States Sentencing Commission. (February 1995). *Report to Congress: Cocaine and federal sentencing policy.* http://www.ussc.gov; See also remarks of Senator Hatch (UT). "Statements on Introduced Bills and Joint Resolutions … S. 1685. A Bill to Reduce the Sentencing Disparity Between Power and Crack Cocaine Violations." *Congressional Record (Daily Edition)* 153:110 (June 25, 2007) S8358–S8359. http://www.gpo.gov/fdsys

91　Staff. "Election-Year Anti-Drug Bill Enacted," 93.

92　Shipley, A. (February 2, 2009). "Phelps Will Not Face Any Sanctions." *Washington Post.* http://www.washingtonpost.com; Verhovek, S. H. (April 29, 2006). "Limbaugh Deal Avoids Drug Prosecution, Defense Says." *Los Angeles Times.* http://articles.latimes.com; Cooperman, A. (January 5, 2007). "Sedative Withdrawal Made Rehnquist Delusional in '81." *Washington Post.* http://www.washingtonpost.com; Kovaleski, S. F. (February 9, 2008). "Old Friends Say Drugs Played Bit Part in Obama's Young Life." *New York Times.* http://www.nytimes.com

93　Data in Figure 6.6 from: Johnston, L. D., O'Malley, P. M., Bachman, J. G., Schulenberg, J. E., Institute for Social Research, University of Michigan. (2013) *Demographic Subgroup Trends among Adolescents for Fifty-One Classes of Licit and Illicit Drugs, 1975–2012* (Monitoring the Future Occasional Paper 79). http://www.monitoringthefuture.org, tables 25, 38, 41, 47, 63, and 74.

94　Substance Abuse and Mental Health Services Administration and the National Opinion Research Center. (April 1998). *Prevalence of Substance Use among Racial & Ethnic Subgroups in the U.S.* (No. 283-95-0002). http://www.samhsa.gov/data/nhsda/ethnic/toc.htm, chapter 1.

95　Substance Abuse and Mental Health Services Administration and the National Opinion Research Center. *Prevalence of Substance Use among Racial & Ethnic Subgroups,* chapter 1.

96　MTF data on crack use extend from 1986 onward.

97　Data in Figure 6.7 from: Johnston, L. D., O'Malley, P. M., Bachman, J. G., Schulenberg, J. E., Institute for Social Research, University of Michigan. (2013) *Demographic Subgroup Trends among Adolescents for Fifty-One Classes of Licit and Illicit Drugs, 1975–2012* (Monitoring the Future Occasional Paper 79). http://www.monitoringthefuture.org, tables 38, 41, and 47.

98　Data in Figure 6.8 from; Johnston, L. D., O'Malley, P. M., Bachman, J. G., Schulenberg, J. E., Institute for Social Research, University of Michigan. *Demographic Subgroup Trends among Adolescents for Fifty-One Classes of Licit and Illicit Drugs,* tables 38 and 41.

99 Johnston, L. D., O'Malley, P. M., Bachman, J. G., and Schulenberg, J. E., Institute for Social Research, University of Michigan. *Demographic Subgroup Trends among Adolescents for Fifty-One Classes of Licit and Illicit Drugs*, table 63.

100 Chapter 4 details at length this perception as a primary driver behind initial enactment of the 100-to-1 crack cocaine penalty structure and its subsequent amendment.

101 Data in Figure 6.9 from: Bureau of Justice Statistics. (June 2013). *Arrest in the United States, 1980–2011* (Arrest Data Analysis Tool). http://www.bjs.gov

102 Data in Figure 6.10 from: Bureau of Justice Statistics. (May 1991). *Race of Prisoners Admitted to State and Federal Institutions, 1926–1986* (NCJ-125618). https://www.ncjrs.gov

103 Source: Data for 1925–1986 from: Bureau of Justice Statistics. *Race of Prisoners Admitted to State and Federal Institutions*, table 7.

104 Data for 1980–1994 in Figure 6.11 obtained from Bureau of Justice Statistics (BJS). (June 1996). *Correctional Populations in the United States, 1994* (NCJ-160091), table 1.8; Data for 1995–1997 from BJS. (August 1999). *Prisoners in 1998* (NCJ 175687), table 11; Data for 2000–2008 from BJS. (December 2009). *Prisoners in 2008* (NCJ 228417), table 5. http://www.bjs.gov

105 Data in Table 6.4 from: Bositis, D. A., Joint Center for Political and Economic Studies. (2012). *Blacks and the 2012 Democratic National Convention*. http://www.jointcenter.org

106 See Tate, K. (1993). *From Protest to Politics: The New Black Voters in American Elections*. Cambridge, MA: Harvard University Press and Marable, M. (2007). *Race, Reform, and Rebellion: The Second Reconstruction in Black America* (3rd ed.). University of Mississippi Press.

107 Smith, R. C. (1996). *We Have No Leaders: African Americans in the post-Civil Rights Era*. Albany, NY: State University of New York Press, 268.

108 Maguire, K. (January 5, 2003). "The Rev. Al Sharpton: Democratic Party Needs Me to Run for President." *Free Republic*. http://www.freerepublic.com

109 Limbaugh, R. (July 26, 2012). "Why Democrats Get the Black Vote." http://www.rushlimbaugh.com/daily/2012/07/26/why_democrats_get_the_black_vote

7 Public Origins: What Americans Believe about Race, Crime, and Criminal Justice Policy

1 Schuman, H., Steeh, C., Bobo, L., and Krysan, M. (1997). *Racial Attitudes in America: Trends and Interpretation*. Cambridge, MA: Harvard University Press, 59.

2 Data in Table 7.1 from: Maguire, K. (ed.). *Sourcebook of Criminal Justice Statistics* http://www.albany.edu/sourcebook, Table 2.26; Gallup, Inc. (June–July 2008). "Race Relations." http://www.gallup.com

3 Newport, F. (December 9, 1999). "Racial Profiling is Seen as Widespread, Particularly among Young Black Men." http://www.gallup.com; Ludwig, J. (May 13, 2003). "Americans See Racial Profiling as Widespread." http://www.gallup.com

4　Unnever, J. D. (2008). "Two Worlds Far Apart: Black-White Differences in Beliefs about Why African-American Men Are Disproportionately Imprisoned." *Criminology*, 46, 511–538.

5　Newport, F. (July 16, 2013). "In U.S., 24% of Young Black Men Say Police Dealings Unfair." http://www.gallup.com

6　Gallup, Inc. "Race Relations."

7　Dowler, K. and Sparks, R. 2008. "Victimization, Contact with Police, and Neighborhood Conditions: Reconsidering African American and Hispanic Attitudes toward the Police." *Police Practice and Research*, 9, 395–415; Howell, S., Perry, H. L. and Vile, M. (2004). "Black Citizens/White Cities: Evaluating the Police." *Political Behavior*, 26, 45–68; Hurwitz, J. and Peffley, M. (2005). "Explaining the Great Racial Divide: Perceptions of Fairness in the U.S. Criminal Justice System." *Journal of Politics*, 67, 762–783; Miller, F. and Foster, E. (2002). "Youths' Perceptions of Race, Class, and Language Bias in the Courts." *Journal of Negro Education*, 71, 193–204; Weitzer, R. (2000). "Racialized Policing: Residents' Perceptions in Three neighborhoods." *Law and Society*, 34, 129–155; Weitzer, R. (1999). "Citizens' Perceptions of Police Misconduct: Race and Neighborhood Contexts." *Justice Quarterly*, 16, 819–846; Brunson, R. K. (2007). "Police Don't Like Black People: African-American Young Men's Accumulated Police Experiences." *Criminology and Public Policy*, 6, 71–102.

8　Bobo, L. D. and Thompson, V. (2006). "Unfair by Design: The War on Drugs, Race, and the Legitimacy of the Criminal Justice System." *Social Research*, 73, 445–470.

9　Weitzer, R. and Tuch, S. A. (2004). "Race and Perceptions of Police Misconduct." *Social Problems*, 51, 305–325, 314.

10　Data in Table 7.2 from: Maguire (ed.), *Sourcebook of Criminal Justice Statistics*, tables 2.0001.2005, 2.0002.2005, 2.0005.2011, 2.0017.2010, 2.10.2011, 2.11.2011, 2.12.2011, 2.17.2010, 2.17.2011, 2.21.2011, 2.45, 2.54.2011; Jones, J. M. (November 10, 2005). "Confidence in Local Police Drops to 10-Year Low." http://www.galllup.com; Pew Research Center. (January 12, 2010). *A Year after Obama's Election: Blacks Upbeat about Black Progress, Prospects*. http://www.pewsocialtrends.org; Gallup, Inc., "Race Relations."

11　Maguire (ed.), *Sourcebook of Criminal Justice Statistics*, table 2.17.2011.

12　Maguire (ed.), *Sourcebook of Criminal Justice Statistics*, table 2.10.2011.

13　Maguire (ed.), *Sourcebook of Criminal Justice Statistics*, table 2.20.2011.

14　Maguire (ed.), *Sourcebook of Criminal Justice Statistics*, table 2.0016.2010.

15　Welch argues that racial stereotyping serves as a subtle rationale for racial profiling. See Welch, K. (2007). "Black Criminal Stereotypes and Racial Profiling." *Journal of Contemporary Criminal Justice*, 23, 276–288.

16　See also Jolls, C. and Sunstein, C. R. (2006). "The Law of Implicit Bias." *California Law Review*, 94, 945–996; Rachlinski, J. J., Johnson, S. L., Wistich, A. J., and Guthrie, C. (2009). "Does Unconscious Racial Bias Affect Trial Judges?" *Notre Dame Law Review*, 84, 1195–1246.

17　Bobo, L., Kluegel, J. R., and Smith, R. A. (1997). "Laissez-Faire Racism: The Crystallization of a Kinder, Gentler, Anti-Black Ideology." In S. A. Tuch and

J. K. Martin (eds.), *Racial Attitudes in the 1990s: Continuity and Change.* Westport, CT: Greenwood Publishing Group, Inc. See also Virtanen, S. V. and Huddy, L. (1998). "Old-Fashioned Racism and New Forms of Racial Prejudice." *Journal of Politics,* 60, 311–332.

18 Dovidio, J. F., Gaertner, S. L., Kawakami, K., and Hodson, G. (2002). "Why Can't We Just Get Along? Interpersonal Biases and Interracial Distrust." *Cultural Diversity and Ethnic Minority Psychology,* 8, 88–102; Dovidio, J. F. and Gaertner, S. L. (2000). "Aversive Racism and Selection Decisions." *Psychological Science,* 11, 315–319.

19 Sniderman, P. M., Piazza, T., Tetlock, P. E., and Kendrick, A. (1991). "The New Racism." *American Journal of Political Science,* 35, 423–447.

20 Quillian, L. and Pager, D. (2001). "Black Neighbors, Higher Crime? The Role of Racial Stereotypes in Evaluations of Neighborhood Crime." *American Journal of Sociology,* 107, 717–767.

21 Data in Table 7.3 from: Smith, T. W., Marsden, P. V., and Hout, M. *General Social Survey, 1972–2010.* ICPSR31521-v1. Storrs, CT: Roper Bibliographic Citation: Center for Public Opinion Research, University of Connecticut/Ann Arbor, MI: Inter-university Consortium for Political and Social Research.

22 Gergen, D. (May 10, 1996). "Harvard's 'Talented Tenth.'" *U.S. News & World Report* http://www.usnews.com

23 Anderson, K. J. (2010). *Benign Bigotry: The Psychology of Subtle Prejudice.* New York, NY: Cambridge University Press, 115.

24 Reeves, J. L. and Campbell, R. (1994). *Cracked Coverage: Television News, the Anti-Cocaine Crusade, and the Reagan Legacy.* Durham, NC: Duke University Press; Beckett, K. and Sasson, T. (2004). *The Politics of Injustice* (2nd ed.). Beverly Hills, CA: Sage; Roberts, D. E. (1999). "Foreword: Race, Vagueness and the Social Meaning of Order-Maintenance of Policing." *Journal of Criminal Law and Criminology,* 89, 775–836.

25 For an earlier similar analysis, see Kluegel, J. R and Smith, E. R. (1982). "Whites' Beliefs about Blacks' Opportunity." *American Sociological Review,* 47, 518–532.

26 Data in Table 7.4 from: Pew Research Center, *Blacks Upbeat*; Smith, Marsden, and Hout, *General Social Survey*; Newport, F. (July 19, 2013). "Fewer Blacks in the United States See Bias in Jobs, Income, and Housing." http://www.gallup.com.

27 Newport, "Fewer Blacks in the United States See Bias."

28 McGarty, C., Yzerbyt, V. Y., and Spears, R. (2002). *Stereotypes as Explanations: The Formation of Meaningful Beliefs about Social Groups.* New York: Cambridge University Press, 161.

29 Data in Table 7.5 from: Moore, N. (May 2009). "Reason Blacks Have Higher Arrest Rates." YouGov Omnibus.

30 Newport, "Fewer Blacks in the United States See Bias."

31 Moore, N. "Reason Blacks Have Higher Arrest Rates." Respondents #89, 106, 148, 243, and 554.

32 Dubois, W. E. B. (1903). *The Souls of Black Folk.* Chicago: A.C. McClurg & Co.

33 Schuman, S., Steeh, C., Bobo, L., and Krysan, M. (1997). *Racial Attitudes in America: Trends and Interpretations* (Rev. ed.). Cambridge, MA: Harvard University Press.

34 Data in Table 7.6 from: Pew Research Center, *Blacks Upbeat*; Gallup, Inc., "Race Relations"; Smith, Marsden, and Hout, *General Social Survey*.

35 Data in Table 7.7 from; Gallup, Inc., "Race Relations"; Pew Research Center, *Blacks Upbeat*.

36 Pew Research Center, *Blacks Upbeat*, Q.21F1.

37 Data in Table 7.8 from: Gallup, Inc., "Race Relations"; Pew Research Center, *Blacks Upbeat*.

38 Barras, J. R. (November 9, 2008). "He Leapt the Tallest Barrier. What Does It Mean for Black America?" *Washington Post*. http://www.washingtonpost.com

39 Williams, J. (November 30, 2007). "Obama's Color Line." *New York Times*. http://www.nytimes.com; Valbrun, M. (February 2, 2008). "Race Matters. So Does Hope." *Washington Post* (Regional ed.); Dowd, M. (March 19, 2008). "Black, White & Gray." *New York Times*; Healy, P. (October 13, 2008). "Race Remains Campaign Issue, but Not a Clear One." *New York Times*; Hoagland, J. (November 2, 2008). "The Post-Racial Election." *Washington Post*; Rodriguez, G. (November 17, 2008). "The Ugly Side of 'Beyond Race': The Romantic Narrative that All Minorities Are Locked Arm and Arm in a Collective Struggle against Oppression Simply Isn't True." *Hutchinson News*. http://www.hutchnews.com

40 Thernstrom, A. (November 6, 2008). "Great Black Hope? The Reality of President-Elect Obama." An NRO symposium. *National Review Online*. http://www.thernstrom.com/articles

41 Thernstrom, A. and Thernstrom, S. (November 11, 2008). "Racial Gerrymandering is Unnecessary." *Wall Street Journal*. http://www.onlinewsj.com

42 Thernstrom and Thernstrom, "Racial Gerrymandering is Unnecessary."

43 Democratic Party Platform (2012). G. Peters and J. T. Wooley (eds.), *American Presidency Project*. http://www.presidency.ucsb.edu

44 politicalticker ... (July 14, 2010). "Sarah Palin Responds to Allegations of Tea Party Racism." http://politicalticker.blogs.cnn.com

45 Pew Research Center, *A Year after Obama's Election*, Q5.

46 Pew Research Center, *A Year after Obama's Election*, Q62F2.

47 Saad, L. (July 18, 2013). "In the United States, 52 Percent of Blacks Unhappy with Societal Treatment." http://www.gallup.com

48 Barack Obama: Remarks on the Verdict in *State of Florida v. George Zimmerman*. (July 19, 2013). *American Presidency Project*.

49 Shapiro, R. (July 21, 2013). "Tavis Smiley on Obama's Trayvon Martin Speech: He Was Pushed to that Podium." *The Huffington Post*. http://www.huffingtonpost.com

50 Eurpublisher. (July 21, 2013). "Smiley Dissed for Dissing Obama's Trayvon Zimmerman Response." http://www.eurweb.com

51 Barack Obama: Remarks on the Verdict in *State of Florida v. George Zimmerman*. (July 19, 2013). *American Presidency Project*.

52 For more on this, see also Barack Obama: Remarks on the Verdict in *State of Florida v. George Zimmerman*. (July 19, 2013). *American Presidency Project*.

53 Among the book-length works that address this point are: Carmines, E. and Stimson, J. (1989). *Issue Evolution: Race and the Transformation of American Politics*. Princeton, NJ: Princeton University Press; Shull, S. A. (1989). *The President and Civil Rights Policy: Leadership and Change*. Westport, CT: Greenwood Press, Inc.; Riley, R. L. (1999). *The Presidency and the Politics of Racial Inequality: Nation-Keeping from 1831 to 1965*. New York: Columbia University Press.

54 King, M. L., Jr. (April 16, 1963). *Letter from a Birmingham Jail*. In Washington, J. M. (ed.). (1986). *The Essential Writings and Speeches of Martin Luther King, Jr*. New York: HarperCollins Publishers.

55 Reed, Jr., A. (1986). *The Jesse Jackson Phenomenon: The Crisis of Purpose in Afro-American Politics*. New Haven, CT: Yale University Press, 37.

56 Barras, "He Leapt the Tallest Barrier."

57 Limbaugh, R. (July 26, 2012). "Why Democrats Get the Black Vote." http://www.rushlimbaugh.com/daily/2012/07/26/why_democrats_get_the_black_vote).

58 Moore, N. "Reason Blacks Have Higher Arrest Rates." Respondents #3, 21, 221, 225, 338, 502, and 559.

59 Data in Table 7.9 from: Smith, Marsden, and Hout, *General Social Survey*; Pew Research Center, *Blacks Upbeat*; Gallup, Inc., "Race Relations."

60 Data in Table 7.10 from: Maguire (ed.), *Sourcebook of Criminal Justice Statistics*, table 2.39.2011; Smith, Marsden, and Hout, *General Social Survey*.

61 Data in Table 7.11 from: Maguire (ed.), *Sourcebook of Criminal Justice Statistics*, table 2.40.2007.

62 Data in Table 7.12 from: Bureau of Justice Statistics. *Criminal Victimization in the United States, 2008 Statistical Tables*. http://www.bjs.gov, tables 1, 5, 16.

63 NCVS data necessarily exclude murder, as the survey is based on responses from actual victims.

64 Data in Table 7.13 from: Maguire (ed.), *Sourcebook of Criminal Justice Statistics*, tables 2.0015.2009, 2.33.2011, 2.34.2011, 2.35.2011, 2.36.2011, 2.44.2011; Smith, Marsden, and Hout, *General Social Survey*; Unpublished demographics for 2009 "drug problem" and 2011 "coping" data provided directly by Kathleen Maguire (ed.), *Sourcebook of Criminal Justice Statistics*. State University of New York at Albany.

65 Cole, D. (1999). *No Equal Justice: Race and Class in the American Criminal Justice System*. New York: The New Press.

66 Smith, T. W. (1985). "The Polls: America's Most Important Problems." *Public Opinion Quarterly*, 49, 268–274.

67 Pew Research Center, *Blacks Upbeat*.

68 Gallup, Inc. (March 28, 2012). "Economic Issues Still Dominate Americans' National Worries." http://www.gallup.com

69 Pew Research Center *Blacks Upbeat*.

70 Gaubatz, K. T. (1995). *Crime in the Public Mind*. Ann Arbor, MI: University of Michigan Press.

71 Data in Table 7.14 from: Smith, Marsden, and Hout, *General Social Survey*; Maguire (ed.), *Sourcebook of Criminal Justice Statistics*, tables 2.0013.2010, 2.28.2010, 2.48, 2.49.2010, 2.52.2011, 2.55; Pew Research Center. (November 5, 2003). *Evenly Divided and Increasingly Polarized: 2004 Political Landscape.* http://www.people-press.org; Pew Research Center. (January 6, 2012). *Continued Majority Support for Death Penalty.* http://www.people-press.org

72 Maguire, K. (ed.) *Sourcebook of Criminal Justice Statistics*, table 2.51.2011.

73 Sears, D. S. (1988). "Symbolic Racism." In P. A. Katz and D. A. Taylor (eds.), *Eliminating Racism: Profiles in Controversy.* New York: Plenum; Cohn, S. F., Barkan, S. E., and Halteman, W. A. (1991). "Public Attitudes Toward Criminals: Racial Consensus or Racial Conflict." *Social Problems*, **38**, 287–296; Kinder, D. R. and Mendelberg, T. (1995). "Cracks in American Apartheid: The Political Impact of Prejudice among Desegregated Whites." *Journal of Politics*, **57**, 402–424; Kinder, D. R. and Sanders, L. M. (1996). *Divided by Color: Racial Politics and Democratic Ideals.* Chicago: University of Chicago Press; Peffley, M., Hurwitz, J. and Sniderman, P. M. (1997). "Racial Stereotyping and Whites' Political Views of Blacks in the Context of Welfare and Crime." *American Journal of Political Science*, **41**, 30–60; Gilens, M. (1999). *Why Americans Hate Welfare: Race, Media, and the Politics of Antipoverty Policy.* Chicago: University of Chicago Press; Gilliam, F. D. and Iyengar, S. (2000). "Prime Suspects: The Influence of Local Television News on the Viewing Public." *American Journal of Political Science*, **44**, 560–573; Mendelberg, T. (2001). *The Race Card.* Princeton, NJ: Princeton University Press; Peffley, M. and Hurwitz, J. (2002). "The Racial Components of Race-Neutral Crime Policy Attitudes." *Political Psychology*, **23**, 59–75; Federico, C. M. and Holmesm, J. W. (2005). "Education and the Interface between Racial Perceptions and Criminal Justice Attitudes." *Political Psychology*, **26**, 47–75; Unnever, J. D. and Cullen, F. T. (2007). "The Racial Divide in Support for the Death Penalty: Does White Racism Matter?" *Social Forces*, **85**, 1281–1301; Johnson, D. (2008). "Racial Prejudice, Perceived Injustice, and the Black-White Gap in Punitive Attitudes." *Journal of Criminal Justice*, **36**, 198–206.

74 Unnever, J. D., Cullen, F. T., and Lero Jonson, C. N. (2008). "Race, Racism, and Support for Capital Punishment." In M. T. Tonry (ed.), *Crime and Justice: A Review of Research*, Vol. 37. Chicago, IL: University of Chicago Press, 53.

75 Zubrinsky, C. L. and Bobo, L. D. (1996). "Prismatic Metropolis: Race and Residential Segregation in the City of Angels." *Social Science Research*, **25**, 335–352.

76 Bobo, L. D. and Gilliam, Jr., F. D. (1990). "Race, Socio-Political Participation, and Black Empowerment." *American Political Science Review*, **84**, 377–393.

77 Bobo, L. D. and Johnson, D. (2004). "A Taste for Punishment: Black and White Americans' Views on the Death Penalty and the War on Drugs." *Du Bois Review*, **1**, 151–180, 171–172.

78 Newport, "Fewer Blacks in the United States See Bias."

79 Hurwitz, J. and Peffley, M. (1997). "Public Perceptions of Race and Crime: The Role of Racial Stereotypes." *American Journal of Political Science*, 41, 375–401.

80 Young argues that black support for the death penalty is a function of trust in the police, while white support is a function of responsibility attribution. Young, R. L. (1991). "Race, Conceptions of Crime and Justice, and Support for the Death Penalty." *Social Psychology Quarterly*, 54, 67–75.

81 For more on this theme, see Cullen, F. T., Fisher, B. S., and Applegate, B. K. (2000). "Public Opinion about Punishment and Corrections." *Crime and Justice*, 27, 1–79.

82 Sniderman, P. M. and Carmines, E. G. (1997). *Reaching beyond Race*. Cambridge, MA: Harvard University Press, 103. See also Sniderman, P., Piazza, T., and Harvey, H. H. (1998). "Prejudice and Politics: An Intellectual Biography of a Research Project." In J. Hurwitz and M. Peffley (eds.), *Perception Prejudice: Race and Politics in the United States*. New Haven, CT: Yale University Press.

83 Data in Table 7.15 from: Pew Research Center. 2003. *Evenly Divided*; Gallup, Inc., "Race Relations"; Smith, Marsden, and Hout, *General Social Survey*; Jeffrey M. Jones. July 24, 2013. "In U.S., Most Reject Considering Race in College Admissions." http://www.gallup.com

84 McConahay, J. B. (1986). "Modern Racism, Ambivalence, and the Modern Racism Scale." In J. F. Dovidio and Samuel L. Gartner (eds.), *Prejudice, Discrimination, and Racism*. Orlando, FL: Academic Press, Inc., 92.

85 Smith, Marsden, and Hout, *General Social Survey*. ICPSR31521-VI. Storrs, CT: Roper Bibliographic Citation: Center for Public Opinion Research, University of Connecticut/Ann Arbor, MI: Inter-university Consortium for Political and Social Research.

86 Pew Research Center. (January 23, 2012). *Public Priorities: Deficit Rising, Terrorism Slipping*. http://www.people-press.org

87 Data in Table 7.16 from: Moore, N. (May 2010) "Policymakers' Priority." YouGov Omnibus.

88 The 2011 survey was administered to a nationally representative sample of 1,030 adults in the United States.

89 Respondents were instructed as follows: "Drag your choice onto the numbered boxes on the right to rank each of the characteristics below."

90 Data in Table 7.17 from: Moore, N. (May 2011). "Race and Crime Survey." YouGov Omnibus.

91 Data in Table 7.18 from: Moore, N. "Race and Crime Survey."

8 Streams of Thought: Belief Options Concerning Race, Crime, and Justice

1 Eberhardt, J. L., Goff, P. A., Purdie, V. J., and Davis, P. G. (2004). "Seeing Black: Race, Crime and Visual Processing." *Journal of Personality and Social Psychology*, 87, 876–893.

2 Plant, A. E., Peruche, B. M., and Butz, D. A. (2005). "Eliminating Automatic Racial Bias: Making Race Non-Diagnostic for Responses to Criminal Suspects." *Journal of Experimental Social Psychology*, 42, 141–156.

3 Beckett, K., Nyrop, K., Pfingst, L., and Bowen, M. (2005). "Drug Use, Drug Possession Arrests, and the Question of Race: Lessons from Seattle." *Social Problems*, 52, 419–441.

4 Guervara, L., Spohn, C., and Herz, D. (2004). "Race, Legal Representation, and Juvenile Justice: Issues and Concerns." *Crime and Delinquency*, 50, 344–371.

5 Bridges, G. S. and Steen, S. (1998). "Racial Disparities in Official Assessments of Juvenile Offenders: Attributional Stereotypes as Mediating Mechanisms." *American Sociological Review*, 63, 554–570.

6 Engen, R. L., Steen, S., and Bridges, G. S. (2002). "Racial Disparities in the Punishment of Youth: A Theoretical and Empirical Assessment of the Literature." *Social Problems*, 49, 194–220, 194.

7 Rachlinski, J. J., Johnson, S. L., Wistich, A. J., and Guthrie, C. (2009). "Does Unconscious Racial Bias Affect Trial Judges?" *Notre Dame Law Review*, 84, 1195–1246.

8 Bodenhausen, G. V. and Wyer, Jr, R. S. (1985). "Effects of Stereotypes on Decision Making and Information-Processing Strategies." *Journal of Personality and Social Psychology*, 48, 267–282.

9 Rector, N. A., Bagby, R. M., Nicholson, R. (1993). "The Effect of Prejudice and Judicial Ambiguity on Defendant Guilt Ratings." *Journal of Social Psychology*, 133, 651–659.

10 Importantly, however, the authors found that for the tenth offense, where crime-related racial stereotyping was absent, juror verdicts were not influenced by race. See Sunnafrank, M. and Fontes, N. E. (1983). "General and Crime Related Racial Stereotypes and Influence on Juridic Decisions." *Cornell Journal of Social Relations*, 17, 1–15.

11 Pizzi, W. T., Blair, I. V., and Judd, C. M. (2005). "Discrimination in Sentencing on the Basis of Afro-Centric Features." *Michigan Journal of Race and Law*, 10, 327–353, 351.

12 Blair, I. V., Judd, C. M., and Chapleau, K. M. (2004). "The Influence of Afro-Centric Facial Features in Criminal Sentencing." *Psychological Science*, 15, 674–679.

13 Hochschild, J. L. and Weaver, V. M. (2007). "The Skin Color Paradox and the American Racial Order." *Social Forces* 86, 643–670, 646. The original study to which Hochschild and Weaver referred is Burch, T. (2005). *Skin Color and the Criminal Justice System: Beyond Black-White Disparities in Sentencing* (Unpublished master's thesis). Harvard University, Cambridge, MA.

14 Eberhardt, J. L. Davis, P. G., Purdie-Vaughns, V. J., and Johnson, S. L. (2006). "Looking Deathworthy: Perceived Stereotypicality of Black Defenders Predicts Capital-Sentencing Outcomes." *Psychological Science*, 17, 383–386.

15 An especially insightful work on the subject is Ifill, S. A. (2007). *Confronting the Legacy of Lynching in the Twenty-First Century*. Boston: Beacon Press.

16 National Association for the Advancement of Colored People. (1919). *Thirty Years of Lynching in the United States 1889–1918*. New York: NAACP.

17 Hampton et al. v. Commonwealth of Virginia, 58 S.E.2d 288, Va. (1950); For a lengthier discussion of the case, see Rise, E. W. (1995). *The Martinsville*

Seven: Race, Rape, and Capital Punishment. Charlottesville: University Press of Virginia.

18 *State v. Culver*, 253 F.2d 507 (5th Cir. 1958).

19 Garfinkel, H. (1949). "Research Note on Inter- and Intra-Racial Homicides." *Social Forces*, 27, 369–381.

20 Bowers, W. and Pierce, G. (1980). "Arbitrariness and Discrimination under Post- *Furman* Capital Statutes." *Crime & Delinquency*, 26, 563–635.

21 *McCleskey v. Kemp*, 481 U.S. 279 (1987).

22 Baldus, D. C., Woodworth, G., and Pulaski, Jr, C. A. (1990). *Equal Justice and the Death Penalty: A Legal and Empirical Analysis*. Boston: Northeastern University Press, 150.

23 Gross, S. R. and Mauro, R. (1989). *Death and Discrimination: Racial Disparities in Capital Sentencing*. Boston: Northeastern University Press.

24 See Arkin, S. (1980). "Discrimination and Arbitrariness in Capital Punishment: An Analysis of Post-*Furman* Murder Cases in Dade County, Florida, 1973–1976." *Stanford Law Review*, 33, 75–101; Baldus, D. C. Woodworth, G., and Pulaski, Jr., C. A. (1985). "Monitoring and Evaluating Contemporary Death Sentencing Systems: Lessons from Georgia." *U. C. Davis Law Review*, 18, 1375–1407; Baldus, D. C., Woodworth, G., and Pulaski, Jr., C. A. (1994). "Reflections on the 'Inevitability' of Racial Discrimination in Capital Sentencing and the 'Impossibility' of its Prevention, Detection, and Correction." *Washington & Lee Law Review*, 51, 359–419; Riedel, M. L. (1976). "Discrimination in the Imposition of the Death Penalty: A Comparison of the Characteristics of Offenders Sentenced Pre-*Furman* and Post-*Furman*." *Temple Law Review*, 49, 261–287; Radelet, M. L. (1981.) "Racial Characteristics and the Imposition of the Death Penalty." *American Sociological Review*, 46, 918–927; Smith, M. D. (1987). Patterns of Discrimination in the Assessment of the Death Penalty: The Case of Louisiana. *Journal of Criminal Justice*, 15, 279–286.

25 Radelet, M. L. and Pierce, G. (1985). "Race and Prosecutorial Discretion in Homicide Cases." *Law and Society Review*, 19, 587–621.

26 Jacoby, J. E. and Paternoster, R. (1982). "Sentencing Disparity and Jury Packing: Further Challenges to the Death Penalty." *Journal of Criminal Law and Criminology*, 73, 379–387.

27 U.S. General Accounting Office. (1990). *Death Penalty Sentencing: Research Indicates Pattern of Racial Disparities* (GAO/GGD-90-57). Report to the Senate and House Committees on the Judiciary. Washington, DC: General Accounting Office, 5.

28 Petri, M. A. and Coverdill, J. E. (2010). "Who Lives and Dies on Death Row? Race, Ethnicity, and Post-Sentence Outcomes in Texas." *Social Problems*, 57, 630–652.

29 Taub, R. P., Dunham, J. D., and Taylor, D.G. (1984). *Paths of Neighborhood Change: Race and Crime in Urban America*. University of Chicago Press.

30 Irving-Jackson, P. (1989). *Minority Group Threat, Crime, and Policing: Social Context and Social Control*. New York: Praeger.

31 Stults, G. J. and Baumer, E. P. (2007). "Racial Threat and Police Force Size: Evaluating the Empirical Validity of the Minority Threat Perspective." *American Journal of Sociology*, 113, 507–546.

32 Myers, M. A. and Talarico, S. M. (1986). "The Social Context of Racial Discrimination in Sentencing." *Social Problems*, 33, 236–251.

33 Jacobs, D., Carmichael, J. T., and Kent, S. L. (2005). "Vigilantism, Current Racial Threat, and Death Sentences." *American Sociological Review*, 70, 656–677. See also Jacobs, D. and Carmichael, J. T. 2002. "The Political Sociology of the Death Penalty: A Pooled Time-Series Analysis." *American Sociological Review*, 67, 109–131.

34 Liska, A. E. and Tausig, M. (1979). "Theoretical Interpretations of Social Class and Racial Differentials in Legal Decision-Making for Juveniles." *Sociological Quarterly*, 29, 197–207.

35 Musto, D. F. (1999). *The American Disease: Origins of Narcotic Control.* New York: Oxford University Press.

36 Whitebread, II, C. H. and Bonnie, R. J. (1974). *The Marihuana Conviction: The History of Marihuana Prohibition in the United States.* Charlottesville: University Press of Virginia.

37 Welch, K. and Payne, A. A. (2010). "Racial Threat and Punitive School Discipline." *Social Problems*, 57, 25–48, 25.

38 Loury, G. C. With Karlan, P. S., Shelby, T., and Wacquant, L. (2008). *Race, Incarceration, and American Values.* Cambridge, MA: MIT Press.

39 Johns, C. J. (1992). *Power, Ideology, and the War on Drugs: Nothing Succeeds Like Failure.* New York: Praeger; Luna, E. (2003). "Race, Crime, and Institutional Design." *Law and Contemporary Design*, 66, 183–220; Stilton, D. J. (2002). "U.S. Prisons and Racial Profiling: A Covertly Racist Nation Rides a Vicious Cycle." *Law & Inequality*, 20, 3–90; Weatherspoon, F. (1994). "The Devastating Impact of the Justice System on the Status of African American Males." *Capital University Law Review*, 23, 27–43.

40 Miller, J. G. (1996). *Search and Destroy: African-American Males in the Criminal Justice System.* New York: Cambridge University Press, 4.

41 See, for example: Blumstein, A., Cohen, J., Martin, S. E., and Tonry, M. H., (eds.). (1983). *Research on Sentencing: The Search for Reform.* Washington, DC: National Academy Press; Petersilia J. and Turner, S. (1985). *Guideline-Based Justice: The Implications for Racial Minorities* (R-3306-NIC). Santa Monica, CA: RAND Corporation.

42 Bureau of Justice Statistics, U.S. Department of Justice. Corrections Statistical Analysis Tool (CSAT) – Prisoners. http://www.bjs.gov/index.cfm?ty=nps.

43 Porter, N. D. and Wright, V. (2011). *Cracked Justice.* Washington, DC: The Sentencing Project.

44 Tonry, M. and Petersilia, J. (eds.). (1999). *Prisons.* University of Chicago Press, 66. See also Beckett, K. (1997). *Making Crime Pay: Law and Order in Contemporary American Politics.* New York: Oxford University Press; Tonry, M. (1995). *Malign Neglect – Race, Crime, and Punishment in America.* New York: Oxford University Press.

45 Tonry, *Malign Neglect.*

46 Tonry, M. and Melewski, M. (2008). "The Malign Effects of Drug and Crime Control Policies on Black Americans." *Crime and Justice*, 37, 1–44, 2 and 31.

47 Tonry and Melewski, "The Malign Effects of Drug and Crime Control," 18 and 31.

48 Nunn, K. B. (2002). "Race, Crime and the Pool of Surplus Criminality: Or Why the "War on Drugs" Was a "War on Blacks." *The Journal of Gender, Race and Justice*, 6, 381–445, 384.

49 Porter and Wright, *Cracked Justice*, 10.

50 Cole, D. (1999). *No Equal Justice: Race and Class in the American Criminal Justice System*. New York: The New Press.

51 Provine, Dori Marie. (2007). *Unequal Under Law: Race in the War on Drugs*. University of Chicago Press.

52 See Alexander, Jr., R.A. and Gyamerah, Jacquelyn. (1997). "Differential Punishing of African Americans and Whites Who Possess Drugs: A Just Policy or a Continuation of the Past?" *Journal of Black Studies*, 28, 97–111.

53 National Institute on Drug Abuse, National Institutes of Health. (1985). "Cocaine Use in America: Epidemiologic and Clinical Perspectives" (Research Monograph 61). Rockville, MD. http://archives.drugabuse.gov/pdf/monographs/download61.html, 74 and 137.

54 National Institute on Drug Abuse, National Institutes of Health. "Cocaine Use in America," 112.

55 U.S. Commission on Sentencing. (May 2002). *Report to the Congress: Cocaine and Federal Sentencing Policy*, v–vi.

56 Reinarman, C. and Levine, H.G. (eds.). (1997.) *Crack in America: Demon Drugs and Social Justice*. Los Angeles, CA: University of California Press.

57 Reinarman and Levine, *Crack in America*, 1.

58 Reinarman and Levine, *Crack in America*, 14.

59 Reinarman and Levine, *Crack in America*, 19.

60 Cole, *No Equal Justice*, 161.

61 Bell, Jr., D. A. (1973). "Racism in American Courts: Cause for Black Disruption or Despair?" *California Law Review*, 61, 165–203, 165 at footnote 2.

62 Glasser, I. (2000). "American Drug Laws: The New Jim Crow." *Albany Law Review*, 63, 703–724.

63 Tonry and Melewski, "The Malign Effects of Drug and Crime Control."

64 Alexander, M. (2010). *The New Jim Crow: Mass Incarceration in the Age of Colorblindness*. New York: The New Free Press, 13.

65 Alexander, *The New Jim Crow*, 212.

66 Alexander, *The New Jim Crow*, 214.

67 Blau, J. R. and Blau, P. M. (1982). "The Cost of Inequality: Metropolitan Structure and Violent Crime." *American Sociological Review*, **47**, 114–129, 123.

68 Blau, P. M. and Golden, R. M. (1986). "Metropolitan Structure and Criminal Violence." *Sociological Quarterly*, **27**, 15–26.

69 Williams, K. R. (1984.) "Economic Sources of Homicide: Reestimating the Effects of Poverty and Inequality." *American Sociological Review*, **49**, 283–289.

70 Corzine, J. and Huff-Corzine, L. (1992). "Racial Inequality and Black Homicide: An Analysis of Felony, Nonfelony and Total Rates." *Journal of Contemporary Criminal Justice*, 8, 150–165.

71 Land, K. C., McCall, P. L., and Cohen, L. E. (1990). "Structural Covariates of Homicide Rates: Are There Any Invariances across Time and Social Space?" *American Journal of Sociology*, **95**, 922–963.

72 Hawkins, D. F. (1993). "Inequality, Culture, and Interpersonal Violence." *Health Affairs*, Winter, 80–95; Parker, K. F. (2001). "A Move Toward Specificity: Examining Urban Disadvantage and Race- and Relationship-Specific Homicide Rates." *Journal of Quantitative Criminology*, 17, 89–110; Parker, K. F. and Pruitt, M. V. (2000.) "Poverty, Poverty Concentration, and Homicide." *Social Science Quarterly*, 81, 555–570.

73 Morenoff, J. D., Sampson, R. J., and Raudenbush, S. W. (2001). "Neighborhood Inequality, Collective Efficacy, and the Spatial Dynamics of Urban Violence." *Criminology*, 39, 517–560, 551.

74 Wooldredge, J. and Thistlethwaite, A. (2003). "Neighborhood Structure and Race-Specific Rates of Intimate Assault." *Criminology*, 41, 393–422, 393.

75 Krivo, L. J. and Peterson, R. D. (1996). Extremely Disadvantaged Neighborhoods and Urban Crime. *Social Forces*, 75, 619–648, 640.

76 Almgren, G., Guest, A., Immerwahr, G., and Spittel, M. (1998). "Joblessness, Family Disruption, and Violent Death in Chicago, 1970–1990." *Social Forces*, 76, 1465–1493.

77 Krivo, L. J. and Peterson, R. D. (2000). "The Structural Context of Homicide: Accounting for Racial Differences in Process." *American Sociological Review*, 65, 547–559, 547.

78 Harer, M. D. and Steffensmeier, D. (1992). "The Differing Effects of Economic Inequality on Black and White Rates of Violence." *Social Forces*, 70, 1035–1054; LaFree, G. and Drass, K. A. (1996). "The Effect of Changes in Intraracial Income Inequality and Educational Attainment on Changes in Arrest Rates for African Americans and Whites, 1957–1990." *American Sociological Review*, 25, 145–168; LaFree, G., Drass, K. A., and O'Day, P. (1992). "Race and Crime in Postwar America: Determinants of African-American and White Rates, 1957–1988." *Criminology*, 30, 157–188; Messner, S. F. and Golden, R. M. (1992). "Racial Inequality and Racially Disaggregated Homicide Rates: An Assessment of Alternative Theoretical Explanations." *Criminology*, 30, 421–447; Parker, K. F. and McCall, P. L. (1999). "Structural Conditions and Racial Homicide Patterns: A Look at the Multiple Disadvantages in Urban Areas." *Criminology*, 37, 447–478; Shihadeh, E. S. and Ousey, G. C. (1996). "Metropolitan Expansion and Black Social Dislocation: The Link between Suburbanization and Center-City Crime." *Social Forces*, 75, 649–666.

79 Shihadeh, E. S. and Shrum, W. (2004). "Serious Crime in Urban Neighborhoods: Is There a Race Effect?" *Sociological Spectrum*, 24, 507–533.

80 McNulty, T. L. (2001). "Assessing the Race-Violence Relationship at the Macro Level: The Assumption of Racial Invariance and the Problem of Restricted Distributions." *Criminology*, 39, 467–490.

81 McNulty, "Assessing the Race-Violence Relationship at the Macro Level," 483; Consistent with this observation concerning the inextricable link between race and class, McNulty and Holloway directly examined spatial differences. Using crime data supplied by the Atlanta Police Department, they concluded that proximity to public housing projects is a factor often missed by critics of racial invariance studies, yet one shown to affect murder, rape, assault, and public order crime. It is well known that crime-ridden public housing projects are more heavily populated by

blacks. See McNulty, T. L. and Holloway, S. R. (2000). "Race, Crime, and Public Housing in Atlanta: Testing a Conditional Effect Hypothesis." *Social Forces*, **79**, 707–729.

82 Massey, D. S. (1995). "Getting Away with Murder: Segregation and Violent Crime in Urban America." *University of Pennsylvania Law Review*, **143**, 1203–1032.

83 Peterson, R. D. and Krivo, L. J. (1993). "Racial Segregation and Black Urban Homicide." *Social Forces*, **71**, 1001–1026.

84 Peterson, R. D. and Krivo, L. J. (1999). "Racial Segregation, the Concentration of Disadvantage, and Black and White homicide Victimization." *Sociological Forum*, **14**, 465–493, 465.

85 Shihadeh, E. S. and Flynn, N. (1996). "Segregation and Crime: The Effect of Black Social Isolation on the Rates of Black Urban Violence." *Social Forces* **74**, 1325–1352.

86 Kubrin, C. E. and Wadworth, T. (2003). Identifying the Structural Correlates of African American Killings. *Homicide Studies*, **7**, 3–35.

87 Lee, M. R. (2000). "Concentrated Poverty, Race, and Homicide." *Sociological Quarterly*, **41**, 189–206.

88 Pattillo-McCoy, M. (1999). *Black Picket Fences: Privilege and Peril among the Black Middle Class*. University of Chicago Press.

89 Smith, M. D., Devine, J. A., and Sheley, J. F. (1992). "Crime and Unemployment: Effects across Age and Race Categories." *Sociological Perspectives*, **35**, 551–572, 565.

90 Shihadeh, E. S. and Ousey, G. C. (1998). "Industrial Restructuring and Violence: The Link between Entry-Level Jobs, Economic Deprivation, and Black and White Homicide." *Social Forces* **77**, 185–206, 185.

91 Crutchfield, R. D., Glusker, A., and Bridges, G. S. (1999). "A Tale of Three Cities: Labor Markets and Homicide." *Sociological Focus* **32**, 65–83, 68.

92 Sampson, R. J. and Groves, W. B. (1989). "Community Structure and Crime: Testing Social-Disorganization Theory." *American Journal of Sociology*, **94**, 774–802, 777.

93 Shaw, C. and McKay, H. (1942). *Juvenile Delinquency and Urban Areas*. University of Chicago Press.

94 Cloward, R. A. and Ohlin, L. E. (1960). *Delinquency and Opportunity: A Theory of Delinquent Gangs*. Glencoe, IL: Free Press.

95 Sampson and Groves, "Community Structure and Crime," 774–802.

96 Phillips, J. A. (1997). "Variation in African-American Homicide Rates: An Assessment of Potential Explanations." *Criminology*, **35**, 527–559.

97 Frazier, E. F. (2002/1939). "Rebellious Youth." In S. L. Gabbidon, H. T. Greene, and V. D. Young, *African American Classics in Criminology and Criminal Justice*. Thousand Oaks, CA, 99.

98 Sampson, R. J. (1987). "Urban Black Violence: The Effect of Male Joblessness and Family Disruption." *American Journal of Sociology*, **93**, 348–382.

99 Parker, K. F. and Johns, T. (2002). "Urban Disadvantage and Types of Race-Specific Homicide: Assessing the Diversity in Family Structures in the Urban Context." *Journal of Research in Crime and Delinquency* **39**, 277–303, 277.

100 Parker and Johns, "Urban Disadvantage and Types of Race-Specific Homicide."

101 Sampson, R. J., Morenoff, J. D., and Raudenbush, S. (2005). "Social Anatomy of Racial and Ethnic Disparities in Violence." *American Journal of Public Health*, 95, 224–232.

102 Wilson, W. J. (1987). *The Truly Disadvantaged: The Inner City, the Underclass, and Public Policy*. University of Chicago Press.

103 Wilson, *The Truly Disadvantaged*, 56.

104 Wilson, *The Truly Disadvantaged*, 58.

105 Wilson, *The Truly Disadvantaged*, 58; for more on why and how certain neighborhoods adjust, see Robert J. Bursik, Jr. and Jim Webb. 1982. "Community Change and Patterns of Delinquency." *American Journal of Sociology* 88: 24–42.

106 Hawkins, "Inequality, Culture, and Interpersonal Violence," 91.

107 Matsueda, R. L., Drakulich, K., and Kubrin, C. E. (2006). "Race and Neighborhood Codes of Violence." In R. D. Peterson, L. J. Krivo, and J. Hagen (eds.), *The Many Colors of Crime: Inequalities of Race, Ethnicity, and Crime in America*. New York University Press.

108 Merton, R. K. (1938). "Social Structure and Anomie." *American Sociological Review* 3, 672–682.

109 Kowalski, G. S., Dittman, Jr., R. L., and Bung, W. L. (1980). "Spatial Distribution of Criminal Offenses by States, 1970–1976." *Journal of Research in Crime and Delinquency* 17, 4–25; Lottier, S. (1938). "Distribution of Criminal Offenses in Sectional Regions." *The Journal of Criminal Law and Criminology* 29, 329–44; Porterfield, A. L. (1949). "Indices of Suicide and Homicide in States and Cities: Some Southern-Non-Southern Contrasts with Implications for Research." *American Sociological Review* 14, 481–490; Shannon, L. W. (1954). "The Spatial Distribution of Criminal Offenses by States." *The Journal of Criminal Law, Criminology and Police Science* 45, 264–273.

110 Wolfgang, M. E. and Ferracuti, F. (1967). *The Subculture of Violence: Towards an Integrated Theory in Criminology*. London: Tavistock Publications, 99–100.

111 Wolfgang and Ferracuti, *The Subculture of Violence*, 264.

112 Bailey, W. C. (1984). "Poverty, Inequality, and City Homicide Rates: Some Not So Unexpected Findings." *Criminology* 22, 531–550, 541.

113 Huff-Corzine, L., Corzine, J., and Moore, D. C. (1986). "Southern Exposure: Deciphering the South's Influence on Homicide Rates." *Social Forces* 64, 906–924, 913, 917.

114 Curtis, L. A. (1975). *Violence, Race, and Culture*. Lexington, MA: Lexington Books, 18.

115 Messner, S. F. (1983). "Regional and Racial Effects on the Urban Homicide Rate: The Subculture of Violence Revisited." *American Journal of Sociology* 88, 997–1007

116 Messner, "Regional and Racial Effects on the Urban Homicide Rate," 1005–1006.

117 Messner, S. F. (1983). "Regional Differences in the Economic Correlates of the Urban Homicide Rate." *American Society of Criminology* 21, 477–488.

118 Covington, J. (1999). "African-American Communities and Violent Crime: The Construction of Race Differences." *Sociological Focus* 32, 7–24, 18.

119 Sampson, R. J. (1985). "Race and Criminal Violence: A Demographically Disaggregated Analysis of Urban Homicide." *Crime & Delinquency* 31, 57–82, 58.

120 Hanner, U. (1969). *Soulside: Inquiries into Ghetto Culture and Community*. New York: Columbia University Press.

121 Anderson, E. (1994). "The Code of the Streets." *Atlantic Monthly: Digital Edition*, 273, 80–94, 80. See also Anderson, E. (1999). *Code of the Street: Decency, Violence, and the Moral Life of the Inner City*. New York: Norton.

122 Anderson, "The Code of the Streets," 80.

123 Anderson, "The Code of the Streets," 80.

124 Massey, D. S. and Denton, N. A. (1993). *American Apartheid: Segregation and the Making of the Underclass*. Cambridge, MA: Harvard University Press, 8.

125 Kubrin, C. E. and Weitzer, R. (2003). "Retaliatory Homicide: Concentrated Disadvantage and Neighborhood Culture." *Social Problems* 50, 157–180.

126 Sampson, R. J. and Bartusch, D. J. (1998). "Legal Cynicism and (Subcultural?) Tolerance of Deviance: The Neighborhood Context of Racial Differences." *Law & Society Review* 32, 777–804, 800.

127 Sampson and Bartusch, "Legal Cynicism and (Subcultural?) Tolerance of Deviance," 800, 801.

128 Matsueda, R. L., Drakulich, K., and Kubrin, C. E. (2006). "Race and Neighborhood Codes of Violence." In Peterson, Krivo, and Hagen (eds.), *The Many Colors of Crime*.

129 McCord, J. and Ensminger, M. E. (2003). "Racial Discrimination and Violence." In D. F. Hawkins (ed.), *Violent Crime: Assessing Race and Ethnic Differences*. New York: Cambridge University Press.

130 Sampson, R. J. and Wilson, W. J. (1995). "Toward a Theory of Race, Crime and Urban Inequality." In J. Hagan and R. D. Peterson (eds.), *Crime and inequality*. Stanford, CA: Stanford University Press, 38.

131 Sampson and Wilson, "Toward a Theory of Race, Crime and Urban Inequality," 41.

132 Wilson, *The Truly Disadvantaged*, 61.

133 Sampson and Wilson, "Toward a Theory of Race, Crime and Urban Inequality," 52.

134 Blumstein, A. and Graddy, E. (1982). "Prevalence and Recidivism in Index Arrests: A Feedback Model." *Law and Society Review* 16, 265–290.

135 Blumstein, A. J. (1982). "On the Racial Disproportionality of U.S. Prison Populations." *Journal of Criminal Law and Criminology* 73, 1259–1281.

136 Blumstein, A. J. (1993). "Racial Disproportionality of U.S. Prison Populations Revisited." *University of Colorado Law Review* 64, 743–760.

137 Blumstein, Cohen, Martin, and Tonry (eds.), *Summary Report – Research on Sentencing*, 13.

138 Wilbanks, W. (1987). *The Myth of a Racist Criminal Justice System*. Monterey, CA: Brooks Cole.

139 Klein, S. P., Turner, S., and Petersilia, J. (1988). *Racial Equity in Sentencing*. R-3599-RC. Santa Monica, CA: RAND Corporation.

140 Steffensmeier, D. and Demuth, S. 2000. "Ethnicity and Sentencing Outcomes in U.S. Federal Courts: Who Is Punished More Harshly?" *American Sociological Review* 65, 705–729.

141 Pope, C. E. and Snyder, H. N. (2003). "Race as a Factor in Juvenile Arrests." *Juvenile Justice Bulletin* (NCJ 189180). Washington, DC: U.S. Department of Justice, Office of Justice Programs, Office of Juvenile Justice and Delinquency Prevention. https://www.ncjrs.gov/pdffiles1/ojjdp/189180.pdf.

142 D'Alessio, S. J. and Stolzenberg, L. (2003). "Race and the Probability of Arrest." *Social Forces* 81, 1381–1397.

143 Federal Bureau of Investigation, U.S. Department of Justice. (2009). "The Nation's Two Crime Measures." In *Crime in the United States 2009*. http://www.ucrdatatool.gov

144 See Coarmae Richey Mann, C. R. (1993). *Unequal Justice: A Question of Color*. Bloomington: Indiana University Press; Free, Jr., M. D. (ed.) (2003). *Racial Issues in Criminal Justice: The Case of African Americans*. Westport, CT: Praeger Publishers; Provine, *Unequal under Law*.

145 Federal Bureau of Investigation, U.S. Department of Justice. "The Nation's Two Crime Measures." In *Crime in the United States 2009*.

146 Bureau of Justice Statistics. (2008). *Criminal Victimization in the United States, 2008 – Statistical Tables*, table 40. http://www.bjs.gov/content/pub/pdf/cvus08.pdf

147 Wilson, *The Truly Disadvantaged*.

148 Madhubuti, H. R. and Karenga, M. (1996). *Million Man March/Day of Absence: A Commemorative Anthology; Speeches, Commentary, Photography, Poetry, Illustrations, Documents*. Chicago: Third World Press.

149 Williams, J. (2006). *Enough: The Phony Leaders, Dead-End Movements, and Culture of Failure that are Undermining Black America – and What We Can Do about It*. New York: Crown Publishers, 8.

150 Williams, *Enough: The Phony Leaders, Dead-End Movements, and Culture of Failure*, 47.

151 Barack Obama: Interview of the President by Jay Leno on *The Tonight Show*. (August 6, 2013). Peters, G. and Wooley, J. T. (eds.). *The American Presidency Project*. http://www.presidency.ucsb.edu

152 See Table 1.27 in Chapter 1.

153 Wolfgang and Ferracuti, *The Subculture of Violence*, 264.

154 Gross and Mauro, *Death and Discrimination*, foreword.

155 Wilson, W. J. (1980). *The Declining Significance of Race: Blacks and Changing American Institutions*. University of Chicago Press.

156 Wilson, *The Truly Disadvantaged*, 32–33.

157 Sampson and Wilson, "Toward a Theory of Race, Crime and Urban Inequality," 43.

158 Peterson, R. D. and Krivo, L. J. (2005). "Macrostructural Analyses of Race, Ethnicity, and Violent Crime: Recent Lessons and New Directions for Research." *Annual Review of Sociology* 31, 331–356, 348.

159 Ronald Reagan: Remarks Announcing Federal Initiatives Against Drug Trafficking and Organized Crime. (October 14, 1982). *American Presidency Project.*

160 Ronald Reagan: Remarks Announcing Federal Initiatives Against Drug Trafficking and Organized Crime.

161 "Lawmakers Enact $30.2 Billion Anti-Crime Bill." (1994). *Congressional Quarterly Almanac: 1994.* Washington, DC: CQ Press, 279.

162 "Lawmakers Enact $30.2 Billion Anti-Crime Bill." *Congressional Quarterly Almanac: 1994,* 284.

163 Lydia Saad. (July 8, 2013). "TV is Americans' Main Source of News." Gallup, Inc. http://www.gallup.com/poll/163412/americans-main-source-news.aspx

164 Much of this increase is attributable to eighteen to twenty-nine year olds; Pew Research Center for the People and the Press. (January 4, 2011). *Internet Gains on Television as Public's Main News Source.* http://www.people-press.org/files/legacy-pdf/689.pdf

165 Pew Research Center for the People and the Press, *Internet Gains on Television.*

166 Pew Research Center for the People and the Press. (September 27, 2012). *In Changing News Landscape, Even Television Is Vulnerable.* http://www.people-press.org/files/legacy-pdf/2012%20News%20Consumption%20Report.pdf

167 Pew Research Center for the People and the Press. (September 12, 2010). *Americans Spending More Time Following the News.* http://www.people-press.org/files/legacy-pdf/652.pdf

168 Pew Research Center for the People and the Press, *Americans Spending More Time Following the News.*

169 Dutta-Bergman, M. J. (2004). "Complementarity in Consumption of News Types across Traditional and New Media." *Journal of Broadcasting & Electronic Media.* 48, 41–60.

170 Orfield, G. (2001). *Schools More Separate: Consequences of a Decade of Resegregation.* Cambridge, MA: Harvard Civil Rights Project; Gary Orfield, G. and Lee, C. (2007). *Historic Reversals, Accelerating Resegregation, and the Need for New Integration Strategies.* Los Angeles, CA: The Civil Rights Project. See also Logan, J. R., Stults, B. J., and Farley, R. (2004). "Segregation of Minorities in the Metropolis: Two Decades of Change." *Demography* 41, 1–22; Massey and Denton, *American Apartheid.*

171 Bennett, D. C. (1973). "Segregation and Racial Interaction." *Annals of the Association of American Geographers* 63, 48–57; Berry, B. (2006). "Friends for Better or for Worse: Interracial Friendship in the United States as Seen through Wedding Party Photos." *Demography* 43, 491–510; Currarini, S., Jackson, M. O., and Pin, P. (2009). "An Economic Model of Friendship:

Homophily, Minorities, and Segregation." *Econometrica* 77, 1003–1045; Echenique, F. and Fryer, Jr., R. G. (2007). "A Measure of Segregation Based on Social Interactions." *Quarterly Journal of Economics* 122, 441–485; Mouw, T. and Entwisle, B. (2006). "Residential Segregation and Interracial Friendship in Schools." *American Journal of Sociology* 112, 394–441; Sigelman, L., Bledsoe, T., Welch, S., and Combs, M. W. (1996) "Making Contact? Black-White Social Interaction in an Urban Setting." *American Journal of Sociology* 101, 1306–1332.

172 Jaynes, G. D. and Williams, R. M. (1989). "Black Participation in American Society." *Common Destiny: Blacks and American Society.* Washington, DC: National Academy Press; Oliver, M. L. and Shapiro, T. M. (1989). "Race and Wealth." *Review of Black Political Economy* 17, 5–26.

173 Sigelman, L. and Welch, S. (1993). "The Contact Hypothesis Revisited: Black-White Interaction and Positive Racial Attitudes." *Social Forces* 71, 781–796.

174 Entman, R. M. (1993). "Framing: Toward Clarification of a Fractured Paradigm." *Journal of Communication* 43, 51–59, 52.

175 Adams, P. C. (1992). "Television as Gathering Place." *Annals of the Association of American Geographers* 82, 117–135; Frosh, P. (2009). "The Face of Television." *Annals of the American Academy of Political and Social Science* 625, 87–102.

176 Entman, R. M. (1989). "How the Media Affect What People Think: An Information Processing Approach." *Journal of Politics* 51, 347–370.

177 Entman, R. M. (1994). "Representation and Reality in the Portrayal of Blacks on Network Television News." *Journalism Quarterly* 71, 509–520, 509.

178 It is worth noting that the negative imagery of blacks pervasive in mainstream media is not as pervasive in black media outlets. For more on this, see Moody, M. N. (2008). *Black and Mainstream Press' Framing of Racial Profiling.* Lanham, MD: University Press of America, Inc.

179 Colfax, J. D. and Sternberg, S. F. (1972). "The Perpetuation of Racial Stereotypes: Blacks in Mass Circulation Magazine Advertisements." *Public Opinion Quarterly* 36, 8–18; Kliman, B. W. (1978). "The Biscuit Eater: Racial Stereotypes, 1939–1972." *Phylon* 39, 87–96; Levy, D. W. (1970). "Racial Stereotypes in Antislavery Fiction." *Phylon* 31, 265–279; Shuey, A. M., King, N., and Griffith, B. (1953). "Stereotyping of Negroes and Whites: An Analysis of Magazine Pictures." *Public Opinion Quarterly* 17, 281–287; Spoehr, L. W. (1973). "Sambo and the Heathen Chinese: Californians' Racial Stereotypes in the Late 1870s." *Pacific Historical Review* 42, 185–204; Zinar, R. (1975). "Racial Bigotry and Stereotypes in Music Books Recommended for Use by Children." *Black Perspective in Music* 3, 33–39.

180 Greco Larson, S. G. (2006). *Media & Minorities: The Politics of Race in News and Entertainment.* Lanham, MD: Rowman & Littlefield Publishers, Inc. See also Roberts, C. (1975). "The Presentation of Blacks in Network Television Newscasts." *Journalism Quarterly* 52, 50–55; Chaudhary, A. G. (1980). "Press Portrayal of Black Officials." *Journalism Quarterly* 57, 636–641; Herman Gray, H. (1989). "Television, Black Americans and the American Dream." *Critical Studies in Mass Communication* 6, 376–386;

Mann, C. R., Zatz, M. S., and Rodriguez, N. (2006). *Images of Color, Images of Crime: Readings* (3rd ed.). Los Angeles, CA: Roxbury Publishing Company.

181 Gilens, M. (1996). "Race and Poverty in America: Public Misperceptions and the American News Media." *Public Opinion Quarterly* 60, 515–541.

182 See also McConahay, J. B. (1986). "Modern Racism, Ambivalence, and the Modern Racism Scale." In J. F. Dovidio and S. Gaertner (eds.), *Prejudice, Discrimination, and Racism: Theory and Research*. New York: Academic Press; Sears, D. O. (1988). "Symbolic Racism." In P. Katz and D. Taylor (eds.), *Eliminating Racism*. New York: Plenum Press.

183 Entman, R. M. (1990). "Modern Racism and the Images of Blacks in Local Television News." *Critical Studies in Mass Communications* 7, 332–345; Entman, R. M. 1992. "Blacks in the News: Television, Modern Racism and Cultural Change." *Journalism Quarterly* 69, 341–361.

184 For fuller exploration, see Dovidio, J. F. (2001). "On the Nature of Contemporary Prejudice: The Third Wave." *Journal of Social Issues* 57, 829–849; Dovidio, J. F., Gaertner, S. L., Kawakami, K., and Hudson, G. (2002). "Why Can't We Just Get Along? Interpersonal Biases and Interracial Distrust." *Cultural Diversity and Ethnic Minority Psychology* 8, 88–102.

185 Hurwitz, J. and Peffley, M. (2005). "Playing the Race Card in the Post-Willie Horton Era: The Impact of Racialized Code Words on Support for Punitive Crime Policy." *Public Opinion Quarterly* 69, 99–112.

186 Russell-Brown, K. (2009). *The Color of Crime: Racial Hoaxes, White Fear, Black Protectionism, Police Harassment, and Other Macroaggressions* (2nd ed.). New York University Press, 15–16.

187 Russell-Brown, *The Color of Crime*.

188 For an excellent micro-context study, see Owens-Patton, T. and Snyder-Yuly, J. (2007). "Any Four Black Men Will Do: Rape, Race, and the Ultimate Scapegoat." *Journal of Black Studies* 37, 859–895.

189 Entman, R. M., Langford, B. H., Burns-Melican, D., Munoz, I., Boayue, S., Raman, A., Kenner, B., and Merrit, C. (1998). *Mass Media and Reconciliation*. Cambridge, MA: Kennedy School of Government, 19.

190 Entman, "Modern Racism and the Images of Blacks in Local Television News"; Entman, "Blacks in the News," 341–361.

191 Entman, "Representation and Reality in the Portrayal of Blacks," 511.

192 Chiricos, T. and Eschholz, S. (2002). "The Racial and Ethnic Typification of Crime and the Criminal Typification of Race and Ethnicity in Local Television News." *Journal of Research in Crime and Delinquency* 39, 400–420.

193 Poindexter, P. M., Smith, L., and Heider, D. (2003). "Race and Ethnicity in Local Television News: Framing, Story Assignments, and Source Selections." *Journal of Broadcasting and Electronic Media* 47, 524–536.

194 Dixon, T. L. and Linz, D. (2000). "Overrepresentation and Underrepresentation of African Americans and Latinos as Lawbreakers on Television News." *Journal of Communication* 50, 131–154.

195 Tierney, K., Bevc, C., and Kugligowski, E. (2006). "Metaphors Matter: Disaster Myths, Media Frames, and Their Consequences in Hurricane

Katrina." *Annals of the American Academy of Political and Social Science* 604, 57–81.

196 Beckett, K. (1994). "Setting the Public Agenda: 'Street Crime' and Drug Use in American Politics." *Social Problems* 41, 425–447, 425.

197 Barlow, M. H., Barlow, D. E., and Chiricos, T. G. (1990). "Economic Conditions and Ideologies of Crime in the Media: A Content Analysis of Crime News." *Crime and Delinquency* 41, 3–19; Dixon, T. L., Azocar, C. L., and Casas, M. (2003). "The Portrayal of Race and Crime on Television Network News." *Journal of Broadcasting & Electronic Media* 47, 498–523; Dixon Linz, "Overrepresentation and Underrepresentation of African Americans and Latinos"; Dixon, T. L. and Linz, D. (2000). "Race and the Misrepresentation of Victimization on Local Television News." *Communication Research* 27, 547–573.

198 Russell-Brown, *The Color of Crime*, 22.

199 Wilson, *The Truly Disadvantaged*, 21.

200 Gamson, W. A., Croteau, D., Hoynes W., and Sasson, T. (1992). "Media Images and the Social Construction of Reality." *Annual Review of Sociology* 18, 373–393, 391.

201 Larson, *Media & Minorities*, 31.

202 For an excellent discussion of this theme, see C. F. Exoo's review of the following five books in "Elections and the Media." *Polity* 16, 343–353: Barber, J. D. (1980). *The Pulse of Politics: Electing Presidents in the Media Age*. New York: W. W. Norton and Company; Paletz, D. L. and Entman, R. M. (1981). *Media-Power-Politics*. New York: Macmillan Publishing Co.; Patterson, T. E. (1980). *The Mass Media Election: How Americans Choose Their President*. New York: Praeger Publishers; Rubin, R. L. (1981). *Press, Party and Presidency*. New York: W. W. Norton and Co.; and, Weaver, D. H., Graber, D. A., McCombs, M. E., and Eyal, C. E. (1981). *Media Agenda-Setting in a Presidential Election*. New York: Praeger Publishers. See also Champlin, D. P. and Knoedler, J. T. (2006). "The Media, the News, and Democracy: Revisiting the Dewey-Lippman Debate." *Journal of Economic Issues* 40, 135–152.

203 Iyengar, S. (1991). *Is Anyone Responsible?* Chicago: University of Chicago Press.

204 Pew Research Center for the People and the Press, *Americans Spending More Time Following the News*.

205 Pew Research Center for the People and the Press, *Internet Gains on Television*.

206 Pew Research Center for the People and the Press, *Americans Spending More Time Following the News*.

207 Entman, R. M. and Rojecki, A. (2000). *The Black Image in the White Mind: Media and Race in America*. University of Chicago Press; Henderson, J. J. and Baldasty, G. J. (2003). "Race, Advertising, and Prime-Time Television." *Howard Journal of Communications* 14, 97–112; Larson, *Media & Minorities*; Russell-Brown, *The Color of Crime*.

208 Perkins, W. E. (1996). "The Rap Attack: An Introduction." In W. E. Perkins (ed.), *Droppin' Science: Critical Essays on Rap Music and Hip Hop Culture*. Philadelphia, PA: Temple University Press.

209 Krims, A. (2000). *Rap Music and the Poetics of Identity*. New York: Cambridge University Press; Perullo, A. (2005). "Hooligans and Heroes: Youth Identity and Hip-Hop in Dar Es Salaam, Tanzania." *Africa Today* 51, 75–101; Sullivan, R. E. (2003). "Rap and Race: It's Got a Nice Beat, but What about the Message?" *Journal of Black Studies* 33, 605–622.

210 Allen, Jr., E. (1996). "Making the Strong Survive: The Contours and Contradictions of Message Rap." In Perkins (ed.), *Droppin' Science*; Kelley, R. D. G. (1996). "Kickin' Reality, Kickin' Ballistics: Gangsta Rap and Postindustrial Los Angeles." In Perkins (ed.), *Droppin' Science*; Keyes, C. L. (2002). *Rap Music and Street Consciousness*. Urbana, IL: University of Illinois Press; Krims, *Rap Music and the Poetics of Identity*.

211 Kubrin, C. E. (2005). "Gangstas, Thugs, and Hustlas: Identity and the Code of the Street in Rap Music." *Social Problems* 52, 360–378.

212 For example, see Adams, T. M and Fuller, D. B. (2006). "The Words Have Changed but the Ideology Remains the Same: Misogynistic Lyrics in Rap Music." *Journal of Black Studies* 36, 938–957; Barongan, C. and Nagayama Hall, G. C. (1995). "The Influence of Misogynous Rap Music on Sexual Aggression Against Women." *Psychology of Women Quarterly* 19, 195–207; Wester, S. R., Crown, C. L., Quatman, G. L., and Heesacker, M. (1997). "The Influence of Sexually Violent Rap Music on Attitudes of Men with Little Prior Exposure." *Psychology of Women Quarterly* 21, 497–508.

213 Sullivan, "Rap and Race."

214 For further discussion of rap music, see Arnett, J. (1992). "The Soundtrack of Recklessness: Musical Preferences and Reckless Behavior among Adolescents." *Journal of Adolescent Research* 7, 313–331; Martinez, T. A. (1993). "Recognizing the Enemy: Rap Music in the Wake of the Los Angeles Riots." *Explorations in Ethnic Studies* 16, 115–127; Martinez, T. A. (1997). "Popular Culture: Rap as Resistance." *Sociological Perspectives* 40, 265–286; Rose, T. (1991). "Fear of a Black Planet: Rap Music and Black Cultural Politics in the 1990s." *Journal of Negro Education* 60, 276–290.

215 Russell-Brown, *The Color of Crime*, 14.

216 Russell-Brown, *The Color of Crime*.

217 See Altheide, D. L. (1997). "The News Media, the Problem Frame, and the Production of Fear." *Sociological Quarterly* 38, 647–668; Domke, D., McCoy, K., and Torres, M. (1999). "News Media, Racial Perceptions, and Political Cognition." *Communication Research* 26, 507–607; Entman, "Blacks in the News," 241–261; Entman and Rojecki, *The Black Image in the White Mind*.

218 Gilliam, Jr., F. D. and Iyengar, S. (2000). "Prime Suspects: The Impact of Local Television News on Attitudes about Crime and Race." *American Journal of Political Science* 44, 560–573.

219 Domke, D. (2001). "Racial Cues and Political Ideology: An Examination of Associative Priming." *Communication Research* 28, 772–801.

220 Bjornstrom, E. E. S., Kaufman, R. L., Peterson, R. D., and Slater, M. D. (2010). "Race and Ethnic Representations of Lawbreakers and Victims in Crime News: A National Study of Television Coverage." *Social Problems* 57, 269–293, 288.

221 Owens and Snyder-Yuly, "Any Four Black Men Will Do."

222 Mutz, D. C. (2007). "Effects of 'In-Your-Face' Television Discourse on Perceptions of a Legitimate Opposition." *American Political Science Review* 101, 621–635.

223 Abrajano, M. and Singh, S. (2009). "Examining the Link between Issue Attitudes and News Source: The Case of Latinos and Immigration Reform." *Political Behavior* 31, 1–30; Barabas, M. and Jerit, J. (2009) "Estimating the Causal Effects of Media Coverage on Policy-Specific Knowledge." *American Journal of Political Science* 53, 73–89; Blondheim, M. and Liebes, T. (2009). "Television News and Nation: The End?" *Annals of the American Academy of Political and Social Sciences* 625, 182–198; Chiricos, T., Eschholz, S. and Gerta, M. (1997). "News and Fear of Crime: Toward an Identification of Audience Effects." *Social Problems* 44, 342–357; Mazur, A. (2006). "Risk Perception and News Coverage across Nations." *Risk Management* 8, 149–174; Mutz, D. C. (1994). "Contextualizing Personal Experience: The Role of Mass Media." *Journal of Politics* 56, 689–714; Page, B. I., Shapiro, R. Y., and Dempsey, G. R. (1987). "What Moves Public Opinion?" *American Political Science Review* 81, 23–44

224 Gilliam Jr., F. D., Valentino, N. A., and Beckmann, M. N. (2002) "Where You Live and What You Watch: The Impact of Racial Proximity and Local Television News on Attitudes about Race and Crime." *Political Research Quarterly* 55, 755–780, 755.

225 Jamieson, K. H. (1992). *Dirty Politics: Deception, Distraction, and Democracy.* New York: Oxford University Press.

226 Warren, P. Y. and Farrell, A. (2009). "The Environmental Context of Racial Profiling." *Annals of the American Academy of Political and Social Science* 623, 52–63; Weitzer, R. and Tuch, S. A. (2005). "Racially Biased Policing: Determinants of Citizen Perceptions." *Social Forces* 83, 1009–1030.

227 For a fuller explanation of the rational public thesis see Page, B. I. and Shapiro, R. I. (1992). *The Rational Public: Fifty Years of Trends in America's Policy Preferences.* University of Chicago Press.

228 Iyengar, R. (1991). *Is Anyone Responsible? How Television Frames Political Issues.* University of Chicago Press.

229 Page, Shapiro, and Dempsey, "What Moves Public Opinion?" 31.

230 Page, Shapiro, and Dempsey, "What Moves Public Opinion?" 32.

231 Page, Shapiro, and Dempsey, "What Moves Public Opinion?" 35.

232 Page, Shapiro, and Dempsey, "What Moves Public Opinion?" 36.

233 Jerit, J. (2009). "Understanding the Knowledge Gap: The Role of Experts and Journalists." *Journal of Politics* 71, 442–456.

234 Ben-Porath, E. N. (2007). "Internal Fragmentation of the News: Television News in Dialogical Format and Its Consequences for Journalism." *Journalism Studies* 8, 414–431; Blondheim and Liebes, "Television News and Nation: The End?" 182–198.

235 Champlin and Knoedler, "The Media, the News, and Democracy," 135–152.

236 Jamieson, *Dirty Politics*, 24.

237 Patterson, T. E. (1998). "Time and News: The Media's Limitations as an Instrument of Democracy." *International Political Science Review* **19**, 55–67.

238 Entman, "Modern Racism and the Images of Blacks in Local Television News."

239 Pew Research Center for the People and the Press. (March 18, 2013) *The State of the News Media 2013: An Annual Report on American Journalism.* http://stateofthemedia.org.

240 Gilliam, Jr. and Iyengar, "Prime Suspects."

241 Jamieson, *Dirty Politics*, 24.

242 Klinenberg, E. (2005). "Convergence: News Production in a Digital Age." *Annals of the American Academy of Political and Social Science* **597**, 48–64, 60.

243 Klinenberg, "Convergence: News Production in a Digital Age," 53.

244 Lotz, A. D. (2009). "What Is U.S. Television Now?" *Annals of the American Academy of Political and Social Science* **625**, 49–59, 51.

245 Pew Research Center for the People and the Press. *The State of the News Media 2013*.

246 Pew Research Center for the People and the Press. *The State of the News Media 2013*.

247 Pew Research Center for the People and the Press. *The State of the News Media 2013*.

248 Pew Research Center for the People and the Press. *The State of the News Media 2013*.

249 Pew Research Center for the People and the Press. *The State of the News Media 2013*.

250 Entman, "Blacks in the News," 341–361, 345.

251 Entman, "Representation and Reality in the Portrayal of Blacks."

252 Nylund, M. (2003). "Asking Questions, Making Sound-Bites: Research Reports, Interviews and Television News Stories." *Discourse Studies* **5**, 517–533.

253 Gamson, Croteau, Hoynes, and Sasson, "Media Images and the Social Construction of Reality," 389.

254 Erbring, L., Goldenberg, E. N., and Miller, A. H. (1980). "Front-Page News and Real-World Cues: A New Look at Agenda-Setting by Media." *American Journal of Political Science* **24**, 16–49, 45.

255 Gentzkow, M. and Shapiro, J. M. (2010). "What Drives Media Slant? Evidence from U.S. Daily Newspapers." *Econometrica* **78**, 35071, 56–58.

256 Gentzkow, and Shapiro, "What Drives Media Slant?" 35 and 37. See also Turner, J. (2007). "The Messenger Overwhelming the Message: Ideological Cues and Perceptions of Bias in Television News." *Political Behavior* **29**, 441–464.

257 Thorson, E. (2008). "Changing Patterns of News Consumption and Participation." *Information, Communication & Society* **11**, 473–489.

258 Pew Research Center for the People and the Press. *The State of the News Media 2013*.

259 Sniderman, P. and Hagen, M. G. (1985). *Race and Inequality: A Study in American Values*. Chatham, NJ: Chatham House Publishers, 97.

260 Sniderman and Hagen, *Race and Inequality*, 97.

261 Kluegel, J. R. (1990). "Trends in Whites' Explanations of the Black-White Gap in Socioeconomic Status, 1977–1989." *American Sociological Review* 55, 512–525.

262 Horatio Alger. (n.d.) *Encyclopaedia Britannica Online*. http://www.britannica.com/EBchecked/topic/14993/Horatio-Alger.

263 The data in Table 8.1 are from: Pew Research Center for the People & the Press. (March 2, 2012). *For the Public, it's Not about Class Warfare, but Fairness*. http://www.people-press.org.

264 The data in Table 8.2 are from: Smith, T. W., Marsden, P. V., and Hout, M. *General Social Survey, 1972–2010*. ICPSR31521-v1. Storrs, CT: Roper Bibliographic Citation: Center for Public Opinion Research, University of Connecticut/Ann Arbor, MI: Inter-university Consortium for Political and Social Research.

Index